Waterlilies and Lotuses

Waterlilies and Lotuses

Species, Cultivars, and New Hybrids

Perry D. Slocum

TIMBER PRESS
Portland · Cambridge

Half-title: Victoria 'Longwood Hybrid;
frontispiece: Nyphaea 'Soux';
this page: Victoria 'Cruziana'.
Photos by Perry D. Slocum

Published in 2005 by
Timber Press, Inc.
The Haseltine Building
133 S.W. Second Avenue, Suite 450
Portland, Oregon 97204-3527, U.S.A.

Timber Press
2 Station Road
Swavesey
Cambridge CB4 5Q J, U.K.

www.timberpress.com

Printed in China

Note that copper and redwood are toxic
to plants and fish and such containers
should be used only in conjunction with
a plastic or other fish-safe liner.

Library of Congress Cataloging-in-Publication Data

Slocum, Perry D.
  Waterlilies and lotuses : species, cultivars, and new hybrids / Perry
D. Slocum.
       p. cm.
    Includes bibliographical references and index.
    ISBN 0-88192-684-1 (hardback)
   1. Lilies. 2. Lotus. I. Title.
    SB413.L7S55 2005
    635.9'3329—dc22

                                                       2004015834

A catalog record for this book is also available from the British Library.

Contents

Overleaf: Nelumbo 'Alba Grandiflora'. Perry D. Slocum

Preface

IN THE DECADE since I wrote "An Encyclopedia of Water Lily and Lotuses" for my 1996 book with Peter Robinson, *Water Gardening: Water Lilies and Lotuses*, tremendous new developments have taken place in the field. This new book describes nearly 500 waterlily and lotus species and cultivars. It covers all six members of the waterlily family, as well as all the species, all the best cultivars, and the best new hybrids—all 123 of them. The lotuses have been given a family of their own: Nelumbonaceae, and ten new lotus hybrids are included. Most important, I am pleased to provide an update of the taxonomy of the genus *Nymphaea*.

Most plant descriptions include standardized color numbers from the *Royal Horticultural Society (RHS) Colour Chart*. When this was not possible for some new hybrids, please refer to the color photographs. Comments on each plant also include reference to suitable pool size. Although there are no hard rules differentiating pool sizes, general guidelines are:

tub garden:	up to 3 ft. (0.9 m) in diameter
small:	4–6 ft. (1.2–1.8 m) in diameter
medium:	7–9 ft. (2.1–2.7 m) in diameter
large:	10 ft. (3 m) or larger in diameter
natural pond:	dirt- or mud-bottom pond of any size

Note that copper and redwood are toxic to plants and fish and should be used only in conjunction with a plastic or other fish-safe liner.

Acknowledgments

I thank Dr. John H. Wiersema of the Systemic Botany and Mycology Laboratory, USDA-ARS, Beltsville, Maryland, for use of material excerpted from his *A Monograph of Nymphaea Subgenus Hydrocallis (Nymphaeaceae)*, volume 16 of *Systematic Botany Monographs*, published in 1987 by the American Society of Plant Taxonomists. The Carnegie Institution, Washington, D.C., and *Systemic Botany Monographs* and The American Society of Plant Taxonomists, University of Michigan Herbarium, Ann Arbor, Michigan, generously contributed visual materials for this book.

I also want to thank the following people and companies for supplying slides of their new hybrids for use in this new edition of the book: Norman Bennett, former owner of Bennett's Water Gardens, England; Franz and Monica Berthold, Germany; Leeann Connelly, owner of Tropical Pond and Garden, Florida; Ernst Epple, Germany; Reg Henley, Wychwood Waterlily Farm, England; Fritz Junge, Germany; Kitt and Ben Knotts, Florida; Kenneth Landon, Texas; Lilypons Water Gardens, Maryland; Dean McGee, owner of Strawn Water Gardens, Texas; Brad and Bruce McLane, Florida Aquatic Nursery; John Mirgon, Denver; J. Craig Presnell, Luster Aquatic Nursery, Florida; Rich Sacher and Bill Dailey, owners of American Aquatic Gardens, Louisiana; Dr. Ed. Schneider, director of the Santa Barbara Botanic Gardens; Stuart Schuck, owner of Charleston Aquatic Nursery, South Carolina; and Van Ness Water Gardens, California.

PLATE 1. A raised display pool at the Slocum home in North Carolina contains hardy and tropical waterlilies and lotuses. Perry D. Slocum

PLATE 2. *Nymphaea gigantea.* Perry D. Slocum

PLATE 3. *Nymphaea gigantea* var. *alba.* Kenneth C. Landon

PLATE 4. *Nymphaea gigantea* var. *neorosea.* Perry D. Slocum

PLATE 5. *Nymphaea gigantea* var. *purpurea.* Kenneth C. Landon

Plate 6. *Nymphaea gigantea* var. *violacea*. Perry D. Slocum

Plate 7. *Nymphaea gigantea* 'Albert de Lestang'. Kenneth C. Landon

Plate 8. *Nymphaea gigantea* 'Blue Cloud'. Kenneth C. Landon

Plate 9. *Nymphaea gigantea* 'Hudsoniana'. Kenneth C. Landon

Plate 10. *Nymphaea ampla*. Perry D. Slocum

Plate 11. *Nymphaea caerulea*. Perry D. Slocum

Plate 12. *Nymphaea capensis*. Perry D. Slocum

Plate 13. *Nymphaea capensis* var. *zanzibariensis*, blue variation. Perry D. Slocum

Plate 14. *Nymphaea capensis* var. *zanzibariensis* 'Rosea'. Perry D. Slocum

Plate 15. *Nymphaea colorata*. Perry D. Slocum

Plate 16. *Nymphaea elegans*. Kenneth C. Landon

Plate 17. *Nymphaea flavovirens*. Kenneth C. Landon

Plate 18. *Nymphaea togoensis*. Kenneth C. Landon

Plate 19. *Nymphaea lotus*. Kenneth C. Landon

Plate 20. *Nymphaea rubra*. Perry D. Slocum

Plate 21. *Nymphaea spontanea*. Kenneth C. Landon

11

PLATE 22. Sprouted tropical waterlily tuber. Peter Slocum

PLATE 24. Planting a tropical waterlily. Perry D. Slocum

PLATE 23. Tropical waterlily plants showing tuber attached (left) and with tuber removed (right). Perry D. Slocum

PLATE 25. *Nymphaea* 'Afterglow'. Perry D. Slocum

PLATE 26. *Nymphaea* 'Albert Greenberg'. Perry D. Slocum

PLATE 27. *Nymphaea* 'Alexis'. Stuart Schuck

PLATE 28. *Nymphaea* 'American Beauty'. Perry D. Slocum

PLATE 29. *Nymphaea* 'August Koch'. Perry D. Slocum

PLATE 30. *Nymphaea* 'Aviator Pring'. Perry D. Slocum

Plate 31. *Nymphaea* 'Bagdad'. Perry D. Slocum

Plate 33. *Nymphaea* 'Bellachika', the darkest red star waterlily. Kenneth C. Landon

Plate 32. *Nymphaea* 'Barbara Barnett'. Florida Aquatic Nursery

PLATE 34. *Nymphaea* 'Bill Yohn'. Perry D. Slocum

PLATE 35. *Nymphaea* 'Blue Anemone'. Leeann Connelly

PLATE 36. *Nymphaea* 'Blue Beauty'. Perry D. Slocum

PLATE 37. *Nymphaea* 'Blue Spider'. Florida Aquatic Nursery

PLATE 38. *Nymphaea* 'Bob Trickett'. Perry D. Slocum

PLATE 39. *Nymphaea* 'Carla's Sonshine'. Florida Aquatic Nursery

15

PLATE 41. *Nymphaea* 'Chaz'. Stuart Schuck

PLATE 40. *Nymphaea* 'Casey Lee Slocum'. Perry D. Slocum

PLATE 42. *Nymphaea* 'Christine Lingg'. Van Ness Water Gardens

PLATE 43. *Nymphaea* 'Daubeniana'. Perry D. Slocum

PLATE 44. *Nymphaea* 'Daubeniana' showing plantlet in center of leaf. Perry D. Slocum

PLATE 45. *Nymphaea* 'Director George T. Moore'. Perry D. Slocum

PLATE 46. *Nymphaea* 'Dorothy Pearl'. Perry D. Slocum

PLATE 47. *Nymphaea* 'Eldorado'. Perry D. Slocum

PLATE 48. *Nymphaea* 'Enchantment'. Perry D. Slocum

PLATE 49. *Nymphaea* 'Evelyn Randig'. Perry D. Slocum

PLATE 50. *Nymphaea* 'Eve's Solitaire'. Kenneth C. Landon

PLATE 51. *Nymphaea* 'Foxfire'. Louis Belloisy

17

PLATE 52. *Nymphaea* 'Gene Joyner'. Peggy Sampson

PLATE 53. *Nymphaea* 'General Pershing', second-day flower. Perry D. Slocum

PLATE 54. *Nymphaea* 'Golden Fascinator'. Perry D. Slocum

PLATE 55. *Nymphaea* 'Golden West'. Perry D. Slocum

PLATE 56. *Nymphaea* 'Green Smoke'. Van Ness Water Gardens

PLATE 57. *Nymphaea* 'Helen Nash'. Peggy Sampson

PLATE 58. *Nymphaea* 'Ineta Ruth'. Perry D. Slocum

PLATE 59. *Nymphaea* 'Innocence'. Florida Aquatic Nursery

PLATE 60. *Nymphaea* 'Islamorada'. Florida Aquatic Nursery

PLATE 61. *Nymphaea* 'Jack Wood'. Perry D. Slocum

PLATE 62. *Nymphaea* 'Janice C. Wood'. Perry D. Slocum

PLATE 63. *Nymphaea* 'Jo Ann'. Van Ness Water Gardens

PLATE 64. *Nymphaea* 'Joseph Baynard Shearouse'. Leeann Connelly

PLATE 65. *Nymphaea* 'Josephine'. Florida Aquatic Nursery

PLATE 67. *Nymphaea* 'Kathy McLane'. Florida Aquatic Nursery

PLATE 66. *Nymphaea* 'Judge Hitchcock'. Perry D. Slocum

PLATE 68. *Nymphaea* 'Key Largo'. Florida Aquatic Nursery

PLATE 69. *Nymphaea* 'Key Lime'. Florida Aquatic Nursery

PLATE 70. *Nymphaea* 'King of Blues'. Perry D. Slocum

PLATE 71. *Nymphaea* 'King of Siam'. Rich Sacher

PLATE 72. *Nymphaea* 'Leopardess'. Perry D. Slocum

PLATE 73. *Nymphaea* 'Lone Star'. Kenneth C. Landon

PLATE 74. *Nymphaea* 'Mahogany Rose'. Rich Sacher

PLATE 75. *Nymphaea* 'Mary Mirgon'. John Mirgon

PLATE 76. *Nymphaea* 'Miami Rose'. Florida Aquatic Nursery

PLATE 77. *Nymphaea* 'Midnight'. Perry D. Slocum

PLATE 78. *Nymphaea* 'Midnight Embers'. J. Craig Presnell

PLATE 79. *Nymphaea* 'Midnight Serenade'. J. Craig Presnell

PLATE 80. *Nymphaea* 'Moon Shadow'. Florida Aquatic Nursery

PLATE 81. *Nymphaea* 'Mr. Martin E. Randig'. Perry D. Slocum

PLATE 82. *Nymphaea* 'Mrs. Edwards Whitaker'. Perry D. Slocum

PLATE 83. *Nymphaea* 'Mrs. George H. Pring'. Perry D. Slocum

PLATE 84. *Nymphaea* 'Mrs. Martin E. Randig'. Perry D. Slocum

Plate 85. *Nymphaea* 'Pamela'. Perry D. Slocum

Plate 86. *Nymphaea* 'Panama Pacific'. Perry D. Slocum

Plate 87. *Nymphaea* 'Paul Stetson'. Perry D. Slocum

Plate 88. *Nymphaea* 'Perry's Blue Heaven'. Perry D. Slocum

Plate 89. *Nymphaea* 'Pink Champagne'. Florida Aquatic Nursery

Plate 90. *Nymphaea* 'Pink Passion'. Florida Aquatic Nursery

PLATE 91. *Nymphaea* 'Pink Pearl'. Perry D. Slocum

PLATE 92. *Nymphaea* 'Pink Platter'. Perry D. Slocum

PLATE 93. *Nymphaea* 'Red Beauty'. Perry D. Slocum

PLATE 94. *Nymphaea* 'Rhonda Kay'. Perry D. Slocum

PLATE 95. *Nymphaea* 'Robert Strawn'. Perry D. Slocum

PLATE 96. *Nymphaea* 'Ron G. Landon'. Kenneth C. Landon

Plate 97. *Nymphaea* 'Rose Star'. Perry D. Slocum

Plate 98. *Nymphaea* 'Sarah Ann'. Perry D. Slocum

Plate 99. *Nymphaea* 'Serendipity'. J. Craig Presnell

Plate 100. *Nymphaea* 'Starlight'. Rich Sacher

Plate 101. *Nymphaea* 'Star of Zanzibar'. Rich Sacher

Plate 102. *Nymphaea* 'St. Louis'. Perry D. Slocum

Plate 103. *Nymphaea* 'St. Louis Gold'. Perry D. Slocum

Plate 104. *Nymphaea* 'Stormy Weather'. Peggy Sampson

Plate 105. *Nymphaea* 'Ted Uber'. Perry D. Slocum

Plate 106. *Nymphaea* 'Tina'. Perry D. Slocum

Plate 107. *Nymphaea* 'White Lightning'. Florida Aquatic Nursery

PLATE 108. *Nymphaea* 'William McLane'. Florida Aquatic
Nursery

PLATE 109. *Nymphaea* 'Wood's Blue Goddess' Perry
D. Slocum

PLATE 110. *Nymphaea* 'Yellow Dazzler'. Perry D. Slocum

PLATE 111. *Nymphaea* 'Antares'. Perry D. Slocum

PLATE 112. *Nymphaea* 'Catherine Marie'. Perry D. Slocum

28

PLATE 113. *Nymphaea* 'Elysian Fields'. Rich Sacher

PLATE 114. *Nymphaea* 'Emily Grant Hutchings'. Perry D. Slocum

PLATE 115. *Nymphaea* 'Jennifer Rebecca'. Perry D. Slocum

PLATE 116. *Nymphaea* 'Juno'. Perry D. Slocum

PLATE 117. *Nymphaea* 'Leanne Connelly'. Perry D. Slocum

PLATE 118. *Nymphaea* 'Maroon Beauty'. Perry D. Slocum

PLATE 119. *Nymphaea* 'Missouri'. Perry D. Slocum

PLATE 120. *Nymphaea* 'Mrs. George C. Hitchcock'. Perry D. Slocum

PLATE 121. *Nymphaea* 'Red Cup'. Perry D. Slocum

PLATE 122. *Nymphaea* 'Red Flare'. Perry D. Slocum

PLATE 123. *Nymphaea* 'Texas Shell Pink'.
George Thomas III

PLATE 124. *Nymphaea* 'Trudy Slocum'. Perry D. Slocum

Plate 125. Hardy waterlily rhizomes. From top to bottom: upright, or pineapple; Marliac; odorata; tuberosa; and finger, or thumb

Plate 127. *Nymphaea alba*. Perry D. Slocum

Plate 126. *Nymphaea tetragona*. Perry D. Slocum

PLATE 128. *Nymphaea candida*. Perry D. Slocum

PLATE 130. *Nymphaea odorata*. Perry D. Slocum

PLATE 129. *Nymphaea odorata* growing naturally in a lake in south Georgia. Perry D. Slocum

33

Plate 131. *Nymphaea odorata* var. *gigantea*. Perry D. Slocum

Plate 132. *Nymphaea tuberosa*. Perry D. Slocum

Plate 133. *Nymphaea mexicana*. Perry D. Slocum

Plate 134. *Nymphaea mexicana* f. *canaveralensis* (*N. mexicana* 'Cape Canaveral'). Perry D. Slocum

Plate 135. *Nymphaea* 'Almost Black'. Perry D. Slocum

Plate 136. *Nymphaea* 'Amabilis'. Perry D. Slocum

Plate 137. *Nymphaea* 'American Star'. Perry D. Slocum

Plate 138. *Nymphaea* 'Anna Epple'. Ernst Epple

Plate 139. *Nymphaea* 'Apple Blossom Pink'. Perry D. Slocum

Plate 140. *Nymphaea* 'Arc-en-Ciel'. Perry D. Slocum

PLATE 141. *Nymphaea* 'Atropurpurea'. Perry D. Slocum

PLATE 142. *Nymphaea* 'Attraction'. Perry D. Slocum

PLATE 143. *Nymphaea* 'Aurora', first-day flower (left), second-day flower (bottom right), third-day flower (top). Perry D. Slocum

Plate 144. *Nymphaea* 'Berit Strawn'. Perry D. Slocum

Plate 145. *Nymphaea* 'Berthold'. Reg Henley

Plate 146. *Nymphaea* 'Black Princess', first-day (upper right), second-day (bottom), and third-day flower (upper left). Perry D. Slocum

Plate 147. *Nymphaea* 'Bleeding Heart'. Perry D. Slocum

Plate 148. *Nymphaea* 'Blushing Bride'. Perry D. Slocum

Plate 149. *Nymphaea* 'Carolina Sunset'. Perry D. Slocum

PLATE 150. *Nymphaea* 'Charlene Strawn'. Perry D. Slocum

PLATE 151. *Nymphaea* 'Charlie's Choice'. Perry D. Slocum

PLATE 152. *Nymphaea* 'Chrysantha', first-day flower (upper left), third-day flower (bottom). Perry D. Slocum

38

PLATE 153. *Nymphaea* 'Clyde Ikins'. Perry D. Slocum

PLATE 154. *Nymphaea* 'Colonel A. J. Welch'. Perry D. Slocum

PLATE 155. *Nymphaea* 'Colonel A. J. Welch' showing new growth from old blossom. Perry D. Slocum

PLATE 156. *Nymphaea* 'Colorado'. Perry D. Slocum

PLATE 157. *Nymphaea* 'Comanche', first-, second-, and third-day flowers (clockwise from top). Perry D. Slocum

PLATE 158. *Nymphaea* 'Darwin' (syn. 'Hollandia'). Perry D. Slocum

PLATE 159. *Nymphaea* 'Doll House'. Perry D. Slocum

PLATE 160. *Nymphaea* 'Ernst Epple sen'. Ernst Epple

PLATE 161. *Nymphaea* 'Escarboucle'. Perry D. Slocum

Plate 162. *Nymphaea* 'Fiesta'. Reg Henley

Plate 163. *Nymphaea* 'Fireball'. Perry D. Slocum

Plate 164. *Nymphaea* 'Firecrest'. Perry D. Slocum

Plate 165. *Nymphaea* 'Florida Sunset'. Perry D. Slocum

Plate 166. *Nymphaea* 'Franz Berthold'. Monica Berthold

PLATE 167. *Nymphaea* 'Fritz Junge'. Reg Henley

PLATE 168. *Nymphaea* 'George L. Thomas'. Lilypons Water Gardens

PLATE 169. *Nymphaea* 'Georgia Peach'. Perry D. Slocum

PLATE 170. *Nymphaea* 'Gladstoniana'. Perry D. Slocum

PLATE 171. *Nymphaea* 'Gloire du Temple-sur-Lot'. Perry D. Slocum

PLATE 172. *Nymphaea* 'Gloriosa'. Perry D. Slocum

PLATE 173. *Nymphaea* 'Gold Medal'. Perry D. Slocum

PLATE 174. *Nymphaea* 'Gonnère'. Perry D. Slocum

PLATE 175. *Nymphaea* 'Gregg's Orange Beauty'. Perry D. Slocum

PLATE 176. *Nymphaea* 'Helvola'. Perry D. Slocum

PLATE 177. *Nymphaea* 'Hermine'. Perry D. Slocum

PLATE 178. *Nymphaea* 'Indiana'. Perry D. Slocum

44

PLATE 179. *Nymphaea* 'Inner Light'. Lilypons Water Gardens

PLATE 180. *Nymphaea* 'James Brydon'. Perry D. Slocum

PLATE 181. *Nymphaea* 'Jasmine'. Reg Henley

PLATE 182. *Nymphaea* 'Jim Saunders'. Reg Henley

PLATE 183. *Nymphaea* 'Joey Tomocik'. Perry D. Slocum

PLATE 184. *Nymphaea* 'Karl Epple'. Ernst Epple

PLATE 185. *Nymphaea* 'Laydekeri Fulgens'. Perry D. Slocum

PLATE 186. *Nymphaea* 'Laydekeri Rosea'. Perry D. Slocum

46

PLATE 187. *Nymphaea* 'Lemonade'. Lilypons Water Gardens

PLATE 188. *Nymphaea* 'Lemon Chiffon'. Perry D. Slocum

PLATE 189. *Nymphaea* 'Lily Pons'. Perry D. Slocum

PLATE 190. *Nymphaea* 'Marie Clara'. Reg Henley

PLATE 191. *Nymphaea* 'Marliacea Rosea'. Perry D. Slocum

PLATE 192. *Nymphaea* 'Martha'. Perry D. Slocum

PLATE 193. *Nymphaea* 'Masaniello'. Perry D. Slocum

PLATE 194. *Nymphaea* 'Mayla'. Perry D. Slocum

PLATE 195. *Nymphaea* 'Meteor'. Perry D. Slocum

PLATE 196. *Nymphaea* 'Michael Berthold'. Monica Berthold

PLATE 197. *Nymphaea* 'Moon Dance'. Florida Aquatic Nursery

PLATE 198. *Nymphaea* 'Moorei'. Perry D. Slocum

PLATE 199. *Nymphaea* 'Mrs. C. W. Thomas'. Lilypons
Water Gardens

PLATE 200. *Nymphaea* 'Mt. Shasta'. Perry D. Slocum

PLATE 202. *Nymphaea* 'Norma Gedye'. Perry D. Slocum

PLATE 201. *Nymphaea* 'Newton'. Perry D. Slocum

PLATE 203. *Nymphaea* 'Peaches and Cream'. Perry D. Slocum

PLATE 204. *Nymphaea* 'Perry's Autumn Sunset'.
Perry D. Slocum

PLATE 205. *Nymphaea* 'Perry's Baby Pink'. Perry D. Slocum

PLATE 206. *Nymphaea* 'Perry's Baby Red'. Perry D. Slocum

PLATE 207. *Nymphaea* 'Perry's Black Opal', first-day flower (top), third-day flower (bottom). Perry D. Slocum

PLATE 208. *Nymphaea* 'Perry's Cactus Pink'. Perry D. Slocum

PLATE 209. *Nymphaea* 'Perry's Double White'. Perry D. Slocum

PLATE 210. *Nymphaea* 'Perry's Double Yellow'. Perry D. Slocum

PLATE 211. *Nymphaea* 'Perry's Fire Opal'. Perry D. Slocum

PLATE 212. *Nymphaea* 'Perry's Magnificent'. Perry D. Slocum

PLATE 213. *Nymphaea* 'Perry's Orange Sunset'. Perry D. Slocum

PLATE 214. *Nymphaea* 'Perry's Pink'. Perry D. Slocum

PLATE 216. *Nymphaea* 'Perry's Red Beauty'. Perry D. Slocum

PLATE 215. *Nymphaea* 'Perry's Pink Heaven'. Perry D. Slocum

PLATE 217. *Nymphaea* 'Perry's Red Bicolor'. Perry D. Slocum

PLATE 218. *Nymphaea* 'Perry's Red Wonder'. Perry D. Slocum

PLATE 219. *Nymphaea* 'Perry's Rich Rose'. Perry D. Slocum

PLATE 220. *Nymphaea* 'Perry's Strawberry Pink'. Perry D. Slocum

PLATE 221. *Nymphaea* 'Perry's Super Red'. Perry D. Slocum

PLATE 222. *Nymphaea* 'Perry's Super Rose'. Perry D. Slocum

Plate 223. *Nymphaea* 'Perry's Super Yellow'. Perry D. Slocum

Plate 224. *Nymphaea* 'Perry's Vivid Rose'. Perry D. Slocum

Plate 225. *Nymphaea* 'Perry's Viviparous Pink', first-day flower in bloom, faded flower in hand showing new plant-let attached to the peduncle. Perry D. Slocum

Plate 226. *Nymphaea* 'Perry's White Star'. Perry D. Slocum

Plate 227. *Nymphaea* 'Peter Slocum'. Perry D. Slocum

PLATE 228. *Nymphaea* 'Pink Beauty'. Perry D. Slocum

PLATE 229. *Nymphaea* 'Pink Grapefruit'. Perry D. Slocum

Plate 230. *Nymphaea* 'Pink Sensation'. Perry D. Slocum

Plate 231. *Nymphaea* 'Red Paradise'. Perry D. Slocum

Plate 232. *Nymphaea* 'Red Queen'. Perry D. Slocum

Plate 234. *Nymphaea* 'Red Spider'. Perry D. Slocum

Plate 233. *Nymphaea* 'Red Sensation'. Perry D. Slocum

PLATE 235. *Nymphaea* 'Regann'. Reg Henley

PLATE 236. *Nymphaea* 'Rose Arey'. Perry D. Slocum

PLATE 237. *Nymphaea* 'Rosy Morn'. Perry D. Slocum

PLATE 238. *Nymphaea* 'Rubra'. Perry D. Slocum

PLATE 239. *Nymphaea* 'Ruby Red'. Perry D. Slocum

PLATE 240. *Nymphaea* 'Sioux', first-day flower (bottom), second-day flower (right), third-day flower (top left). Perry D. Slocum

PLATE 241. *Nymphaea* 'Splendida'. Perry D. Slocum

PLATE 242. *Nymphaea* 'Sultan'. Perry D. Slocum

PLATE 243. *Nymphaea* 'Sunrise'. Perry D. Slocum

PLATE 244. *Nymphaea* 'Texas Dawn'. Perry D. Slocum

PLATE 245. *Nymphaea tuberosa* 'Richardsonii'. Perry D. Slocum

PLATE 246. *Nymphaea* 'Venus'. Perry D. Slocum

PLATE 247. *Nymphaea* 'Vesuve'. Perry D. Slocum

PLATE 248. *Nymphaea* 'Virginalis'. Perry D. Slocum

PLATE 249. *Nymphaea* 'Virginia', third-day flower. Perry D. Slocum

PLATE 250. *Nymphaea* 'Walter Pagels'. Perry D. Slocum

PLATE 251. *Nymphaea* 'Weymouth Red'.
Norman Bennett

PLATE 252. *Nymphaea* 'White Sensation'. Perry D. Slocum

PLATE 253. *Nymphaea* 'White 1000 Petals'. Perry D. Slocum

PLATE 254. *Nymphaea* 'Wow'. Perry D. Slocum

PLATE 255. *Nymphaea* 'Yellow Princess'. Perry D. Slocum

PLATE 256. *Nymphaea* 'Yellow Queen'. Perry D. Slocum

PLATE 257. *Nymphaea* 'Yellow Sensation'. Perry D. Slocum

PLATE 258. *Nymphaea* 'Yogi Gi'. Dean McGee

Plate 259. *Nymphaea* 'Yuh-Ling'. Dean McGee

Plate 260. *Nuphar japonica*, third-day flower and new floating leaf. Perry D. Slocum

Plate 261. *Nuphar lutea* subsp. *macrophylla*, Lake Pierce, Florida. Perry D. Slocum

Plate 262. First-day flower of *Victoria* 'Adventure'. Kit Knotts

Plate 263. Second-day flower of *Victoria* 'Adventure'. Kit Knotts

PLATE 264. *Victoria amazonica*, first-day flower. Perry D. Slocum

PLATE 265. *Victoria amazonica*, second-day flower. Perry D. Slocum

PLATE 266. *Victoria cruziana*, first-day flower. Perry D. Slocum

PLATE 267. *Victoria* 'Longwood Hybrid', first-day flower. Perry D. Slocum

PLATE 268. *Victoria* 'Longwood Hybrid', second-day flower. Perry D. Slocum

PLATE 269. *Euryale ferox*, leaf coverage. Perry D. Slocum

PLATE 270. *Euryale ferox*. Perry D. Slocum

PLATE 271. *Euryale ferox*, underside of leaf. Perry D. Slocum

Plate 272. *Barclaya longifolia*. Perry D. Slocum

Plate 274. *Ondinea purpurea* subsp. *petaloidea*. Ed Schneider

Plate 273. *Ondinea* tubers. Ed Schneider

Plate 275. *Nelumbo nucifera*, rhizomes of the "edible lotus" variant. Perry D. Slocum

Plate 276. *Nelumbo* 'Alba Grandiflora' (Asiatic lotus). Perry D. Slocum

Plate 277. *Nelumbo* 'Alba Striata', first-day flower. Perry D. Slocum

PLATE 278. *Nelumbo* 'Alba Striata', second-day flower. Perry D. Slocum

PLATE 279. *Nelumbo* 'Angel Wings'. Perry D. Slocum

PLATE 280. *Nelumbo* 'Baby Doll' growing in an Aqualite pool. Perry D. Slocum

Plate 281. *Nelumbo* 'Ben Gibson'. Perry D. Slocum

Plate 282. *Nelumbo* 'Charles Thomas'. Perry D. Slocum

Plate 283. *Nelumbo* 'Chawan Basu'. Perry D. Slocum

Plate 284. *Nelumbo* 'First Lady'. Perry D. Slocum

Plate 285. *Nelumbo* 'Gregg Gibson'. Perry D. Slocum

Plate 286. *Nelumbo* 'Lavender Lady'. Perry D. Slocum

PLATE 287. *Nelumbo* 'Linda'. Perry D. Slocum

PLATE 288. *Nelumbo* 'Little Tom Thumb'. Perry D. Slocum

PLATE 289. *Nelumbo* 'Louise Slocum'. Perry D. Slocum

PLATE 290. *Nelumbo* 'Louise Slocum' and Louise Slocum. Perry D. Slocum

PLATE 291. *Nelumbo* 'Louise Slocum'. Perry D. Slocum

PLATE 292. *Nelumbo lutea*. Perry D. Slocum

PLATE 293. *Nelumbo lutea* 'Yellow Bird'. Perry D. Slocum

PLATE 294. *Nelumbo* 'Maggie Belle Slocum' and Maggie Belle Slocum. Perry D. Slocum

PLATE 295. *Nelumbo* 'Momo Botan'. Perry D. Slocum

PLATE 296. *Nelumbo* 'Mrs. Perry D. Slocum'. Perry D. Slocum

PLATE 297. *Nelumbo* 'Night and Day'. Perry D. Slocum

PLATE 298. The author's granddaughter, Nikki Gibson, with *Nelumbo* 'Nikki Gibson', first-day (left) and third-day flower (right). Perry D. Slocum

PLATE 299. *Nelumbo nucifera*. Perry D. Slocum

PLATE 301. *Nelumbo nucifera* var. *rosea*, second-day flower. Perry D. Slocum

PLATE 300. *Nelumbo nucifera* var. *caspicum*. Perry D. Slocum

PLATE 302. *Nelumbo nucifera* 'Alba Plena' (Shiroman lotus). Perry D. Slocum

PLATE 303. *Nelumbo nucifera* 'Shirokunshi' (tulip lotus). Perry D. Slocum

PLATE 304. *Nelumbo nucifera* 'Waltzing Matilda' showing a new red leaf. Perry D. Slocum

PLATE 305. *Nelumbo* 'Patricia Garrett'. Perry D. Slocum

PLATE 306. Owner Ben Gibson and a display bed of *Nelumbo* 'Pekinensis Rubra' at Perry's Water Gardens, Franklin, North Carolina. Perry D. Slocum

PLATE 307. *Nelumbo* 'Pekinensis Rubra', first-day flower. Perry D. Slocum

PLATE 308. *Nelumbo* 'Pekinensis Rubra', second-day flower. Perry D. Slocum

PLATE 309. *Nelumbo* 'Pekinensis Rubra', third-day flower. Perry D. Slocum

PLATE 310. *Nelumbo* 'Perry's Double Red Lotus'. Perry D. Slocum

PLATE 311. Lacy Houston holding a flower of *Nelumbo* 'Perry's Giant Sunburst'. Perry D. Slocum

PLATE 312. *Nelumbo* 'Perry's Super Star', first-day flower. Perry D. Slocum

PLATE 313. *Nelumbo* 'Perry's Super Star', second-day flower. Perry D. Slocum

PLATE 314. *Nelumbo* 'Perry's Super Star', third-day flower. Perry D. Slocum

PLATE 315. *Nelumbo* 'Pink and Yellow'. Perry D. Slocum

PLATE 316. *Nelumbo* 'Rosea Plena'. Perry D. Slocum

PLATE 318. *Nelumbo* 'Strawberry Blonde', first-day flower. Perry D. Slocum

PLATE 317. *Nelumbo* 'Sharon'. Perry D. Slocum

PLATE 319. *Nelumbo* 'Strawberry Blonde', second-day flower. Perry D. Slocum

PLATE 320. *Nelumbo* 'Strawberry Blonde', third-day flower. Perry D. Slocum

PLATE 321. *Nelumbo* 'Suzanne'. Perry D. Slocum

PLATE 322. *Nelumbo* 'Sweetheart'. Perry D. Slocum

PLATE 323. *Nelumbo* 'The President'. Perry D. Slocum

CHAPTER 1

The Genus *Nymphaea*

THE WATERLILY family, Nymphaeaceae, includes six genera: *Nymphaea, Nuphar, Victoria, Euryale, Barclaya* (syn. *Hydrostemma*), and *Ondinea* (Figure 1). The classification of these plants has been considerably confused, and the present taxonomy represents a painstaking attempt to sort out the identification and nomenclature of the various species and cultivars. For some plant groups, further study is needed before the taxonomy can be considered authoritative.

In recent years some important changes have been made in established classifications: the genera *Barclaya* and *Ondinea* have been added to the family Nymphaeaceae and the former waterlily genera *Brasenia* and *Cabomba* are now in the Cabombaceae. In addition, anatomical, morphological, phytochemical, and other studies demonstrate that *Nelumbo* (lotus) should not be considered a member of the waterlily family. Molecular studies of the Nymphaeaceae (*Water Garden Journal*, Winter 1993) show that *Nelumbo* does not have the same *rbc*L gene sequence in the chloroplast that *Nymphaea, Nuphar, Victoria, Euryale*, and *Barclaya* possess. (*Ondinea* was not studied for this report.) Therefore,

Nelumbo has now been placed in a family by itself: Nelumbonaceae. Descriptions of the waterlily genera *Nuphar, Victoria, Euryale, Barclaya*, and *Ondinea* are given in chapter 7, while chapter 8 describes the lotuses, *Nelumbo*.

A most basic distinction can be made between tropical waterlilies, those native to tropical or semi-tropical climates, and hardy waterlilies, which are native to cooler climates. The blooms of all hardy waterlilies open during the daytime, whereas tropical species and cultivars can be distinguished as day blooming or night blooming. The tropical flowers of night bloomers in the subgenus *Hydrocallis* bloom in the middle of the night for a short time (only two hours in some species). Flowers of the night bloomers in the subgenus *Lotos* open around dusk and stay open to nearly noon on the following day. On cloudy or cool days these blooms may stay open all day. Typically *Lotos* flowers are large and showy.

Tropical waterlily blooms are usually raised several inches above the water. Last-day flowers usually float. So-called star lilies, whose parentage includes *Nymphaea flavovirens* (syn. *N. gracilis*) or *N. capensis* var. *zanzibariensis*, are day bloomers that may raise

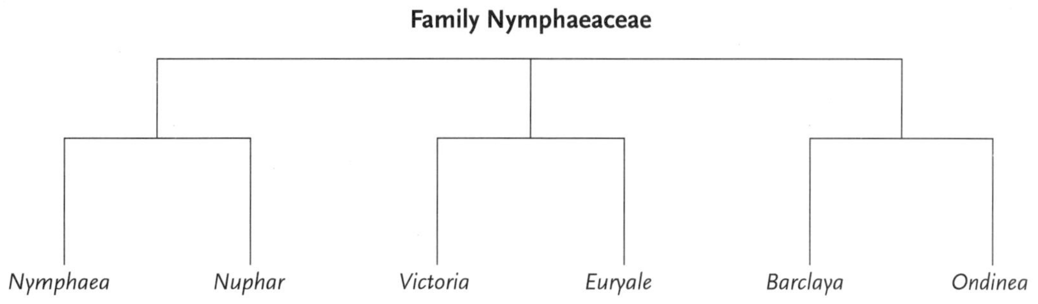

Family Nymphaeaceae

Nymphaea — Nuphar — Victoria — Euryale — Barclaya — Ondinea

FIGURE 1. The six genera of the waterlily family.

their flowers 12 in. (30 cm) or more above water. Hardy waterlilies generally raise their blooms only slightly above the water or allow them to float. The hardy exceptions include the cultivars *N.* 'Pink Starlet' (1970) and *N.* 'Texas Dawn' (1985), with blooms held 9 and 10 in. (23 and 25 cm) above the water, respectively.

An interesting and unusual method of viviparous reproduction (bearing young plants) occurs in a few tropical species. *Nymphaea micrantha* and many of its hybrids form new young plants (or plantlets) on their leaves at the junction to the petiole. These plantlets may bloom while still attached to the mother plant. Another type of viviparous reproduction occurs in two species of the *Hydrocallis* group: *N. lasiophylla* and *N. prolifera* form new plants from tubers developing in the flowers.

No species of hardy waterlily is considered viviparous, although *Nymphaea* 'Colonel A. J. Welch' is a possible exception. This is a Marliac introduction, and little is known about when it was introduced or its parentage. Hybridizer Reg Henley of Odiham, Hampshire, England, considers this plant a species because it produces young plants with rhizomes from many of its flowers (several hardy cultivars do this also). Henley has presented programs on his hybridizing efforts to the International Water-

lily and Water Gardening Society and is widely acclaimed for his work. The hardy waterlily cultivars that occasionally develop plantlets from old flowers are *N.* 'Perry's Pink Delight', *N.* 'Perry's Red Star', and *N.* 'Perry's Viviparous Pink'.

Nymphaea species, not necessarily the cultivars, may be broadly described as follows: Petals number 12–40; there are usually four sepals, rarely three or five; stamens can be numerous, 20–700 in number; carpels number 8–35; the stigma is broad, concave, and radiate; fruit is spongy and ripens underwater; seeds mature with floating sacks (Figure 2). Reproduction by seed involves ripe seeds bursting to the top of the water by means of a buoyant aril (the floating sack), a spongy, gelatinous mass of tissue covering each seed. This tissue stays intact for two to three days while wind or waves move seeds to new areas. The sacks dissolve and the seeds sink to the bottom to initiate germination.

Dr. Henry S. Conard, who published his authoritative *The Waterlilies: A Monograph of the Genus Nymphaea* (1905), described these plants as "aquatic herbs" with perennial elongated or tuberous rhizomes that root in mud at the bottom of streams, ponds, lakes, and other bodies of water. The lovely blossoms are white or various shades of blue, red, or yellow. The colors orange (in hardies) and green,

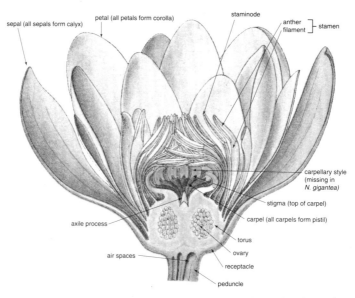

FIGURE 2. Cross section of a hardy waterlily flower. After a plate from *The Waterlilies: A Monograph of the Genus Nymphaea* by Henry S. Conard (1905).

violet, and purple (in tropicals) also are seen in cultivars.

The New Species

After several talks with Kenneth Landon, an expert on waterlily species, I believe that Conard's taxonomy of waterlilies provides a good working basis. Yet it is necessary to add a few species discovered since Conard's studies to bring the taxonomy up to date.

In 1929 B. D. Burtt, botanist for the Tse Tse Research Bureau, Kondoa, Tanganyika Territory, Africa, discovered *Nymphaea burtii* Pring & Woodson. In 1951, Dr. George Pring determined that *N. burtii* and *N. stuhlmannii* were actually the same species—a judgment I accept.

In 1939 the Royal Botanic Gardens, Kew, England, received seeds of a new waterlily from Africa. These seeds were forwarded to the Missouri Botanical Garden by R. S. Trickett. The name *Nymphaea colorata* Peter was assigned, as A. Peter had originally described this plant in 1928.

In 1986 Kenneth Landon discovered a white day-blooming tropical with features that set it apart from similar species in the rain pools, rivers, and streams of the Togo region of Africa. He assigned it the name *Nymphaea togoensis* Landon. A night-blooming tropical, *N. spontanea* Landon, has recently been elevated to species status.

Dr. John H. Wiersema of the USDA-ARS's Systemic Botany and Mycology Laboratory, Beltsville, Maryland, has done extensive research on the subgenus *Hydrocallis*. His studies have resulted in dropping three species, *Nymphaea blanda* Meyer, *N. stenaspidota* Caspary, and *N. gibertii* Morong, from Conard's listing and adding seven new species: *N. belophylla* Trickett, *N. conardii* Wiersema, *N. glandulifera* Rodschied, *N. lingulata* Wiersema, *N. novogranatensis* Wiersema, *N. potamophila* Wiersema, and *N. prolifera* Wiersema.

Still other species have been proposed during the years since Conard's comprehensive studies in the *Anecphya* and *Nymphaea gigantea* complex. Further research must be done on the subgenus *Anecphya* in order to properly interpret its variants. The following is a list of seven published species closely related to *Nymphaea gigantea* that may or may not attain species rank upon further study. The first five were briefly described in the March 1989 *Water Garden Journal* by Dr. Surrey Jacobs, Royal Botanic Gardens, Sydney, Australia:

1. *Nymphaea dictyophlebia* Merrill & Perry; blue or white flowers; native to the Northern Territory and Queensland, Australia, and Papuasia;
2. *Nymphaea hastifolia* Domin; small white flowers; native to north Australia;
3. *Nymphaea macrosperma* Merrill & Perry; blue flowers; native to the north of the Northern Territory, Australia, and Papuasia;
4. *Nymphaea minima* Jacobs; small blue flowers; native to northeast Queensland, Australia;
5. *Nymphaea violacea* Lehman; blue, white, or pink flowers, usually deep blue; most widespread of the five species described by Dr. Jacobs, native to the north and parts of central Australia and Papuasia;
6. *Nymphaea brownii* F. M. Bailey; pale bluish white flowers; plant is being grown at Longwood Gardens, Pennsylvania; according to Patrick Nutt, foreman of plant propagation at Longwood Gardens, *N. brownii* has no commercial value but could be used in hybridizing; native to Australia;
7. *Nymphaea casparyi* (Rehnelt & Henkel) Carrière; light to medium blue flowers, similar to the *N. gigantea* type but with divergent sinus margins; native to Australia.

Dr. Kirk Strawn, former owner of Strawn Water Gardens, believes that Jacobs was correct in referring the first five taxa to species rank. However, Kenneth Landon, who has researched the group extensively for many years, considers these seven so-called species to be varieties or forms of the *Nymphaea gigantea* complex, because they do not breed true from seed—a requirement for species status. This latter is the view to which I subscribe.

Taxonomy of the Genus *Nymphaea*

The genus *Nymphaea* is divided into two main groups, which in turn divide into five subgenera, according to Dr. Henry Conard (1905). Group *Apocarpiae* includes the subgenera *Anecphya* and *Brachy-*

ceras, and group *Syncarpiae* consists of the subgenera *Hydrocallis, Lotos,* and *Nymphaea* (syn. *Castalia*).

Group *Apocarpiae* consists entirely of *Nymphaea gigantea* and the other tropical day-blooming waterlilies. Conard placed the hardy waterlilies of subgenus *Nymphaea* in group *Syncarpiae* with the night-blooming tropicals (*Hydrocallis* and *Lotos*) because his studies revealed a closer botanical rela-tionship between hardy waterlilies and night-blooming tropicals than with day-blooming tropicals. The *Nymphaea* subgenera are enumerated below. Plants of all the subgenera are described in chapter 2, except subgenus *Nymphaea*, which is de-scribed in chapter 5. By the summer of 2003, the name *N. mexicana* 'Cape Canaveral' was accepted and being used for *N. mexicana* f. *canaveralensis*.

Group *Apocarpiae*
Subgenus *Anecphya*
Nymphaea gigantea Hooker
- *N. gigantea* var. *alba* (Bentham) Landon
- *N. gigantea* var. *neorosea* Landon
- *N. gigantea* var. *purpurea*
- *N. gigantea* var. *violacea* (Lehman) Conard

Subgenus *Brachyceras*
N. ampla (Salisbury) de Candolle
- *N. ampla* var. *pulchella* (de Candolle) Caspary
- *N. ampla* var. *speciosa* (Martius & Zuccarini) Caspary

N. caerulea Savigny
N. calliantha Conard
- *N. calliantha* var. *tenuis* Conard

N. capensis Thunberg
- *N. capensis* var. *alba* Landon
- *N. capensis* var. *madagascariensis* (de Candolle) Conard
- *N. capensis* var. *zanzibariensis* (Caspary) Conard

N. colorata Peter
N. elegans Hooker
N. flavovirens Lehmann
N. heudelotii Planchon
- *N. heudelotii* var. *nana*

N. micrantha Guillemin & Perrottet
N. nouchali Burman f.
- *N. nouchali* var. *cyanea* (Hooker f. & Thomson) Almeida
- *N. nouchali* var. *versicolor* (Roxburgh) Hooker f. & Thomson

N. ovalifolia Conard
N. stuhlmannii (Engler) Schweinfurth & Gilg
N. sulfurea Gilg
N. togoensis Landon

Group *Syncarpiae*
Subgenus *Hydrocallis*
N. amazonum subsp. *amazonum* Martius & Zuccarini
- *N. amazonum* subsp. *pedersenii* Wiersema

N. belophylla Trickett
N. conardii Wiersema
N. gardneriana Planchon
N. glandulifera Rodschied
N. jamesoniana Planchon
N. lasiophylla Martius & Zuccarini
N. lingulata Wiersema
N. novogranatensis Wiersema
N. oxypetala Planchon
N. potamophila Wiersema
N. prolifera Wiersema
N. rudgeana G. Meyer
N. tenerinervia Caspary

Subgenus *Lotos*
N. lotus Linnaeus
N. pubescens Willdenow
N. rubra Roxburgh
N. spontanea Landon
N. zenkeri Gilg

Subgenus *Nymphaea*
Section *Chamaenymphaea*
N. tetragona Georgi
- *N. tetragona* var. *angusta* Caspary
- *N. tetragona* var. *lata* Caspary
- *N. tetragona* var. *leibergii* (Morong) Porsild

Section *Eucastalia*
N. alba Linnaeus
- *N. alba* var. *rubra* Lönnroth

N. candida Presl
N. odorata Aiton
- *N. odorata* var. *gigantea* Tricker
- *N. odorata* var. *minor* Sims
- *N. odorata* var. *rosea* Pursh

N. tuberosa Paine
Section *Xanthantha*
N. mexicana Zuccarini
- *N. mexicana* f. *canaveralensis* Frase

CHAPTER 2

Tropical Waterlily Species

FIVE TROPICAL waterlily species that grow well in water gardens are widely available in the aquatic nursery trade (see Sources for Plants and Equipment at end of the book). These species are *Nymphaea capensis, N. colorata, N. gigantea, N. lotus,* and *N. rubra. Nymphaea capensis* (cape waterlily) from the Cape of Good Hope region in Africa is often listed as "blue capensis." There are many commonly available cultivars of *N. capensis* from Zanzibar, many of them selections of variety *zanzibariensis. Nymphaea colorata* is a very choice and desirable waterlily for small or medium pools, and it is comparable to its hybrids *N.* 'Director George T. Moore' and *N.* 'Midnight'. *Nymphaea gigantea,* listed as 'Blue Gigantea' in William Tricker's catalog, is quite large, very beautiful, and very impressive. It does require water of 80°F (27°C) to grow and bloom; otherwise, it enters dormancy. Two night bloomers, *N. lotus* and *N. rubra,* are also being grown and sold in nurseries. (*Nymphaea* 'Juno' is usually considered to be *N. lotus,* and *N.* 'Trudy Slocum' was selected from a group of *N.* 'Juno'.) Most of the other species have similar counterparts in cultivars that are superior in performance, and the species not currently in cultivation are generally considered inferior to hybrids and are therefore not marketed.

This chapter contains a complete listing of tropical day-blooming and night-blooming waterlily species, varieties, forms, and named selections. The arrangement follows the taxonomy of the genus *Nymphaea* as discussed in chapter 1. First, I give a brief summary of the group characteristics and then describe the plants.

The species are arranged alphabetically by specific epithet with descriptions of related plants (vari-

eties, forms, and named selections) immediately following; author and date of discovery are given when known. Synonyms are given after the botanical name, followed by common names, if any. In descriptions of several rare species, when I could not compare live specimens (or sharp photos) with the *RHS Colour Chart,* standard color references are omitted.

In the species descriptions in this book the stamen consists of the anther (bearing pollen), a typically slender filament holding the anther, and often an appendage, or "tip," just above the anther (Figure 3). "Stamen color" refers to the color of the filament portion of the stamen, and "anther color" to the various colors of the anther and tip. "Leaf size" refers either to the diameter of the leaf of a mature plant or to the measurements of its length × width, in that order. "Leaf spread" refers to the diameter of the area on the water's surface covered by a mature plant. See Figure 4 for the variety of forms and characteristics *Nymphaea* leaves may have.

Plant tropical waterlilies only when the water temperature averages 75°F (24°C) or above. Planting too early may induce dormancy. Refer to the hardiness zone maps at the end of the book and follow this general planting timetable:

In North America		In Europe	
Zone 10	March–early April	Zone 10	mid–late May
Zone 9	early April	Zone 9	June
Zone 8	mid April	Zones 8–4	conservatory
Zone 7	mid–late May		planting, where
Zone 6	late May–early June		water can be
Zone 5	early–mid June		heated to 75°F
Zone 4	mid–late June		(24°C) or higher

Group *Apocarpiae* Caspary

In general, species in the group *Apocarpiae* display carpels that are free from one another at the sides, fused along part of the suture with the axis of the flower, and fused dorsally with the perigynous torus. These are tropical species with diurnal flowers ranging in color from blue through pink to white. Blooms are raised 3–12 in. (8–30 cm) above the water. Peduncles are stiff. Rhizomes are upright, tuberous, and round (or nearly so). Tubers are dormant during the dry season in their native habitat; growth initiates with the rainy season. Cold weather (60–68°F, 16–20°C for two or three days) may also induce dormancy. Viviparous varieties and night-blooming varieties can take more cold than others.

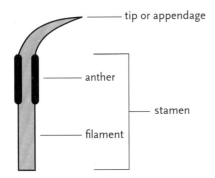

FIGURE 3. The stamen of a tropical waterlily. The tip, or appendage, is characteristic of day-blooming tropical waterlilies.

Subgenus *Anecphya* Caspary

The subgenus *Anecphya* consists of a single species, *Nymphaea gigantea*, which is native to Australia and New Guinea. The species includes three varieties. Carpellary styles are generally absent. Stamens are plentiful with narrow filaments and short, curved anthers without appendages. Kenneth Landon (*Phytologia*, September 1978) described other *N. gigantea* variants as follows: "In a given colony of *N. gigantea* where various varieties and forms exist, crosses between plants are sure to eventuate with the resulting progeny giving rise to natural hybrids some of which may be individualized enough to warrant separate distinction. The vast majority of such hybrids, however, are seldom self-sustaining seed-producers, and after a short time their identity is often lost. The typical blue *N. gigantea*, along with several other variants (such as variety *violacea*), produce self-fertile seedlings, some of which evolve as botanical mutants (sports), creating other distinct variants. Generally, however, such progenal differences are so slight as to be subordinate to botanical varieties or even forms with regard to classification."

Nymphaea gigantea Hooker

Native to north Australia, New Guinea

PLATE 2

CHARACTERISTICS. Day blooming, nonviviparous, free flowering; flowers held 12 in. (30 cm) above water.

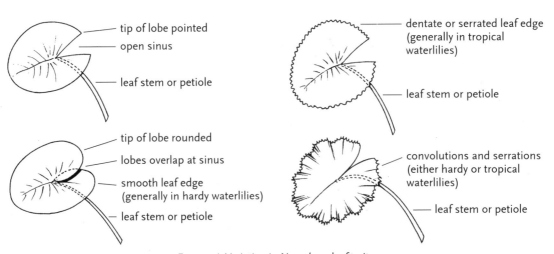

FIGURE 4. Variation in *Nymphaea* leaf traits.

FLOWERS. Petal color: Inner petals, pale blue-violet (*RHS* 92C); outer, deeper blue-violet (*RHS* 92A,B). Sepal color: Medium violet-purple (*RHS* 92A). Anther color: Deep yellow (*RHS* 5B). Stamen color: Yellow. Flower shape: Large, globular star. Flower size: 10–12 in. (25–30 cm). Fragrance: Slight. Number of petals: 24. Number of sepals: 4.

LEAVES. Color: Top, green; underside, purplish. Leaf egg-shaped; sinus, a half-open V. Leaf size: 15 × 13 in. (38 × 33 cm). Leaf spread: 7–8 ft. (2.1–2.4 m). Stem color: Peduncle, bright green; petiole, green, many tiny purple specks and dots. No pubescence on peduncle or petiole.

COMMENTS. *Nymphaea gigantea* is a magnificent species. The large, unique flowers are stunning. Blooms are held high above the water and the abundance of yellow stamens is very striking. This is a fine plant for the collector with a large pool in a warm climate or with a heated conservatory. Both white and pink variants exist. At least one nursery (William Tricker, Inc.) offers *N. gigantea* under the name 'Blue Gigantea'.

Nymphaea gigantea var. *alba* (Bentham) Landon
Syn. *Nymphaea gigantea* f. *alba* Bentham & Müller
PLATE 3
FLOWERS. Average 3.5–4 in. (9–10 cm) in diameter; petals (about 20) are a dazzling white within and without; four sepals white inside; 350–500 stamens have bright yellow anthers.

LEAVES. On mature plants nearly round, averaging 14 in. (35 cm) in diameter, green above and below. Leaf margin is dentate with short, acute teeth.

COMMENTS. Variety *alba* is self-sustaining from seed, yet is sometimes variable.

Nymphaea gigantea var. *neorosea* Landon
Syn. *Nymphaea gigantea* f. *neorosea*
PLATE 4
FLOWER. Diameter 3–5 in. (8–13 cm); petals (average 25), are long, narrow at base, longer than sepals, and, unlike most waterlily blooms, not entirely covered by sepals after first-day closing. Deep rose, darkest at apex and lighter toward base. Outer petals are deepest rose, innermost petals lightest. Four sepals are rose-colored and slightly darker rose

at margins. Stamens (about 412) have bright yellow anthers.

LEAVES. Nearly orbicular, averaging 14 × 13 in. (35 × 33 cm); dentate, green above with maroon spots, and green on underside with maroon perimeter. Sinus is open.

COMMENTS. Variety *neorosea* is self-sustaining from seed.

Nymphaea gigantea var. *purpurea*
PLATE 5
COMMENTS. This variety is not only one of the darkest of the *N. gigantea* complex but, according to Ken Landon, who has done a lot of work and study of the giganteas and their forms and variations, it is one of the two *gigantea* varieties that is consistent from seed (the other is *N. gigantea* var. *neorosea*). Even though *Nymphaea gigantea* var. *purpurea* and *N. gigantea* var. *neorosea* have nearly a 100 percent "true to form" germination from seed, Landon feels that they should still be considered varieties and not species.

Nymphaea gigantea var. *violacea* (Lehman)
Conard
PLATE 6
FLOWERS. Average more than 5 in. (13 cm) in diameter; petals average 27, with outermost dark violet or purple and innermost paler. Four sepals are dark violet on the interior side, green (as with most waterlilies) on the exterior. Flowers contain 500 stamens on average.

LEAVES. Ovate, 15 in. (38 cm) average diameter, green above, and deep purple below; margin dentate.

COMMENTS. This variety is self-sustaining from seed yet produces some variant progeny. Seedlings sometimes develop a lighter colored bloom.

Nymphaea gigantea 'Albert de Lestang'
Pring 1946
PLATE 7
FLOWERS. Average 6 in. (15 cm) in diameter; petals (average 33) predominantly white streaked with purplish blue, becoming darker at base; outer petals streaked a deeper purplish blue; inner petals white except for purple at point of attachment; overall appearance bluish white. Purplish blue coloring fades

in later days, becoming deep rose after spent flower submerges into the water. Stamens average 500.

LEAVES. Leaf of mature plant is nearly round, averaging 20 in. (50 cm) in diameter. Margin wavy with dentate yellow- or brown-tipped teeth. Green on top and green tinged with brownish violet below.

COMMENTS. The bluish white flowers are the largest (8–10 in., 20–25 cm) of the *Nymphaea gigantea* variants.

Nymphaea gigantea 'Blue Cloud' Landon 2001

Preselected seedling of *N. gigantea* × *N. gigantea* var. *violacea*

PLATE 8

CHARACTERISTICS. Very free flowering, nonviviparous.

FLOWERS. Petal color: Blue to dark blue to purple. Sepal color: Inner, light purple; outer, yellow green. Anther color: Inner, yellow; outer, yellow. Stamen color: Yellow. Flower shape: Globe. Flower size: 12 in. (30 cm). Fragrance: None. Number of petals: 30. Number of sepals: 4.

LEAVES. Color: Top, green to yellow-green; underside, violet with prominent green veins beneath. Sinus open (30 degrees). Leaf size: 22 × 20 in. (55 × 50 cm). Leaf spread: 15–20 ft. (4.5–6 m). Stem color: Olive green. Faint pubescence on peduncle and petiole when young.

COMMENTS BY KEN LANDON. This hybrid is slightly fertile, producing an abundance of very showy well-shaped broad-petaled flowers of exceptional color and contrast.

Nymphaea gigantea 'Hudsoniana' Hudson 1893

PLATE 9

COMMENTS. The blue flowers of *N.* 'Hudsoniana' are larger than those of variety *violacea*, averaging 6–8 in. (15–20 cm) in diameter. Original accounts describe dark to medium blue flowers.

Nymphaea gigantea intermediate forms 1 and 2

Landon

COMMENTS. Forms 1 and 2 are unnamed forms indigenous to Australia. The distinguishing characteristics of form 1 are the large flowers colored a rich royal purplish blue. The distinguishing characteristics of form 2 are its medium- to large-sized flowers,

which at a distance appear totally white but upon closer examination are white lightly streaked with purplish blue.

Subgenus *Brachyceras* Caspary

Subgenus *Brachyceras* includes 14 species distributed throughout the tropics. In general, carpellary styles are present; styles are short, stiff, and fleshy. Stamens are numerous. Anthers are long and usually have sturdy appendages. Filaments are flat. The day-blooming tropical cultivars commonly seen today were derived from this group through hybridizing. Two of the species, *Nymphaea capensis* and *N. colorata*, are grown extensively in water gardens around the world.

Nymphaea ampla (Salisbury) de Candolle

Native to south Texas, Mexico, Central America, south to central Brazil, Antilles, and the Bahamas

PLATE 10

CHARACTERISTICS. Day blooming, nonviviparous, very free flowering.

FLOWERS. Petal color: White (*RHS* 155D); outermost petals flushed yellowish green (*RHS* 149D). Sepal color: White (*RHS* 155A), flushed green (*RHS* 145D). Anther color: Yellow, white tips (*RHS* 4A; tips, 155D). Stamen color: Yellow. Flower shape: Stellate. Flower size: 4–5.5 in. (10–14 cm). Fragrance: Pronounced. Number of petals: 7–21. Number of sepals: 4.

LEAVES. Color: Top, new leaves bronzy red, soon bronzy green, then green; underside, reddish purple, prominent veins and numerous small black specks. Leaf usually slightly longer than wide, dentate, many long teeth and serrations, wavy perimeter; sinus usually open. Leaf size: 15–20 in. (38–50 cm). Leaf spread: 8 ft. (2.4 m). Stem color: Greenish brown. No pubescence on peduncle or petiole.

COMMENTS. *Nymphaea ampla*, if available, is suitable only for the collector with a medium or large pool.

Nymphaea ampla var. *pulchella* (de Candolle)

Caspary

Native to tropical and subtropical America

COMMENTS. Flowers have fewer stamens and

are smaller than average for the species. Leaf edges are less wavy.

Nymphaea ampla var. *speciosa* (Martius & Zuccarini) Caspary
Native to Mexico, West Indies, and Brazil

COMMENTS. Blooms are white but smaller than the type. Leaves sharply dentate with a relatively soft texture.

Nymphaea caerulea Savigny
Native to north and central Africa

PLATE 11

CHARACTERISTICS. Day blooming, nonviviparous, free flowering.

FLOWERS. Petal color: Base, nearly white (*RHS* paler than 91C); tip, light violet blue (*RHS* 91C). Sepal color: White (*RHS* 155A). Anther color: Yellow, light blue tips (*RHS* 158A; tips, 91C). Stamen color: Yellow. Flower shape: Stellate. Flower size: 3–6 in. (8–15 cm). Fragrance: Very faint. Number of petals: 14–20. Number of sepals: 4.

LEAVES. Color: Top, green; underside, green, small purple spots. Leaf egg-shaped; lobes usually overlap at sinus. Leaf size: 12–16 in. (30–40 cm). Leaf spread: 8–10 ft. (2.4–3 m). Stem color: Brownish green. No pubescence on peduncle or petiole.

COMMENTS. *Nymphaea caerulea* is known as the "blue lotus of the Nile," though actually there is no such thing as a blue lotus. *Nymphaea caerulea* produces seeds easily and is a parent of *N.* 'Blue Beauty'. Due to the large leaves, the large coverage, and the small flowers, I recommend this species only for the collector with a large pool.

Nymphaea calliantha Conard
Native to central and southwest Africa

CHARACTERISTICS. Day blooming, nonviviparous, free flowering.

FLOWERS. Petal color: Pink, violet-blue, or light blue. Sepal color: Base, white; apex, tippled rose-pink for 0.6–0.75 in. (1.5–2 cm). Anther color: Yellow. Stamen color: Yellow. Flower shape: Stellate. Flower size: 4–6 in. (10–15 cm). Fragrance: Pleasant. Number of petals: 17. Number of sepals: 4.

LEAVES. Color: Top, green; underside, purplish margin shading to green. Leaf nearly egg-shaped;

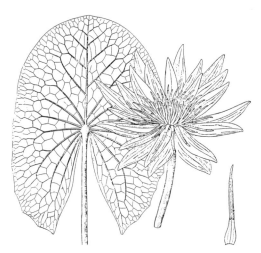

FIGURE 5. *Nymphaea calliantha*, flower and underside of leaf reduced; outer stamen enlarged. From *The Waterlilies: A Monograph of the Genus Nymphaea* by Henry S. Conard (1905).

wide-open lobes form a pronounced V. Leaf size: 5–11 × 3.5–9 in. (13–28 × 9–23 cm). Leaf spread: 6–8 ft. (1.8–2.4 m). Stem color: Greenish. No pubescence on peduncle or petiole.

COMMENTS. This species is not currently listed in nursery catalogs and is quite rare. Charles Masters, who has done extensive research on waterlilies, believes *N. calliantha* would probably become popular if introduced.

Nymphaea calliantha var. *tenuis* Conard
Native to central and southwest Africa

FLOWERS. White or light blue, 3.5–5.5 in. (9–14 cm) in diameter.

LEAVES. Green above, dark purple on underside, 3–4 × 3–3.5 in. (8–10 × 8–9 cm).

COMMENTS. Conard (1905) stated that *Nymphaea calliantha* var. *tenuis* should prove a valuable acquisition for the water garden. A century later, this has yet to happen.

Nymphaea capensis Thunberg
Cape waterlily, blue capensis

Native to the Cape of Good Hope region, Africa

PLATE 12

CHARACTERISTICS. Day blooming, nonviviparous, very free flowering; flower usually held 8–10 in. (20–25 cm) above water.

FLOWERS. Petal color: Light blue (*RHS* 92C). Sepal color: Pale blue or light green (*RHS* 92D or 128D). Anther color: Violet-blue (*RHS* 92C). Stamen color: Deep yellow. Flower shape: Stellate. Flower size: 6–8 in. (15–20 cm). Fragrance: Delightful. Number of petals: 21–38. Number of sepals: 4.

LEAVES. Color: Top, green; underside, green. Leaf nearly round, dentate, serrated; sinus usually closed, may be partly open. Leaf size: 10–16 in. (25–40 cm). Leaf spread: 5–8 ft. (1.5–2.4 m). Stem color: Green. No pubescence on peduncle or petiole.

COMMENTS. Because this plant will adapt to a limited growing area, it can be planted in pools of nearly any size. Although this is a fine waterlily for the collector, much more colorful cultivars are now available for water gardeners.

Nymphaea capensis var. *alba* Landon

Native to the Okavango River Delta, Kalahari Desert, Botswana, Africa

COMMENTS. This recently discovered variety differs from the type by having white flowers, 5 in. (13 cm) in diameter. Differences include young leaves displaying maroon blotches, and leaf undersides are violet or dark purple. As there are several better (larger-flowered) white cultivars available, I recommend this waterlily for the collector only.

Nymphaea capensis var. *madagascariensis* (de Candolle) Conard

Native to Madagascar

COMMENTS. This is a small variety, with leaves about 2.5 in. (6 cm) in diameter.

Nymphaea capensis var. *zanzibariensis*

(Caspary) Conard
Blue Zanzibar
Native to Zanzibar
PLATES 13, 14

COMMENTS. Differs from the type principally in its larger flowers, 7–10 in. (18–25 cm), and fewer petals on average. Like *N. capensis*, this variety is very free flowering and hybridizes readily with other species of the *Brachyceras* group. Seedlings show much variation in flower size and color. Many shades of blue, pink, and even red often develop. The seedlings from a single pod can even display a range of flower color. A choice seedling with light to medium blue flowers is marketed as *N. capensis* var. *zanzibariensis* 'Azurea'; a pink-flowered seedling is *N. capensis* var. *zanzibariensis* 'Rosea' (pink capensis). Other selections, including *N.* 'King of Blues', with deep violet-blue flowers, and the red-flowered *N.* 'Red Beauty', are described in chapter 3.

Nymphaea colorata Peter

Native to Africa
PLATE 15

CHARACTERISTICS. Day blooming, nonviviparous, very free flowering.

FLOWERS. Petal color: Rich, violet-blue, paling (*RHS* 91A then 92C). Sepal color: Violet-blue, veins deeper (*RHS* 92B; veins, 92A). Anther color: Deep reddish blue; tips lighter, purplish (*RHS* 83B; tips, 94C). Stamen color: Purple-black. Flower shape: Cuplike. Flower size: 4.5–5.5 in. (11–14 cm). Fragrance: Slight, if any. Number of petals: 13–15. Number of sepals: 4 or 5.

LEAVES. Color: Top, green; underside, bluish violet, prominent green veins. Leaf nearly round, fairly smooth, wavy edges; sinus usually open, may be one-third to one-half covered by lobes. Leaf size: 8–9 in. (20–23 cm). Leaf spread: 3–6 ft. (0.9–1.8 m). Stem color: Green. No pubescence on peduncle or petiole.

COMMENTS. This species continues to flower when water temperatures drop to 65°F (18°C). I have seen it bloom all winter in central Florida in a small tub. This waterlily is excellent for a tub garden or a small or medium pool. Two fine cultivars derived from *N. colorata* by Dr. George Pring are *N.* 'Director George T. Moore' and *N.* 'Midnight'.

Nymphaea elegans Hooker

Native to south Florida, south Texas, Mexico, Guatemala
PLATE 16

CHARACTERISTICS. Day blooming, nonviviparous, fairly free flowering.

FLOWERS. Petal color: Pale, delicate blue (*RHS* 91D or lighter). Sepal color: Greenish (*RHS* 130D). Anther color: Yellow; tips, pale blue (*RHS* 19A; tips, 91D). Stamen color: Deep yellow. Flower shape: Stellate. Flower size: 3–5 in. (8–13 cm). Fragrance:

Slight. Number of petals: 12–24. Number of sepals: 4 or 5.

LEAVES. Color: Top, green, freckled purple; underside, red or purple (on same plant), green veins, many small purple blotches. Leaf longer than wide; sinus usually an open V. Leaf size: 6–8 in. (15–20 cm). Leaf spread: 4 ft. (1.2 m). Stem color: Red and reddish brown. No pubescence on peduncle or petiole.

COMMENTS. This species is occasionally found growing in south Florida yet is quite scarce. I have collected this species from two south Florida swamps about 100 miles (160 km) apart. When cold weather arrives, this is one of the first tropicals to go dormant in central Florida. For this reason *N. elegans* is not a practical waterlily for the average water garden.

Nymphaea flavovirens Lehmann
Syn. *Nymphaea gracilis* Zuccarini
PLATE 17

CHARACTERISTICS. Day blooming, nonviviparous, very free flowering; flowers held 8–12 in. (20–30 cm) above water.

FLOWERS. Petal color: White (*RHS* 155C). Sepal color: White (*RHS* 155C). Anther color: Yellow; tips white (*RHS* 7A; tips, white 155C). Stamen color: Yellow. Flower shape: Stellate. Flower size: 4–6 in. (10–15 cm). Fragrance: Sweet. Number of petals: 18 or 19. Number of sepals: 4.

LEAVES. Color: Top, green; underside, green. Leaves nearly round, lobe tips rounded; sinus open. Leaf size: 12–18 in. (30–45 cm). Leaf spread: 6–10 ft. (1.8–3 m). Stem color: Olive green. No pubescence on peduncle or petiole.

COMMENTS. Conard considered the status of this species "uncertain." Landon found it growing wild at Toluca, Mexico; Masters believed it to be endemic to Brazil and Peru as well. This species propagates easily from seeds or tubers and also hybridizes readily with other waterlilies, including *N. capensis* var. *zanzibariensis*. Such hybrids are typically colorful and free blooming. Some cultivars of *N. flavovirens* are *N.* 'Red Star', *N.* 'Pink Star', and *N.* 'Blue Star'. (Most of the so-called star lilies include *N. flavovirens* as a parent.) I recommend this species for medium or large pools.

Nymphaea heudelotii Planchon
Native to West Africa, rare

CHARACTERISTICS. Day blooming, nonviviparous, free flowering. Anthers are five to six times as long as the filaments.

FLOWERS. Petal color: Bluish white. Sepal color: White or bluish white. Anther color: Yellow. Stamen color: Yellow. Flower shape: Stellate. Flower size: 1.25–2 in. (3–5 cm). Fragrance: Slight. Number of petals: 5–8. Number of sepals: 4.

LEAVES. Color: Top, green; underside, purplish, spotted violet. Leaf egg-shaped or nearly round; sinus narrow, sometimes nearly closed. Leaf size: 1–3 in. (2.5–8 cm). Leaf spread: 12–16 in. (30–40 cm). Stem color: Greenish. No pubescence on peduncle or petiole.

COMMENTS. This species is scarce even in its native habitat. It probably has no commercial future due to its rarity, poor flower color, and market competition from the similar *N.* 'Daubeniana' (syn. *N.* 'Dauben').

Nymphaea heudelotii var. *nana*
Native to West Africa

COMMENTS. Very small white flowers, 1–1.25 in. (2.5–3 cm). Leaves are round, green, reddish on the underside, 0.75–1.5 in. (2–4 cm) in diameter. This variety failed to attract a market in the United States, and I do not see any commercial future for this plant.

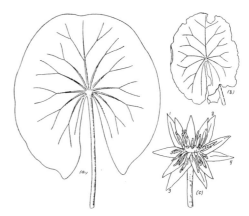

FIGURE 6. *Nymphaea heudelotii*, leaves (a, b); flower (c); sepals (1–4). From *The Waterlilies: A Monograph of the Genus Nymphaea* by Henry S. Conard (1905).

Nymphaea micrantha Guillemin & Perrottet

Native to the west coast of Africa

CHARACTERISTICS. Day blooming, viviparous, free flowering. Young plants develop at top of petiole and may bloom while still on mother plant; petiole decay allows young plants to float to another location. Anthers twice as long as filaments. Rhizomes have soft wool at petiole base.

FLOWERS. Petal color: Pale blue to white. Sepal color: Mostly white. Anther color: Outer, creamy white, tipped blue; inner, creamy white. Stamen color: Creamy white. Flower shape: Cuplike, then stellate. Flower size: 1–4 in. (2.5–10 cm). Fragrance: Faint. Number of petals: 10. Number of sepals: 5.

LEAVES. Color: Top, pale green; underside, reddish, violet-black dots. Leaves nearly round; sinus wide open. Leaf size: 3×2 in. (8×5 cm). Leaf spread: 2–2.5 ft. (0.6–0.8 m). Stem color: Greenish. Pubescence at petiole and peduncle where attached to rhizome.

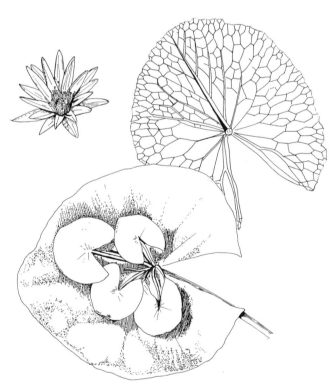

FIGURE 7. *Nymphaea micrantha*, flower (upper left); leaf underside (upper right); plantlet on top of leaf (bottom). After a plate from *The Waterlilies: A Monograph of the Genus Nymphaea* by Henry S. Conard (1905).

COMMENTS. This species is parent to several wonderful hybrids: *Nymphaea* 'August Koch', *N.* 'Charles Thomas' (not to be confused with the lotus 'Charles Thomas'), *N.* 'Daubeniana' (syn. *N.* 'Dauben'), *N.* 'Margaret Mary', *N.* 'Mrs. Martin E. Randig', *N.* 'Panama Pacific', *N.* 'Patricia', *N.* 'Paul Stetson', and new hybrids *N.* 'Islamorada' and *N.* 'Dorothy Pearl'. According to Kenneth Landon, it is doubtful that any true plants of *N. micrantha* are in cultivation in North or South America. Plants grown as such are probably the very similar *N.* 'Daubeniana' (syn. *N.* 'Dauben'); furthermore, the species is thought to be intermixed with *N.* 'Daubeniana'. True *N. micrantha* is most likely limited to the west coast of Africa.

Nymphaea nouchali Burman f.

Syn. *Nymphaea stellata* Willdenow

Native to southern and eastern Asia, Borneo, the Philippines, Sri Lanka

CHARACTERISTICS. Day blooming, nonviviparous, free flowering; blooms held about 12 in. (30 cm) above water.

FLOWERS. Petal color: Usually pale blue (*RHS* 92C); can vary to pink or white. Sepal color: Bluish white, usually (*RHS* 92D). Anther color: Pale yellow, tips blue or same as petals (*RHS* 4D; tips, 92C). Stamen color: Pale yellow. Flower shape: Stellate. Flower size: 2–5 in. (5–13 cm). Fragrance: Nearly absent. Number of petals: 10–16. Number of sepals: 4.

LEAVES. Color: Top, green, faint brownish blotches; underside, pink or blue-violet. Leaf oval to round, sinuate margin; sinus usually open. Leaf size: 5–6 in. (13–15 cm). Leaf spread: 4.5–5 ft. (1.4–1.5 m). Stem color: Greenish. No pubescence on peduncle or petiole.

COMMENTS. This waterlily is often referred to as the "blue lotus of India," but of course it is not a lotus at all. For centuries it has been cultivated in Southeast Asia, especially around temples. It has also been cultivated for food in Sri Lanka as the rhizomes are full of starch and reputedly quite tasty when boiled. In 1899 the plant flowered outdoors in England and received considerable publicity. This species does well in tubs, small pools, or large pools, although it is rarely available in the United States.

Nymphaea nouchali var. *cyanea* (Hooker f. & Thomson) Almeida

Syn. *Nymphaea stellata* var. *cyanea*

Native to southern and eastern Asia, Borneo, the Philippines, Sri Lanka

COMMENTS. The medium-sized flowers are deep or pale blue, with little or no fragrance. Leaves are slightly wavy and margins may or may not be dentate.

Nymphaea nouchali var. *versicolor* (Roxburgh) Hooker f. & Thomson

Syn. *Nymphaea stellata* var. *versicolor*

Native to Sri Lanka, India, Indochina, and the Philippines

FLOWERS. Usually pink but may be white or red, measuring 4–5 in. (10–13 cm).

LEAVES. Green above and pink on underside with some purplish markings, 8 in. (20 cm).

COMMENTS. In autumn a small hard tuber develops at the base of each leaf stem. Particularly in USDA zones 3–8, it is necessary to store tubers indoors during the winter months for use in the spring. Many thousands of tubers are exported annually from Sri Lanka to the aquarium trade in the United States and Europe. When placed in warm water (70–90°F, 21–32°C) for a few weeks, tubers become very attractive "instant" aquarium plants.

Nymphaea ovalifolia Conard

Native to East Africa

CHARACTERISTICS. Day blooming, nonviviparous, free flowering.

FLOWERS. Petal color: White, tipped blue. Sepal color: White or delicate blue. Anther color: Yellow. Stamen color: Yellow. Flower shape: Stellate. Flower size: 5–8 in. (13–20 cm). Fragrance: Very sweet. Number of petals: 16–18. Number of sepals: 4.

LEAVES. Color: Top, light green, brown blotches; underside, green. Leaf oval to elliptical; sinus 4 in. (10 cm) long, sides nearly parallel. Leaf size: 10 × 6 in. (25 × 15 cm). Leaf spread: 5–7 ft. (1.5–2.1 m). Stem color: Greenish. No pubescence on peduncle or petiole.

COMMENTS. *Nymphaea ovalifolia*, even if generally available, would not be a very desirable plant for cultivation due to its poor off-white flower color.

George Pring of the Missouri Botanical Garden nonetheless used it as a parent in producing several outstanding hybrids: *N.* 'General Pershing', *N.* 'Mrs. Edwards Whitaker', and *N.* 'Mrs. George H. Pring'.

Nymphaea stuhlmannii (Engler) Schweinfurth & Gilg

Syn. *Nymphaea burtii* Pring & Woodson

Native to Tanzania, Dodoma District, Mgunda Mkali, Bibisande, Africa

CHARACTERISTICS. Day blooming, nonviviparous, free flowering.

FLOWERS. Petal color: Bright sulfur-yellow. Sepal color: Yellowish green. Anther color: Sulfur-yellow. Stamen color: Orange-yellow. Flower shape: Full, stellate. Flower size: 4–6 in. (10–15 cm). Fragrance: Sweet. Number of petals: 22. Number of sepals: 4.

LEAVES. Color: Top, green; underside, green, prominent veins. Leaves oval to round, rounded tips on lobes; sinus open. Leaf size: 10 × 8 in. (25 × 20 cm). Leaf spread: 5–6 ft. (1.5–1.8 m). Stem color: Green. No pubescence on peduncle or petiole.

COMMENTS. Dr. George Pring used this species in his hybridizing to produce some magnificent yellow tropical waterlilies. One example is *Nymphaea* 'St. Louis'. He was working with a species from East Africa known as *N. burtii* Pring & Woodson. In

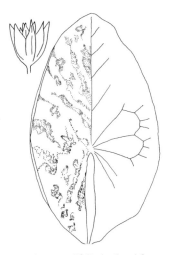

FIGURE 8. *Nymphaea ovalifolia*, leaf and flower. Upper side of leaf displaying mottling (left; note leaf edge fold at margin); underside of leaf showing veins (right). After an illustration from *The Waterlilies: A Monograph of the Genus Nymphaea* by Henry S. Conard (1905).

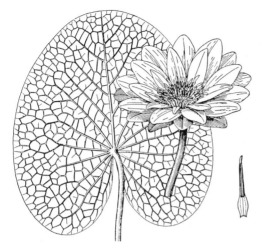

FIGURE 9. *Nymphaea stuhlmannii*, flower, underside of leaf, and outer stamen. From *The Waterlilies: A Monograph of the Genus Nymphaea* by Henry S. Conard (1905).

February 1951, after carefully comparing specimens, Dr. Pring determined that *N. burtii* and *N. stuhlmannii* were the same species. Because *N. stuhlmannii* was discovered in 1890, this name took precedence over *N. burtii*, discovered in 1929.

Nymphaea sulfurea Gilg

Native to south-central Africa

CHARACTERISTICS. Day blooming, nonviviparous, free flowering.

FLOWERS. Petal color: Rich sulfur-yellow. Sepal color: Purplish. Anther color: Bright yellow. Stamen color: Yellow. Flower shape: Stellate. Flower size: 2–3 in. (5–8 cm). Fragrance: Sweet. Number of petals: 13. Number of sepals: 4.

LEAVES. Color: Top, reddish; underside, red. Leaves nearly round; sinus open. Leaf size: 1.75–2.25 in. (4.5–5.5 cm). Leaf spread: 15–20 in. (38–50 cm). Stem color: Reddish or bronzy. No pubescence on peduncle or petiole.

COMMENTS. *Nymphaea sulfurea* is a dwarf type. Dr. George Pring used it in producing *N.* 'St. Louis Gold' and *N.* 'Aviator Pring'.

Nymphaea togoensis Landon

Native to the Togo region of Africa

PLATE 18

CHARACTERISTICS. Day blooming, nonviviparous, very free flowering until onset of fruiting.

FLOWERS. Petal color: White (*RHS* 155D). Sepal color: White (*RHS* 155D). Anther color: Yellow, white tips (*RHS* A; tips, 155D). Stamen color: Yellow. Flower shape: Stellate. Flower size: 4–6 in. (10–15 cm). Fragrance: Faint. Number of petals: 16–18. Number of sepals: 4.

LEAVES. Color: Top, green, few purple flecks; underside, grayish green, suffused purple. Leaves slightly sinuate toward base; sinus varies. Leaf size: 5–10 in. (13–25 cm). Leaf spread: 8 ft. (2.4 m). Stem color: Maroon. No pubescence on peduncle or petiole.

COMMENTS. This is a species recently discovered in coastal swamps, rivers, streams, and rain pools throughout the Togo region of Africa. Kenneth Landon first described this species and supplied the above information.

Group *Syncarpiae* Caspary

In members of group *Syncarpiae*, carpels are completely fused with one another at the sides and are attached to the axis of the flower and to the torus, as in group *Apocarpiae*. Flowers are white, pink, purple, or yellow but never blue. Plants are either day or night blooming.

Subgenus *Hydrocallis* Planchon

In *A Monograph of Nymphaea Subgenus Hydrocallis (Nymphaeaceae)* (1987), Dr. John H. Wiersema listed the 14 species described here, which is four more species than Conard (1905) had listed. Dr. Wiersema dropped *N. blanda*, *N. gibertii*, and *N. stenaspidota* and added *N. belophylla*, *N. conardii*, *N. glandulifera*, *N. lingulata*, *N. novogranatensis*, *N. potamophila*, and *N. prolifera*.

All *Hydrocallis* are night-blooming waterlilies (artificial light has little effect on blooming) native to the tropics of the Western Hemisphere. Flowers open for a short period (about two hours in some varieties) in the middle of the night or very early morning. (Subgenus *Lotos* blooms open from dusk to about 11:00 a.m.) Blooms either float or remain close to the water surface. Petals are usually in whorls of four, and styles are slender and cylindrical with enlarged club-shaped tips. Pollination is frequently accomplished by scarab beetles (*Cyclocephala* spp.). None of the 14 species is suited for the average water garden, as blooms are short-lived and open in the middle of the night. These lilies are for the collector with a medium or large pool.

Note that "Sepal color" in the following *Hydrocallis* descriptions refers to the outside of the sepals not the inside, as with other *Nymphaea* species and cultivars. The inside of the sepals usually matches the petals—creamy white, in most cases.

Nymphaea amazonum subsp. *amazonum*

Martius & Zuccarini

Native to tropical South America, Caribbean Islands, particularly in lowlands near coastal areas; rare in Central America and Mexico

CHARACTERISTICS. Night blooming, nonviviparous, flowers floating, sepals and petals in whorls of four. Propagates by short sprouts, stolons from rhizomes, and seeds. Stamens usually number less than 200.

FLOWERS. Petal color: Creamy white. Sepal color: Green, short black streaks. Anther color: Creamy white. Stamen color: Creamy white. Flower shape: Stellate. Flower size: 4–5 in. (10–13 cm). Fragrance: Strong odor resembling turpentine, xylol, gasoline, or acetone. Number of petals: 16, 20, or 24. Number of sepals: 4.

LEAVES. Color: Top, green, purple spots; underside, purple, small dark flecks. Leaf oval, 1–1.35 times as long as wide; lobes slightly tapered to rounded; sinus open. Leaf size: 13 × 11 in. (33 × 28 cm). Leaf spread: 5–6 ft. (1.5–1.8 m). Stem color: Green. Peduncle usually bare, occasionally pubescent at apex; petioles display ring of pubescence at apex, the remaining bare or occasionally pubescent.

COMMENTS. In its native habitats, this plant is mostly found growing in still water, sometimes in slightly brackish water. This species is mostly for the collector as its nocturnal blooming habit would limit its use in the average water garden: first-day flower opens partially two to three hours before dawn and closes by dawn; second-day flower opens at dusk and closes by an hour after dawn.

Nymphaea amazonum subsp. *pedersenii*

Wiersema

Syn. *Nymphaea amazonum* Martius & Zuccarini

Native to subtropical portions of Argentina and southern Brazil; probably also in adjacent Paraguay and Uruguay

CHARACTERISTICS. Night blooming, nonviviparous, flowers floating, sepals and petals in whorls of four. Appears to propagate mostly by stolons. Stamens usually number more than 225.

FLOWERS. Petal color: Creamy white. Sepal color: Green, short black streaks. Anther color: Creamy white. Stamen color: Creamy white. Flower shape: Stellate. Flower size: About 4 in. (10 cm). Fragrance: Strong aromatic odor. Number of petals: 16, 20, or 24. Number of sepals: 4.

LEAVES. Color: Top, green, usually variegated red; underside, green or somewhat reddened, often splotched deeper red, prominent central veins. Leaf 1.25–1.5 times as long as wide, egg-shaped; lobes end in dull point at apex; sinus open. Leaf size: 13 ×

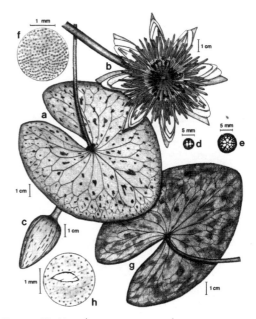

FIGURE 10. *Nymphaea amazonum* subsp. *amazonum* (a–f) and *N. amazonum* subsp. *pedersenii* (g, h). Underside of leaf (a); opened flower (b); unopened flower bud (c); cross section of petiole (d); cross section of peduncle (e); upper side of leaf (f); underside of leaf (g); upper side of leaf (h). From *A Monograph of Nymphaea Subgenus Hydrocallis (Nymphaeaceae)* by John H. Wiersema (1987).

9 in. (33 × 23 cm). Leaf spread: 5–6 ft. (1.5–1.8 m). Stem color: Greenish. Peduncle, bare; petiole apex usually displays ring of pubescence.

COMMENTS. I recommend *Nymphaea amazonum* subsp. *pedersenii* only for the collector because of its nocturnal blooming habit, similar to that of *N. amazonum* subsp. *amazonum*. Requires a medium or large pool.

Nymphaea belophylla Trickett

Native to the Amazon and Orinoco Basins, South America

CHARACTERISTICS. Night blooming, nonviviparous, flowers floating, sepals and petals in whorls of four. Seldom produces seeds.

FLOWERS. Petal color: Creamy white or light yellow; tips greenish changing to creamy white or light yellow. Sepal color: Green. Anther color: Creamy white to light yellow. Stamen color: Creamy white to light yellow. Flower shape: Somewhat stellate. Flower size: 2.5–4 in. (6.3–10 cm). Fragrance: Almondlike. Number of petals: 16 or 20. Number of sepals: 4.

LEAVES. Color: Top, green; underside, green. Leaf more than twice as long as wide, acute lobes at apex; arrow-shaped; sinus long and wide open. Leaf size: 12 × 4.3 in. (30 × 11 cm). Leaf spread: 3–4 ft.

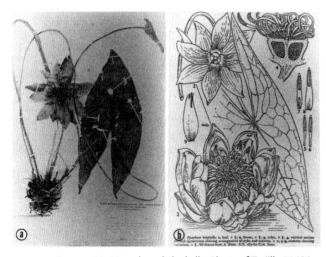

(a)

(b)

FIGURE 11. *Nymphaea belophylla*. Photo of *Trujillo 11430* (MY) from Barinas, Venezuela (a); illustration from the original publication reproduced in Kew Bulletin, vol. 26 (b). From *A Monograph of Nymphaea Subgenus Hydrocallis (Nymphaeaceae)* by John H. Wiersema (1987).

(0.9–1.2 m). Stem color: Green. No pubescence on peduncle or petiole.

COMMENTS. *Belophylla* is Greek for "arrow-shaped leaves." Like the other *Hydrocallis* waterlilies, *Nymphaea belophylla* blooms for a short period in the middle of the night. As such, its use is limited in the average water garden. This species is rare and most studies have been done on museum specimens.

Nymphaea conardii Wiersema

Native to southern Mexico through Central America to northern South America, including Colombia, Venezuela, northern Brazil; also found in Cuba, Hispaniola, and Puerto Rico

CHARACTERISTICS. Night blooming, nonviviparous, flowers floating, sepals and petals in whorls of four. Propagates by seed.

FLOWERS. Petal color: Creamy white. Sepal color: Green. Anther color: Creamy white. Stamen color: Creamy white. Flower shape: Stellate. Flower size: About 6.5 in. (16.3 cm). Fragrance: Strong but pleasant. Number of petals: 12, 16, or 20. Number of sepals: 3–6.

LEAVES. Color: Top, green; underside, green. Leaf 1–1.5 times as long as wide, pronounced web-like venation; lobes acute to rounded at apex with slight protuberance; sinus open. Leaf size: 7 × 5.5 in. (18 × 14 cm). Leaf spread: 2–4 ft. (0.6–1.2 m). Stem color: Green. No pubescence on peduncle or petiole.

COMMENTS. This species, as with other *Hydrocallis* waterlilies, has a limited commercial future due to its short, nocturnal bloom period. Flowers begin opening at dusk and start closing around midnight, being fully closed by 1:00 a.m. Blooms open for two successive nights.

Nymphaea gardneriana Planchon

Native to South America, including Venezuela, Brazil, Bolivia, Paraguay, Argentina

CHARACTERISTICS. Night blooming, nonviviparous, flowers floating, sepals and petals in whorls of four. Propagates by stolons from rhizome.

FLOWERS. Petal color: Creamy white; tips greenish. Sepal color: Green. Anther color: Creamy white. Stamen color: Creamy white. Flower shape: Stellate. Flower size: 3.5–5 in. (9–12.7 cm). Fragrance:

Strong, somewhat sweet. Number of petals: 16–28. Number of sepals: 4.

LEAVES. Color: Top, green; underside, green, often suffused or mottled rusty brown. Leaf 1–1.5 times as long as wide, pronounced weblike venation; lobes acute to rounded at apex; sinus wide open. Leaf size: up to 8.5 in. (21.6 cm) to 6 in. (15cm)

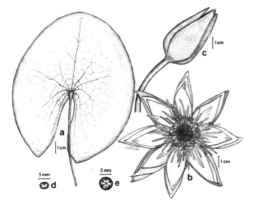

FIGURE 12. *Nymphaea conardii*, underside of leaf (a); opened flower (b); unopened flower bud (c); cross section of petiole (d); cross section of peduncle (e). From *A Monograph of Nymphaea Subgenus Hydrocallis (Nymphaeaceae)* by John H. Wiersema (1987).

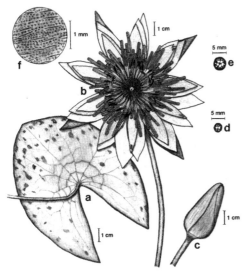

FIGURE 13. *Nymphaea gardneriana*, underside of leaf (a); opened flower (b); unopened flower bud (c); cross section of petiole (d); cross section of peduncle (e); upper side of leaf (f). From *A Monograph of Nymphaea Subgenus Hydrocallis (Nymphaeaceae)* by John H. Wiersema (1987).

wide. Leaf spread: 2–4 ft. (0.6–1.2 m). Stem color: Green. Occasional few hairs on petiole.

COMMENTS. *Nymphaea gardneriana* has limited value for water garden use as flowers open about dusk and close about midnight. Blooms for two consecutive nights.

Nymphaea glandulifera Rodschied

Syn. *Nymphaea blanda* G. Meyer

Native to northern South America and Central America from Amazonas, Brazil, west to northern Peru and Ecuador and north to Guatemala, Belize, Trinidad, and French Guiana

CHARACTERISTICS. Night blooming, nonviviparous, flowers floating, sepals and petals in whorls of four. Propagates by seed.

FLOWERS. Petal color: Creamy white. Sepal color: Green. Anther color: Creamy white. Stamen color: Creamy white. Flower shape: Stellate. Flower size: About 6 in. (15 cm). Fragrance: Not mentioned in report studied. Number of petals: 12–20. Number of sepals: 4.

LEAVES. Color: Top, green; underside, pale green.

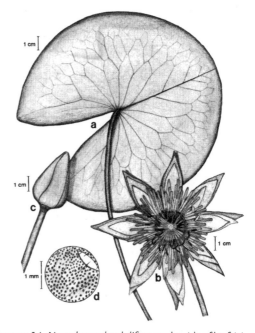

FIGURE 14. *Nymphaea glandulifera*, underside of leaf (a); opened flower (b); unopened flower bud (c); upper side of leaf (d). From *A Monograph of Nymphaea Subgenus Hydrocallis (Nymphaeaceae)* by John H. Wiersema (1987).

Leaf nearly round, lobes obtuse to rounded at apex; sinus open. Leaf size: 8.25×7.5 in. (21×19 cm). Leaf spread: 2–4 ft. (0.6–1.2 m). Stem color: Green. Peduncle and petiole sometimes slightly pubescent.

COMMENTS. Due to its short nightly blooming period (from dusk to midnight), it is not suited for the average water garden.

Nymphaea jamesoniana Planchon

Native to tropical and subtropical America, including Florida, Mexico, Central America, Argentina, Brazil, Colombia, Ecuador, and Paraguay

CHARACTERISTICS. Night blooming, nonviviparous, flowers floating, sepals and petals in whorls of four. Propagates by seed.

FLOWERS. Petal color: Mostly creamy white, greenish tip edges. Sepal color: Green, slender rusty brown lines. Anther color: Creamy white. Stamen color: Creamy white. Flower shape: Stellate. Flower size: 2.5–5 in. (6.4–12.7 cm). Fragrance: Disagreeable odor resembling used motor oil or acetone. Number of petals: 12, 16, or 20. Number of sepals: 4.

LEAVES. Color: Top, green, sometimes with dark flecks; underside, green, sometimes flecked purple. Leaf egg-shaped, prominent venation webbing, lobes usually ending in fairly sharp point; sinus long and open. Leaf size: Up to 9 × 7.25 in. (22.9 ×18.4 cm). Leaf spread: 4–5 ft. (1.2–1.5 m). Stem color: Green. No pubescence on peduncle or petiole.

COMMENTS. In its native habitats, found growing in freshwater ditches, ponds, or slow-moving streams. I recommend this species for the collector with a medium or large pool. This plant is not suited to the average water garden as flowers begin opening about dusk and close about midnight.

Nymphaea lasiophylla Martius & Zuccarini

Native to the coastal regions of eastern Brazil, Rio de Janeiro north to Piauí, with a separate population (probably introduced) on Isla de Margarita, Venezuela

CHARACTERISTICS. Night blooming, viviparous, new growth from submerged tuberiferous flowers. Flowers floating, sepals and petals in whorls of four. Propagation from stolons, seed, and submerged flowers, which later detach.

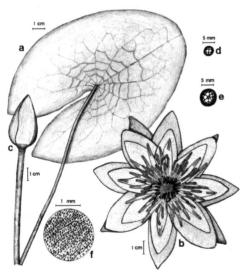

FIGURE 15. Nymphaea jamesoniana, underside of leaf (a); opened flower (b); unopened flower bud (c); cross section of petiole (d); cross section of peduncle (e); upper side of leaf (f). From A Monograph of Nymphaea Subgenus Hydrocallis (Nymphaeaceae) by John H. Wiersema (1987).

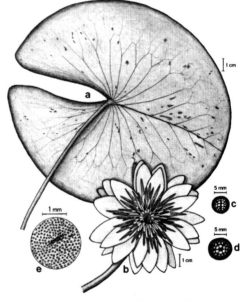

FIGURE 16. Nymphaea lasiophylla, underside of leaf (a); opened flower (b); cross section of petiole (c); cross section of peduncle (d); upper side of leaf (e). From A Monograph of Nymphaea Subgenus Hydrocallis (Nymphaeaceae) by John H. Wiersema (1987).

FLOWERS. Petal color: Creamy white. Sepal color: Green or yellow-green. Anther color: Creamy white. Stamen color: Creamy white. Flower shape: Full, stellate. Flower size: 4 in. (10 cm). Fragrance: Strongly aromatic. Number of petals: 20–26. Number of sepals: 4.

LEAVES. Color: Top, green, often with darker flecks; underside, green, slight reddish tint. Leaf nearly round; prominent, slightly raised veins radiate from center; lobes rounded or with small obtuse protuberance; sinus open. Leaf size: 13 × 12 in. (33 × 30 cm). Leaf spread: 6 ft. (1.8 m). Stem color: Green. No pubescence on peduncle or petiole.

COMMENTS. In its native habitats, usually found growing in stagnant water, frequently in artificial ponds. I recommend *Nymphaea lasiophylla* for the collector with a medium or large pool. Tubers develop from the abortive submerged flowers; they later detach, remain floating briefly, and eventually developing into adult plants. Collectors may find this an interesting process, though with its short bloom period (from midnight to before 4:00 a.m.), it would not be acceptable to most gardeners.

Nymphaea lingulata Wiersema

Native to northeastern Brazil

CHARACTERISTICS. Night blooming, nonviviparous, flowers floating, sepals and outer petals in whorls of four. Propagation mainly by seed, also by stolon production from rhizome.

FLOWERS. Petal color: Creamy white. Sepal color: Yellowish green, sometimes flecked black. Anther color: Creamy white. Stamen color: Creamy white, dark purple base. Flower shape: Stellate, long, narrow petals. Flower size: 5.5 in. (14 cm). Fragrance: Faint. Number of petals: 8–14. Number of sepals: 4.

LEAVES. Color: Top, green; underside, red to reddish purple. Leaf a little longer than wide, lobes rounded or with small obtuse protuberance; sinus open. Leaf size: About 10 × 8 in. (25 × 20 cm). Leaf spread: 3–5 ft. (0.9–1.5 m). Stem color: Green. No pubescence on peduncle or petiole.

COMMENTS. *Nymphaea lingulata* begins to open approximately two hours after dark and closes around 2:00 to 3:00 a.m. For this reason I do not recommend it for most water gardens.

Nymphaea novogranatensis Wiersema

Native to Venezuela and Colombia

CHARACTERISTICS. Night blooming, nonviviparous, flowers floating or slightly emergent, sepals and petals in whorls of four. Propagation by seed.

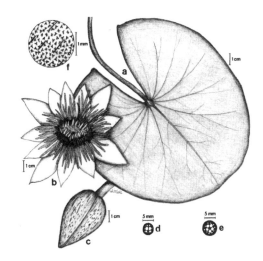

FIGURE 17. *Nymphaea lingulata*, underside of leaf (a); opened flower (b); unopened flower bud (c); cross section of petiole (d); cross section of peduncle (e); upper side of leaf (f). From *A Monograph of Nymphaea Subgenus Hydrocallis (Nymphaeaceae)* by John H. Wiersema (1987).

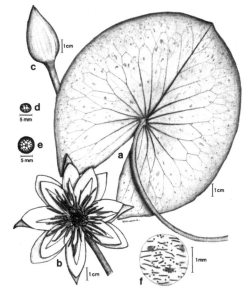

FIGURE 18. *Nymphaea novogranatensis*, underside of leaf (a); opened flower (b); unopened flower bud (c); cross section of petiole (d); cross section of peduncle (e); upper side of leaf (f). From *A Monograph of Nymphaea Subgenus Hydrocallis (Nymphaeaceae)* by John H. Wiersema (1987).

FLOWERS. Petal color: White. Sepal color: Green or somewhat brownish purple. Anther color: Cream. Stamen color: Cream, inner filaments purplish at base. Flower shape: Stellate. Flower size: 2.5–3.5 in. (64–9 cm). Fragrance: Faint. Number of petals: 16 or 20. Number of sepals: 4.

LEAVES. Color: Top, glossy green, new leaves flecked purple; underside, brownish purple, darker flecks evident, especially on younger leaves. Leaf nearly round; quite prominent veins radiate from center; lobes obtuse to rounded with slight protuberance; sinus open. Leaf size: 9.5 × 8 in. (24 × 20 cm). Leaf spread: 3–5 ft. (0.9–1.5 m). Stem color: Green. No pubescence on peduncle or petiole.

COMMENTS. Flowers start opening one to two hours after dark and close by midnight the first night. Second-day flowers begin opening at dusk and close at dawn. I do not recommend it for the average water garden.

Nymphaea oxypetala Planchon

Native to southern Brazil, Ecuador, Venezuela

CHARACTERISTICS. Night blooming, nonviviparous, flowers floating, sepals and outermost petals

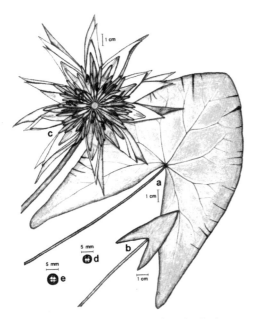

FIGURE 19. *Nymphaea oxypetala*, underside of submerged leaf (a); upper side of floating leaf (b); opened flower (c); cross section of petiole (d); cross section of peduncle (e). From *A Monograph of Nymphaea Subgenus Hydrocallis (Nymphaeaceae)* by John H. Wiersema (1987).

in whorls of four, leaves mostly submerged. Reproduction by seed.

FLOWERS. Petal color: Creamy white; tips greenish. Sepal color: Green. Anther color: Creamy white, suffused purple. Stamen color: Creamy white, suffused purple. Flower shape: Very stellate. Flower size: 5–10 in. (13–25 cm). Fragrance: Strong etherlike aroma. Number of petals: 16–34. Number of sepals: 4.

LEAVES. Color: Top, green; underside, purplish. Floating leaves very small, 1.9–2.5 times as long as wide, acute to rounded at the apex, lobes acute and tapering; sinus open. Submerged leaves large, 1–1.8 times as long as wide, lobes acute to rounded; sinus open. Leaf size: Floating leaves, about 2.5 × 1 in. (6 × 2.5 cm); submerged leaves up to 16 × 13 in. (40 × 33 cm). Leaf spread: 2–3 ft. (0.6–0.9 m). Stem color: Green. No pubescence on peduncle or petiole.

COMMENTS. This species has beautiful underwater foliage. Wiersema believes *Nymphaea oxypetala* might be suitable as an aquarium plant. He notes that it prefers gently flowing fresh water, yet there is a possibility that it would adapt to a clean, well-filtered tank.

Nymphaea potamophila Wiersema

Native to the states of Amazonas and Pará, northern Brazil

CHARACTERISTICS. Night blooming, nonviviparous, flowers floating, sepals and petals in whorls of four. Reproduction by seed.

FLOWERS. Petal color: Creamy white, greenish tips and edges. Sepal color: Green. Anther color: Creamy white. Stamen color: Creamy white. Flower shape: Stellate. Flower size: About 5 in. (12.5 cm). Fragrance: Unknown. Number of petals: 16. Number of sepals: 4.

LEAVES. Color: Top, green, often variegated red; underside, greenish, variegated dark red. Leaf 1.8–2.5 times as long as wide, acute-tapering to somewhat rounded at apex; lobes long and pointed; sinus open. Leaf size: About 8 × 4 in. (20 × 10 cm). Leaf spread: 2–4 ft. (0.6–1.2 m). Stem color: Green. No pubescence on peduncle or petiole.

COMMENTS. This is a rare waterlily and not much is known about the flowering except that it blooms for a short period in the middle of the night. I do not recommend it for the water garden.

Nymphaea prolifera Wiersema

Native to northern Argentina, southern Brazil, western Ecuador, Paraguay, Costa Rica, and El Salvador

CHARACTERISTICS. Night blooming, viviparous, producing tiny tubers from flowers. Flowers floating, sepals and outer petals in whorls of four. Asexual reproduction from tuber-bearing flowers.

FLOWERS. Petal color: Creamy white. Sepal color: Green, sometimes suffused purple, usually short black streaks. Anther color: Cream; inner anthers tinged indigo or purple toward flower center. Stamen color: Cream; inner stamens tinged indigo or purple. Flower shape: Full star. Flower size: About 7 in. (18 cm). Fragrance: Etherlike. Number of petals: 19–35. Number of sepals: 4.

LEAVES. Color: Top, green, often flecked purple; underside, green or purple-tinged with dark flecks. Leaf nearly round, lobes slightly tapering to broadly rounded; sinus open. Leaf size: to 8.7 × 8.25 in. (22 ×

21 cm). Leaf spread: 4–5 ft. (1.2–1.5 m). Stem color: Green. No pubescence on peduncle or petiole.

COMMENTS. In its native habitat, this species is mostly found growing in lowland savannas. Flowers of *Nymphaea prolifera* open for two successive days as follows: initial opening, from one hour after dusk to around 3:00 or 4:00 a.m.; second opening, at dusk, closing one to two hours before dawn. Although watching the tuber-bearing flowers form new plants would be interesting, most gardeners would find that the timing of the flower opening leaves much to be desired. I recommend it only for the collector.

Nymphaea rudgeana G. Meyer

Native to eastern and northern South America, north of the state of Paraná, Brazil, and east of northern Colombia; also in Cuba, Guadeloupe, Jamaica, Martinique, Trinidad, and Nicaragua

CHARACTERISTICS. Night blooming, nonviviparous, flowers floating, sepals and petals in whorls of four. Reproduction by seed.

FLOWERS. Petal color: Creamy white to light yellow, developing pinkish tinge. Sepal color: Green-

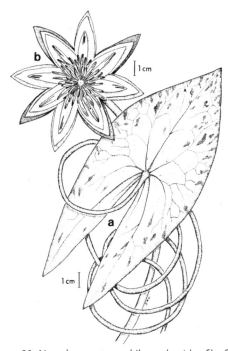

FIGURE 20. *Nymphaea potamophila*, underside of leaf (a); opened flower (b). From *A Monograph of Nymphaea Subgenus Hydrocallis (Nymphaeaceae)* by John H. Wiersema (1987).

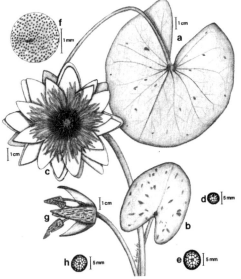

FIGURE 21. *Nymphaea prolifera*, underside of leaf (a); upper side of young leaf (b); opened flower (c); cross section of petiole (d); cross section of peduncle (e); upper side of leaf (f); tuberiferous flower (g); cross section of peduncle of tuberiferous flower (h). From *A Monograph of Nymphaea Subgenus Hydrocallis (Nymphaeaceae)* by John H. Wiersema (1987).

ish, base yellowish; underside, yellowish, tinged red. Anther color: Creamy white to light yellow. Stamen color: Creamy white to light yellow. Flower shape: Stellate. Flower size: 4–7 in. (10–18 cm). Fragrance: Variously described as fruity, aniselike, and reminiscent of acetone. Number of petals: 12–29. Number of sepals: 4.

LEAVES. Color: Top, green, sometimes purplish, occasionally flecked purple; underside, greenish or brownish purple, sometimes darker flecks. Leaf nearly round, irregularly dentate, teeth obtuse, dentate apex on lobes, margins often slightly upturned in larger leaves; sinus open. Leaf size: Up to 14.5 in. (36 cm). Leaf spread: 6–7 ft. (1.8–2.1 m). Stem color: Bronzy green. No pubescence on peduncle or petiole.

COMMENTS. In its native habitats, *Nymphaea rudgeana* is mostly found growing in lowland coastal areas in stagnant, sometimes brackish, or flowing water. It blooms for two or three successive nights. Flowers open at dusk and close between midnight and dawn. This opening period alone makes this waterlily potentially undesirable for the water gar-den. Commercial aquarium-plant grower Don Bryne of Suwannee Laboratories, Lake City, Florida, discovered that under ideal conditions, *N. rudgeana* produces beautiful reddish submerged leaves. Plants would lose the red coloring after a while, however, and die during cooler times of the year.

Nymphaea tenerinervia Caspary

Native to northern Brazil, mostly north Bahia and northern Goiás and east of the Amazon Basin, although also collected in Roraima; common to natural swamps and marshes in northern Piauí and Ceará

CHARACTERISTICS. Night blooming, nonviviparous, flowers floating, sepals and petals in whorls of four. Propagation mostly by stolons from rhizome.

FLOWERS. Petal color: Creamy white to light yellow. Sepal color: Green, short purple streaks. Anther color: Creamy white to light yellow. Stamen color: Creamy white to light yellow. Flower shape: Somewhat stellate. Flower size: 3–7 in. (8–18 cm). Fragrance: Faint. Number of petals: 16 or 20. Number of sepals: 4.

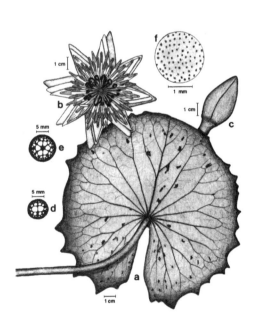

FIGURE 22. *Nymphaea rudgeana*, underside of leaf (a); opened flower (b); unopened flower bud (c); cross section of petiole (d); cross section of peduncle (e); upper side of leaf (f). From *A Monograph of Nymphaea Subgenus Hydrocallis (Nymphaeaceae)* by John H. Wiersema (1987).

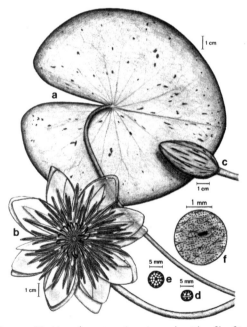

FIGURE 23. *Nymphaea tenerinervia*, underside of leaf (a); opened flower (b); unopened flower bud (c); cross section of petiole (d); cross section of peduncle (e); upper side of leaf (f). From *A Monograph of Nymphaea Subgenus Hydrocallis (Nymphaeaceae)* by John H. Wiersema (1987).

LEAVES. Color: Top, green or occasionally reddish, often flecked purple; underside, purple or red-purple, often short, darker purple flecks. Leaf nearly round; lobes rounded, little or no protuberance; sinus open. Leaf size: Up to 8.5 × 7.5 in. (21 × 19 cm). Leaf spread: 3–5 ft. (0.9–1.5 m). Stem color: Green. Peduncle and petiole bare or slightly pubescent.

COMMENTS. Flowers open two consecutive nights. Initial opening one hour after dusk, closing by midnight; second opening at dusk, remaining until dawn. Such opening periods makes this species undesirable for water gardens.

Subgenus *Lotos* de Candolle

The *Lotos* waterlilies include the night-blooming tropicals that have been hybridized to create the night-blooming cultivars popular in the trade today. Conard (1905) included only four species in the subgenus *Lotos*, but Kenneth Landon has identified one more (*N. spontanea*, closely related to *N. pubescens*), bringing the current total to five.

Plants are native to the tropics of the Old World, the Philippines, Egypt, central and West Africa, Madagascar, and to two isolated warm-water areas of Hungary. In their native habitats many of the *Lotos* group experience a wet season alternating with a dry season. During the end of the wet season, tubers form under the plants, leaves die down, and plants survive the dry season as dormant tubers. In cultivation the somewhat round tubers usually go dormant when cold weather arrives.

Flowers of *Lotos* open about dusk. On warm days blooms close between 11:00 a.m. and noon, opening and closing for three or four successive days. Plants hold their blooms 6–12 in. (15–30 cm) above the water, yet the last-day flowers may float. In autumn, when cool days arrive, the blooms stay open day and night continuously for a few days. Flower scent is generally considered more pungent than pleasing.

Nymphaea lotus Linnaeus
Native to Egypt, central and West Africa,
   Madagascar, and Grosswardein, Hungary
PLATE 19

CHARACTERISTICS. Night blooming, occasionally viviparous from flower, flowers freely, each flower lasts four days.

FLOWERS. Petal color: White (*RHS* 155D). Sepal color: White, 10–16 prominent, creamy white veins (*RHS* 155D; veins 155A). Anther color: Yellow (*RHS* 11B). Stamen color: Yellow. Flower shape: Flat when fully open. Flower size: 6–10 in. (15–25 cm). Fragrance: Slight. Number of petals: 19 or 20. Number of sepals: 4.

LEAVES. Color: Top, green, new leaves reddish; underside, greenish or dull purplish brown. Mature leaf round, dentate, small waves at perimeter; sinus usually open yet lobes may overlap. Leaf size: 8–20 in. (20–50 cm). Leaf spread: 5–10 ft. (1.5–3 m). Stem color: Brownish green. Peduncle pubescent; petiole usually pubescent.

COMMENTS. *Nymphaea lotus* confuses many people because of its name. This "lotus" is in the genus *Nymphaea* (Nymphaeaceae), not in the lotus family, Nelumbonaceae. Most of the white night-blooming waterlily cultivars in use today come from *Nymphaea lotus*. If you can find it, this species makes a fine plant for medium and large pools.

Nymphaea pubescens Willdenow
Hairy waterlily
Native to India, the Philippines, Java, Australia

CHARACTERISTICS. Night blooming, nonviviparous. Rhizomes covered with thick hairs.

FLOWERS. Petal color: White. Sepal color: White. Anther color: Yellow. Stamen color: Yellow. Flower shape: Stellate, opening out flat. Flower size: 6–10 in. (15–25 cm). Fragrance: Moderately sweet. Number of petals: 18–20. Number of sepals: 4

LEAVES. Color: Top, dark green; underside, dull purplish green. Leaf egg-shaped, irregularly dentate, lobe may display small protuberance, whole leaf frequently hairy underneath; sinus either open or closed, margin usually curved. Leaf size: Up to 10 × 8 in. (25 × 20 cm). Leaf spread: 4–5 ft. (1.2–1.5 m). Stem color: Greenish. Pubescence on peduncle and petiole.

COMMENTS. This species is commonly known as the hairy waterlily because its rhizome, stems, and leaf undersides are usually tomentose. There are now hybrids with flowers 10–13 in. (25–33 cm),

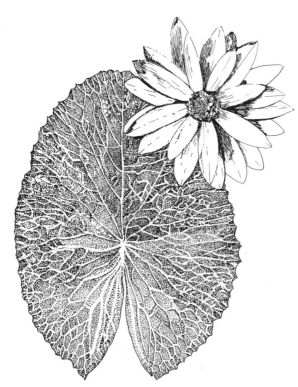

FIGURE 24. *Nymphaea pubescens*, flower and leaf. After a plate from *The Waterlilies: A Monograph of the Genus Nymphaea* by Henry S. Conard (1905).

such as *N.* 'Missouri' and *N.* 'Sir Galahad', which are better suited to the water garden.

Nymphaea rubra Roxburgh

Native to central and southern India

PLATE 20

CHARACTERISTICS. Night blooming, nonviviparous, very free flowering.

FLOWERS. Petal color: Deep purplish red in warm weather, then pink as weather cools (*RHS* 63A then 63C). Sepal color: Dull purplish red (*RHS* 64B). Anther color: Orange-red (*RHS* 168B). Stamen color: Orange-red. Flower shape: Flat, starlike when fully open. Flower size: 6–10 in. (15–25 cm). Fragrance: Slight. Number of petals: 12–20. Number of sepals: 5–7.

LEAVES. Color: Top, reddish brown, very old leaves greenish; underside, dark reddish brown. Leaf nearly round, dentate, underside pubescent, lobes usually pointed; sinus usually open, may be partly closed. Leaf size: 10–18 in. (25–45 cm). Leaf

spread: 6–10 ft. (1.8–3 m). Stem color: Reddish brown. Some pubescence on petiole; occasionally some on peduncle.

COMMENTS. This species is a very good bloomer in small, medium, or large pools and has been used in hybridizing several cultivars with larger and more attractive blooms.

Nymphaea spontanea Landon

Native to Southeast Asia

PLATE 21

CHARACTERISTICS. Night blooming, nonviviparous, very free flowering, and producing much less fruit than *N. pubescens*.

FLOWERS. Petal color: Cerise (*RHS* 63B). Sepal color: Purplish red (*RHS* 70C). Anther color: Cerise (*RHS* 63B). Stamen color: Reddish. Flower shape: Broad, stellate. Flower size: 5–7 in. (13–18 cm). Fragrance: Slight but pungent. Number of petals: 15–17. Number of sepals: 4.

LEAVES. Color: Top, maroon to olive green; underside, maroon to purple. Leaf dentate; sinus open. Leaf size: 8–12 in. (20–30 cm). Leaf spread: 5–7 ft. (1.5–2.1 m). Stem color: Maroon. Occasionally pubescence on peduncle and petiole.

COMMENTS. In regard to Southeast Asian *Nymphaea*, subgenus *Lotos*, Kenneth Landon stated: "The basic white-flowered plants are generally classed as *Nymphaea pubescens* in the wild, while those plants possessing cerise or reddish colored

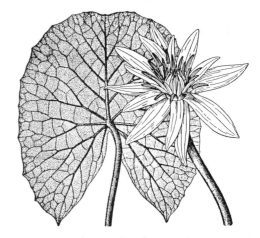

FIGURE 25. *Nymphaea zenkeri*, flower and underside of leaf. From *The Waterlilies: A Monograph of the Genus Nymphaea* by Henry S. Conard (1905).

flowers are referred to as *N. spontanea*. Those with pink petals are considered natural hybrids. It should be noted that all are closely interrelated. The color forms are most likely natural hybrids of *N. pubescens* and *N. rubra*. These forms are often self-perpetuating—sometimes producing numerous intermediates." Because there are many new cultivars that possess larger and more striking flowers than *N. spontanea*, I do not recommend this species for the water garden.

Nymphaea zenkeri Gilg

Native to the former Cameroons, West Africa

CHARACTERISTICS. Night blooming, nonviviparous, very small, free flowering.

FLOWERS. Petal color: White. Sepal color: White. Anther color: Yellow. Stamen color: Yellow. Flower shape: Stellate. Flower size: 2–3 in. (5–8 cm). Fragrance: Slight. Number of petals: 7 or 8. Number of sepals: 4.

LEAVES. Color: Top, green; underside, greenish. Leaf nearly round, prominent veins, short hairs underneath on adult leaves; lobes far apart, protuberance on tips; sinus wide open. Leaf size: 4–6 × 3.5–5 in. (10–15 × 9–13 cm). Leaf spread: 20–24 in. (50–60 cm). Stem color: Greenish. Short hairs on peduncle and petiole.

COMMENTS. *Nymphaea zenkeri* is very rare and so I cannot recommend it for the water garden.

CHAPTER 3

Day-Blooming Tropical Cultivars

FLOWERS of the tropical waterlily cultivars are generally considered the largest and showiest of all waterlilies and are available in just about every color, including green (*Nymphaea* 'Green Smoke'). Flowers of day bloomers open in midmorning and close in late afternoon. Cool autumn days may allow them to remain open for longer periods. Blooms generally open for three to four consecutive days. This chapter includes complete descriptions of the tropical day-blooming waterlily cultivars. (Night-blooming cultivars are described in chapter 4.) Two hybridizers, in particular, deserve thanks for the beautiful tropical waterlily cultivars available today: Dr. George H. Pring, hybridizer at the Missouri Botanical Garden, and Martin E. Randig of San Bernardino, California, who gave his hybrids to Van Ness Water Gardens of Upland, California, for introduction to the public. In recent years, several hybridizers have introduced beautiful new hybrids. You will find these described later in this and other chapters of this book.

The following plant descriptions are arranged alphabetically by cultivar name. This name is followed by any synonyms, the name of the hybridizer or originator, and the date, if known. Some cultivars hold a U.S. plant patent, and these are noted under "Comments." Such patents expire 20 years from issue and are not renewable.

To plant a tropical waterlily, separate the plant from the sprouted tuber and spread the roots out in a depression in the middle of a 0.5- to 1-bushel (18- to 35-L) planter. I prefer to use clay loam or garden soil. If not available, buy an all-black bagged soil (potting soil with white particles is not suitable). Firm the soil and top with 1 in. (2.5 cm) of fine gravel or very coarse sand. Place the planting immediately under 6–12 in. (15–30 cm) of water (Plates 22–24). Plant tropical waterlilies only when the water temperature averages 75°F (24°C) or above. Planting too early may cause plants to go dormant. See the hardiness zone maps at the end of the book and follow this general planting timetable:

In North America		In Europe	
Zone 10	March–early April	Zone 10	mid–late May
Zone 9	early April	Zone 9	June
Zone 8	mid April	Zones 8–4	conservatory
Zone 7	mid–late May		planting, where
Zone 6	late May–early June		water can be
Zone 5	early–mid June		heated to 75°F
Zone 4	mid–late June		(24°C) or higher

Nymphaea 'Afterglow'

Randig 1946

Parentage unknown

PLATE 25

CHARACTERISTICS. Nonviviparous, very free flowering.

FLOWERS. Petal color: Yellow, orange tips (*RHS* 11A; tips, 29B). Sepal color: Deep, pinkish orange (*RHS* 31B). Anther color: Yellow, outer anthers tipped deep pinkish orange (*RHS* 11C; tips, 31B). Stamen color: Golden orange. Flower shape: Like a big sunflower after first day. Flower size: 6–10 in. (15–25 cm). Fragrance: Delightful. Number of petals: 21. Number of sepals: 4.

LEAVES. Color: Top, green; underside, red, prominent green veins. Leaf nearly round, smooth, wavy edges; sinus an open V. Leaf size: 11.5 × 11 in. (29 × 28 cm). Leaf spread: 6–8 ft. (1.8–2.4 m). Stem color: Brownish red. No pubescence on peduncle or petiole.

COMMENTS. One of the most colorful of the

"sunset" tropicals. Worthy of a place in any medium or large pool. Flowers open out flatter than those of N. 'Albert Greenberg', yet the color is quite similar.

Nymphaea 'Albert Greenberg'

Birdsey 1969

Chance seedling, parentage unknown

PLATE 26

CHARACTERISTICS. Nonviviparous, very free flowering.

FLOWERS. Petal color: Yellow, orange-pink tips (RHS 11B; tips, 29B). Sepal color: Outer two-thirds deep pinkish orange, yellowish green base (RHS outer, 32D; base, 144B). Anther color: Yellow, pink tips (RHS 4B; tips, 38C). Stamen color: Deep yellow. Flower shape: Cuplike. Flower size: 6–7 in. (15–18 cm). Fragrance: Very lovely. Number of petals: 20. Number of sepals: 4.

LEAVES. Color: Top, green, heavily blotched purple; underside, green center, pinkish red perimeter, all heavily blotched deep red. Leaf large, nearly round, rounded notches and wavy convolutions along edge; lobes usually overlap completely at sinus. On mature leaves one lobe frequently raised. Leaf size: Up to 19 × 18 in. (48 × 45 cm). Leaf spread: 5–8 ft. (1.5–2.4 m). Stem color: Peduncle bright yellowish green; petiole mostly brown. No pubescence on peduncle or petiole.

COMMENTS. One of the most popular "sunset" tropicals. Flowers are distinctly cup-shaped. Freedom of bloom, rich color, and beautifully mottled leaves make this waterlily very desirable for medium and large pools.

Nymphaea 'Alexis'

Schuck 2001

Seedling of N. 'Pink Pearl'

PLATE 27

CHARACTERISTICS. Free flowering, nonviviparous.

FLOWERS. Petal color: Light purple with whitish staminodes. Anthers develop as small petals. Sepal color: Inner, purple and white, similar to petals; outer, green with red speckles. Flower shape: Stellate. Flower size: 6–7 in. (15–18 cm). Fragrance: Light and pleasant. Number of petals: More than

100 with the anthers, which turn into petals. Number of sepals: 4.

LEAVES. Color: Top, olive green; underside, solid red. Leaf oval with dentate edges; sinus closed with overlapping lobes. Leaf size: 10–12 in. (25.5–30 cm). Leaf spread: 3–4 ft. (0.9–1.2 m). Color of stem: Green. No pubescence on peduncle or petiole.

COMMENTS BY STUART SCHUCK. This plant is very unique in its flower form. There are 100 petals and more. It opens very flat and the staminodes rise above the other petals. Very striking, and it has compact foliage and a vigorous growth habit.

Nymphaea 'Alice Tricker'

Tricker 1937

Possibly a seedling, hybrid, or mutation of N. 'Mrs. George H. Pring'

CHARACTERISTICS. Nonviviparous, very free flowering.

FLOWERS. Petal color: White (RHS 155B). Sepal color: White, greenish gray stripes (RHS 155B; stripes, 193D). Anther color: Yellow, white tips (RHS 7A; tips, 155B). Stamen color: Deep, golden yellow. Flower shape: Stellate with broad petals. Flower size: 7–9 in. (18–23 cm). Fragrance: Delightful. Number of petals: 21. Number of sepals: 4.

LEAVES. Color: Top, green, new leaves mottled purple; underside, green, purplish blue mottles. Leaves egg-shaped; lobes overlap about halfway down sinus. Leaf size: 15 × 12 in. (38 × 30 cm). Leaf spread: 6–8 ft. (1.8–2.4 m). Stem color: Bronzy green underwater; bright green above water. No pubescence on peduncle or petiole.

COMMENTS. An excellent waterlily for medium and large water gardens due to its long blooming period and reliability for good performance.

Nymphaea 'American Beauty'

Pring 1941

Nymphaea colorata × N. 'William Stone'

PLATE 28

CHARACTERISTICS. Nonviviparous, free flowering.

FLOWERS. Petal color: Rich raspberry pink (RHS 70C). Sepal color: Deep pink (RHS 70B). Anther color: Orange-pink, rich raspberry-pink tips (RHS 171D; tips, 70C). Stamen color: Yellow. Flower shape: Cuplike then flat. Flower size: 5–6 in. (13–15 cm). Fragrance: Very sweet. Number of petals: 25. Number of sepals: 4.

LEAVES. Color: Top, green, a few purple blotches on new leaves; underside, red, prominent green veins. Leaf large, nearly round, many serrations and convolutions along edge; sinus occasionally open, generally two-thirds to completely closed due to overlap of lobes. Leaf size: 12 × 10.5 in. (30 × 27 cm). Leaf spread: 6 ft. (1.8 m). Stem color: Bright green. No pubescence on peduncle or petiole.

COMMENTS. A fine waterlily for medium and large pools.

Nymphaea 'Aquarius'

Nutt 1972

Nymphaea 'Judge Hitchcock' × *N. colorata*

CHARACTERISTICS. Nonviviparous, very free flowering, petals somewhat crumpled.

FLOWERS. Petal color: Deep violet-blue (*RHS* 88C). Sepal color: Slightly deeper than petals (*RHS* 88B). Anther color: Brown, almost chocolate, deep violet-blue tips (*RHS* 176C; tips, 88C). Stamen color: Deep yellow. Flower shape: Very full star. Flower size: 8–10 in. (20–25 cm). Fragrance: Slight. Number of petals: 28 or 29. Number of sepals: 4.

LEAVES. Color: Top, dark green, some purple mottling; underside, green, suffused purple, very prominent veins. Leaves oval-shaped, somewhat dentate; sinus usually closed, may be partly open. Leaf size: Up to 18 × 16 in. (45 × 40 cm). Leaf spread: 6–7 ft. (1.8–2.1 m). Stem color: Bronzy green. No pubescence on peduncle or petiole.

COMMENTS. *Nymphaea* 'Aquarius' is a fine waterlily for medium and large pools. It is somewhat similar to *N.* 'Director George T. Moore', but blooms are larger and more double.

Nymphaea 'August Koch'

Koch and Pring 1922

Probably *N.* 'Blue Beauty' × *N.* 'Mrs. Woodrow Wilson'

PLATE 29

CHARACTERISTICS. Viviparous, extremely free flowering.

FLOWERS. Petal color: Rich blue (*RHS* 92C or lighter). Sepal color: Lilac-purple (*RHS* 90D). Anther color: Inner anthers brownish orange, tipped rich blue; outer, lilac-purple, tipped rich blue (*RHS* inner, 166D; outer, 90D; tips, 92C or lighter). Stamen color: Inner, orange-brown; outer, lilac-purple. Flower shape: Cuplike. Flower size: 4.5–5.5 in. (11–14 cm). Fragrance: Very pleasant. Number of petals: 22–25. Number of sepals: 4.

LEAVES. Color: Top, olive green; underside, mostly green, pink on lobes; lobes display prominent green veins. Leaf nearly round, unevenly serrated, some convolutions along edges; sinus usually, yet not always, closed due to overlap of lobes. Leaf size: 12.5 × 12 in. (32 × 30 cm). Leaf spread: 4–6 ft. (1.2–1.8 m). Stem color: Bronzy green; portions of peduncle above water bright green. No pubescence on peduncle or petiole.

COMMENTS. The cross that resulted in *Nymphaea* 'August Koch' was made at Garfield Park, Chicago, Illinois. Since all leaves are viviparous, this waterlily will reproduce well from plantlets that form on leaves if insects are kept from devouring new starts. Aphids love to congregate around tender new growth. *Nymphaea* 'August Koch' is excellent for small or medium pools and will also bloom well in tub gardens. It can withstand crowding.

Nymphaea 'Aviator Pring'

Pring 1956

Nymphaea sulfurea × *N.* 'St. Louis'

PLATE 30

CHARACTERISTICS. Nonviviparous, very free flowering.

FLOWERS. Petal color: Yellow (*RHS* 3B). Sepal color: Yellow (*RHS* 3B). Anther color: Yellow (*RHS* 3B). Stamen color: Yellow. Flower shape: Large, full star. Flower size: 8–10 in. (20–25 cm). Fragrance: Delightful. Number of petals: 25 or 26. Number of sepals: 4.

LEAVES. Color: Top, green; underside, green. Leaf somewhat egg-shaped; sinus usually half open. Leaf size: 12 × 10.5 in. (30 × 27 cm). Leaf spread: 6–8 ft. (1.8–2.4 cm). Stem color: Bronzy green. No pubescence on peduncle or petiole.

COMMENTS. One of the very best yellow tropicals for medium and large pools, and I highly recommend it.

Nymphaea 'Bagdad'

Pring 1941

Nymphaea 'Pink Platter' × unnamed hybrid

PLATE 31

CHARACTERISTICS. Viviparous, very free flowering.

FLOWERS. Petal color: Light blue (wisteria blue, *RHS* 106D). Sepal color: Lavender (*RHS* 76C). Anther color: Butterscotch-yellow, wisteria-blue tips (*RHS* 165D; tips, 106D). Stamen color: Yellow. Flower shape: Full, stellate. Flower size: 8 in. (20 cm). Fragrance: Sweet. Number of petals: 30–32. Number of sepals: 4.

LEAVES. Color: Top, green, heavily mottled and blotched purple and red; underside, dark green, heavily blotched purple. Leaf nearly round; sinus usually partly open. Leaf size: 10–12 in. (25–30 cm). Leaf spread: 6–7 ft. (1.8–2.1 m). Stem color: Bright green. No pubescence on peduncle or petiole.

COMMENTS. I consider *N.* 'Bagdad' a very choice tropical. Since it is viviparous, it can withstand more cold and is not so apt to go dormant in early spring. It has beautiful leaves, a distinct plus. In addition, the light blue color of the flower is very lovely. I highly recommend 'Bagdad' for medium and large pools.

Nymphaea 'Barbara Barnett'

Florida Aquatic Nursery 1997

Parentage unknown

PLATE 32

CHARACTERISTICS. Free flowering, nonviviparous.

FLOWERS. Petal color: Yellow and orange with pink tips. Sepal color: Inner, pinkish orange; outer, green to bronze with black specks. Anther color: Inner, yellow with pink tips; outer, yellow with pink tips. Stamen color: Yellow. Flower shape: Open cup. Flower size: 6–7 in. (15–18 cm). Fragrance: Sweetly scented. Number of petals: Up to 42. Number of sepals: 4.

LEAVES. Color: Top, green, heavily splashed with burgundy; underside, green, heavily blotched with light and dark red. Nearly round leaf, margins with rounded notches; lobes usually meet and push upward at sinus. Leaf size: Up to 11.5–11 in. (29–28 cm). Leaf spread: Up to 6–8 ft. (1.8–2.4 m). Stem

color: Bronze. No pubescence on peduncle or petiole.

COMMENTS BY FLORIDA AQUATIC NURSERY. *Nymphaea* 'Barbara Barnett' is one of a few "sunset" tropical lilies on the market today. The flower is very similar to *N.* 'Albert Greenberg' in size, shape, and color. With its heavily mottled leaves, it's a good addition to any medium to large pool.

Nymphaea 'Bellachika'

Landon 2002

Nymphaea gracillis (*N. flavovirens*) × *N. capensis* var. *zanzibariensis* 'Rosea' (a specially bred plant with dark rose flowers and more petals than average)

PLATE 33

CHARACTERISTICS. Very free flowering, nonviviparous.

FLOWERS. Petal color: Intense crimson. Sepal color: Inner, crimson; outer, dark maroon. Anther color: Inner, reddish orange; outer, bright crimson. Stamen color: Red. Flower shape: Stellate. Flower size: 7 in. (18 cm). Fragrance: Strong. Number of petals: 22. Number of sepals: 4.

LEAVES. Color: Top, bright yellow green with occasional blotches of maroon; underside, bright red with prominent green veins. Sinus closed with overlapping lobes. Leaf size: 12 × 9 in. (30 × 23 cm), Leaf spread: 8 ft. (2.4 m). Stem color: Yellow green. No pubescence on peduncle or petiole.

COMMENTS BY KENNETH LANDON. *Nymphaea* 'Bellachika' is a new intense red star waterlily. Floral color surpasses its red predecessors with the addition of broader and more petals. Plants, while large, are smaller than early previous *N. flavovirens* hybrids.

Nymphaea 'Bill Yohn'

Frase 1989

Nymphaea ampla × *N.* 'Director George T. Moore'

PLATE 34

CHARACTERISTICS. Nonviviparous, very free flowering.

FLOWERS. Petal color: Deep blue then medium blue (*RHS* 94C; last day, 94D). Sepal color: Deep blue (*RHS* 94C). Anther color: Deep yellow (*RHS* 11A); inner rows (about three) also have yellow tips (*RHS* 11A; outer tips, blue 94C). Stamen color: Yellowish brown. Flower shape: Stellate. Flower size: 6–9 in. (15–23 cm). Fragrance: Very pleasant. Number of petals: 19 or 20. Number of sepals: 5 or 6.

LEAVES. Color: Top, green, few purple blotches, perimeter of new leaves purple, especially around sinus; underside, red, green veins. Leaf almost round, serrated edges; sinus usually an open V. Leaf size: 12–15 in. (30–38 cm). Leaf spread: 5–8 ft. (1.5–2.4 m). Stem color: Brownish turning purplish. Heavy, short fuzz on all stems.

COMMENTS. A very striking blue that is bound to make a name for itself among the blue waterlilies. I recommend it for medium or large pools.

Nymphaea 'Black Prince'

Winch 1987

Parentage unknown

CHARACTERISTICS. Nonviviparous, free flowering.

FLOWERS. Petal color: Deep blue (RHS 94B,C). Sepal color: Deep violet (RHS 90D). Anther color: Deep golden yellow, deep blue tips (RHS 12B; tips, 90D). Stamen color: Deep yellow. Flower shape: Stellate. Flower size: 6 in. (15 cm). Fragrance: Pronounced. Number of petals: 21. Number of sepals: 4.

LEAVES. Color: Top, green; underside, green, portion under lobes purple. Leaf nearly round, deeply serrated, sharp teeth around edges; sinus usually half open, sometimes fully open or fully closed on same plant. Leaf size: 15 × 14 in. (38 × 35 cm). Leaf spread: 10 ft. (3 m). Stem color: Green. No pubescence on peduncle or petiole.

COMMENTS. Nymphaea 'Black Prince' is a star waterlily. Flowers, which are rather small in comparison to the large leaves, are held very high above the water. Like most of the star lilies, it performs best when given plenty of room. I recommend N. 'Black Prince' for medium and large pools.

Nymphaea 'Blue Ampla'

Landon 1978

Nymphaea ampla × N. capensis var. zanzibariensis 'Rosea'

CHARACTERISTICS. Nonviviparous, free flowering.

FLOWERS. Petal color: Blue (RHS 100C). Sepal color: Medium blue then pale blue (RHS 106C then 108D). Anther color: Butterscotch-yellow, blue tips (RHS 165D; tips, 100C). Stamen color: Deep, golden yellow. Flower shape: Stellate after first day. Flower size: 8–10 in. (20–25 cm). Fragrance: Very pleasant. Number of petals: 18–22. Number of sepals: 4.

LEAVES. Color: Top, green; underside, red-purple. Leaf longer than wide, very dentate; sinus frequently half open. Leaf size: 12–14 in. (30–35 cm). Leaf spread: 7–8 ft. (2.1–2.4 m). Stem color: Bronzy green. No pubescence on peduncle or petiole.

COMMENTS. Nymphaea 'Blue Ampla', with its very striking deep sky-blue blooms, is a fine waterlily for medium or large water gardens.

Nymphaea 'Blue Anemone'

Connelly 1998

Nymphaea colorata × N. 'Midnight'

PLATE 35

CHARACTERISTICS. Free flowering, nonviviparous.

FLOWERS. Petal color: Medium violet blue. Sepal color: Outside, bronzy green with purple border and flecks; inside, same, but a little lighter. Anthers color: Inner, yellow; outer, yellow. Stamen color: Inner, yellow; outer, light blue and they have become petaloids. Flower shape: Somewhat cup shaped becoming flat. Flower size: 6–7 in. (15–17.5 cm). Fragrance: Spicy sweet. Number of petals: 75–80. Number of sepals: 4.

LEAVES. Color: Top, green; underside, blue-green blended with lavender. Leaf size: 10–12 in. (25.5–30 cm). Leaf spread: 5–7 ft. (1.5–2.1 m). Stem color: Brown. Pubescence on peduncle and petiole.

COMMENTS BY LEEANN CONNELLY. Very good seed parent for modern hybrids of double flowers. This waterlily is best suited for small or medium pools. The petaloid stamens are curly on the second day, and the flower really looks like a blue sea anemone.

Nymphaea 'Blue Beauty'

Syn. 'Pennsylvania'

Conard and Tricker 1897

Nymphaea caerulea × N. capensis var. zanzibariensis

PLATE 36

CHARACTERISTICS. Nonviviparous, very free flowering.

FLOWERS. Petal color: Deep, rich blue (*RHS* 92B). Sepal color: Pale blue background, heavily streaked greenish blue near base (*RHS* 92C; streaks near base, 139D). Anther color: Brownish yellow beginning second day (*RHS* 164C). Stamen color: Deep yellow. Flower shape: Stellate. Flower size: 8–11 in. (20–28 cm). Fragrance: Very sweet. Number of petals: 21–23. Number of sepals: 4.

LEAVES. Color: Top, green, few purple specks and small blotches prominent on newest leaves; underside, purplish brown, numerous small, dark purple mottles. Leaf longer than wide, numerous serrations and waves around edges and 0.5-in. (1.3-cm) projection at each lobe tip; lobes overlap about halfway down sinus. Leaf size: 14 × 13 in. (35 × 33 cm). Leaf spread: 4–7 ft. (1.2–2.1 m). Stem color: Brown. Fuzz and fine hairs on petiole.

COMMENTS. Due to its abundance of flowers and excellent color, I rate *N*. 'Blue Beauty' as one of the greatest waterlilies of all time. If it is planted too early, however, and cold weather arrives, the plant may go dormant and not recover. I recommend this waterlily for medium and large pools.

Nymphaea 'Blue Bird'

William Tricker, Inc. 1946

Parentage unknown

CHARACTERISTICS. Viviparous, very free flowering.

FLOWERS. Petal color: Very brilliant blue (*RHS* 94D). Sepal color: Light blue (*RHS* 92C). Anther color: Rich butterscotch-brown, blue tips (*RHS* 165C; tips, 94D). Stamen color: Deep yellow. Flower shape: Cuplike then flat. Flower size: 5–6 in. (13–15 cm). Fragrance: Sweet. Number of petals: 28–30. Number of sepals 4.

LEAVES. Color: Top, bright olive green; underside, purple, green veins. Leaf nearly round, fairly smooth edges; sinus either closed or partly open. Leaf size: 8–10 in. (20–25 cm). Leaf spread: 5 ft. (1.5 m). Stem color: Stems purplish, short green portion on peduncle just below flower. No pubescence on peduncle or petiole.

COMMENTS. Though this waterlily is currently in scarce supply, it is a fine choice for any size pool.

Nymphaea 'Blue Spider'

Florida Aquatic Nursery 1994

Nymphaea capensis var. *zanzibariensis* × unknown

PLATE 37

CHARACTERISTICS. Free flowering, nonviviparous.

FLOWERS. Petal color: Violet blue. Sepal color: Inner, deep violet blue; outer, dark green with black specks. Anther color: Inner, yellow with blue tips; outer, red purple with violet blue tips. Stamen color: Red purple. Flower shape: Open cup. Flower size: 4–6 in. (10–15 cm). Fragrance: Sweetly scented. Number of petals: 29. Number of sepals: 4.

LEAVES. Color: Top, green with narrow burgundy mottling; underside, olive green covered with purple blotches. Leaf margins serrated and undulating; nearly round leaf; sinus partly closed. Lobes occasionally curling upward, tips are pointed. Leaf size: 12–10 in. (30–25.5 cm). Leaf spread: 4–6 ft. (1.2–1.8 m). Stem color: Green or bronze. No pubescence on peduncle or petiole.

COMMENTS BY FLORIDA AQUATIC NURSERY. *Nymphaea* 'Blue Spider' was the first hybrid released by Florida Aquatic Nursery. Its burgundy mottled leaves set off the deep violet blue flower. Because it is slightly cold tolerant, this is a fine addition to any medium or large pool.

Nymphaea 'Blue Star'

Syn. 'William Stone'

Tricker 1899

Nymphaea flavovirens × unknown (probably *N. capensis* var. *zanzibariensis*)

CHARACTERISTICS. Nonviviparous, very free flowering. Peduncles hold flowers 12–15 in. (30–38 cm) above the water.

FLOWERS. Petal color: Blue (*RHS* 91A). Sepal color: Deeper blue than petals (*RHS* 92A). Anther color: Orange-brown, blue tips (*RHS* 171C; tips, 91A). Stamen color: Deep yellow. Flower shape: Stellate. Flower size: 5–6 in. (13–15 cm). Fragrance: Delightful. Number of petals: 13 or 14. Number of sepals: 4.

LEAVES. Color: Top, green; underside, violet. Leaf a little longer than wide, slightly dentate edges, lobes have pointed tips; sinus open. Leaf size: 12 × 10.5 in. (30 × 27 cm). Leaf spread: 8 ft. (2.4 m). Stem color: Bronzy green or green. No pubescence on peduncle or petiole.

COMMENTS. Like most of the star lilies, *Nymphaea* 'Blue Star' adapts somewhat to the given area. If allowed, however, this plant can fill an 8-ft. (2.4-m) or larger surface area with leaves. For this reason, I recommend it for medium or large pools only.

Nymphaea 'Bob Trickett'

Pring 1949

Nymphaea stellata var. *caerulea* × *N.* 'Mrs. Edwards Whitaker'

PLATE 38

CHARACTERISTICS. Nonviviparous, very free flowering.

FLOWERS. Petal color: Sky blue (*RHS* 92C). Sepal color: Light blue, prominent greenish veins (*RHS* 97D; veins, 138D). Anther color: Butterscotch, sky-blue tips (*RHS* 165D; tips, 92C). Stamen color: Deep yellow. Flower shape: Cuplike then stellate. Flower size: 10–14 in. (25–35 cm). Fragrance: Very pleasing. Number of petals: 36 or 37. Number of sepals: 4.

LEAVES. Color: Top, green; underside, red, green veins. Leaves round; sinus usually open. Leaf size: 12 in. (30 cm). Leaf spread: 6 ft. (1.8 m). Stem color: Green. No pubescence on peduncle or petiole.

COMMENTS. *Nymphaea* 'Bob Trickett' is a very choice waterlily. It was named by George H. Pring to honor a friend who devoted most of his life to studying, working with, and promoting waterlilies. Truly a giant in the field, Bob Trickett became one of the world's experts and richly merits the tribute. I recommend *N.* 'Bob Trickett' for medium and large pools.

Nymphaea 'Carla's Sonshine'

Florida Aquatic Nursery 2001

Unnamed hybrid × *N.* 'Trail Blazer'

PLATE 39

CHARACTERISTICS. Free flowering, viviparous.

FLOWERS. Petal color: Deep yellow. Sepal color: Inner, yellow; outer, green to bronze with dark specks. Anther color: Inner, yellow; outer, yellow. Stamen color: Yellow. Flower shape: Cuplike. Flower size: 5–6 in. (12.5–15 cm). Fragrance: Sweetly scented. Number of petals: Up to 30. Number of sepals: 4.

LEAVES. Color: Top, green with medium burgundy mottling; underside, green with heavy red blotches. Nearly round leaf, margins slightly dentate; sinus open with lobes slightly raised. Leaf size: 12–12.5 in. (30–31 cm). Leaf spread: 4–6 ft. (1.2–1.8 m). Stem color: Bronze. No pubescence on peduncle or petiole.

COMMENTS BY FLORIDA AQUATIC NURSERY. This is the first yellow viviparous waterlily to be hybridized in years and the only one on the market today. Its numerous deep yellow flowers displayed above the mottled leaves makes this a great addition to any size pool.

Nymphaea 'Casey Lee Slocum'

Connelly 1999

Nymphaea ampla × *N.* 'Joseph Baynard Shearouse'

PLATE 40

CHARACTERISTICS. Very free flowering, nonviviparous.

FLOWERS. Petal color: Bright violet sky blue. Sepal color: Inner, sky blue; outer, dark green with purple flecks. Anther color: Inner, yellow with blue tips; outer, yellow with blue tips. Stamen color: Yellow. Flower shape: Stellate. Flower size: 14–15 in. (35–37.5 cm). Fragrance: Very sweet. Number of petals: 23. Number of sepals: 4.

LEAVES. Color: Top, green; underside, blue. Semi-oval leaf; edges very serrated with semi-closed sinus. Leaf size: 18–26 in. (45–65 cm). Leaf spread: 12–18 ft. (3.6–5.4 m). Stem color: Brown. Pubescence on peduncle and petiole.

COMMENTS BY LEEANN CONNELLY. This is the largest *Nymphaea* in the world. It needs a very large pool and can only be described as magnificent. In south Florida, *N.* 'Casey Lee Slocum' almost never has less than two flowers everyday all year. It makes a wonderful cut flower.

Nymphaea 'Charles Thomas'

Wood 1985

Parentage unknown

CHARACTERISTICS. Viviparous, very free flowering.

FLOWERS. Petal color: Sky blue (*RHS* 100C). Sepal color: Light blue, darker blue veins (*RHS* 106D; veins, 106B). Anther color: Yellow, sky-blue tips (*RHS* 11A; tips, blue 100C). Stamen color: Yellow. Flower shape: Stellate. Flower size: 5–6 in. (13–15 cm). Fragrance: Very pleasant. Number of petals: 24 or 25. Number of sepals: 4.

LEAVES. Color: Top, green, heavily mottled and blotched purple; underside, green, purple blotches. Leaf nearly round; sinus usually open. Leaf size: 10–11 in. (25–28 cm). Leaf spread 4–6 ft. (1.2–1.8 m). Stem color: Green. No pubescence on peduncle or petiole.

COMMENTS. With its magnificently mottled leaves, *Nymphaea* 'Charles Thomas' is one of the finest blue tropicals. I recommend it for any size pool, including tub gardens. Being viviparous, it will take more cold in early spring than many of the blue tropicals.

Nymphaea 'Charles Winch'

Winch 1986

Parentage unknown

CHARACTERISTICS. Nonviviparous, very free flowering.

FLOWERS. Petal color: White (*RHS* 155C). Sepal color: White, greenish tips and veins (*RHS* 155C; tips and veins, 145D). Anther color: Butterscotch, white tips (*RHS* 160C; tips, 155C). Stamen color: Deep yellow. Flower shape: Large, cuplike. Flower size: 8–10 in. (20–25 cm). Fragrance: Very sweet. Number of petals: 32–34. Number of sepals: 4.

LEAVES. Color: Top, green; underside, bronzy green. Leaf a little longer than wide, lobes usually overlap about halfway; sinus varies, usually partly open. Leaf size: 10–12 in. (25–30 cm). Leaf spread: 6 ft. (1.8 m). Stem color: Green or bronzy. No pubescence on peduncle or petiole.

COMMENTS. Probably the very best white day-blooming tropical. Many of the petals (especially the inner ones) are beautifully rolled, creating a unique and very pleasing effect. This plant adapts to available space, so I recommend it for any size pool.

Nymphaea 'Chaz'

Schuck 2002

Nymphaea colorata × *N.* 'Queen of Siam'

PLATE 41

CHARACTERISTICS. Free flowering, nonviviparous.

FLOWERS. Petal color: Smoky blue. Sepal color: Inner, smoky blue; outer, green with maroon specks. Anther color: Inner, yellow on smoky blue; outer, yellow on smoky blue. Stamen color: Blue and yellow. Flower shape: Cuplike. Flower size: 8–11 in. (20–28 cm). Fragrance: Pleasant. Number of petals: 21. Number of sepals: 4.

LEAVES. Color: Top, mahogany leaves with olive green variegation; color does not fade and remains dark; underside, red with yellow veins. Nearly round leaf with dentate edges; sinus is closed and lobes overlap. Leaf size: 10–12 in. (25.5–30 cm). Leaf spread: 3–4 ft. (0.9–1.2 m).

COMMENTS BY STUART SCHUCK. *Nymphaea* 'Chaz' is beautiful with its contrast between the smoky blue flowers and dark red leaves. The variegation between the mahogany and green leaves makes it impressive. It has a compact growing habit and the leaves do not fade with time. This hybrid won the Banksian Award given by the International Waterlily and Water Gardening Society in 2002.

Nymphaea 'Christine Lingg'

Lingg, year unknown

Parentage unknown

PLATE 42

CHARACTERISTICS. Nonviviparous, very free flowering.

FLOWERS. Petal color: Lavender-blue (*RHS* 92B). Sepal color: Pale lavender (*RHS* 84C). Anther color: Rich butterscotch-yellow, lavender-blue tips (*RHS* 11A and 165C; tips, 92B). Stamen color: Deep yellow. Flower shape: Large, cuplike. Flower size: 6–8 in. (15–20 cm). Fragrance: Delightful. Number of petals: 54–56. Number of sepals: 4.

LEAVES. Color: Top, green, heavily mottled purple; underside, red, maroon blotches. Leaves nearly round, somewhat dentate; sinus usually closed. Leaf size: 10–12 in. (25–30 cm). Leaf spread: 5–6 ft. (1.5–1.8 m). Stem color: Pinkish red. No pubescence on peduncle or petiole.

COMMENTS. One of the choicest of all the tropical lilies for any size pool except the tub garden. The magnificent leaves alone make it well worthwhile. The very double lavender-blue blooms add to its charm.

Nymphaea 'Clint Bryant'

Wood 1980

Parentage unknown

CHARACTERISTICS. Nonviviparous, free flowering, long flower stem.

FLOWERS. Petal color: Violet-blue (*RHS* 98D). Sepal color: Bluish purple (*RHS* 96D). Anther color: Purplish brown, violet-blue tips (*RHS* 185C; tips, 98D). Stamen color: Yellow. Flower shape: Cuplike. Flower size: 7–8 in. (18–20 cm). Fragrance: Lovely. Number of petals: 28. Number of sepals: 4.

LEAVES. Color: Top, green; underside, blushed pink. Leaves nearly round, highly dentate; sinus usually open. Leaf size: 10–12 in. (25–30 cm). Leaf spread: 6–7 ft. (1.8–2.1 m). Stem color: Greenish. No pubescence on peduncle or petiole.

COMMENTS. An excellent free-blooming waterlily for medium and large pools. The plant does quite well in shaded or partly shaded areas.

Nymphaea 'Daubeniana'

Syn. 'Dauben' (in the United States)

Daubeny 1863

Probably *N. micrantha* × *N. caerulea*

PLATES 43, 44

CHARACTERISTICS. Highly viviparous, very free flowering.

FLOWERS. Petal color: Light blue, slightly darker tips (*RHS* 92D; tips, 92C). Sepal color: Light blue, striped green (*RHS* 108D or lighter; stripes, 138D). Anther color: Yellow, blue tips (*RHS* 13B; tips, 92C). Stamen color: Golden yellow. Flower shape: Cuplike. Flower size: 4–6 in. (10–15 cm). Fragrance: Very highly scented. Number of petals: 21. Number of sepals: 4.

LEAVES. Color: Top, green; underside, green, many small purple specks. Leaf egg-shaped, edges wavy, convoluted; almost all leaves produce a fast-growing plantlet; sinus a wide-open V. Leaf size: Up to 12 × 10 in. (30 × 25 cm). Leaf spread: 3–7 ft. (0.9–2.1 m). Stem color: Peduncle, reddish brown; petiole, brownish. No pubescence on peduncle or petiole.

COMMENTS. Nearly every leaf develops a plantlet that frequently blooms while still attached to the mother plant. This waterlily is ideal for the tub garden or small pool as it adapts readily to a small planting area. Like other viviparous tropicals, it withstands more cold than most tropical lilies without going dormant.

Nymphaea 'Director George T. Moore'

Pring 1941

Nymphaea 'Judge Hitchcock' × *N. colorata*

PLATE 45

CHARACTERISTICS. Nonviviparous, very free flowering.

FLOWERS. Petal color: Deep violet-blue (*RHS* 94B). Sepal color: Deep violet (*RHS* 90A). Anther color: Purple, deep violet-blue tips (*RHS* 89D; tips, 94B). Stamen color: Deep violet-blue. Flower shape: Wide-open star after first day. Flower size: 7–10 in. (18–25 cm). Fragrance: Delightful. Number of petals: 13–26. Number of sepals: 4 or 5.

LEAVES. Color: Top, green, a few purple blotches and mottles; underside, rich royal purple, green veins. Leaf almost round; lobes overlap broadly at sinus. Leaf size: 10–12 in. (25–30 cm). Leaf spread 5–8 ft. (1.5–2.4 m). Stem color: Varies from green to purple. A few short hairs on peduncle and petiole; bare on above-water portion of peduncle.

COMMENTS. *Nymphaea* 'Director George T. Moore' is one of my two favorite tropicals (the other is *N.* 'William McLane'). The blooms are of the richest violet imaginable and are borne very freely. It is somewhat similar to *N.* 'Aquarius' but much deeper in color. I highly recommend it for medium or large pools.

Nymphaea 'Dorothy Pearl'

Slocum Water Gardens 1999

Natural hybrid, *N.* 'August Koch' probable parent

PLATE 46

CHARACTERISTICS. Free flowering, viviparous.

FLOWERS. Petal color: White. Sepal color: Inner, greenish white with green stripes; outer, olive green. Anther color: Inner, yellow; outer, yellow. Stamen color: Yellow with white tips. Flower shape: Cuplike. Flower size: 4–6 in. (10–15 cm). Fragrance: Very pronounced. Number of petals: 19 or 20. Number of sepals: 4.

LEAVES. Color: Top, green; underside, green with lots of yellow green veins. Nearly round leaf with a variable sinus, which is either partly or mostly open. Leaf size: 8.5–10 in. (21.5–25.5 cm). Leaf spread: 3–7 ft. (0.9–2.1 m). Stem color: Brownish. No pubescence on peduncle or petiole.

COMMENTS. Virgil Smith, a long-time employee at Slocum Water Gardens, discovered this waterlily blooming in a bed of *Nymphaea* 'August Koch'. He asked to name it after his grandmother. *Nymphaea* 'Dorothy Pearl' is a fast propagator from its viviparous leaves and has all the excellent qualities of *N.* 'August Koch'. A great waterlily for any size pool, especially the small pool or tub garden.

Nymphaea 'Edward D. Uber'
Van Ness Water Gardens 1985
Parentage unknown

CHARACTERISTICS. Viviparous, very free flowering.

FLOWERS. Petal color: Pinkish purple (*RHS* 63C). Sepal color: Pinkish purple (*RHS* 63C). Anther color: Butterscotch, pinkish purple tips (*RHS* 26C; tips, 63C). Stamen color: Deep yellow. Flower shape: Stellate, long sepals. Flower size: 8 in. (20 cm). Fragrance: Delightful. Number of petals: 18–22. Number of sepals: 4.

LEAVES. Color: Top, deep green; underside, pinkish, small maroon flecks. Leaves a little longer than wide; sinus open. Leaf size: 10 in. (25 cm). Leaf spread: 5–6 ft. (1.5–1.8 m). Stem color: Pinkish red. No pubescence on peduncle or petiole.

COMMENTS. Being a viviparous variety, *Nymphaea* 'Edward D. Uber' can take more cold and shade than most tropicals and still bloom well. Also, it can be planted a little earlier in the spring than nonviviparous varieties. I highly recommend it for any size pool.

Nymphaea 'Eldorado'
Randig 1963
Parentage unknown
PLATE 47

CHARACTERISTICS. Nonviviparous, very free flowering.

FLOWERS. Petal color: Medium lemon yellow (*RHS* 13B). Sepal color: Lemon yellow, edges frequently tinted pinkish orange (*RHS* 12C; edges, 31D or lighter). Anther color: Yellow, medium lemon-yellow tips (*RHS* 14B; tips, 13B). Stamen color: Deep golden orange. Flower shape: Large, stellate. Flower size: 9–11 in. (23–28 cm). Fragrance: Very lovely. Number of petals: 20–22. Number of sepals: 4.

LEAVES. Color: Top, green, numerous purple blotches, new leaves bronzy; underside, green, heavily blotched deep violet-purple. Leaf large, egg-shaped, smooth edges; sinus usually an open V. Leaf size: Up to 12 × 10 in. (30 × 25 cm). Leaf spread: 6 ft. (1.8 m). Stem color: Reddish brown. No pubescence on peduncle or petiole.

COMMENTS. Among the best of the yellow tropicals. With its heavily mottled leaves, *Nymphaea* 'Eldorado' can be among the prettiest of any yellow tropical; its rich yellow flowers are nearly as large as the leaves, and it performs well even in a small pool. Its only drawback is that leaves often disintegrate around the center of pads. I recommend it for any size pool.

Nymphaea 'Enchantment'
Randig 1963
Parentage unknown
PLATE 48

CHARACTERISTICS. Nonviviparous, free flowering.

FLOWERS. Petal color: Rich medium pink (*RHS* 75B,C). Sepal color: Medium pink (*RHS* 75B,C). Anther color: Pinkish orange, rich medium pink tips (*RHS* 31C; tips, 75B,C). Stamen color: Yellow. Flower shape: Round, flat. Flower size: 7–10 in. (18–25 cm). Fragrance: Delightful. Number of petals: 24 or 25. Number of sepals: 4.

LEAVES. Color: Top, bright green; underside, yellow-green. Leaf large, oval, some serrations and many convolutions along edges; lobes overlap completely along sinus; on older leaves one lobe raised 1 in. (2.5 cm). Leaf size: Up to 15 × 13.5 in. (38 × 34 cm). Leaf spread: 5–9 ft. (1.5–2.7 m). Stem color: Green. No pubescence on peduncle or petiole.

COMMENTS. To my mind, *Nymphaea* 'Enchantment' is tops for a medium pink tropical. The color is terrific, flowers are large, and blooms are plentiful. I highly recommend it for medium or large pools.

Nymphaea 'Evelyn Randig'

Randig 1931

Parentage unknown

PLATE 49

CHARACTERISTICS. Nonviviparous, excellent bloomer.

FLOWERS. Petal color: Deep raspberry pink (*RHS* 72C). Sepal color: Outer two-thirds, deep raspberry pink (*RHS* 72C); base, greenish, with many tiny purple lines or veins (*RHS* base, 144C; veins, 72B). Anther color: Inner, yellow, outer, purple; tips, deep raspberry pink (*RHS* 2B; outer, 72B; tips, 72C). Stamen color: Deep yellow. Flower shape: Cuplike then full star. Flower size: 7–9 in. (18–23 cm). Fragrance: Slight. Number of petals: 25. Number of sepals: 4.

LEAVES. Color: Top, deep green, large purple blotches cover more than half the leaf; underside, greenish yellow, numerous red blotches. Leaf almost round, smooth or nearly smooth edges; sinus usually closed due to overlapping lobes; some young leaves have partly open sinuses. Leaf size: 14–15 in. (35–38 cm). Leaf spread: 5–7 ft. (1.5–2.1 m). Stem color: Brown, short green portion on peduncle just below flower. No pubescence on peduncle or petiole.

COMMENTS. With its rich raspberry-pink blooms and magnificent mottled leaves, this waterlily has to be considered one of the most beautiful and desirable lilies. Suitable for medium and large pools.

Nymphaea 'Eve's Solitaire'

Landon 1998

Nymphaea 'Evelyn Randig' × *N. capensis* var. zanzibariensis 'Purpurea'

PLATE 50

CHARACTERISTICS. Free flowering, nonviviparous.

FLOWERS. Petal color: Intense iridescent bright blue to purple. Sepal color: Inner, bright blue; outer, speckled purplish black. Anther color: Inner, blue; outer, dark blue. Stamen color: Lavender. Flower shape: Stellate, well defined. Flowers open less than flat (20 degrees above horizontal). Flower size: 5 in. (12.5 cm). Fragrance: Average. Number of petals: 22. Number of sepals: 4.

LEAVES. Color: Top, strongly blotched dark maroon on green; underside, mosaic pattern, purple on green with prominent green veins. Leaves round; sinus closed, margins closed and strongly converging, producing a raised sail 2–3 in. (5–7.5 cm) above leaf. Leaf size: 12 in. (30 cm). Leaf spread: 6–8 ft. (1.8–2.4 m). Stem color: Olive green. No pubescence on peduncle or petiole.

COMMENTS BY KENNETH LANDON. *Nymphaea* 'Eve's Solitaire' is an exceptional medium-sized plant with striking leaves in a compact arrangement. The vivid infertile flowers are born in profusion.

Nymphaea 'Foxfire'

Presnell 2003

Unnamed seedling × *N. ampla*

PLATE 51

CHARACTERISTICS. Free flowering, nonviviparous.

FLOWERS. Petal color: Long outer petals, medium blue; short inner petals, pink. Sepal color: Inner, white; outer, dark green, very heavily covered with black speckles. Flower shape: Stellate then flat. Flower size: 8–9 in. (20–23 cm). Fragrance: Slight. Number of petals: 150. Number of sepals: 4.

LEAVES. Color: Top, maroon with green mottling; underside, pink blotches with prominent green veins. Oval leaf with heavily serrated margins; sinus is usually closed with lobes overlapping. Leaf size: 19 × 17 in. (49 × 43 cm). Leaf spread: About 10 ft. (3 m). Stem color: Brown. Pubescence on underwater portion of peduncle and petiole.

COMMENTS BY J. CRAIG PRESNELL. The numerous pink inner petals contrast sharply with the blue outer petals, providing a sensational flower that is bound to impress all flower lovers. This waterlily is one of the earliest to open and is best displayed in a large pool.

Nymphaea 'Gene Joyner'

Connelly 1999

Nymphaea ampla × unnamed hybrid

PLATE 52

CHARACTERISTICS. Free flowering, nonviviparous.

FLOWERS. Petal color: Bright sky blue. Sepal color: Inner, sky blue; outer, medium green with purple flecks. Anther color: Inner, butterscotch yellow with blue tips; outer, yellow with blue tips. Stamen color: Yellow. Flower shape: Stellate. Flower size: 12–13 in. (30–32.5 cm). Fragrance: Very sweet. Number of petals: 23–28. Number of sepals: 4.

LEAVES. Color: Top, green with some very sparse purple flecks; new leaves have slight copper color; underside, red. Semi-oval leaf; sinus usually closed. Leaf size: 18–24 in. (45–60 cm). Leaf spread: 12–15 ft. (3.6–4.5 m). Stem color: Brown. Pubescence on peduncle and petiole.

COMMENTS BY LEEANN CONNELLY. This water-lily is a sister seedling to Nymphaea 'Casey Lee Slocum'. It was selected because it makes an excellent cut flower—there exists no finer waterlily for cutting. Unlike some other waterlilies, this one stands up very well in a vase.

Nymphaea 'General Pershing'

Pring 1920

Nymphaea 'Mrs. Edwards Whitaker' × *N.* 'Castaliflora'

PLATE 53

CHARACTERISTICS. Nonviviparous, very free flowering.

FLOWERS. Petal color: Lavender-pink (*RHS* 75C). Sepal color: Lavender-pink, green base (*RHS* 73D; base, 138D). Anther color: Deep yellow, lavender-pink tips (*RHS* 12B; tips, 75C). Stamen color: Deep yellow. Flower shape: Cuplike then flat. Flower size: 8–11 in. (20–28 cm). Fragrance: Wonderfully sweet. Number of petals: 25–27. Number of sepals: 4.

LEAVES. Color: Top, olive green, many small purple blotches; underside, bronzy pink, many small red flecks and mottles. Leaf almost round, smooth, wavy edges; sinus usually closed or barely open. Leaf size: 9.5–10.5 in. (24–27 cm). Leaf spread: 5–6 ft. (1.5–1.8 m). Stem color: Brown. No pubescence on peduncle or petiole.

COMMENTS. *Nymphaea* 'General Pershing' has always been one of my favorite waterlilies. The orchid-pink color (from parent *N.* 'Castaliflora') and mottled leaves are especially lovely, and the blooms are pleasantly large (from parent *N.* 'Mrs. Edwards Whitaker') in relation to the medium-sized leaves. I recommend this waterlily for any size pool except the tub garden.

Nymphaea 'Golden Fascinator'

Randig 1946

Parentage unknown

PLATE 54

CHARACTERISTICS. Nonviviparous, very free flowering.

FLOWERS. Petal color: Yellow, orange-pink outer petals and tips (*RHS* 13B; outer petals and tips, 37A). Sepal color: Pinkish orange, reddish tips (*RHS* 13B flushed by 29A; tips, 37A). Anther color: Yellow, pink tips (*RHS* 13C; tips, 37A). Stamen color: Deep yellow. Flower shape: Cuplike at first and then stellate. Flower size: 6.5–9 in. (16–23 cm). Fragrance: Wonderful. Number of petals: 18–22. Number of sepals: 4.

LEAVES. Color: Top, green; underside, deep red, prominent green veins. Leaf a little longer than wide, a few jagged points and waves around edges; sinus mostly closed due to overlap of lobes. Leaf size: 11–12 in. (28–30 cm). Leaf spread: 6–7 ft. (1.8–2.1 m). Stem color: Peduncle mostly brown; petiole red. No pubescence on peduncle or petiole.

COMMENTS. This is a beautiful waterlily for medium or large pools. Blooms are striking and quite large in relation to the leaves.

Nymphaea 'Golden West'

Randig 1936

Seedling of *N.* 'St. Louis'

PLATE 55

CHARACTERISTICS. Nonviviparous, extremely free flowering.

FLOWERS. Petal color: Peach (*RHS* 38C). Sepal color: Peach, prominent greenish gray lengthwise veins (*RHS* 36C; veins, 193C). Anther color: Yellow-orange, peach tips (*RHS* 22B; tips, 38C). Stamen color: Deep, golden yellow. Flower shape: Cuplike at first and then flat. Flower size: 8–10 in. (20–25 cm). Fragrance: Very sweet. Number of petals: 21. Number of sepals: 4.

LEAVES. Color: Top, green, new leaves heavily mottled purple; underside, pink or greenish, heavily mottled red. Leaf a little longer than wide; sinus usually open, sometimes halfway open. Leaf size: 10–11 in. (25–28 cm). Leaf spread: 5–6 ft. (1.5–1.8 m). Stem color: Bright green. No pubescence on peduncle or petiole.

COMMENTS. A beautiful waterlily for medium and large pools.

Nymphaea 'Green Smoke'

Randig 1965

Parentage unknown

PLATE 56

CHARACTERISTICS. Nonviviparous, flowers quite freely.

FLOWERS. Petal color: Inner petals, greenish yellow, tipped blue; outer petals blue (RHS inner, 142D; tips and outer petals, 92B). Sepal color: Outer two-thirds light blue, greenish yellow base (RHS outer, 92C; base, 142D). Anther color: Golden yellow, greenish yellow tips (RHS 11A; tips, 142D). Stamen color: Yellow. Flower shape: Cuplike. Flower size: 5–6 in. (13–15 cm). Fragrance: Pleasant. Number of petals: 21 or 22. Number of sepals: 5.

LEAVES. Color: Top, greenish, faint purple blotches, new leaves bronzy, faintly blotched purple; underside, green, prominent violet mottling, new leaves pinkish, many violet flecks and mottles. Leaves egg-shaped, a little longer than wide, wavy edges, rounded teeth; sinus wide-open V; on new leaves lobes usually overlap. Leaf size: Up to 12 × 10.5 (30 × 27 cm). Leaf spread: 5–6 ft. (1.5–1.8 m). Stem color: Peduncle, mostly yellow-green; petiole green, base brown. No pubescence on peduncle or petiole.

COMMENTS. Nymphaea 'Green Smoke' has a most unusual color, making it very desirable for medium and large pools. Nurseries currently have a hard time keeping up with the demand for this waterlily.

Nymphaea 'Helen Nash'

Connelly 1996

Tropical white seedling × N. 'General Pershing'

PLATE 57

CHARACTERISTICS. Free flowering, nonviviparous.

FLOWERS. Petal color: Very deep raspberry pink with lavender overtones. Sepal color: Inner, slightly lighter color than petals; outer, light green with some bronze and purple flecks. Anther color: Inner, golden; outer, raspberry pink. Stamen color: Bright yellow. Flower shape: Stellate, then semi-flat. Flower size: 6–8 in. (15–20 cm). Fragrance: Delightful. Number of petals: 35. Number of sepals: 4.

LEAVES. Color: Top, olive green with dramatic purple mottling and a plum color border. Nearly round leaf with partly open sinus. Leaf size: 12–14 in. (30–35 cm). Leaf spread: 6–8 ft. (1.8–2.4 m). Stem color: Bright green. No pubescence on peduncle or petiole.

COMMENTS BY LEEANN CONNELLY. This waterlily is unusual because the pollen used to pollinate the seed parent came from a pollen bank that I developed. The International Waterlily and Water Gardening Society gave the 1998 Banksian Award to Nymphaea 'Helen Nash'.

Nymphaea 'Henry Shaw'

Pring 1917

Seedling of N. 'Castaliflora', itself a seedling of N. capensis var. zanzibariensis 'Rosea'

CHARACTERISTICS. Nonviviparous, free flowering.

FLOWERS. Petal color: Campanula blue (RHS 84C,D). Sepal color: Lighter blue than petals (RHS 84D). Anther color: Inner, lemon-chrome; outer, brownish purple; all tipped campanula blue (RHS inner, 12C; outer, 186D; tips, 84C,D). Stamen color: Deep yellow. Flower shape: Cuplike then flat. Flower size: 8–10 in. (20–25 cm). Fragrance: Very sweet. Number of petals: 28–30. Number of sepals: 4.

LEAVES. Color: Top, green, new leaves sparsely spotted light brown; underside, light green, suffused pink. Leaf oval, indented wavy margin; sinus one-third open. Leaf size: Up to 15 × 13.5 in. (38 × 34 cm). Leaf spread: 6–8 ft. (1.8–2.4 m). Stem color: Brown. No pubescence on peduncle or petiole.

COMMENTS. This plant honors the founder of the Missouri Botanical Garden, Henry Shaw. This very charming plant is worthy of a place in any medium or large pool.

Nymphaea 'Ineta Ruth'

Syn. 'Yellow Star'

Landon 1990

Nymphaea flavovirens × N. 'St. Louis Gold'

PLATE 58

CHARACTERISTICS. Nonviviparous, free flowering.

FLOWERS. Petal color: Yellow (*RHS* 8C). Sepal color: Yellowish green, greenish veins (*RHS* 1C; veins, 145C). Anther color: Dark yellow, lighter yellow tips (*RHS* 12A; tips, 8C). Stamen color: Deep yellow. Flower shape: Stellate. Flower size: 7–8 in. (18–20 cm). Fragrance: Delightful. Number of petals: 15–20. Number of sepals: 4.

LEAVES. Color: Top, green; underside, green, suffused purple or violet, prominent green veins. Leaf a little longer than wide; sinus usually open. Leaf size: 13 in. (33 cm), much smaller than most star lilies. Leaf spread: 4–8 ft. (1.2–2.4 m), average 6 ft. (1.8 m). Stem color: Pale olive green. No pubescence on peduncle or petiole.

COMMENTS. Kenneth Landon selected *Nymphaea* 'Ineta Ruth' as the very best of 85 seedlings. Blooms open early and stay open until late afternoon—an average of 14 hours per day. This was the first true yellow star waterlily to be hybridized. Flowers are produced in profusion. I highly recommend it for medium and large pools.

Nymphaea 'Innocence'

Florida Aquatic Nursery 2001
Unnamed hybrid × *N.* 'Trail Blazer'
PLATE 59

CHARACTERISTICS. Very free flowering, viviparous.

FLOWERS. Petal color: White. Sepal color: inner, white; outer, green to bronze with black specks. Anther color: Inner, yellow with white tips; outer, yellow with white tips. Stamen color: Yellow with white tips. Flower shape: Stellate. Flower size: 5–7 in. (12.5–17.8 cm). Fragrance: Sweetly scented. Number of petals: Up to 26. Number of sepals: 4.

LEAVES. Color: Top, green with large burgundy splashes; underside, olive green covered with red and purple blotches. Oval with round-toothed margins; sinus open. Leaf size: 11–12 in. (28–30 cm). Leaf spread: 5–7 ft. (1.5–2.1 m). Stem color: Bronze. No pubescence on peduncle or petiole.

COMMENTS BY FLORIDA AQUATIC NURSERY. The unusually large, pure white flower that stands high on a large stem with mottled foliage sets this plant apart from other white lilies. We recommend this plant for any medium to large pool.

Nymphaea 'Isabell Pring'

Pring 1941
Parentage unknown

CHARACTERISTICS. Viviparous, very free flowering.

FLOWERS. Petal color: Creamy white (*RHS* 155C). Sepal color: Creamy white (*RHS* 155C). Anther color: Yellow, creamy white tips (*RHS* 4B; tips, 155C). Stamen color: Yellow. Flower shape: Large star. Flower size: 7–10 in. (18–25 cm). Fragrance: Delightful. Number of petals: 23 or 24. Number of sepals: 4.

LEAVES. Color: Top, green, scattering of purple flecks; underside, green, flecked reddish brown. Leaves nearly round, quite dentate; lobes usually overlap considerably at sinus. Leaf size: 12–14 in. (30–35 cm). Leaf spread: 5–7 ft. (1.5–2.1 m). Stem color: Peduncle, bronzy green; petiole brownish. No pubescence on peduncle or petiole.

COMMENTS. A fine white tropical waterlily for medium and large pools. Being viviparous, it can withstand more cold and more shade than most other white day-blooming tropicals.

Nymphaea 'Islamorada'

Florida Aquatic Nursery 1998
Nymphaea 'Micrantha' × *N.* 'Calliantha'
PLATE 60

CHARACTERISTICS. Very free flowering, viviparous.

FLOWERS. Petal color: Purple with white spots throughout. Sepal color: Inner, violet blue; outer, green to bronze. Anther color: Inner, purple with a yellow base and violet blue tips; outer, purple with a yellow base and violet blue tips. Stamen color: Purple with a yellow base. Flower shape: Stellate. Flower size: 4–6 in. (10–15 cm). Fragrance: Sweetly scented. Number of petals: 23. Number of sepals: 4.

LEAVES. Color: Top, olive green; underside, red purple covered with dark purple specks. Oval leaf with toothed margins; sinus open; lobes long and pointed. Leaf size: 10 × 9 in. (25.5 × 23 cm). Leaf spread: 3–5 ft. (0.9–1.5 m). Stem color: Brown. No pubescence on peduncle or petiole.

COMMENTS BY FLORIDA AQUATIC NURSERY. Named after one of the Florida Keys, *Islamorada* means purple isle. This deep purple flower with white spots is unique, and no other waterlily, hardy or tropical, has duplicated it. It is very strongly viviparous and somewhat cold tolerant, which makes it a fine addition to any size pool.

Nymphaea 'Jack Wood'

Wood 1972
Parentage unknown
PLATE 61

CHARACTERISTICS. Nonviviparous, very free flowering.

FLOWERS. Petal color: Raspberry red (*RHS* 66C). Sepal color: Deep red (*RHS* 53C). Anther color: Brownish orange, raspberry-red tips (*RHS* 172C; tips, 66C). Stamen color: Bright yellow. Flower shape: Stellate, long sepals. Flower size: 8–10 in. (20–25 cm). Fragrance: Lovely. Number of petals: 25 or 26. Number of sepals: 4.

LEAVES. Color: Top, green, some purple blotches on new leaves; underside, reddish, dark purple blotches. Leaves nearly round, dentate edges; lobes overlap at sinus. Leaf size: 10–12 in. (25–30 cm). Leaf spread: 6–7 ft. (1.8–2.1 m). Stem color: Bronzy green. No pubescence on peduncle or petiole.

COMMENTS. This is one of the most striking waterlilies ever developed. I highly recommend *Nymphaea* 'Jack Wood' for medium and large pools. It can even be used in small pools if planted in a 10-in. (25-cm) pot to restrict growth. In most pools I recommend building a pedestal out of blocks or bricks so that there is 8–10 in. (20–25 cm) of water over the pot. Blooms will be produced freely if fertilizer tablets are added once a month.

Nymphaea 'Janice C. Wood'

Wood 1982
Parentage unknown
PLATE 62

CHARACTERISTICS. Nonviviparous, free flowering.

FLOWERS. Petal color: White (*RHS* 155D). Sepal color: White (*RHS* 155D). Anther color: Yellow, white tips (*RHS* 5C; tips, 155D). Stamen color: Yellow. Flower shape: Stellate. Flower size: 7–8 in. (18–20 cm). Fragrance: Very nice, sweet. Number of petals: 25 or 26. Number of sepals: 4.

LEAVES. Color: Top, very heavily blotched and mottled purple, smaller areas of green or yellow; underside, greenish, very heavily blotched purple. Leaf nearly round, slightly serrated; sinus usually closed yet about 1 in. (2.5 cm) may be open. Leaf size: 12 in. (30 cm). Leaf spread: 6 ft. (1.8 m). Stem color: Greenish bronze. No pubescence on peduncle or petiole.

COMMENTS. *Nymphaea* 'Janice C. Wood' has magnificent leaves—among the most beautiful of any day-blooming tropical. I recommend it for any medium or large pool.

Nymphaea 'Jo Ann'

Van Ness Water Gardens 1981
Parentage unknown
PLATE 63

CHARACTERISTICS. Nonviviparous, very free flowering.

FLOWERS. Petal color: Raspberry red (*RHS* 64D). Sepal color: Deeper red than petals (*RHS* 60B). Anther color: Orange, raspberry-red tips (*RHS* 26A; tips, 64D). Stamen color: Glowing yellow. Flower shape: Cuplike. Flower size: 7–8 in. (18–20 cm). Fragrance: Very pleasant. Number of petals: 32 or 33. Number of sepals: 4.

LEAVES. Color: Top, deep green; underside, pinkish red. Leaf large, nearly round; sinus usually open. Leaf size: 10–13 in. (25–33 cm). Leaf spread: 5–6 ft. (1.5–1.8 m). Stem color: Pink. A few hairs on petiole and on underwater portion of peduncle.

COMMENTS. A fine waterlily for medium and large pools. It will do well in semi-shaded pools.

Nymphaea 'Joseph Baynard Shearouse'

Connelly 1999
Nymphaea 'Blue Anemone' × *N.* 'Director Moore'
PLATE 64

CHARACTERISTICS. Very free flowering, nonviviparous.

FLOWERS. Petal color: Rich violet. Sepal color: Inner, lavender; outer, olive green with purple flecks and thin lavender border. Anther color: Inner, golden yellow; outer, golden yellow. Stamen color: Lighter lavender giving the flower a two-tone effect. Flower shape: Cuplike at first, then becoming stellate. Flower size: 6–8 in. (15–20 cm). Fragrance: Very sweet. Number of petals: 55. Number of sepals: 4.

LEAVES. Color: Top, green; underside, green mixed with purple. Nearly round leaf, usually with partly closed sinus. Leaf size: 10–12 in. (25.5–30 cm). Leaf spread: 6–7 ft. (1.8–2.1 m). Stem color: Bright green. No pubescence on peduncle or petiole.

COMMENTS BY LEEANN CONNELLY. This is an extraordinary flower. It is fully double and grows fairly compact. The lighter petaloids give a very pleasing two-tone effect. *Nymphaea* 'Joseph Baynard Shearouse' will do well in any size pool.

Nymphaea 'Josephine'

Florida Aquatic Nursery 1997
Nymphaea 'Paul Stetson' × unknown
PLATE 65

CHARACTERISTICS. Free flowering, viviparous.

FLOWERS. Petal color: White. Sepal color: Inner, white; outer, green with some bronze. Anther color: Inner, yellow; outer, yellow with white tips. Stamen color: Yellow with white tips. Flower shape: Cuplike. Flower size: 3–4 in. (7.5–10 cm). Fragrance: Sweetly scented. Number of petals: 26. Number of sepals: 4.

LEAVES. Color: Top, green; underside, green. Ovate, nearly round leaf; sinus open. Margins dentate, lobes curl upward slightly, tips sharply pointed. Leaf size: 8.5 × 8 in. (21.5 × 20 cm). Leaf spread: 2–3 ft. (0.6–0.9 m). Stem color: Light brown. No pubescence on peduncle or petiole.

COMMENTS BY FLORIDA AQUATIC NURSERY. Joe Tomocik at Denver Botanic Gardens was given the right to name this plant; Josephine is his greenhouse manager's mother's name. With the compact shape and size, this plant fits into any garden including a small tub garden.

Nymphaea 'Judge Hitchcock'

Pring 1941
Nymphaea stuhlmannii probably one parent
PLATE 66

CHARACTERISTICS. Nonviviparous, very free flowering.

FLOWERS. Petal color: Blue, nearly purple (*RHS* 91A). Sepal color: More purplish than petals, 12–14 prominent gray or greenish lengthwise veins (*RHS* 95A; veins, 190C). Anther color: Butterscotch, purplish blue tips (*RHS* 26C; tips, 91A). Stamen color:

Yellow. Flower shape: Cuplike, full. Flower size: 6–8 in. (15–20 cm). Fragrance: Very strongly scented. Number of petals: 24. Number of sepals: 4.

LEAVES. Color: Top, green, many purple blotches radiating from center; underside, pinkish, many purple mottles. Leaf nearly round, slightly longer than wide, slight indentation at apex opposite main vein; lobes overlap about halfway down sinus. Leaf size: 10 in. (25 cm). Leaf spread: 5 ft. (1.5 m). Stem color: Brown. No pubescence on peduncle or petiole.

COMMENTS. A medium-sized tropical that can be used in pools of any size, including small pools. In central Florida (zone 9a), this waterlily has performed well in half-shade.

Nymphaea 'Kathy McLane'

Florida Aquatic Nursery 2000
Parentage unknown
PLATE 67

CHARACTERISTICS. Free flowering, nonviviparous.

FLOWERS. Petal color: Rosy red. Sepal color: Inner, deep red; outer, yellow green, covered with burgundy dashes. Anther color: Inner, dark red with rosy red tips; outer, dark red with rosy red tips. Stamen color: Golden yellow. Flower shape: Open cup. Flower size: 5–7 in. (12.5–18 cm). Fragrance: Sweetly scented. Number of petals: 48. Number of sepals: 4.

LEAVES. Color: Top, green covered with splashes of burgundy; underside, light red with dark red blotches. Oval leaf, margins dentate; sinus closed, lobes overlapping. Leaf size: 12 × 11 in. (30 × 28 cm). Leaf spread: 5–7 ft. (1.5–2.1 m). Stem color: Brown. No pubescence on peduncle or petiole.

COMMENTS BY FLORIDA AQUATIC NURSERY. *Nymphaea* 'Kathy McLane' compliments any size water garden. The full flowers, supporting up to 48 petals each, stay open later than most tropical waterlilies.

Nymphaea 'Key Largo'

Florida Aquatic Nursery 2001
Nymphaea 'Panama Pacific' × unknown
PLATE 68

CHARACTERISTICS. Free flowering, viviparous.

FLOWERS. Petal color: Lavender. Sepal color: Inner, lavender; outer, green with black specks. Anther color: Inner, purple with lavender tips; outer, purple with lavender tips. Stamen color: Purple with a yellow base and lavender tips. Flower shape: Open cup. Flower size: 4–6 in. (10–15 cm). Fragrance: Sweetly scented. Number of petals: 26. Number of sepals: 4.

LEAVES. Color: Top, olive green, covered with thin burgundy streaks; underside, green, covered with raspberry spots. Nearly round leaf with serrated margins; sinus is usually open, lobes may overlap. Leaf size: 12 × 11 in. (30 × 28 cm). Leaf spread: 4–6 ft. (1.2–1.8 m). Stem color: Yellow green. No pubescence on peduncle or petiole.

COMMENTS BY FLORIDA AQUATIC NURSERY. *Nymphaea* 'Key Largo' is one of a few lavender lilies on the market today. Its compact growth habit and slight cold tolerance makes it a nice addition to any size pool.

Nymphaea 'Key Lime'

Florida Aquatic Nursery 1999
Nymphaea 'Crystal' × *N.* 'Trail Blazer'
PLATE 69

CHARACTERISTICS. Free flowering, nonviviparous.

FLOWERS. Petal color: Bright yellow. Sepal color: Inner, yellow; outer, green to bronze. Anther color: Inner, golden with yellow tips; outer, golden with yellow tips. Stamen color: Golden with yellow tips. Flower shape: Stellate. Flower size: 6–8 in. (15–20 cm). Fragrance: Sweet. Number of petals: 34. Number of sepals: 4.

LEAVES. Color: Top, rich green with wide burgundy splashes; underside, light green with red and purple blotches. Nearly round, margins mildly dentate; sinus is an open V. Leaf size: 14 × 13 in. (35 × 32.5 cm). Leaf spread: 6–8 ft (1.9–2.4 m). Stem color: Light green. No pubescence on peduncle or petiole.

COMMENTS BY FLORIDA AQUATIC NURSERY. This waterlily won first place in its category at the International Waterlily and Water Gardening Society 2000 Banksian Trials. The bright yellow flowers tower 12–14 in. (30–35 cm) above beautifully mottled pads. This plant is a good addition for any medium to large pool.

Nymphaea 'King of Blues'

Slocum 1955
Seedling of *N. capensis* var. *zanzibariensis*
PLATE 70

CHARACTERISTICS. Nonviviparous, very free flowering.

FLOWERS. Petal color: Very deep violet-blue (*RHS* 90D). Sepal color: Deep violet-blue (*RHS* 87C). Anther color: Butterscotch, deep violet-blue tips (*RHS* 26C; tips, 90D). Stamen color: Deep yellow. Flower shape: Stellate, full. Flower size: 7–9 in. (18–23 cm). Fragrance: Very delightful. Number of petals: 26–28. Number of sepals: 4.

LEAVES. Color: Top, yellowish green, some purple blotches; underside, purple, prominent green veins. Leaf egg-shaped, longer than wide, edges convoluted, dully serrated; sinus either open or fully closed. Leaf size: Up to 13 × 11 in. (33 × 28 cm). Leaf spread: 6–8 ft. (1.8–2.4 m). Stem color: Yellowish green. No pubescence on peduncle or petiole.

COMMENTS. I selected this magnificent seedling for propagation and feel it is truly one of the most beautiful blues for a medium or large pool. It readily produces seeds, and some seedlings may develop pink flowers as well as various shades of blue.

Nymphaea 'King of Siam'

Hybridizer unknown, introduced from Thailand in 2000 by Sakata and Sacher
PLATE 71

CHARACTERISTICS. Free flowering, nonviviparous.

FLOWERS. Petal color: Deep blue. Sepal color: Inner, blue; outer, green. Anther color: No anthers. Stamen color: No stamens. Flower shape: Flat, stellate. Flower size: 5–6 in. (12.5–15 cm). Fragrance: Pleasant. Number of petals: 80–100. Number of sepals: 6.

LEAVES. Color: Top, green; underside, violet. Oval; sinus is closed with overlapping lobes. Leaf size: 8–10 in. (20–25.5 cm). Leaf spread: 4–5 ft. (1.2–1.5 m). Stem color: Rosy brown. No pubescence on peduncle or petiole.

COMMENTS BY RICH SACHER. In the Deep South of the United States, some petals burn on older flowers during the heat of July and August. Growing the plant where it gets afternoon shade can minimize this. In the north, no petal burn occurs, even in 100°F (37°C) summer temperatures.

COMMENTS BY RICH SACHER. *Nymphaea* 'King of Siam' is the very first truly double tropical waterlily, giving an exciting new flower shape for tropical day bloomers. It is sterile and does not seed.

Nymphaea 'Laura Frase'

Frase 1960

Nymphaea 'Blue Beauty' × *N.* 'Panama Pacific'

CHARACTERISTICS. Nonviviparous, free flowering.

FLOWERS. Petal color: Medium dark blue (*RHS* 100C). Sepal color: Lighter blue than petals (*RHS* 97B). Anther color: Yellow, medium dark blue tips (*RHS* 8C; tips, 100C). Stamen color: Yellow. Flower shape: Somewhat cuplike. Flower size: 8–11 in. (20–28 cm). Fragrance: Delightful. Number of petals: 36. Number of sepals: 4.

LEAVES. Color: Top, green, blotched purple, new leaves bronzy; underside, red, purple blotches, prominent green veins. Leaf nearly round; sinus open on new leaves, overlapped by lobe on older leaves. Leaf size: 12–14 in. (30–35 cm). Leaf spread: 6–8 ft. (1.8–2.4 m). Stem color: Olive green. No pubescence on peduncle or petiole.

COMMENTS. *Nymphaea* 'Laura Frase' is a beautiful shade of forget-me-not blue that strongly impresses most viewers. Bill Frase named this cultivar after his wife. I recommend it for medium and large pools.

Nymphaea 'Leopardess'

Randig 1931

Parentage unknown

PLATE 72

CHARACTERISTICS. Nonviviparous, free flowering; noted for its remarkably beautiful leaves.

FLOWERS. Petal color: Clear blue, purple tips (*RHS* 97C; tips, 78B). Sepal color: Clear blue (*RHS* 97C). Anther color: Yellowish (*RHS* 8D). Stamen color: Yellow. Flower shape: Cuplike. Flower size: 4–5 in. (10–13 cm). Fragrance: Slight. Number of petals: 30. Number of sepals 4.

LEAVES. Color: Top, purple, green blotches; underside, green, heavily speckled purple. Leaf nearly round; lobes usually overlap at sinus. Leaf size: 10–

12 in. (25–30 cm). Leaf spread: 4–5 ft. (1.2–1.5 m). Stem color: Gray-brown. No pubescence on peduncle or petiole.

COMMENTS. With its magnificent purple mottled leaves and clear blue flowers, *Nymphaea* 'Leopardess' commands instant attention. I highly recommend it for any size pool.

Nymphaea 'Lone Star'

Landon 1997

Nymphaea ampla var. *plumieri* (largest variety of the species) × *N. capensis* var. *zanzibariensis*

PLATE 73

CHARACTERISTICS. Very free flowering, nonviviparous.

FLOWERS. Petal color: Satiny rich pastel purplish white fading to pale purple. Petals wide, 1–1.5 in. (2.5–3.8 cm). Sepal color: Inner, faintly purplish white; outer, dark yellow green with fine lines and small dots. Anther color: Inner, purple; outer, purple. Stamen color: Purple. Flower shape: Round with excellent symmetry from above, opens flat. Flower size: 9 in. (23 cm). Fragrance: Like vanilla. Number of petals: 20. Number of sepals: 4.

LEAVES. Color: Top, dark yellow-green; underside, suffused violet with prominent green veins. Round to slightly oval leaf; sinus slightly open (20 degrees). Leaf size: 15 × 15 in. (35 × 35 cm). Leaf spread: 6–8 ft. (1.8–2.1 m). Stem color: Maroon. Pubescence on peduncle and petiole.

COMMENTS BY KENNETH LANDON. *Nymphaea* 'Lone Star' is a striking waterlily. Foliage is very tight and compact. The bright yellow-green leaves are produced in excellent symmetry, offering a most attractive background for the stellate flowers. Infertile blossoms are produced in profusion with colors from dark, medium, to light pastel purple all on the same plant at the same time, offering a unique contrast. The parent *N. ampla* var. *plumieri* is the largest variety of the species.

Nymphaea 'Louella G. Uber'

Van Ness Water Gardens 1970

Parentage unknown

CHARACTERISTICS. Nonviviparous, very free flowering; blooms stay open later than most tropicals.

FLOWERS. Petal color: White (*RHS* 155D). Sepal color: White, prominent grayish green veins (*RHS* 155D; veins, 195C). Anther color: Yellow, white tips (*RHS* 13A; tips, 155D). Stamen color: Yellow. Flower shape: Stellate. Flower size: 8–10 in. (20–25 cm). Fragrance: Very pleasant. Number of petals: 16–18. Number of sepals: 4.

LEAVES. Color: Top, green; underside, pink, flecked maroon. Leaves nearly round, quite dentate; sinus either open or closed. Leaf size: 10–12 in. (25–30 cm). Leaf spread: 6 ft. (1.8 m). Stem color: Pink. No pubescence on peduncle or petiole.

COMMENTS. A fine waterlily for medium and large water gardens.

Nymphaea 'Mahogany Rose'

Sacher 2001

Parentage unknown

PLATE 74

CHARACTERISTICS. Free flowering, nonviviparous.

FLOWERS. Petal color: Light to medium pink. Sepal color: Inner, pink; outer, pink. Anther color: Inner, pink; outer, pink. Stamen color: Pink. Flower shape: Stellate. Flower size: 5–6 in. (12.5–15 cm). Fragrance: Pleasant. Number of petals: 38–40. Number of sepals: 4 full sepals plus 4 narrow sepals.

LEAVES. Color: Top, dark mahogany; underside, red with green flecks. Oval; sinus open. Leaf size: 10–12 in. (25.5–30 cm). Leaf spread: 4–5 ft. (1.2–1.5 m). Stem color: Green. No pubescence on peduncle or petiole.

COMMENTS BY RICH SACHER. This is the first day-blooming tropical with almost entirely dark maroon leaves, which make a great contrast with the light pink flowers. Flowers fertile and set seed easily.

Nymphaea 'Margaret Mary'

George L. Thomas Jr. 1964

Parentage unknown

CHARACTERISTICS. Moderately viviparous, extremely free flowering.

FLOWERS. Petal color: Deep, rich blue (*RHS* 94C). Sepal color: Lighter blue than petals (*RHS* 92C). Anther color: Deep, rich yellow (*RHS* 13B). Stamen color: Yellow. Flower shape: Cuplike then stellate. Flower size: 5–6.5 in. (13–16 cm). Fragrance: Delightful. Number of petals: 24. Number of sepals: 4.

LEAVES. Color: Top, green, new leaves lightly mottled purple; underside, purple, green veins. Leaf longer than wide; lobes usually overlap sinus halfway to completely, occasionally an open V. Leaf size: 10 × 9 in. (25 × 23 cm). Leaf spread: 4–5 ft. (1.2–1.5 m). Stem color: Brown to purplish brown. Tiny hairs on underwater portions of peduncle and petiole.

COMMENTS. The beautiful blue color is similar to that of *Nymphaea* 'Blue Beauty'. This is one of my favorites for a small pool or a tub garden. For many years, I have used this waterlily for a bathtub pool in a North Carolina display garden in a spot that receives shade for over half the day. Once it starts to bloom it is practically always with flower—frequently more than one at a time. This lily held U.S. plant patent 2453 given to George L. Thomas Jr.

Nymphaea 'Margaret Randig'

Randig 1939

Parentage unknown

CHARACTERISTICS. Nonviviparous, very free flowering.

FLOWERS. Petal color: Blue (*RHS* 91C). Sepal color: Blue (*RHS* 91C). Anther color: Inner, yellowish orange, tips blue; outer, deeper blue-purple (*RHS* 26C; tips, 91C; outer, 90D). Stamen color: Golden yellow. Flower shape: Very large, round, flat. Flower size: 8–11 in. (20–28 cm). Fragrance: Delightful. Number of petals: 22. Number of sepals: 4.

LEAVES. Color: Top, deep green; underside, purplish, darker in lobes, prominent green veins. Leaves nearly round, large round serrations; younger leaves may not show serrations; sinus varies, usually about two-thirds open. Leaf size: Up to 13 × 12 in. (33 × 30 cm). Leaf spread: 8–9 ft. (2.4–2.7 m). Stem color: Peduncle, reddish brown, green closest to flower; petiole, brown. No pubescence on peduncle or petiole.

COMMENTS. Flower color is the same, even shade throughout each flower. *Nymphaea* 'Margaret Randig' is a great waterlily for medium and large pools.

Nymphaea 'Marian Strawn'

Strawn 1969

Nymphaea 'Mrs. George H. Pring' × unknown

CHARACTERISTICS. Nonviviparous, very free flowering.

FLOWERS. Petal color: White (*RHS* 155D). Sepal color: White (*RHS* 155D). Anther color: Yellow, white tips (*RHS* 4C; tips, 155D). Stamen color: Yellow. Flower shape: Stellate, full. Flower size: 8–10 in. (20–25 cm). Fragrance: Lovely. Number of petals: 22. Number of sepals: 6.

LEAVES. Color: Top, green, many irregular purple blotches radiate from center; underside, light green, mottled reddish purple. Leaf longer than wide, convoluted, serrated, lightly dentate; lobes overlap at sinus. Leaf size: Up to 13 × 11 in. (33 × 28 cm). Leaf spread: 7–8 ft. (2.1–2.4 m). Stem color: Green or bronzy green. No pubescence on peduncle or petiole.

COMMENTS. A very fine tropical for medium and large pools.

Nymphaea 'Mark Pullen'

Winch 1987

Parentage unknown

CHARACTERISTICS. Nonviviparous, free flowering.

FLOWERS. Petal color: Rich violet-blue (*RHS* 91A). Sepal color: Pale bluish green (*RHS* 123C). Anther color: Inner, yellow, violet-blue tips; outer, violet-blue (*RHS* 13B; tips and outer, 91A). Stamen color: Yellow. Flower shape: Cuplike then stellate, full. Flower size: 7–8 in. (18–20 cm). Fragrance: Lightly scented. Number of petals: 37–44. Number of sepals: 4 or 5.

LEAVES. Color: Top, green; underside, purplish red, small red freckles, prominent green veins. Leaf nearly round, edges wavy; lobes overlap at sinus, one lobe usually raised slightly. Leaf size: Up to 12 × 11.5 in. (30 × 29 cm). Leaf spread: 5–6 ft. (1.5–1.8 m). Stem color: Peduncle brown, green above water; petiole mostly brown, greenish near leaf. No pubescence on peduncle or petiole.

COMMENTS. *Nymphaea* 'Mark Pullen' is an introduction from Charles Winch of Sydney, Australia, and was named after his grandson. The color is terrific, one of my favorite blues, and the flower is very double. I highly recommend this waterlily for medium and large pools.

Nymphaea 'Mary Mirgon'

Winch 1988

Nymphaea 'Cup Pink' × unknown

PLATE 75

CHARACTERISTICS. Nonviviparous, very free flowering.

FLOWERS. Petal color: Lavender-purple (*RHS* 70B,C). Sepal color: Slightly deeper lavender-purple than petals (*RHS* 70B). Anther color: Butterscotch, lavender-purple tips (*RHS* 167B; tips, 70B,C). Stamen color: Deep yellow. Flower shape: Cuplike, full. Flower size: 6–8 in. (15–20 cm). Fragrance: Sweet, reminiscent of raspberries. Number of petals: 32. Number of sepals: 4.

LEAVES. Color: Top, medium green, slightly mottled near sinus; underside, blushed red. Leaves heart-shaped, undulating edges; lobes open at sinus. Leaf size: Up to 10 in. (25 cm). Leaf spread: 3–4 ft. (0.9–1.2 m). Stem color: Deep green. No pubescence on peduncle or petiole.

COMMENTS. *Nymphaea* 'Mary Mirgon', a beautifully colored tropical, is a magnificent introduction from Australia. It will do well in any size pool. It is named in honor of the wife of John Mirgon, founder and first president of the Colorado Water Lily Society, the first such society in the United States.

Nymphaea 'Miami Rose'

Florida Aquatic Nursery 1999

Nymphaea 'Ruby' × N. 'Renegade'

PLATE 76

CHARACTERISTICS. Free flowering, nonviviparous.

FLOWERS. Petal color: Raspberry red. Sepal color: Inner, light red purple; outer, green to bronze. Anther color: Inner, raspberry red; outer, raspberry red. Stamen color: Golden yellow. Flower shape: Stellate. Flower size: 4–6 in. (10–15 cm). Fragrance: Sweetly scented. Number of petals: more than 50. Number of sepals: 4.

LEAVES. Color: Top, rich green heavily splashed with burgundy; underside, light green covered with burgundy and purple blotches. Oval leaf, margins are serrated and undulating; sinus is an open V. Leaf size: 12–11 in. (30–28 cm). Leaf spread: 4–5 ft. (1.2–1.5 m). Stem color: Yellow green. No pubescence on peduncle or petiole.

COMMENTS BY FLORIDA AQUATIC NURSERY. The heavily petaled flowers are a full star, which is somewhat unique and eye catching. This plant is a good addition to any size pool.

Nymphaea 'Midnight'
Pring 1941
Nymphaea colorata × N. capensis var. *zanzibariensis*
PLATE 77

CHARACTERISTICS. Nonviviparous, very free flowering. Anthers develop as small petals.

FLOWERS. Petal color: Deep violet-blue (*RHS* 94B). Sepal color: Deep violet-blue (*RHS* 94B). Anther color (not true anthers): Deep violet-blue (*RHS* 94B). Stamen color: Yellow. Flower shape: Stellate, full. Flower size: 6–8 in. (15–20 cm). Fragrance: Slight. Number of petals: 95–123. Number of sepals: 4.

LEAVES. Color: Top, bright green; underside, violet. Nearly round, quite dentate; lobes overlap at sinus. Leaf size: 9–10 in. (23–25 cm). Leaf spread: 4–6 ft. (1.2–1.8 m). Stem color: Bronzy to purple. A few hairs on underwater portions of peduncle and on petiole.

COMMENTS. *Nymphaea* 'Midnight' is unique among tropical cultivars in that the stamen tops have become small petals. These displace the anthers and create a delicate fringe in the center of the blooms. This is a good choice for any size pool.

Nymphaea 'Midnight Embers'
Presnell 2003
Unnamed seedling × *N.* 'Ampla'
PLATE 78

CHARACTERISTICS. Free flowering, nonviviparous.

FLOWERS. Petal color: Long outer, blue; short inner, yellow with pink margins. Sepal color: Inner, light blue; outer, light green heavily speckled with black. Flower shape: Stellate, then flat. Flower size: 10 in. (25.5 cm). Fragrance: Slight. Number of petals: Long outer petals, 42; short inner petals, 140. Number of sepals: 4.

LEAVES. Color: Top, green with maroon speckling; underside, light purple blotches on green with prominent green veins. Oval with serrate margins, sinus is usually closed with lobes overlapping. Leaf size: 23 × 19 in. (58–48 cm). Leaf spread: About 10 ft. (3 m). Stem color: Brown. Pubescence on underwater portion of peduncle and petiole.

COMMENTS BY J. CRAIG PRESNELL. An abundance of small inner petals form a thick, plush cushion around the flower's center. This waterlily is one of the earliest to open and is best displayed in a large pond.

Nymphaea 'Midnight Serenade'
Presnell 2000
Parentage unknown
PLATE 79

CHARACTERISTICS. Free flowering, nonviviparous.

FLOWERS. Petal color: Purple. Sepal color: Inner, purple; outer, bright green with black streaks. Flower shape: Stellate, then flat. Flower size: 6–8 in. (15–20 cm). Fragrance: Slight. Number of petals: 145–155. Number of sepals: 4.

LEAVES. Color: Top, green with maroon mottling; underside, green with pink and purple blotches. Round with wavy margins; lobes usually overlap at sinus. Leaf size: 11 × 11 in. (28 × 28 cm). Leaf spread: 6 ft. (1.8 m). Stem color: Green. No pubescence on peduncle or petiole.

COMMENTS BY J. CRAIG PRESNELL. *Nymphaea* 'Midnight Serenade' was the winner of the Banksian Award given by the International Waterlily and Water Gardening Society in 2002 for best medium/large tropical waterlily. This waterlily is recommended for a medium or large pond.

Nymphaea 'Moon Shadow'
Florida Aquatic Nursery 1999
Nymphaea 'Trail Blazer' × unknown
PLATE 80

CHARACTERISTICS. Free flowering, nonviviparous.

FLOWERS. Petal color: Yellow, green and blue. Sepal color: Inner, yellow; outer, green. Anther color: Inner, yellow with blue tips. Flower shape: Stellate. Flower size: 6–8 in. (15–20 cm). Fragrance:

Sweetly scented. Number of petals: 22. Number of sepals: 4.

LEAVES. Color: Top, light green; underside, olive green. Oval leaf, margins dentate and undulating; sinus closed at apex, lobes overlap. Leaf size: 15 × 14 in. (37.5 × 35 cm). Leaf spread: 6–8 ft. (1.8–2.4 m). Stem color: Yellow green. No pubescence on peduncle or petiole.

COMMENTS BY FLORIDA AQUATIC NURSERY. The unique flower color of this plant inspired the name 'Moon Shadow'. Its smoky blue color is rare in tropical lilies, until now seen only in *Nymphaea* 'Green Smoke' and *N.* 'Anna Emmet'. Its free flowering characteristics and large flower size makes it a good choice for any medium to large pool.

Nymphaea 'Mr. Martin E. Randig'
Randig 1967
Parentage unknown
PLATE 81

CHARACTERISTICS. Nonviviparous, free flowering.

FLOWERS. Petal color: Deep pink (*RHS* 68B). Sepal color: Slightly deeper pink than petals (*RHS* 70B). Anther color: Yellowish orange, deep pink tips (*RHS* 23B; tips, 68B). Stamen color: Deep yellow. Flower shape: Cuplike then almost flat. Flower size: 6–8 in. (15–20 cm). Fragrance: Pleasant. Number of petals: 20 or 21. Number of sepals: 4.

LEAVES. Color: Top, olive green, heavily mottled deep purple; underside, red, heavily mottled deep red-purple. Nearly round, rounded projections at perimeter; lobes usually overlap completely at sinus. Leaf size: Up to 12 × 10.5 in. (30 × 27 cm). Leaf spread: 5–6 ft. (1.5–1.8 m). Stem color: Bronzy green. No pubescence on peduncle or petiole.

COMMENTS. Wonderful flower color and marvelous leaves with particularly beautiful markings make this a fine choice for medium and large pools.

Nymphaea 'Mrs. Charles Winch'
Winch 1986
Parentage unknown

CHARACTERISTICS. Nonviviparous, free flowering.

FLOWERS. Petal color: Bright yellow (*RHS* 4A). Sepal color: Greenish yellow (*RHS* 1B). Anther color: Greenish yellow (*RHS* 1B). Stamen color: Yellow. Flower shape: Stellate. Flower size: 6 in. (15 cm). Fragrance: Very pleasant. Number of petals: 16. Number of sepals: 6.

LEAVES. Color: Top, green, variegated blue and red; underside, green, mottled blue. Oval leaf; sinus closed. Leaf size: 6–8 in. (15–20 cm). Leaf spread: 6 ft. (1.8 m). Stem color: Bronze. No pubescence on peduncle or petiole.

COMMENTS. *Nymphaea* 'Mrs. Charles Winch' needs heat to get established. It should not be placed outdoors until temperatures reach 75°F (24°C). Like most yellow tropicals, it opens late and closes late. I recommend it for medium or large pools.

Nymphaea 'Mrs. Edwards Whitaker'
Pring 1917
Nymphaea ovalifolia × *N.* 'Castaliflora'
PLATE 82

CHARACTERISTICS. Nonviviparous, extremely free flowering.

FLOWERS. Petal color: Light blue (*RHS* 92D). Sepal color: Light blue, green tips (*RHS* 92D; tips, 143D). Anther color: Yellow, light blue tips (*RHS* 13B; tips, 92D). Stamen color: Deep yellow. Flower shape: Stellate, large. Flower size: 9–12 in. (23–30 cm). Fragrance: Pronounced. Number of petals: 21. Number of sepals: 4.

LEAVES. Color: Top, green, some small purple mottles; underside, green, purple blotches. Leaf a little longer than wide; lobes usually overlap at sinus. Leaf size: Up to 13 × 12 in. (33 × 30 cm). Leaf spread: 6–7 ft. (1.8–2.1 m). Stem color: Green. No pubescence on peduncle or petiole.

COMMENTS. One of the older tropical waterlilies and still one of the best for medium and large pools. The huge flowers are very impressive.

Nymphaea 'Mrs. George H. Pring'
Pring 1922
Nymphaea ovalifolia × *N.* 'Mrs. Edwards Whitaker'
PLATE 83

CHARACTERISTICS. Nonviviparous, very free flowering.

FLOWERS. Petal color: Creamy white, greenish gray stripes in outer petals (*RHS* 155B; stripes, 190C). Sepal color: Creamy white, greenish gray stripes (*RHS* 155B; stripes, 190C). Anther color: Yellow, creamy white tips (*RHS* 7A; tips, 155B). Stamen color: Deep golden yellow. Flower shape: Stellate. Flower size: 7–8 in. (18–20 cm). Fragrance: Pleasant, delicate. Number of petals: 21. Number of sepals: 4.

LEAVES. Color: Top, green, new leaves blotched purple; underside, green, purple blotches on old leaves fade somewhat. Leaf egg-shaped, longer than wide, smooth edges; extra-long lobes sometimes overlap completely at sinus, sometimes leave sinus partly open. Leaf size: Up to 16.5 × 13 in. (42 × 33 cm). Leaf spread: 6–9 ft. (1.8–2.7 m). Stem color: Peduncle, above water bright green, below water bronzy green; petiole, bronzy green. No pubescence on peduncle or petiole. Fuzzy algae frequently accumulate on stems and can easily be mistaken for pubescence.

COMMENTS. This waterlily is the "old reliable" of white day-blooming tropicals. It is still hard to beat for all-around performance. Often an established plant will have five or six blooms at a time. I recommend it for medium or large pools.

Nymphaea 'Mrs. Martin E. Randig'

Randig 1938

Includes *N.* 'Panama Pacific', *N.* 'Daubeniana', *N.* 'Lilac Queen', *N.* 'Royal Zanzibar', *N.* 'Indigo Zanzibar', and *N.* 'Amethyst'

PLATE 84

CHARACTERISTICS. Viviparous, very free flowering.

FLOWERS. Petal color: Deep violet-blue (*RHS* 91A). Sepal color: Purple (*RHS* 75A). Anther color: Deep yellow (*RHS* 13B). Stamen color: Yellow. Flower shape: Somewhat cuplike. Flower size: 4.5–6 in. (11–15 cm). Fragrance: Very lovely. Number of petals: 23 or 24. Number of sepals: 4.

LEAVES. Color: Top, green; underside, deep red, prominent bright green veins on new pads. Leaf nearly round; sinus usually an open V. Leaf size: 10 × 8 in. (25 × 20 cm). Leaf spread: 3–5 ft. (0.9–1.5 m). Stem color: Brown. Fine fuzz and hair on underwater portions of peduncle or petiole.

COMMENTS. The second U.S. plant patent ever issued for a waterlily was given to Martin E. Randig in 1938 for this cultivar. This is one of his finest

waterlilies. Like other viviparous varieties, it will withstand more cold weather than most blue tropicals. I recommend it for any size pool, including tub gardens.

Nymphaea 'Noelene'

Winch 1972

Parentage unknown

CHARACTERISTICS. Nonviviparous, free flowering.

FLOWERS. Petal color: Lavender-pink (*RHS* 75B,C). Sepal color: Lavender-pink (*RHS* 75B). Anther color: Deep yellow (*RHS* 13B). Stamen color: Yellow. Flower shape: Stellate. Flower size: 6–9 in. (15–23 cm). Fragrance: Very sweet. Number of petals: 16. Number of sepals: 4.

LEAVES. Color: Top, bright green, maroon mottles; underside, yellow-green, maroon mottles. Leaf nearly round, convoluted along perimeter; lobes overlap at sinus. Leaf size: 8–10 in. (20–25 cm). Leaf spread: 5–7 ft. (1.5–2.1 m). Stem color: Bright green. No pubescence on peduncle or petiole.

COMMENTS. *Nymphaea* 'Noelene' is an Australian introduction in the rare color class of lavender (others include *N.* 'Christine Lingg', *N.* 'Helen Nash', and *N.* 'Key Largo'). It is a very worthwhile waterlily. I recommend it for medium and large pools. Like all tropicals in northern areas, it should not be planted outside until all danger of cold is past.

Nymphaea 'Pamela'

Koch 1931

Parentage unknown

PLATE 85

CHARACTERISTICS. Nonviviparous, very free flowering.

FLOWERS. Petal color: Rich sky blue (*RHS* 97B). Sepal color: Rich sky blue (*RHS* 97B). Anther color: Yellow (*RHS* 12B). Stamen color: Outer, blue, base yellow; inner, yellow. Flower shape: Stellate, round, flat. Flower size: 8–13 in. (20–33 cm). Fragrance: Very sweet. Number of petals: 21–27. Number of sepals: 4.

LEAVES. Color: Top, green, new leaves heavily blotched purple; underside, reddish, new leaves green, display many red blotches, prominent green veins on older leaves. Leaf longer than wide; both lobes frequently rise up 1 in. (2.5 cm) at junction or overlap. Leaf size: Up to 15 × 13.5 in. (38 × 34 cm). Leaf spread: 5–8 ft. (1.5–2.4 m). Stem color: Mostly brown; peduncle green above water. Fine fuzz and hairs on older petioles and peduncles below water; none on peduncles above water.

COMMENTS. *Nymphaea* 'Pamela' is one of my favorite blues. The color of the flower is terrific, the leaves are magnificent, and the plant is a profuse bloomer. This waterlily is ideal for medium or large pools.

Nymphaea 'Panama Pacific'
Tricker 1914
Parentage unknown
PLATE 86
CHARACTERISTICS. Viviparous, very free flowering.

FLOWERS. Petal color: Deep violet-purple (*RHS* 82C). Sepal color: Purple (*RHS* 87D). Anther color: Yellow, violet tips (*RHS* 11A; tips, 77C). Stamen color: Yellow. Flower shape: Cuplike then stellate. Flower size: 4.5–6 in. (11–15 cm). Fragrance: Very sweet. Number of petals: 21 or 22. Number of sepals: 4.

LEAVES. Color: Top, green; underside, purple, new leaves green then red, all heavily mottled purple. Leaves nearly round; sinus an open V or lobes may overlap up to halfway down sinus. Leaf size: 9–11 in. (23–28 cm). Leaf spread: 4–6 ft. (1.2–1.8 m). Stem color: Brown. Fine fuzz and tiny hairs on peduncle and petiole.

COMMENTS. One of the viviparous varieties and among the hardiest of the tropicals. Produces young plants freely in the middle of its pads. I recommend it for any size pool, including a tub garden.

Nymphaea 'Patricia'
Tricker pre-1940
Nymphaea colorata × unknown
CHARACTERISTICS. Viviparous, free flowering, small leaf spread.

FLOWERS. Petal color: Pinkish red (*RHS* 70C). Sepal color: Slightly darker than petals (*RHS* 70B, C). Anther color: Yellowish orange, pinkish red tips (*RHS* 26B; tips, 70C). Stamen color: Yellow. Flower shape: Cuplike then stellate. Flower size: 3–5 in. (8–

13 cm). Fragrance: Faint yet noticeably sweet. Number of petals: 19 or 20. Number of sepals: 4.

LEAVES. Color: Top, yellowish green; underside, red, many purplish red specks and blotches, prominent green veins. Leaf a little longer than wide, moderately dentate, many small convolutions; sinus usually an open V. Leaf size: 9–10 in. (23–25 cm). Leaf spread: 3–5 ft. (0.9–1.5 m). Stem color: Reddish brown. Tiny hairs scattered on petiole and underwater portion of peduncle.

COMMENTS. More viviparous than most viviparous lilies as every leaf develops a plantlet. An excellent waterlily for the tub garden or small pool. Performs well in medium and large pools, too.

Nymphaea 'Paul Stetson'
Wood 1984
Parentage unknown
PLATE 87
CHARACTERISTICS. Viviparous, very free flowering.

FLOWERS. Petal color: Sky blue (*RHS* 92D,C). Sepal color: Light blue, darker blue veins (*RHS* 92D; veins, 92C). Anther color: Yellowish orange (*RHS* 26C). Stamen color: Yellow. Flower shape: Stellate. Flower size: 4–6 in. (10–15 cm). Fragrance: Lovely. Number of petals: 18. Number of sepals: 4.

LEAVES. Color: Top, bright green, spotted maroon; underside, yellowish green, maroon mottles. Leaf nearly round, lobe tips pointed; lobes overlap at sinus. Leaf size: 6–9 in. (15–23 cm). Leaf spread: 3–4 ft. (0.9–1.2 m). Stem color: Brownish red. No pubescence on peduncle or petiole.

COMMENTS. A wonderful cultivar for the tub garden or small or medium pool. It can be kept small by planting it in an 8- to 10-in. (20- to 25-cm) pot or plastic dishpan. This waterlily frequently produces two or more blooms at a time.

Nymphaea 'Peach Blow'
Pring 1941
Parentage unknown
CHARACTERISTICS. Viviparous, very free flowering.

FLOWERS. Petal color: Inner petals, light pink; outer petals medium pink (*RHS* inner, 65C; outer, 65A). Sepal color: Greenish yellow (*RHS* 150D).

Anther color: Yellow, light pink tips (*RHS* 4C; tips, 65C). Stamen color: Yellow. Flower shape: Full, peony-style. Flower size: 8–10 in. (20–25 cm). Fragrance: Lovely. Number of petals: 34–36. Number of sepals: 4 or 5.

LEAVES. Color: Top, light green, new leaves sparsely flecked purple; underside, light green, flushed red. Leaves nearly round, somewhat dentate; lobes overlap at sinus. Leaf size: Up to 12 in. (30 cm). Leaf spread: 7–8 ft. (2.1–2.4 m). Stem color: Green. No pubescence on peduncle or petiole.

COMMENTS. A two-toned pink waterlily displaying a large yellow center when the flower opens after the first day. The lovely pink-and-yellow combination makes one think of the peace rose or the *Nelumbo* 'Mrs. Perry D. Slocum' lotus. I highly recommend it for medium and large pools.

Nymphaea 'Perry's Blue Heaven'

Slocum 1994
Nymphaea caerulea × *N.* 'Evelyn Randig'
PLATE 88

CHARACTERISTICS. Free flowering, nonviviparous.

FLOWERS. Petal color: Medium blue, becoming paler with age. Sepal color: Inner, medium to light blue; outer, bright green and covered with purple short vertical lines and speckles. Anther color: Inner, medium yellow; outer, yellow to bluish. Stamen color: Bright medium yellow. Flower shape: Cuplike at first, opening out flat by second day. Flower size: 8–10 in. (20–25 cm). Fragrance: Pronounced and delightful. Number of petals: 16 or 17. Number of sepals: 4.

LEAVES. Color: Top, all new leaves are green, heavily blotched with purple, becoming all green after a few weeks; underside, pinkish, heavily blotched with purple. Leaf nearly round; sinus sometimes wide open, often partly closed. Leaf size: 10 in. (25.5 cm). Leaf spread: 5–6 ft. (1.5–1.8 m). Stem color: Green. Pubescence on petiole but not peduncle.

COMMENTS. The bloom of *Nymphaea* 'Perry's Blue Heaven' is very similar to *N.* 'Blue Beauty', being about one shade lighter. However, due to its mottled leaves, 'Perry's Blue Heaven' is very distinctive from 'Blue Beauty'. I recommend it for medium and large pools.

Nymphaea 'Persian Lilac'

Pring 1941
Parentage unknown

CHARACTERISTICS. Nonviviparous, very free flowering.

FLOWERS. Petal color: Pinkish lilac (*RHS* 69A, B). Sepal color: Paler than petals (*RHS* 69C,D). Anther color: Butterscotch, pinkish lilac tips (*RHS* 164B; tips, 75B). Stamen color: Deep yellow. Flower shape: Very full, peony-style. Flower size: 8–10 in. (20–25 cm). Fragrance: Delightful. Number of petals: 41 or 42. Number of sepals: 4.

LEAVES. Color: Top, light green, new leaves sparsely flecked brownish red; underside, red. Leaf a little longer than wide, dentate; sinus usually closed, lobes overlapping. Leaf size: Up to 10 in. (25 cm). Leaf spread: 5–6 ft. (1.5–1.8 m). Stem color: Bronzy green. No pubescence on peduncle or petiole.

COMMENTS. The flower is very full and the color is wonderful. I recommend *Nymphaea* 'Persian Lilac' for any size pool.

Nymphaea 'Pink Champagne'

Florida Aquatic Nursery 1997
Parentage unknown
PLATE 89

CHARACTERISTICS. Very free flowering, nonviviparous.

FLOWERS. Petal color: Pink. Sepal color: Inner, pink; outer, green to bronze with dark specks. Anther color: Inner, dark pink; outer, dark pink. Stamen color: Dark pink with golden yellow base and lighter pink tips. Flower shape: Cuplike. Flower size: 4–6 in. (10–15 cm). Fragrance: Sweet. Number of petals: 28. Number of sepals: 4.

LEAVES. Color: Top, new leaves bronze with splashes of green and burgundy; older leaves more green with burgundy splashes; underside, light green with reddish blotches. Ovate leaf, margins dentate, sinus closed, undulating lobes overlapping or curling upward. Leaf size: 13.5 × 12 in. (34 × 30 cm). Leaf spread: 4–6 ft. (1.2–1.8 m). Stem color: Yellow green. No pubescence on peduncle or petiole.

COMMENTS BY FLORIDA AQUATIC NURSERY. *Nymphaea* 'Pink Champagne' has been an outstanding performer at the Denver Botanic Gardens trials for years. It is a vigorous plant and an above-average bloomer. Having uniquely colored solid pink flowers, it is one of Joe Tomocik's favorite tropicals. This plant is a good addition to any medium or large pool.

Nymphaea 'Pink Passion'

Florida Aquatic Nursery 1998
Parentage unknown
PLATE 90

CHARACTERISTICS. Very free flowering, nonviviparous.

FLOWERS. Petal color: Solid pink. Sepal color: Inner, solid pink; outer, green. Anther color: Dark pink with golden yellow base and pink tips. Flower shape: Open cup. Flower size: 6–8 in. (15–20 cm). Fragrance: Sweetly scented. Number of petals: More than 50. Number of sepals: 4.

LEAVES. Color: Top, green; underside, reddish pink. Oval leaf with dentate margins; sinus partially closed, lobes may push each other upward. Leaf size: 14 × 12 in. (35 × 30 cm). Leaf spread: 5–7 ft. (1.5–2.1 m). Stem color: Green. No pubescence on peduncle or petiole.

COMMENTS BY FLORIDA AQUATIC NURSERY. The large, solid pink, double flowers with more than 50 petals are quite striking. Its vigorous habit and slight cold tolerances make this plant a good addition to any medium to large pool.

Nymphaea 'Pink Pearl'

Koch, year unknown
Nymphaea 'Mrs. George H. Pring' × unknown
PLATE 91

CHARACTERISTICS. Nonviviparous, very free flowering; blooms held up to 12 in. (30 cm) above water.

FLOWERS. Petal color: Pinkish lavender (RHS 75B,C). Sepal color: Pale lavender with grayish green veins (RHS 73D; veins, 193B). Anther color: Butterscotch, pinkish lavender tips (RHS 163A; tips, 75B,C). Stamen color: Deep yellow-orange. Flower shape: Cuplike. Flower size: 7–8 in. (18–20 cm). Fragrance: Very pleasant. Number of petals: 40–42. Number of sepals: 4.

LEAVES. Color: Top, deep green; underside, reddish brown. Leaf nearly round, undulating perime-

ter; sinus either open or partly open. Leaf size: Up to 10 in. (25 cm). Leaf spread: 4–5 ft. (1.2–1.5 m). Stem color: Deep green. No pubescence on peduncle or petiole.

COMMENTS. Flowers are quite double and the color is excellent. Nymphaea 'Pink Pearl' is a fine waterlily for any size pool.

Nymphaea 'Pink Perfection'

Lingg 1951
Parentage unknown

CHARACTERISTICS. Nonviviparous, very free flowering.

FLOWERS. Petal color: Lavender-pink (RHS 75B). Sepal color: Pale lavender-pink (RHS 75D). Anther color: Yellow, lavender-pink tips (RHS 11A; tips, 75B). Stamen color: Yellow. Flower shape: Stellate, long, pointed sepals. Flower size: 8–10 in. (20–25 cm). Fragrance: Very sweet. Number of petals: 24–26. Number of sepals: 4.

LEAVES. Color: Top, heavily variegated reddish purple and green; underside, green, purple blotches. Nearly round, somewhat dentate; sinus usually open, sometimes closed. Leaf size: 10–12 in. (25–30 cm). Leaf spread: 5–7 ft. (1.5–2.1 m). Stem color: Greenish. No pubescence on peduncle or petiole.

COMMENTS. Its magnificent leaves and gorgeous lavender-pink blooms with prominent yellow centers make Nymphaea 'Pink Perfection' a beautiful addition to any medium or large pool.

Nymphaea 'Pink Platter'

Pring 1941
Parentage unknown
PLATE 92

CHARACTERISTICS. Slightly to moderately viviparous, very free flowering.

FLOWERS. Petal color: Medium pink (RHS 37C,D). Sepal color: Deeper pink than petals (RHS 37C). Anther color: Inner, yellow, pink tips; outer, orange-pink (RHS inner, 12B; tips, 37C,D; outer, 31C). Stamen color: Deep yellow. Flower shape: Large, round, flat. Flower size: 7–10 in. (18–25 cm). Fragrance: Some. Number of petals: 26–30. Number of sepals: 4.

LEAVES. Color: Top, olive green, lightly mottled purple (mottles more prominent on new leaves);

underside, green, perimeter pink, new leaves pinkish, prominent green veins. Nearly round, wavy, somewhat serrated; sinus usually an open V on young plants, lobes overlap on older plants. Leaf size: 9–10 in. (23–25 cm). Leaf spread: 5–6 ft. (1.5–1.8 m). Stem color: Peduncle green above water, mostly brown below water; petiole brown, green near leaf. No pubescence on peduncle or petiole.

COMMENTS. *Nymphaea* 'Pink Platter' is moderately viviparous when conditions are right (70–85°F [21–30°C] with good rich soil). On one plant I once found four leaves with small plantlets starting. Like other viviparous lilies, this plant will take more cold than most day-blooming varieties, especially in spring. It is an excellent choice for medium and large pools.

Nymphaea 'Pink Star'

Syn. 'Stella Gurney'
Gurney 1900–1905(?)
Chance seedling of N. 'Mrs. C. W. Ward'

CHARACTERISTICS. Nonviviparous, very free flowering.

FLOWERS. Petal color: Pink (*RHS* 73C). Sepal color: Slightly deeper pink than petals (*RHS* 73B). Anther color: Yellowish brown, pink tips (*RHS* 167B; tips, 73C). Stamen color: Orange-yellow. Flower shape: Stellate. Flower size: 7–8 in. (18–20 cm). Fragrance: Pleasant. Number of petals: 17 or 18. Number of sepals: 4.

LEAVES. Color: Top, green; underside, green, usually flushed pinkish. Leaf longer than wide, dentate; sinus usually open. Leaf size: 17 × 15.5 in. (43 × 39 cm). Leaf spread: Up to 10–12 ft. (3–3.6 m). Stem color: Green. No pubescence on peduncle or petiole.

COMMENTS. Like other star lilies, *Nymphaea* 'Pink Star' withstands more cold than many of the other tropicals. Prolific leaf production. It is an excellent plant, but only for the large water garden.

Nymphaea 'Red Beauty'

Slocum 1966
Seedling of N. *capensis* var. *zanzibariensis*
PLATE 93

CHARACTERISTICS. Nonviviparous, free flowering.

FLOWERS. Petal color: Deep pinkish red (*RHS*

77B). Sepal color: Dark red-purple (*RHS* 70A). Anther color: Inner, yellow, red-purple tips; outer, red-purple (*RHS* inner, 13C, tips, 77B; outer, 64B,C). Stamen color: Yellow. Flower shape: Cuplike. Flower size: 5–6 in. (13–15 cm). Fragrance: Delightful. Number of petals: 34. Number of sepals: 4.

LEAVES. Color: Top, green, few faint purple blotches; new leaves on young plants bronzy, purple mottles. Underside color varies widely; some mostly green, some red or pinkish at perimeter with green center and prominent green veins. Leaf longer than wide, convoluted, serrated; sinus variable, either an open V or partially closed. Leaf size: 12.5–14 in. (32–35 cm). Leaf spread: 5–6 ft. (1.5–1.8 m). Stem color: Top several inches green, lower portions light brown. No pubescence on peduncle or petiole.

COMMENTS. *Nymphaea* 'Red Beauty' has excellent color and is a good choice for medium or large pools. It does have a rather small flower relative to its large leaves, however.

Nymphaea 'Red Star'

Syn. 'Mrs. C. W. Ward'
Tricker 1899(?)
Nymphaea flavovirens × unknown

CHARACTERISTICS. Nonviviparous, very free flowering; blooms held 12 in. (30 cm) above water.

FLOWERS. Petal color: Reddish pink (*RHS* 64D). Sepal color: Slightly deeper reddish pink than petals (*RHS* 64B). Anther color: Orange, reddish pink tips (*RHS* 31B; tips, 64D). Stamen color: Yellow. Flower shape: Stellate. Flower size: 6–8 in. (15–20 cm). Fragrance: Sweet and lovely. Number of petals: 15 or 16. Number of sepals: 4.

LEAVES. Color: Top, green; underside, red, maroon spots. Leaves large, egg-shaped, somewhat convoluted; sinus generally open. Leaf size: 12–15 in. (30–38 cm). Leaf spread: 8 ft. (2.4 m). Stem color: Bronzy red. No pubescence on peduncle or petiole.

COMMENTS. Where space allows, *Nymphaea* 'Red Star' is a fine addition to medium or large pools.

Nymphaea 'Rhonda Kay'

Landon 1984
Nymphaea capensis var. *zanzibariensis* 'Purpurea' × N. *flavovirens*
PLATE 94

CHARACTERISTICS. Nonviviparous, very free flowering; blooms held 12 in. (30 cm) above water.

FLOWERS. Petal color: Violet-blue (*RHS* 96B). Sepal color: Deeper violet than petals (*RHS* 96A). Anther color: Butterscotch (*RHS* 167B). Stamen color: Deep yellow. Flower shape: Stellate. Flower size: 6 in. (15 cm). Fragrance: Sweet. Number of petals: 23. Number of sepals: 4.

LEAVES. Color: Top, green; underside, green. Leaf a little longer than wide; lobes overlap at sinus. Leaf size: 11–12 in. (28–30 cm), very small for a star waterlily. Leaf spread: 6–9 ft. (1.8–2.7 m). Stem color: Green or bronzy green. No pubescence on peduncle or petiole.

COMMENTS. Blooms, held very high above the water, have a most striking color. This is an excellent tropical cultivar and a terrific bloomer as well. I highly recommend it for medium or large pools.

Nymphaea 'Robert Strawn'

Strawn 1969

Nymphaea elegans × unknown

PLATE 95

CHARACTERISTICS. Nonviviparous, free flowering; blooms held 12 in. (30 cm) above water.

FLOWERS. Petal color: Deep lavender-blue (*RHS* 85A). Sepal color: Outer two-thirds deep lavender-blue, light green base (*RHS* outer, 85A; base, 192D). Anther color: Orange, lavender-blue tips (*RHS* 179D; tips, 85A). Stamen color: Yellow. Flower shape: Stellate. Flower size: 5–6 in. (13–15 cm). Fragrance: Slight. Number of petals: 19–21. Number of sepals: 4–6.

LEAVES. Color: Top, green, small purple blotches; underside, purple, deep purple blotches, prominent green veins. Leaf longer than wide; lobes usually overlap about halfway down sinus. Leaf size: Up to 15 × 13 in. (38 × 33 cm). Leaf spread: 6–8 ft. (1.8–2.4 m). Stem color: Purplish red. A few tiny hairs on underwater stems.

COMMENTS. Dr. Kirk Strawn named this waterlily after his father. Flower stems are very long, holding flowers high above the water. I consider this only a fair plant for medium and large pools, however, as its leaf spread is huge compared with its medium-sized flowers.

Nymphaea 'Ron G. Landon'

Landon 1999

Nymphaea ampla var. *plumieri* × *N. capensis* var. *zanzibariensis purpurea*

PLATE 96

CHARACTERISTICS. Very free flowering, nonviviparous.

FLOWERS. Petal color: Intense dark satiny blue to purple. Sepal color: Inner, light blue; outer, olive green with purple lines. Anther color: Inner, purple; outer, dark purple. Stamen color: Purple. Flower shape: Opens wide, slightly cup-shaped (20 degrees above horizontal) with wide petals arching toward the center. Flower size: 9–12 in. (23–30 cm), held 18–22 in. (45–56 cm) above water's surface. Fragrance: Average. Number of petals: 28. Number of sepals: 4.

LEAVES. Color: Top, dark green; underside, dark purplish red with green veins. Large and oval; sinus closed with overlapping lobes. Leaf size: 26 × 24 in. (65 × 60 cm). Leaf spread: 25 ft. (7.5 m). Stem color: Dark olive green. Pubescence on peduncle and petiole.

COMMENTS. The parent *Nymphaea ampla* var. *plumieri* is the largest variety of the species. This hybrid is one of the largest Brachyceras types. Plants are vigorous and impressive, however it will adapt to smaller cultural conditions. The large bright blue flowers are infertile and are born in profusion.

Nymphaea 'Rose Pearl'

Wood 1976

Parentage unknown

CHARACTERISTICS. Nonviviparous, very free flowering.

FLOWERS. Petal color: Raspberry red (*RHS* 63B). Sepal color: Deeper raspberry red than petals (*RHS* 63A). Anther color: Orange-red, pink tips (*RHS* 37A; tips, 63C). Stamen color: Yellow. Flower shape: Broad stellate. Flower size: 8–10 in. (20–25 cm). Fragrance: Very pleasant. Number of petals: 28. Number of sepals: 4.

LEAVES. Color: Top, green; underside, green. Leaves large, dentate, prominent light green veins on top; sinus usually open, sometimes partly closed. Leaf size: Up to 15 in. (38 cm). Leaf spread: 6–8 ft.

(1.8–2.4 m). Stem color: Greenish. No pubescence on peduncle or petiole.

COMMENTS. *Nymphaea* 'Rose Pearl', with its magnificent raspberry-red blossoms, is a fine waterlily for medium and large pools.

Nymphaea 'Rose Star'

Sturtevant pre-1905

One parent probably *N. flavovirens*, common to most star lilies

PLATE 97

CHARACTERISTICS. Nonviviparous, very free flowering; blooms held 12–15 in. (30–38 cm) above water.

FLOWERS. Petal color: Rosy pink, sometimes purplish near tips (*RHS* 65B; tips, 67B). Sepal color: Same as petals. Anther color: Orange, purple-pink tips (*RHS* 26B; tips, 67C). Stamen color: Inner stamens, burnt orange; outer, purplish. Flower shape: Stellate. Flower size: 7–8 in. (18–20 cm). Fragrance: Very nice. Number of petals: 19–21. Number of sepals: 4.

LEAVES. Color: Top, green, a few purple mottles; underside, pinkish, a few purple blotches, prominent green veins. New leaves are red. Leaves large, oval, convoluted, dentate; sinus varies from half open to fully closed. Leaf size: Up to 17 × 15.5 in. (43 × 39 cm). Leaf spread 10–12 ft. (3–3.6 m). Stem color: Bright yellowish green, bronzy underwater. No pubescence on peduncle or petiole.

COMMENTS. Plants can be very impressive, especially well-established plants that produce a great many flowers. The huge leaf spread limits *Nymphaea* 'Rose Star' to very large pools.

Nymphaea 'Sarah Ann'

Volunteer at Slocum Water Gardens 1987

Parentage unknown

PLATE 98

CHARACTERISTICS. Free flowering, viviparous.

FLOWERS. Petal color: Pinkish red. Sepal color: Inner, top three-fifths rose, base greenish; outer, green with rose edging. Anther color: Inner, yellowish; outer, yellowish purple. Stamen color: Yellow and purple. Flower shape: Cuplike. Flower size: 4.5–6 in. (11.5–15 cm). Fragrance: Sweet. Number of petals: 15 or 16. Number of sepals: 4.

LEAVES. Color: Top, green; underside, light red pink. Leaf shape: Nearly round. Sinus shape: Mostly open. Leaf size: 10.5 in. (26.5 cm). Leaf spread: 3–5 ft. (0.9–1.5 m). Stem color: Brownish green. No pubescence on peduncle or petiole.

COMMENTS BY SLOCUM WATER GARDENS. My son, Peter, named this waterlily after his wife. *Nymphaea* 'Sarah Ann' is very free blooming, and the smooth leaves have attractive wavy edges. It does well in any size pool.

Nymphaea 'Serendipity'

Presnell 2001

Unnamed hybrid × *N.* 'Green Smoke'

PLATE 99

CHARACTERISTICS. Free flowering, nonviviparous.

FLOWERS. Petal color: Soft purple. Sepal color: Inner, light blue; outer, dark green with many dark speckles. Anther color: Yellow with light blue tips. Stamen color: Yellow. Flower shape: Stellate. Flower size: 6 in. (15 cm). Fragrance: Very pleasant. Number of petals: 30. Number of sepals: 4.

LEAVES. Color: Top, green with maroon mottling; underside, green with purple blotches, prominent green veins. Oval with serrate margins; sinus usually closed with lobes overlapping. Leaf size: 13 × 11.5 in. (33 × 28 cm). Leaf spread: 6 ft. (1.8 m). Stem color: Green. No pubescence on peduncle or petiole.

COMMENTS BY J. CRAIG PRESNELL. *Nymphaea* 'Serendipity' was the winner of the International Waterlily and Water Gardening Society Banksian Award in 2001 for the best waterlily. This waterlily is recommended for medium or large ponds.

Nymphaea 'Starlight'

Sacher 2000

Nymphaea 'Morning Star' × *N.* 'Purple Zanzibar'

PLATE 100

CHARACTERISTICS. Free flowering, nonviviparous, compact growth habit.

FLOWERS. Petal color: Light blue, becoming white at base. Sepal color: Inner, greenish white; outer, green with dark lines. Anther color: Inner, pale blue; outer, pale blue. Stamen color: Yellow. Flower shape: Stellate. Flower size: 6–8 in. (15–20 cm). Fragrance: Pleasant. Number of petals: 38–40. Number of sepals: 4 full size, 2 narrow.

LEAVES. Color: Top, green splashed with maroon; underside, green with purple flecks. Round leaf, closed sinus with raised leaf lobe. Leaf size: 10 × 12 in. (25.5 × 30 cm). Leaf spread: 4–5 ft. (1.2–1.5 m). Stem color: Rosy brown. No pubescence on peduncle or petiole.

COMMENTS BY RICH SACHER. The flowers of Nymphaea 'Starlight' are larger than most tropicals. The subtlety of the large, ice blue flower, held against variegated leaves on this compact plant make it one of our favorites. It is a heavy bloomer, often having three flowers open at the same time.

Nymphaea 'Star of Zanzibar'
Sacher 2000
Nymphaea 'Morning Star' × N. 'Purple Zanzibar'
PLATE 101
CHARACTERISTICS. Nonviviparous, free flowering, very compact habit.

FLOWERS. Petal color: Dark blue. Sepal color: Inner, dark blue; outer, green with black lines. Anther color: Inner, blue; outer, blue. Stamen color: Yellow. Flower shape: Stellate. Flower size: 5–6 in. (12.5–15 cm). Fragrance: Strong. Number of petals: 30–34. Number of sepals: 4.

LEAVES. Color, top, green with small splashes of maroon; underside, green with purple flecks. Oval leaf; closed sinus, raised leaf lobes. Leaf size: 10–12 in. (25.5–30 cm). Leaf spread: 5–6 ft. (1.5–1.8 m). Stem color: Plum. No pubescence on peduncle or petiole.

COMMENTS BY RICH SACHER. A vigorous, free-blooming waterlily with striking flowers. The lengthwise crease in the flower petals gives the flower a very sturdy appearance. A very compact plant no matter how large it grows. Nymphaea 'Star of Zanzibar' won the 2000 Banksian Award given by the International Waterlily and Water Gardening Society.

Nymphaea 'St. Louis'
Pring 1932
Nymphaea stuhlmannii × N. 'Mrs. George H. Pring'
PLATE 102
CHARACTERISTICS. Nonviviparous, very free flowering.

FLOWERS. Petal color: Lemon yellow (RHS 2D). Sepal color: Lemon yellow, lengthwise green stripes (RHS 2D; stripes, 130D). Anther color: Dark yellow, lemon-yellow tips (RHS 11A; tips, 2C). Stamen color: Deep golden yellow. Flower shape: Stellate. Flower size: 8–11 in. (20–28 cm). Fragrance: Very pleasant. Number of petals: 29–31. Number of sepals: 4.

LEAVES. Color: Top, green, new leaves delicately blotched purple; underside, green. Leaves very large, nearly round, smooth, edges somewhat wavy; sinus usually an open V. Leaf size: Up to 20 × 19 in. (50 × 48 cm). Leaf spread: 8–10 ft. (2.4–3 m). Stem color: Underwater stems bronzy brown; peduncle yellowish green above water. No pubescence on peduncle or petiole.

COMMENTS. In 1933 George H. Pring was issued a plant patent for N. 'St. Louis', making it the first waterlily in the United States to be patented. This waterlily is one of the best performers of all the tropicals and very striking for medium or large pools.

Nymphaea 'St. Louis Gold'
Pring 1956
Nymphaea sulfurea × N. 'African Gold'
PLATE 103
CHARACTERISTICS. Nonviviparous, free flowering.

FLOWERS. Petal color: Deep yellow (RHS 20A). Sepal color: Deep yellow (RHS 20A). Anther color: Yellow-orange, deep yellow tips (RHS 14B; tips, 20A). Stamen color: Deep yellowish orange. Flower shape: Stellate. Flower size: 5–6 in. (13–15 cm). Fragrance: Slightly sweet. Number of petals: 20–22. Number of sepals: 4.

LEAVES. Color: Top, olive green, new leaves bronzy, covered with small purple blotches, prominent light green veins; underside, green, new leaves light purple. Leaf oval-shaped; sinus slightly open. Leaf size: 8–10 in. (20–25 cm). Leaf spread: 4–5 ft. (1.2–1.5 m). Stem color: Purplish brown. No pubescence on peduncle or petiole.

COMMENTS. Flowers of Nymphaea 'St. Louis Gold' open late and close late. A magnificent waterlily for any size pool and an especially good choice for the small pool due to its restricted leaf spread.

Nymphaea 'Stormy Weather'

Connelly 1999

Nymphaea 'Green Smoke' × *N.* 'August Koch'

PLATE 104

CHARACTERISTICS. Free flowering, nonviviparous.

FLOWERS. Petal color: Grayish green with yellow base. Sepal color: Inner, blue-gray; outer, olive and black. Anther color: Inner, lavender; outer, blue. Stamen color: Golden. Flower shape: Semi-open. Flower size: 6–7 in. (15–17.5 cm).

LEAVES. Color: Top, new leaves red turning to green; underside, green with pink and purple speckles. Leaves oval. Leaf size: 10–12 in. (25.5–30 cm). Leaf spread: 6–8 ft. (1.8–2.4 m). Stem color: Bright green. Pubescence on peduncle and petiole.

COMMENTS BY LEEANN CONNELLY. *Nymphaea* 'Stormy Weather' is a lovely lily with very unusual leaves. I recommend it for medium and large ponds.

Nymphaea 'Tammie Sue Uber'

Van Ness Water Gardens 1970

Parentage unknown

CHARACTERISTICS. Nonviviparous, extremely free flowering.

FLOWERS. Petal color: Fuchsia pink (*RHS* 73B). Sepal color: Lighter than petals (*RHS* 73D). Anther color: Yellow, fuchsia tips (*RHS* 2B; tips, 73B). Stamen color: Yellow. Flower shape: Cuplike. Flower size: 7–8 in. (18–20 cm). Fragrance: Pronounced. Number of petals: 18. Number of sepals: 4.

LEAVES. Color: Top, green, new leaves heavily mottled purple; underside, green. Leaf nearly round, fairly smooth edges; sinus open. Leaf size: 10 in. (25 cm). Leaf spread: 5–6 ft. (1.5–1.8 m). Stem color: Brown or bronze. No pubescence on peduncle or petiole.

COMMENTS. Due to its restricted leaf spread, *Nymphaea* 'Tammie Sue Uber' can be used in any size pool.

Nymphaea 'Ted Uber'

Randig 1965

Parentage unknown

PLATE 105

CHARACTERISTICS. Nonviviparous, very free flowering.

FLOWERS. Petal color: White (*RHS* 155D). Sepal color: White (*RHS* 155A). Anther color: Yellow, white tips (*RHS* 13B; tips, 155D). Stamen color: Yellow. Flower shape: Large, cuplike then round, flat. Flower size: 8–10 in. (20–25 cm). Fragrance: Very pronounced, pleasant. Number of petals: 24. Number of sepals: 4.

LEAVES. Color: Top, green; underside, green, new leaves red, turning to pink under lobes. Leaf a little longer than wide, slightly serrated; lobes usually overlap at sinus, one lobe frequently raised. Leaf size: 11.5–12.5 in. (29–32 cm). Leaf spread: 6–8 ft. (1.8–2.4 m). Stem color: Peduncle, purplish brown above water, green below water; petiole green. No pubescence on peduncle or petiole.

COMMENTS. *Nymphaea* 'Ted Uber' is a wonderful waterlily when it grows properly, yet some growers complain that misshapen leaves develop. For the most part, this is an excellent choice for medium or large pools.

Nymphaea 'Tina'

Van Ness Water Gardens 1974

Parentage unknown

PLATE 106

CHARACTERISTICS. Viviparous, very free flowering.

FLOWERS. Petal color: Deep violet-purple (*RHS* 91A). Sepal color: Outer two-thirds purple, base greenish (*RHS* outer, 76B; base, 144D). Anther color: Yellow, purple tips (*RHS* 13C; tips, 90C). Stamen color: Yellow. Flower shape: Cuplike. Flower size: 4.5–6 in. (11–15 cm). Fragrance: Very nice. Number of petals: 15 or 16. Number of sepals: 4.

LEAVES. Color: Top, green, new leaves bronzy; underside, light red or pink, new leaves red, prominent green veins. Leaf slightly longer than wide, smooth, wavy edges; sinus usually wide open. Leaf size: 10.5 × 9.5 in. (27 × 24 cm). Leaf spread: 3–5 ft. (0.9–1.5 m). Stem color: Reddish purple. No pubescence on peduncle or petiole.

COMMENTS. Although this waterlily has relatively few petals, it is one of the most satisfactory waterlilies for the small pool or tub garden. It is a great favorite at some water gardens in Australia, where it outsells all other waterlilies, both hardies and tropicals. (Because it is tropical, however, *Nym-*

phaea 'Tina' has a limited market in the cooler climate of south Australia.) *Nymphaea* 'Tina' is a good performer in medium and large pools as well.

Nymphaea 'White Delight'
Winch 1984

Parentage unknown

CHARACTERISTICS. Nonviviparous, extremely free flowering.

FLOWERS. Petal color: Light yellow, center petals slightly deeper yellow; occasionally older flowers tipped pink (*RHS* inner, 2C; outer, 4D or paler; tips, 65B,C). Sepal color: Whitish yellow, pink-tipped on older blooms, prominent greenish gray veins (*RHS* 155A; tips, 65B,C; veins, 193C). Anther color: Deep yellow (*RHS* 6A). Stamen color: Deep yellow. Flower shape: Stellate. Flower size: 10–12 in. (25–30 cm). Fragrance: Pronounced. Number of petals: 26–29. Number of sepals: 4.

LEAVES. Color: Top, green, new leaves heavily mottled purple; underside, greenish, pink under lobes, heavily mottled. Leaves large, egg-shaped; lobes overlap sinus, one lobe frequently raised. Leaf size: Up to 13 × 12 in. (33 × 30 cm). Leaf spread: 6–7 ft. (1.8–2.1 m). Stem color: Greenish bronze. No pubescence on peduncle or petiole.

COMMENTS. *Nymphaea* 'White Delight', with its huge and numerous blooms, is one of the finest recent introductions. I highly recommend it for medium and large pools.

Nymphaea 'White Lightning'
Florida Aquatic Nursery 1996

Nymphaea capensis × unknown

PLATE 107

CHARACTERISTICS. Very free flowering, nonviviparous.

FLOWERS. Petal color: White. Sepal color: Inner, white; outer, green. Anther color: Inner, creamy yellow with white tips; outer, creamy yellow with white tips. Stamen color: Creamy yellow with a golden yellow base and white tips. Flower shape: Stellate. Flower size: 6–10 in. (15–25.5 cm). Fragrance: Sweet. Number of petals: 32. Number of sepals: 4.

LEAVES. Color: Top, green with burgundy streaks; underside, green covered with red blotches. Nearly round leaf, margins dentate; sinus closed, lobes

overlap or push each other up. Leaf size: 14 × 13 in. (35 × 33 cm). Leaf spread: 6–8 ft. (1.8–2.4 m). Stem color: Green. No pubescence on peduncle or petiole.

COMMENTS BY FLORIDA AQUATIC NURSERY. *Nymphaea* 'White Lightning' got its name from the white flower and the irregular mottling on the pads. With its pure white flower, this plant makes a nice addition to any medium to large pool.

Nymphaea 'William C. Uber'
Van Ness Water Gardens 1970

Parentage unknown

CHARACTERISTICS. Nonviviparous, very free flowering.

FLOWERS. Petal color: Fuchsia red (*RHS* 58C). Sepal color: Fuchsia red (*RHS* 58C). Anther color: Reddish orange, pink tips (*RHS* 31B; tips, 73C). Stamen color: Deep yellow. Flower shape: Cuplike, full. Flower size: 8–9 in. (20–23 cm). Fragrance: Pleasant. Number of petals: 18 or 19. Number of sepals: 4.

LEAVES. Color: Top, green; underside, green. Leaf nearly round, fairly smooth edge; sinus open. Leaf size: 10–12 in. (25–30 cm). Leaf spread: 5–6 ft. (1.5–1.8 m). Stem color: Bronzy green. No pubescence on peduncle or petiole.

COMMENTS. A beautiful, splendidly colored cultivar. This is one I can recommend for pools of every size, especially medium and large pools.

Nymphaea 'William McLane'
Florida Aquatic Nursery 1997

Parentage unknown

PLATE 108

CHARACTERISTICS. Free flowering, nonviviparous.

FLOWERS. Petal color: Purple. Sepal color: Inner, deep violet blue; outer, green to bronze. Anther color: Inner, violet blue; outer, violet blue. Stamen color: Violet blue with yellow base and purple tips. Flower shape: Open cup. Flower size: 5–7 in. (12.5–18 cm). Fragrance: Sweet. Number of petals: 48. Number of sepals: 4.

LEAVES. Color: Top, dark chocolate brown with green blotches; underside, purple with green veins. Oval shaped leaf, margins dentate; sinus closed, lobes overlap or push each other upward. Leaf size:

14 × 13 in. (35 × 33 cm). Leaf spread: 4–5 ft. (1.2–1.5 m). Stem color: Brown. No pubescence on peduncle or petiole.

COMMENTS BY FLORIDA AQUATIC NURSERY. Named after the founder of Florida Aquatic Nurseries, Dr. William McLane, this waterlily was the first to win the prestigious Banksian Award given by the International Waterlily and Water Gardening Society in 1997. The flower is striking because of its large size, deep color, and numerous petals. *Nymphaea* 'William McLane' makes a good centerpiece for any medium to large pool.

COMMENTS BY PERRY SLOCUM. *Nymphaea* 'William McLane' is my wife's favorite waterlily and also one of mine.

Nymphaea 'Wood's Blue Goddess'

Wood 1989

Nymphaea ampla is one parent

PLATE 109

CHARACTERISTICS. Nonviviparous, free flowering. Forms bulblets around main tuber, similar to *N. colorata*.

FLOWERS. Petal color: Deep sky blue then lighter blue in bright sunny weather (*RHS* 104B–D). Sepal color: Generally lighter blue than petals (*RHS* 104D). Anther color: Very deep violet, sky-blue tips (*RHS* 94A; tips, 104B–D). Stamen color: Deep violet. Flower shape: Stellate. Flower size: 10–12 in. (25–30 cm). Fragrance: Faint. Number of petals: 20. Number of sepals: 4.

LEAVES. Color: Top, olive green; underside, purple-blue. Leaf nearly round, sharply serrated; sinus usually closed. Leaf size: 12–13 in. (30–33 cm). Leaf spread: 8 ft. (2.4 m). Stem color: Reddish brown. No pubescence on peduncle or petiole.

COMMENTS. This is a unique waterlily—its large blue flowers with very dark, almost black, violet stamens give a very striking effect. *Nymphaea* 'Wood's Blue Goddess' was voted most outstanding tropical waterlily introduction at the 1987 International Waterlily and Water Gardening Society Symposium, where it was on display as *N.* 'Blue Ampla' (a name already assigned to a waterlily by Landon in 1978). I recommend it for medium or large pools.

Nymphaea 'Yellow Dazzler'

Randig 1938

Parentage unknown

PLATE 110

CHARACTERISTICS. Nonviviparous, free flowering.

FLOWERS. Petal color: Lemon yellow (*RHS* 2C). Sepal color: Yellowish green, prominent darker yellowish green veins (*RHS* 150D; veins, 148D). Anther color: Golden yellow, lemon-yellow tips (*RHS* 7B; tips, 2C). Stamen color: Deep golden yellow. Flower shape: Stellate, large. Flower size: 8–10 in. (20–25 cm). Fragrance: Very pleasant. Number of petals: 23. Number of sepals: 4.

LEAVES. Color: Top, green, a few purple blotches; underside, green, faint purplish or bluish tinge. Leaves large, egg-shaped, edges quite smooth, some convolutions; sinus usually closed. Leaf size: Up to 17 × 14.5 in. (43 × 37 cm). Leaf spread: 6–8 ft. (1.8–2.4 m). Stem color: Brownish red. No pubescence on peduncle or petiole.

COMMENTS. *Nymphaea* 'Yellow Dazzler' is an excellent waterlily for medium and large pools. Flowers can seem rather small relative to the leaves.

CHAPTER 4

Night-Blooming Tropical Cultivars

THE CULTIVARS of night-blooming tropical water-lilies usually open around dusk and close between 11:00 a.m. and noon the following day. Cold autumn days can cause them to remain open for longer periods. Like the day bloomers, the flowers of these cultivars usually open and close for three or four successive days.

The following plant descriptions are arranged alphabetically by cultivar name. This name is followed by any synonyms, the name of the hybridizer or originator, and the date, if known.

Plant tropical waterlilies only when the water temperature averages 75°F (24°C) or above. Planting too early may induce dormancy. See the hardiness zone maps at the end of the book and follow this general planting timetable:

In North America		In Europe	
Zone 10	March–early April	Zone 10	mid–late May
Zone 9	early April	Zone 9	June
Zone 8	mid April	Zones 8–4	conservatory
Zone 7	mid–late May		planting, where
Zone 6	late May–		water can be
	early June		heated to 75°F
Zone 5	early–mid June		(24°C) or higher
Zone 4	mid–late June		

Nymphaea 'Antares'

Longwood Gardens 1962

Nymphaea 'H. C. Haarstick' × *N.* 'Emily Grant Hutchings'

PLATE 111

CHARACTERISTICS. Nonviviparous, free flowering.

FLOWERS. Petal color: Dark rosy red (*RHS* 50A). Sepal color: Dark rosy red (*RHS* 50A). Anther color: Deep red (*RHS* 31C). Stamen color: Orange. Flower shape: Cuplike. Flower size: 6–10 in. (15–25 cm). Fragrance: Pungent. Number of petals: 30–36. Number of sepals: 4.

LEAVES. Color: Top, green, newest leaves bronzy with green veins; underside, brown. Leaf round, perimeter undulating, pointed projections; sinus open. Leaf size: 10–12 in. (25–30 cm). Leaf spread: 5–7 ft. (1.5–2.1 m). Stem color: Reddish brown. Very short hairs on peduncle and petiole.

COMMENTS. This is an exceptional night-blooming tropical with excellent color. *Nymphaea* 'Antares' was developed at Longwood Gardens by Patrick Nutt. I recommend this waterlily for medium and large pools.

Nymphaea 'Brazos White'

Strawn 1998

Parentage unknown

CHARACTERISTICS. Nonviviparous, very free flowering.

FLOWERS. Petal color: Bright white; outer, white flushed green. Sepal color: Inner, white; outer, dark green. Anther color: Inner, soft yellow; outer, soft yellow. Stamen color: Soft yellow. Flower shape: Large round, then opens flat. Flower size: 6–8 in. (15–20 cm). Fragrance: Pungent. Number of petals: 19 or 20. Number of sepals: 4.

LEAVES. Color: Top, medium green, newer leaves lighter green with light flecking on perimeter; underside, olive green, heavily blotched purple. Mature leaves longer than wide, rounded notches and wavy convolutions on edges, sinus slightly open. Leaf size: 12–14 in. (30–35 cm). Leaf spread: 5–6 ft. (1.5–1.8 m). Stem color: Olive green. Short pubescence on peduncle and petiole.

COMMENTS BY DEAN MCGEE. The large white

bloom stands well over 1 ft. (0.3 m) out of the water. Great for large ponds.

Nymphaea 'Catherine Marie'

Landon 1990
Nymphaea 'Wood's White Knight' × *N.* 'Red Flare'
PLATE 112

CHARACTERISTICS. Nonviviparous, free flowering.

FLOWERS. Petal color: Rich pink (*RHS* 68A). Sepal color: Maroon (*RHS* 47C). Anther color: Orange-red (*RHS* 42B). Stamen color: Pale yellow. Flower shape: Round, full, somewhat flat across top when fully open. Flower size: 8–10 in. (20–25 cm). Fragrance: Very pungent. Number of petals: 30. Number of sepals: 4.

LEAVES. Color: Top, olive green; underside, olive green. Leaf nearly round; lobes slightly divergent or overlap at sinus. Leaf size: 12–14 in. (30–35 cm). Leaf spread: 6–8 ft. (1.8–2.4 m). Stem color: Maroon. Occasionally faint pubescence on peduncle and petiole.

COMMENTS. Kenneth Landon selected this cultivar out of many seedlings due to its outstanding beauty and performance. This raving beauty has gone far in the water garden world. I recommend it for medium and large pools.

Nymphaea 'Elysian Fields'

Sacher 2001
Nymphaea 'Missouri' × *N.* 'Antares'
PLATE 113

CHARACTERISTICS. Free flowering, with broad petals.

FLOWERS. Petal color: Medium pink in summer, pale apple blossom pink in greenhouse in winter. Sepal color: Inner, pink; outer, bronze with pink veins. Anther color: Inner, yellow to brown; outer, tan. Stamen color: Dark pink. Flower shape: Broad bowl shape. Flower size: 6–8 in. (15–20 cm). Fragrance: None. Number of petals: 30–32. Number of sepals: 4.

LEAVES. Color: Top, copper bronze in sun; underside, green with purple flecks. Round leaf with closed sinus. Leaf size: 10–12 in. (25.5–30 cm). Leaf spread: 5–6 ft. (1.5–1.8 m). Stem color: Plum. Pubescence on peduncle and petiole.

COMMENTS BY RICH SACHER. This hybrid shows characteristics of each parent: the wide petals of *Nymphaea* 'Missouri' and pink flowers of *N.* 'Antares'. Leaves are a striking copper color when grown in full sun and hold that color until they turn yellow.

Nymphaea 'Emily Grant Hutchings'

Pring 1922
Nymphaea 'C. E. Hutchings' × unknown
PLATE 114

CHARACTERISTICS. Nonviviparous, very free flowering.

FLOWERS. Petal color: Dark pink (*RHS* 66D). Sepal color: Dark pink (*RHS* 67B). Anther color: Dark orange-pink (*RHS* 39B). Stamen color: Red. Flower shape: Large, cuplike. Flower size: 6–8 in. (15–20 cm). Fragrance: Slight. Number of petals: 20. Number of sepals: 4.

LEAVES. Color: Top, bronzy green; underside, olive green. Leaves round, undulating; lobes overlap at sinus. Leaf size: 10–12 in. (25–30 cm). Leaf spread: 6–7 ft. (1.8–2.1 m). Stem color: Bronze. Short hairs on peduncle and petiole.

COMMENTS. *Nymphaea* 'Emily Grant Hutchings' is an excellent night bloomer that propagates very freely. Tubers send out short runners, developing new plants at the tips. This cultivar blooms earlier in the season than most other night-blooming varieties. I highly recommend it for medium and large pools; alternatively, by using an 8- to 10-in. (20- to 25-cm) pot, its growth can be restricted and yet it will still produce plenty of blooms for the small pool.

Nymphaea 'H. C. Haarstick'

Gurney 1922
Nymphaea 'Mrs. D. R. Francis' × unknown

CHARACTERISTICS. Nonviviparous, very free flowering.

FLOWERS. Petal color: Red (*RHS* 61C). Sepal color: Red (*RHS* 61C). Anther color: Orange-red (*RHS* 47B). Stamen color: Orange-red. Flower shape: Large, round, flat. Flower size: 10–12 in. (25–30 cm). Fragrance: Pungent. Number of petals: 22–24. Number of sepals: 4.

LEAVES. Color: Top, reddish brown; underside, purple. Leaf round, dentate, small convolutions at perimeter; sinus usually open or partly open. Leaf size: Up to 16 in. (40 cm). Leaf spread: 6–12 ft. (1.8–3.6 m). Stem color: Purple. Tiny hairs on underwater stems.

COMMENTS. This cultivar was produced at the Missouri Botanical Garden and was one of the first night bloomers developed. It remains an excellent choice for medium or large pools.

Nymphaea 'Jennifer Rebecca'

Landon 1990

Nymphaea 'Wood's White Knight' × N. 'Red Flare'

PLATE 115

CHARACTERISTICS. Nonviviparous, free flowering.

FLOWERS. Petal color: Dark red (RHS 67B,C). Sepal color: Dark maroon (RHS 47A). Anther color: Dark maroon (RHS 46B). Stamen color: Deep pink. Flower shape: Resembling a sunflower. Flower size: 8–10 in. (20–25 cm). Fragrance: Quite pungent. Number of petals: 32. Number of sepals: 4.

LEAVES. Color: Top, reddish brown; underside, reddish brown. Leaves nearly round, sharply dentate, perimeter wavy on older leaves; sinus closed. Leaf size: 15 in. (38 cm). Leaf spread: 7–9 ft. (2.1–2.7 m). Stem color: Dark maroon. Slight pubescence on peduncle and petiole.

COMMENTS. Nymphaea 'Jennifer Rebecca' is one of the most striking red night bloomers I have ever seen. With its amazing color and plentiful blooms, it is sure to stand out in a water garden. I recommend it for medium and large pools.

Nymphaea 'Juno'

Unknown 1906

Nymphaea lotus is one parent

PLATE 116

CHARACTERISTICS. Nonviviparous, free flowering.

FLOWERS. Petal color: White (RHS 155B). Sepal color: White (RHS 155A). Anther color: Yellow (RHS 12B). Stamen color: Yellow. Flower shape: Cuplike then flat. Flower size: 6–10 in. (15–25 cm). Fragrance: Pungent. Number of petals: 19 or 20. Number of sepals: 4.

LEAVES. Color: Top, green, new leaves green or bronzy, a few purple blotches; underside, brown or purplish, prominent greenish yellow veins. Leaf nearly round, dentate; sinus usually open, lobes may overlap partially or completely. Leaf size: 13 × 12 in. (33 × 30 cm). Leaf spread: 5–6 ft. (1.5–1.8 m). Stem color: Mostly brown; peduncle above water usually greenish. Short fuzz on peduncle and petiole.

COMMENTS. Although its hybridizer is unknown, Nymphaea 'Juno' was first offered for sale in 1906, according to waterlily researcher and author Charles Masters. It performs well in any size pool.

Nymphaea 'Leeann Connelly'

Connelly 1984

Nymphaea 'Wood's White Knight' × N. 'Mrs. George Hitchcock'

PLATE 117

CHARACTERISTICS. Free flowering, changeable, from white to pink.

FLOWERS. Petal color: Nearly white on first day, turning to light pink on second day. Sepal color: Inner, mostly white, turning to pink; outer, bronzy green with darker flecks. Anther color: Inner, orange; outer, yellow. Stamen color: Orange to yellow. Flower shape: Very flat. Flower size: 10–12 in. (25.5–30.5 cm). Fragrance: None. Number of petals: 15 or 16. Number of sepals: 4 or 5.

LEAVES. Color: Top, bronzy green at first, then olive green; underside, bronzy purple with purple speckles. Round leaf with serrated edging; sinus closed. Leaf size: 10–15 in. (25.5–38 cm). Leaf spread: 5–6 ft. (1.5–1.8 m). Stem color: Underwater portions bronzy purple; above usually dark green. Pubescence on underwater parts of peduncle and petiole.

COMMENTS BY LEEANN CONNELLY. This is a very pleasing, free-blooming night bloomer that changes color.

Nymphaea 'Maroon Beauty'

Slocum 1950

Seedling of N. 'H. C. Haarstick'

PLATE 118

CHARACTERISTICS. Nonviviparous, free flowering.

FLOWERS. Petal color: Deep red (RHS 64B). Sepal color: Deep red (RHS 63A). Anther color: Chocolate, tipped red (RHS 178B; tips, 64B). Stamen color: Inner stamens reddish brown, outer red. Flower shape: Huge, round, flat. Flower size: 10–12 in. (25–30 cm). Fragrance: Pungent. Number of petals: 24–26. Number of sepals: 4.

LEAVES. Color: Top, reddish brown; underside, purple. Leaf round, dentate, perimeter convoluted; sinus an open V. Leaf size: Up to 16 in. (40 cm). Leaf spread: 6–12 ft. (1.8–3.6 m). Stem color: Purple. Tiny hairs on underwater stems.

COMMENTS. *Nymphaea* 'Maroon Beauty', a magnificent, striking waterlily, is best suited to medium and larger pools because of its large leaf spread.

Nymphaea 'Missouri'

Pring 1932

Probably *N*. 'Mrs. George C. Hitchcock' × *N*. 'Sturtevantii'

PLATE 119

CHARACTERISTICS. Nonviviparous, fairly free flowering.

FLOWERS. Petal color: White (*RHS* 155B). Sepal color: White (*RHS* 155B). Anther color: Deep yellow (*RHS* 13C). Stamen color: Yellow. Flower shape: Flat, platelike. Flower size: 10–14 in. (25–35 cm). Fragrance: Pungent. Number of petals: 31. Number of sepals: 4.

LEAVES. Color: Top, green, new leaves bronze; underside, green, flecked purple. Leaves large, a little longer than wide, very dentate, margins wavy; lobes usually overlap at sinus or sinus may be partly open. Leaf size: Up to 14 × 12 in. (35 × 30 cm). Leaf spread: 6–10 ft. (1.8–3 m). Stem color: Bronzy. Tiny short hairs on peduncle and petiole.

COMMENTS. *Nymphaea* 'Missouri' can produce blooms larger than those of any other night bloomer, if planted in a large container with at least 2 cu. ft. (0.05 m³) of soil and given plenty of fertilizer. I recommend it only for the large pool due to its extensive leaf spread.

Nymphaea 'Mrs. George C. Hitchcock'

Pring 1926

Seedling of *N*. 'Omarana'

PLATE 120

CHARACTERISTICS. Nonviviparous, very free flowering, seed production profuse.

FLOWERS. Petal color: Light to medium pink (*RHS* 65A). Sepal color: Darker pink than petals (*RHS* 66D). Anther color: Burnt orange (*RHS* 34D).

Stamen color: Burnt orange, same as anthers. Flower shape: Large, flat. Flower size: 10–11 in. (25–28 cm). Fragrance: Pungent. Number of petals: 20. Number of sepals: 4.

LEAVES. Color: Top, bronzy, newer pads darker bronze, some purple blotches; underside, purple. Leaves longer than wide, serrated, perimeter convoluted; sinus closed on newer leaves, open on older leaves. Leaf size: Up to 15 × 13.5 in. (38 × 34 cm). Leaf spread: 7–8 ft. (2.1–2.4 m). Stem color: Peduncle, orange-brown; petiole brownish. Very short fuzz on peduncle and petiole.

COMMENTS. A true show waterlily. Blooms usually open around dark and close toward midday, yet they will stay open all day on cool, overcast days. This is a fine choice for a medium or large pool.

Nymphaea 'Red Cup'

Strawn 1986

Nymphaea 'Red Flare' × unknown

PLATE 121

CHARACTERISTICS. Nonviviparous, free flowering.

FLOWERS. Petal color: Dark red then deep pink in late summer and autumn (*RHS* 67A then 67B). Sepal color: Dark red then deep pink in late summer and autumn (*RHS* 67A then 67B). Anther color: Red (*RHS* 50A). Stamen color: Red. Flower shape: Cuplike. Flower size: 5–8 in. (13–20 cm). Fragrance: Slightly pungent. Number of petals: 18–20. Number of sepals: 4.

LEAVES. Color: Top, bronzy brown; underside, purple. Leaves oval, heavily serrated, wavy edges; sinus open. Leaf size: 13–18 in. (33–45 cm). Leaf spread: 5–12 ft. (1.5–3.5 m). Stem color: Peduncle purple; petiole purple, browning. Very short fuzz on peduncle and petiole.

COMMENTS. This cultivar has a unique vaselike bloom and excellent petal color and foliage. I recommend it for medium or large pools.

Nymphaea 'Red Flare'

Randig 1938

Parentage unknown

PLATE 122

CHARACTERISTICS. Nonviviparous, very free flowering; blooms held 12 in. (30 cm) above water.

FLOWERS. Petal color: Deep red (*RHS* 67A). Sepal color: Deep red (*RHS* 67A). Anther color: Reddish brown (*RHS* 175B). Stamen color: Light pink or yellowish. Flower shape: Large, round, flat. Flower size: 7–10 in. (18–25 cm). Fragrance: Faint but pungent. Number of petals: 19–20. Number of sepals: 4.

LEAVES. Color: Top, reddish bronze, fading only slightly, few small purple blotches; underside, purple. Young leaves much longer than wide; older leaves nearly round, heavily serrated, wavy edges; sinus usually a wide-open V. Leaf size: 10–12 in. (25–30 cm). Leaf spread: 5–6 ft. (1.5–1.8 m). Stem color: Peduncle, reddish brown; petiole brown. Tiny short hairs on peduncle and petiole.

COMMENT. This is one of the very best red night bloomers for any size pool.

Nymphaea 'Sir Galahad'

Randig 1965

Parentage unknown

CHARACTERISTICS. Nonviviparous, free flowering; flowers held 10–11 in. (25–28 cm) above water.

FLOWERS. Petal color: White (*RHS* 155D). Sepal color: White (*RHS* 155D). Anther color: Rich yellow (*RHS* 14A). Stamen color: Rich yellow. Flower shape: Round, flat. Flower size: 9–12 in. (23–30 cm). Fragrance: Pungent. Number of petals: 28. Number of sepals: 4.

LEAVES. Color: Top, green; underside, green, tinted purple. Leaf nearly round, sharply serrated; lobes usually overlap at sinus except for outer 1–2 in. (2.5–5 cm). Leaf size: 13–15 in. (33–38 cm). Leaf spread: 6–9 ft. (1.8–2.7 m). Stem color: Peduncle, green; petiole, purplish green. Very short fuzz on all underwater stems.

COMMENTS. *Nymphaea* 'Sir Galahad' is a wonderful plant. Its stout peduncles hold massive flowers high above the water. This waterlily is dramatic and beautiful, once it is established producing several blooms at a time. I recommend it for large pools.

Nymphaea 'Texas Shell Pink'

Nelson 1979

Parentage unknown

PLATE 123

CHARACTERISTICS. Nonviviparous, free flowering.

FLOWERS. Petal color: Creamy white, tips reddish purple (*RHS* 155D; tips, 65A). Sepal color: Basal third white; tips (outer two-thirds) red-purple (*RHS* base, 155D; tips, 65B). Anther color: Grayish orange (*RHS* 166A). Stamen color: Yellowish green. Flower shape: Platelike. Flower size: Up to 8 in. (20 cm). Fragrance: Like cinnamon. Number of petals: 16–20. Number of sepals: 4.

LEAVES. Color: Top, dark yellow-green, grayish brown cast; underside, greenish. Leaf a little longer than wide; sinus open. Leaf size: 13–15 in. (33–38 cm). Leaf spread: 5–6 ft. (1.5–1.8 m). Stem color: Dark gray-green at base, gray-brown near flower and leaf. Very fine hairs on peduncle and petiole.

COMMENTS. The blending of white to a soft red-purple gives this flower a glowing effect. I recommend it for medium and large pools.

Nymphaea 'Trudy Slocum'

Slocum 1948

Seedling of N. 'Juno'

PLATE 124

CHARACTERISTICS. Nonviviparous, very free flowering.

FLOWERS. Petal color: White (*RHS* 155B). Sepal color: White (*RHS* 155A). Anther color: Yellow, brown vertical stripes (*RHS* 11A; stripes, 176C). Stamen color: Deep yellow. Flower shape: Round, nearly flat. Flower size: 6–8 in. (15–20 cm). Fragrance: Pungent. Number of petals: 19–29. Number of sepals: 4.

LEAVES. Color: Top, green, new leaves green or brownish, lightly blotched purple; underside, brown or purplish, prominent greenish veins. Leaf nearly round; sinus usually open, lobes may overlap partially or completely. Leaf size: 13.5 × 12.5 in. (34 × 32 cm). Leaf spread: 5–6 ft. (1.5–1.8 m). Stem color: Mostly brown, peduncle greenish above water. Short fuzz on peduncle and petiole.

COMMENTS. *Nymphaea* 'Trudy Slocum' was named after my first wife. It is outstanding in beauty and performance. It readily produces seed and the variable seedlings grow easily. One plant may develop into a clump containing several plants by the end of the season. This waterlily is suited for any size pool.

Nymphaea 'Wood's White Knight'

Wood 1977

Nymphaea 'Sir Galahad' and *N*. 'Missouri' included in parentage

CHARACTERISTICS. Nonviviparous, very free flowering.

FLOWERS. Petal color: White (*RHS* 155A). Sepal color: White, flushed green (*RHS* 155A; flush, 142D and lighter). Anther color: Yellow (*RHS* 162A). Stamen color: Yellow. Flower shape: Full, peony-style. Flower size: 10–12 in. (25–30 cm). Fragrance: Pungent. Number of petals: 28–30. Number of sepals: 4.

LEAVES. Color: Top, green; underside, greenish, variegated. Leaves nearly round, scalloped, edges somewhat wavy; sinus usually open. Leaf size: 12–15 in. (30–38 cm). Leaf spread: 8–10 ft. (2.4–3 m). Stem color: Greenish brown. Tiny hairs on all underwater stems.

COMMENTS. Blooms are quite double. *Nymphaea* 'Wood's White Knight' is an excellent waterlily for medium and large pools.

CHAPTER 5

Hardy Waterlily Species

ALL THE HARDY waterlily species described in this chapter are listed in one or more aquatic nursery catalogs (see Sources for Plants and Equipment at the end of the book). Most hardy waterlily species now have counterparts in cultivars that are superior in garden performance; the collector will find the species worthwhile, however. The flowers of *Nymphaea odorata, N. mexicana,* and hybrids from these species are pleasantly fragrant. Flowers of the other hardy species are not at all or are only slightly scented. Figure 26 illustrates the parts of a hardy waterlily flower.

The arrangement of this chapter follows the taxonomy of the genus *Nymphaea* as outlined in chapter 1. Following each taxonomic section are the plant descriptions arranged alphabetically by specific epithet with descriptions of related plants (varieties, forms, and named selections) immediately following. All plant names are given with their author and year of discovery when known. Common names, if any, appear after the botanical name. "Characteristics" includes the type of rhizome, as described below. "Stamen color" refers to the color

found on the basal portion of the stamen (the filament) and the base of the staminodes.

Plant hardy waterlilies only when the water temperature reaches 60°F (16°C) or above. Refer to the hardiness zone maps at the end of the book and follow this general planting timetable:

In North America and Europe

Zone 10	any time of year
Zone 9	March–September
Zone 8	April–September
Zone 7	April–August
Zone 6	mid April–August
Zone 5	late April/early May–mid August
Zone 4	mid May–early August

Group *Nymphaea Syncarpiae* Caspary

In general, species in the group *Syncarpiae* display carpels that are completely fused with one another at the sides; they are also attached to the axis of the flower and to the torus, as in day-blooming tropicals. Flowers are diurnal and colored white, rose, or yellow, but not blue.

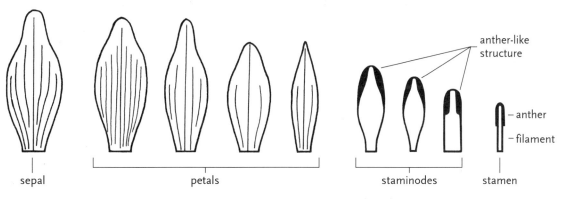

sepal   petals   staminodes   stamen

anther-like structure

— anther

— filament

FIGURE 26. Size and shape transition in hardy *Nymphaea* floral parts.

Subgenus *Nymphaea* de Candolle

Subgenus *Nymphaea* (syn. *Castalia*) comprises the hardy waterlily species. This subgenus consists of six species divided into three sections, *Chamaenymphaea, Eucastalia,* and *Xanthantha,* according to variations. All plants in subgenus *Nymphaea* bloom during the day. Sepals frequently have prominent veins. Leaves usually have smooth edges, lacking the dentation of many tropical waterlilies. Rhizomes vary considerably and may be separated into five types: upright, or pineapple; Marliac; odorata; tuberosa; and finger, or thumb (also grows upright). Plate 125 shows all five types.

The upright, or pineapple, rhizome is tuberous and may be 4 in. (10 cm) thick. As its name implies, it grows upright and is the approximate shape of a pineapple. In general, waterlilies with upright rhizomes are very vigorous growers and very free flowering. At least a bushel (35 L) of soil is recommended for waterlilies of this group, which includes *Nymphaea mexicana*. Some growers recommend planting these rhizomes upright. I have had good success planting them horizontally (the same as most waterlily rhizomes are planted) with the crown just peeking through the soil.

The Marliac rhizome grows a thick, horizontally traveling main root. Frequently this rhizome is 2 in. (5 cm) thick. Waterlilies with Marliac rhizomes are among the freest blooming hardies. Plants are also heavy feeders and do best in a bushel (35 L) or more of soil. *Nymphaea alba* and *N. candida* are in this group. Both are very easy to grow.

The odorata rhizome is long and more slender than the upright or Marliac types. The thickness varies from 1 to 1.5 in. (2.5 to 4 cm). Usually several small, new, firmly attached rhizomes (known as eyes) form along the main rhizome. This rhizome is called a "crawling root" in England because it spreads so rapidly. New plants develop from the eyes. Odorata rhizomes need room to spread out and develop a colony of several plants to become free bloomers. This may take two or more months. I recommend planting in a container 24 × 24 × 12 in. (60 × 60 × 30 cm).

The tuberosa rhizome is usually 0.75–1 in. (2–2.5 cm) thick, being more slender than the odorata type, which it closely resembles. A very noticeable difference is that the side rhizomes are joined by a very slender attachment and nearly all detach when the main rhizome is pulled. Like odorata rhizomes, tuberosa rhizomes need room to spread out and develop colonies to become free bloomers. *Nymphaea tuberosa* is in this group.

The last of the five types, the finger or thumb rhizome, is small—finger size in poor soil, thumb size in rich loamy soil with regular fertilization. The rhizome grows upright and very seldom divides. A half bushel (17.5 L) is enough soil for this miniature. *Nymphaea tetragona* is in this group.

Section *Chamaenymphaea* Planchon

Flowers of species in section *Chamaenymphaea* are white or rosy, opening around noon and closing in late afternoon. Leaves are egg-shaped to oval, and leaf edges are smooth. Rhizomes are upright and short. It includes one species that is native to the north temperate regions of North America, China, Japan, Siberia, Finland, and eastern Europe.

Nymphaea tetragona Georgi

Native to circumboreal regions mostly: in North America from Maine along the Canadian border to the West Coast, from Quebec to Lake Superior and western Canada; also Finland, Japan, China, much of Asia, eastern Europe, and Australia

PLATE 126

CHARACTERISTICS. Day blooming, finger rhizome, free flowering when conditions are suitable.

FLOWERS. Petal color: White (*RHS* 155C). Sepal color: White (*RHS* 155C). Anther color: Yellow (*RHS* 6A). Stamen color: Yellow. Flower shape: Cuplike. Flower size: 1–2 in. (2.5–5 cm). Fragrance: Slight. Number of petals: 8–13. Number of sepals: 4.

LEAVES. Color: Top, green, blotched purple, new leaves purplish; underside, purple. Leaf longer than wide; sinus an open V. Leaf size: 2.75 × 2 in. (7 × 5 cm), 1–2 in. (2.5–5 cm) larger in rich soil. Leaf spread: 10–15 in. (25–38 cm), up to 30 in. (75 cm) in rich soil. Stem color: Green. Tiny hairs on petiole.

COMMENTS. *Nymphaea tetragona* is the tiniest of all waterlilies and is well suited to a small tub garden. Flowers do not open until late morning or early afternoon, yet they do stay open late. For many years *N. fennica* was believed to be a separate species, but Pertti Uotila, professor of botany at the University of Helsinki, Finland, ascertained that *N. fennica* Mela is really one of several variants of *N. tetragona* Georgi from around the world (see others, following). *Nymphaea tetragona* is parent of *N.* 'Helvola' (syn. *N.* 'Yellow Pygmy') and probable parent to several cultivars of the *N.* 'Laydekeri' hybrid group. Because of their need for cold water temperatures, *N. tetragona* var. *lata* and var. *leibergii* are best suited for northern climates, whereas var. *angusta* does well in warm climates.

Nymphaea tetragona var. *angusta* Caspary
Native to China and Japan

COMMENTS. Sepals and petals are larger and narrower than the type. Sinus is equal to or exceeds half the length of the leaf. Leaves are bright olive green on plants that I grew in North Carolina from seeds sent by Kenneth Landon. (Landon's original stock came from France, though Walter Pagels believes the French stock is actually from China.) After being stored in the refrigerator for a few months, the seeds were sown outside in April. Germination and growth was fast. Blooms appeared in August without any transplanting. The young plants flowered in profusion in September and October. It also bloomed freely for Landon in San Angelo, Texas, where summer temperatures reach 100°F (38°C) or higher. This variety has an excellent commercial future.

Nymphaea tetragona var. *lata* Caspary
Native to Siberia, Manchuria, and the Ural
Mountains

COMMENTS. Sepals and petals are shorter and broader than the type. Sinus is less than half the length of the leaf. I have never grown this variety.

Nymphaea tetragona var. *leibergii* (Morong)
Porsild
Native to southeastern and east-central Alaska and
northwestern North America

COMMENTS. Leaves are quite wavy around the perimeter; sinus is usually wide open; a few purple blotches are prominent in new leaves. I tried growing two Alaskan specimens sent to me by Walter Pagels. Plants arrived in beautiful shape with flowers and seed pods ready to burst. I collected some seeds and let some seeds drop. Seeds were stored in a refrigerator. The following year only a few seeds germinated and they, along with the two tubers, produced only a rosette of underwater leaves close to the rhizome. No surface leaves or blooms developed. My conclusion is that the commercial future of variety *leibergii* is nil.

Section *Eucastalia* Planchon

The four species included in section *Eucastalia* represent the majority of hardy waterlilies of subgenus *Nymphaea*. Flowers are white, pink, or red, opening in early morning and closing around midafternoon. Some species have fragrant flowers. Leaves are nearly round with solid color on top. Rhizomes grow horizontally and are long and branching. These waterlilies are native to the north temperate regions of North America and Europe, south to North Africa and Guyana.

Nymphaea alba Linnaeus
Native to Europe and northern Africa
PLATE 127

CHARACTERISTICS. Day blooming, Marliac rhizome, very free flowering; usually produces two to four flowers at a time.

FLOWERS. Petal color: White (*RHS* 155C). Sepal color: Green, white tips (*RHS* 136D–135D; tips, 155C). Anther color: Light yellow (*RHS* 6B). Stamen color: Yellow. Flower shape: Cuplike then stellate. Flower size: 4–5 in. (10–13 cm). Fragrance: Slight, on first day only. Number of petals: 12–28. Number of sepals: 4.

LEAVES. Color: Top, green; underside, yellowish green, margins tinged red. Leaf orbicular; sinus usually an open V. Leaf size: 8–10 in. (20–25 cm). Leaf spread: 5.5 ft. (1.7 m). Stem color: Green. No pubescence on peduncle or petiole.

COMMENTS. This species was used extensively by Joseph Bory Latour-Marliac in hybridizing. As a result, many fine cultivars have *Nymphaea alba* parentage. This waterlily is suitable for small, medium, or large pools.

Nymphaea alba var. rubra Lönnroth

Swedish red waterlily

Native to two very cold lakes (Fayer and Fagertarn)
near Nerike, Hammar Parish, Sweden

COMMENTS. Flowers are pale pink on opening, changing to rose-pink or red, often with a bluish flush. Third-day flowers have the richest color. Blooms are deepest pink in the center, becoming progressively lighter toward the outer petals. Flowers are 3–6 in. (8–15 cm) in diameter. Leaves and rhizomes resemble those of the species. Reputedly this variety was used by Marliac to develop his red, pink, and changeable hardy waterlilies.

Nymphaea alba Australian variant

COMMENTS. This distinct variant of *N. alba* produces rather small blooms, 3–3.5 in. (8–9 cm) in diameter. Leaves are medium size, and the sinus is an open V. The plant produces seeds profusely, an indication of a species. Rhizome is Marliac.

Nymphaea alba New Zealand variant

COMMENTS. This distinct variant produces large blooms, 5–6 in. (13–15 cm) in diameter. Leaves are also large, with lobes that overlap at sinus. The plant produces seeds in quantity, an indication of a species. Rhizome is a thick Marliac. The New Zealand variant has been a parent of many fine commercially available hybrids, such as *Nymphaea* 'Perry's Pink Beauty', *N.* 'Perry's Pink Bicolor', *N.* 'Perry's Strawberry Pink', *N.* 'Perry's White Wonder', and *N.* 'Yellow Sensation'.

Nymphaea candida Presl

Native to northern and central Europe, northern Asia
PLATE 128

CHARACTERISTICS. Day blooming, Marliac rhizome, very free flowering; stigmas yellow, red, or violet.

FLOWERS. Petal color: White (*RHS* 155D). Sepal color: White, blushed pink, green borders and tips (*RHS* 155D; blush, 65D or paler; borders and tips, 193B). Anther color: Yellow (*RHS* 3A). Stamen color: Yellow. Flower shape: Cuplike. Flower size: 3 in. (8 cm). Fragrance: None or very slight. Number of petals: 12–20. Number of sepals: 4 or 5.

LEAVES. Color: Top, green; underside, reddish purple, prominent green veins. Leaves a little longer than wide; lobes may overlap halfway down sinus or sinus open. Leaf size: 7 × 6 in. (18 × 15 cm). Leaf spread: 30–36 in. (75–90 cm). Stem color: Mostly purple-bronze, peduncle a little paler than petiole. Many fine hairs on peduncle and petiole.

COMMENTS. *Nymphaea candida* can be grown successfully in a tub garden or a small pool. Blooms are relatively small compared to the leaves. Fertilizing seems to enhance this relative difference, yielding 10-in. (25-cm) leaves and 4-in. (10-cm) blooms. I think there are better whites for medium and large pools, such as *N.* 'Marliacea Albida', *N.* 'Perry's Double White', *N.* 'Perry's White Star', *N.* 'Perry's White Wonder', *N.* 'Queen of Whites', *N.* 'Venus', *N.* 'Virginalis'.

Nymphaea odorata Aiton

Fragrant waterlily

Native to eastern North America from Newfoundland south through Florida, west to northeastern Texas, Kansas, Michigan, and Indiana; also Mexico, West Indies, and the Guianas

Plates 129, 130

CHARACTERISTICS. Day blooming, odorata rhizome, fairly free flowering when established.

FLOWERS. Petal color: White, outer petals occasionally develop pink blush (*RHS* 155C; blush, 65D or lighter). Sepal color: White or pale pink (*RHS* 155C, 65D or lighter). Anther color: Yellow (*RHS* 3A). Stamen color: Yellow. Flower shape: Stellate. Flower size: 2–4.5 in. (5–11 cm). Fragrance: Delightful. Number of petals: 24–32. Number of sepals: 4 or 5.

LEAVES. Color: Top, green; underside, varies widely from bronze to pink, purple, red. Some leaves wider than long, some round; sinus usually wide open. Leaf size: 6–8 in. (15–20 cm). Leaf spread: 3–4 ft. (0.9–1.2 m). Stem color: Usually green or greenish purple. No pubescence on peduncle or petiole.

COMMENTS. This species has considerable variation. In some ponds in southern Georgia flower petals are narrow; in Maine petals may be very broad. Likewise, in some ponds in Georgia sepals are quite pink, while in Maine some flowers have pink at the base of all the petals. Leaves also vary considerably. Some southern Georgia specimens have brilliant red undersides, while bronze is the predominant color elsewhere. Some tiny plants growing naturally in Georgia develop flowers only 2–3 in. (5–8 cm) in diameter, yet flowers develop twice that size when planted in rich soil at a nursery. *Nymphaea odorata* is suitable for any size pool but must form a colony of rhizomes before blooming freely.

Nymphaea odorata var. *gigantea* (Tricker) Conard

Native to Florida, Oklahoma, Missouri, Texas, Louisiana, Cuba, Mexico, and the Guianas; reported in eastern states as far north as Delaware

PLATE 131

COMMENTS. Flowers, are much larger than the type, 6–8 in. (15–20 cm) across. Blooms are also more double, with 36–38 petals. Leaves average much larger, 11–12 in. (28–30 cm) across, with leaf sinus two-thirds to three-fourths closed, and leaf spread is likewise much larger at 5–7 ft. (1.5–2.1 m). This variety is especially suited to natural ponds. It can be used in a large pool if planted in a large container. This waterlily varies considerably; occasionally a plant develops blooms similar to many tropicals, with long, lanceolate petals, sepals that fold down, and blooms held 6–8 in. (15–20 cm) above the water. *Hopatcong* is a Native American name for this plant.

Nymphaea odorata var. *minor* Sims

Native habitat limited to several shallow ponds in New Jersey

COMMENTS. Flowers are pure white, only 2–3 in. (5–8 cm) in diameter, and very fragrant. Leaves are 2–5 in. (5–13 cm) across, green on top and dark red on underside. Peduncles are deep reddish brown. This is an interesting plant for small pools or for the collector.

Nymphaea odorata var. *rosea* Pursh

Native to the northeastern and north-central United States

COMMENTS. Flowers are 5–6 in. (13–15 cm) in diameter and very fragrant. Petals and sepals are a beautiful clear pink. Leaves are round with an open sinus. Leaf color is initially reddish purple on top, turning to green with age. Leaf undersides are a very brilliant red. Leaves are 8–9 in. (20–23 cm) in diameter with a leaf spread of 4–5 ft. (1.2–1.5 m). Stems are green with light fuzz on petiole but none on peduncle. This variety makes a fine plant for medium and large pools when planted in a large container, but many cultivars now available would give more blooms.

Nymphaea tuberosa Paine

Native to Ontario and Quebec and west of the Appalachian Mountains from Lake Champlain west through the Great Lakes to Minnesota and south to Arkansas; also found growing in New Jersey and Maryland

PLATE 132

CHARACTERISTICS. Day blooming, tuberosa rhizome, fairly free flowering, very fast propagator.

FLOWERS. Petal color: Pure white (*RHS* 155D). Sepal color: Pure white (*RHS* 155D). Anther color: Yellow (*RHS* 3A). Stamen color: Yellow. Flower shape: Cuplike. Flower size: 4–9 in. (10–23 cm). Fragrance: Slight. Number of petals: 27–31. Number of sepals: 4.

LEAVES. Color: Top, green, new leaves purplish; underside, green. Leaf round or wider than long; sinus usually a wide-open V; lobes may overlap along the first 0.75 in. (2 cm). Leaf size: 7–10 in. (18–25 cm). Leaf spread: 4–6 ft. (1.2–1.8 m). Stem color: Petiole green, striped brownish purple; peduncle green. Fine fuzz on petiole.

COMMENTS. *Nymphaea tuberosa* is an interesting species for the collector. A unique feature is a pink spot about the size of a pinhead right in the middle of the stigma. This is most prominent in the first-day flower. *Nymphaea* 'Perry's Pink', a chance seedling with probable *N. tuberosa* genes, has a similar red dot in the same place. If planted in a large container *N. tuberosa* could be used in a large pool. Many freer-blooming white cultivars are now available for the water garden.

Section *Xanthantha* Caspary

Section *Xanthantha* includes only one species, *Nymphaea mexicana*. Flowers are yellow, opening about noon and closing in late afternoon. Floating new leaves have blotches of reddish brown. The upright rhizomes are usually short; long white stolons develop laterally all summer and send up new plants like a strawberry plant. In autumn tiny white runners are sent straight downward from these stolons and tiny clusters of banana-shaped structures, about 1–2 in. (2.5–5 cm) in length, form about 6 in. (15 cm) under the main plant. In the spring, these structures form new plants. This species tends to be invasive when grown in a natural pond. A variant, which produces larger flowers than the type, has been identified in the Cape Canaveral area of Florida.

Nymphaea mexicana Zuccarini

Syn. *Nymphaea mexicana* No. 1

Banana waterlily

Native to Mexico, South Carolina, Georgia, Florida, along the Gulf of Mexico to Texas

PLATE 133

CHARACTERISTICS. Semihardy, day blooming, upright rhizome produces runners (stolons), fairly free flowering.

FLOWERS. Petal color: Deep yellow (*RHS* 2B). Sepal color: Greenish yellow (*RHS* 9A). Anther color: Deep yellow (*RHS* 9A). Stamen color: Deep yellow. Flower shape: Cuplike then stellate. Flower size: 3–4.5 in. (8–11 cm). Fragrance: Very sweet. Number of petals: 20–23. Number of sepals: 4.

LEAVES. Color: Top, green, new leaves olive green, heavily splashed purple or reddish brown; underside, bronzy red, small purple specks. Leaf egg-shaped, slightly serrated; sinus usually open. Leaf size: 7.5–9 in. (19–23 cm). Leaf spread: 3.5–4 ft. (1.1–1.2 m). Stem color: Greenish yellow. No pubescence on peduncle or petiole.

COMMENTS. Flowers do not open until midday. *Nymphaea mexicana* No. 1 is hardy in zones 6–10, semihardy in zones 3–5. It is parent to many yellow and orange changeable hardies and is a desirable waterlily, although very difficult to eradicate once planted in a natural pond. Its invasive qualities can be checked by planting in a container in a concrete or liner pond.

Nymphaea mexicana f. *canaveralensis* Frase

Syn. *Nymphaea mexicana* No. 2, *N. mexicana* 'Cape Canaveral'

Native to the Cape Canaveral area of Florida

PLATE 134

COMMENTS. Its hardiness is the same as that of *N. mexicana* No. 1. The principal difference between this and the type is the larger flower, 6–8 in. (15–20 cm) across with 21–23 petals. Blooms are a very deep yellow, opening at midday and lasting two days. A novelty for the collector or hybridizer, this waterlily is beautiful when grown in a large container and properly fertilized. In a small planter, with less space and nourishment, blooms are smaller and flower color weaker. This plant is a parent of *N.* 'Yellow Sensation' and a probable parent of *N.* 'Sunrise'. I recommend this plant for the collector or hybridizer with a medium or large pool, but *Nymphaea mexicana* f. *canaveralensis* is unsuitable for the natural pond as it can take over and become a pest. By the summer of 2003, the name *Nymphaea mexicana* 'Cape Canaveral' was already accepted and being used (sometimes with *mexicana* dropped).

CHAPTER 6

Hardy Waterlily Cultivars

ONE HYBRIDIZER of hardy waterlilies in particular deserves recognition for many of the fine cultivars available today, Joseph Bory Latour-Marliac. He was born in 1830 at Granges, Lot-et-Garonne, France, and did most of his hybridizing work between 1880 and 1910 at Temple-sur-Lot, about 80 miles (130 km) east of Bordeaux. After his death in 1911, his son-in-law, Maurice Laydeker, continued operating the Latour-Marliac Nursery. Two generations of Laydekers succeeded Maurice until the Latour-Marliac Nursery was finally sold to Stapeley Water Gardens of Nantwich, Cheshire, England, in 1991. More than 100 Marliac varieties resulted from Latour-Marliac's work. Many of these are still grown and sold by aquatic nurseries worldwide, and they still rank among the best varieties currently available.

The term *hardy*, when used to describe waterlily cultivars, generally means that the plant will survive winter temperatures as long as the rhizome itself does not freeze. All hardy waterlilies are day blooming. Many of the finest descend from *Nymphaea alba* var. *rubra*, the Swedish red waterlily, native to ponds and two cold lakes (Lakes Fayer and Fagertarn) in Nerike, Hammar Parish, Sweden. Descendants include red-, pink-, white-, yellow-, and orange-flowering cultivars. In the southern United States some of the hardy waterlilies, particularly the red- and pink-flowered, do not thrive, probably because of their Swedish ancestry. Nearly all hardy waterlilies are perennials except for some that are killed by crown rot in northern states and Europe or that cannot take intense heat.

The term *changeable* indicates that flower color changes after the bloom opens, usually from light to darker shades of the same hue. In first-day flowers, opening time varies depending mainly on air temperatures. Warm days initiate flower opening earlier than cooler ones. The flowers of some cultivars, however, such as *Nymphaea* 'Helvola', and the species *N. tetragona* and *N. mexicana* Nos. 1 and 2, do not open until midday. The first-day flower contains a pool of nectar (slightly sweet to the taste), topping the pistil in the flower center. This nectar serves to attract pollinating insects. Small insects such as sweat bees (*Halictus* spp.) or even honeybees (*Apis mellifera*) sometimes drown in this pool of nectar. The carpellary appendages (lacking in *N. gigantea*) encircling the nectar pool are erect. Frequently, first-day flowers do not open completely and remain somewhat cup-shaped.

In second-day flowers, the pool of nectar disappears. Any nectar not drunk by visiting insects has evaporated. Carpellary appendages turn inward, as do the stamens and inner rows of staminodes. Pollen on the anthers is now ripe, and pollen on the outer rows of staminodes may or may not be ripe. Bees can pick up this ripe pollen and carry it to a first-day flower. Fertilization will occur on species flowers or the rare seed-producing cultivar. Although bees consume most of this protein-laden pollen, enough is carried on their bodies to serve fertilization.

In third-day flowers, the stamens and staminodes circling the flower center bend into the center as much as possible. In the case of changeable lilies, this is the day when petals reach their deepest color. Only a slight darkening can be noticed in sepal color. Third-day flowers usually float or are held slightly above the water.

With few exceptions, the fourth-day flower does not open and sinks down into the water. In species flowers and seed-producing cultivars, the seeds start development inside the ovaries if the flower was fertilized. In other situations, the fourth-day flower sinks into the water and becomes a jellylike mass, disintegrating in a few days.

Some cultivars will not bloom freely or blooming will be interrupted when air temperatures remain in the 80–90°F (27–32°C) range for prolonged periods. For example, *Nymphaea* 'William Falconer' is a free bloomer in zones 3–5, but when grown in zones 6 and 7, it stops blooming completely in midsummer and resumes blooming in autumn when cooler weather arrives. When grown in zones 8–10 *Nymphaea* 'William Falconer' will produce few blooms to no blooms at all. Other cultivars unsuitable for zones 8–10 include *N.* 'Atropurpurea', *N.* 'Chrysantha', *N.* 'Conqueror', *N.* 'Ellisiana', *N.* 'Gloire du Temple-sur-Lot', *N.* 'Gonnère', *N.* 'Helvola', *N.* 'Laydekeri Purpurata', *N.* 'Maurice Laydeker', and *N.* 'Norma Gedye'.

Another climatic effect resulting from high summer temperatures is petal "burning" or "melting." During hot days when summer temperatures reach 85–90°F or more (29–32°C or more), flower petals may blacken. Blooming is not necessarily interrupted and the burning of the petals stops with cooler weather. Some of the cultivars most susceptible to petal burning are *Nymphaea* 'Atropurpurea', *N.* 'Conqueror', *N.* 'Perry's Red Beauty' (slightly susceptible), *N.* 'Perry's Wildfire', and *N.* 'William Falconer'. *Nymphaea* 'Atropurpurea' (in zones 8–10) and *N.* 'William Falconer' (in zones 6–10) can be expected to have their blooms interrupted due to high temperatures along with petal burning.

This chapter includes a full description of hardy waterlily cultivars as noted in nursery catalogs from around the world (see Sources for Plants and Equipment at the end of the book). Plants are listed alphabetically by published name, followed by any synonyms. Next, the author and year of introduction are given, when known. Common names, if any, follow. Some of these cultivars are my own introductions, developing largely from work carried out in North Carolina (zone 6b). I have been told that the summer climate there is very similar to that of the area in southern France where Marliac did much of his work. Although many of my introductions resulted from hand-pollination, others are the result of natural (bee) crosses; it is thought that many of Marliac's originations developed from bee crosses, too.

"Characteristics" includes type of rhizome; the five rhizome types are described in chapter 5. "Stamen color" refers to the color found on the basal portion of the stamen, also known as the filament. As hardy waterlilies also have staminodes, located just outside the stamens, my reference to stamens also includes the base portion of the staminodes. "Leaf size" refers either to the diameter of the leaf of a mature plant or to the measurements of its length × width, in that order. "Leaf spread" refers to the diameter of the area on the water's surface covered by the leaves of the mature plant.

Plant hardy waterlily cultivars only when the water temperature reaches 60°F (16°C) or above. Refer to the hardiness zone maps at the end of the book and follow this general planting timetable:

In North America and Europe

Zone 10	any time of year
Zone 9	March–September
Zone 8	April–September
Zone 7	April–August
Zone 6	mid April–August
Zone 5	late April/early May–mid August
Zone 4	mid May–early August

Nymphaea 'Alba Plenissima'

Formerly 'Hermine' No. 2

Parentage unknown

CHARACTERISTICS. Tuberosa rhizome, moderately free flowering.

FLOWERS. Petal color: White (*RHS* 155C). Sepal color: Greenish white (*RHS* 145D). Anther color: Yellow (*RHS* 10A). Stamen color: Yellow. Flower shape: Cuplike then stellate. Flower size: 4.5–5 in. (11–13 cm). Fragrance: Pleasant. Number of petals: 28 or 29. Number of sepals: 4.

LEAVES. Color: Top, green, newest leaves bronzy; underside, bronzy purple. Leaves nearly round; lobes usually overlap sinus or sinus may be open 1 in. (2.5 cm) or wide open. Generally there is a tip at the end of each leaf lobe. Leaf size: 6–7 in. (15–18 cm). Leaf spread: 4 ft. (1.2 m). Stem color: Reddish brown. Thick fuzz on peduncle and petiole.

COMMENTS. This is a small- to medium-growing tuberosa best suited to small or medium pools.

Blooms are not plentiful until a colony of several plants has formed in a large planter. *Nymphaea* 'Alba Plenissima' tends to develop an abundance of leaves.

Nymphaea 'Albatross'
Marliac 1910

Parentage unknown

CHARACTERISTICS. Marliac rhizome, very free flowering.

FLOWERS. Petal color: White (*RHS* 155C). Sepal color: White (*RHS* 155C). Anther color: Yellow (*RHS* 6B). Stamen color: Yellow. Flower shape: Stellate. Flower size: 6–8 in. (15–20 cm). Fragrance: None. Number of petals: 29 or 30. Number of sepals: 5.

LEAVES. Color: Top, olive green with a few purple blotches; underside, red. Leaf round; sinus half to two-thirds open. Leaf size: 8–10 in. (20–25 cm). Leaf spread: 3–5 ft. (0.9–1.5 m). Stem color: Yellowish. A few very fine hairs on peduncle and petiole.

COMMENTS. Pointed petal tips distinguish this waterlily from the cultivar with rounded petal tips that is sometimes mislabeled "Albatross" in European nurseries. The true *N.* 'Albatross' is a fine plant for any size pool.

Nymphaea 'Almost Black'
Slocum 1994

Nymphaea 'Perry's Fire Opal' × *N.* 'Blue Beauty'

PLATE 135

CHARACTERISTICS. Free flowering, Marliac rhizome, perennial.

FLOWERS. Petal color: Color varies from nearly black in center to redder in outer petals. It becomes darker as flower ages. Sepal color: Inner, pinkish red; outer, greenish brown frequently with wide pink margin. Anther color: Inner, dark yellow; outer, orange-yellow. Stamen color: Orange to red (outer). Flower shape: Cuplike becoming flatter with age. Flower size: 5–6 in. (12.7–15.2 cm). Fragrance: Pleasant. Number of petals: 38–40. Number of sepals: 4.

LEAVES. Color: Top, newest leaves are purple and soon turn to green; underside, reddish purple with prominent green veins. Leaves are nearly round. Sinus is usually closed but may be partly open. Leaf size: About 8 in. (20.3 cm). Leaf spread: 3.5–5 ft. (1–1.5 m). Stem color: peduncle brownish, petiole greenish brown. Short fuzz on all stems.

COMMENTS. *Nymphaea* 'Almost Black' is a nearly unbelievable waterlily—I hybridized a tropical waterlily with an odorata and came up with a Marliac rhizome. (I made a somewhat similar cross in hybridizing *N.* 'Black Princess' and produced a Marliac rhizome as well.) Some skeptics said it could not be done; however, one reason I was able to do it may be because *N.* 'Perry's Fire Opal' already had some tropical ancestry in it put there by me in 1987. (I was able to cross *N.* 'Peter Slocum' × *N.* 'Director George T. Moore'.) *Nymphaea* 'Almost Black' has one bad feature: its center petals burn during really hot weather in the Deep South. *Nymphaea* 'Almost Black' receives lots of praise from visitors to Perry's Water Gardens. I highly recommend it, except in the southern states, for any size pool.

Nymphaea 'Amabilis'
Syn. 'Pink Marvel'

Latour-Marliac Nursery 1921

Parentage unknown

PLATE 136

CHARACTERISTICS. Marliac rhizome, fairly free flowering.

FLOWERS. Petal color: Medium pink, tips light pink (*RHS* 63D; tips, 65D). Sepal color: Silvery pink (*RHS* 65C,D). Anther color: Deep yellow (*RHS* 13A). Stamen color: Deep yellow. Flower shape: Stellate. Flower size: 6–7.5 in. (15–19 cm). Fragrance: Slight to medium. Number of petals: 20–23. Number of sepals: 4.

LEAVES. Color: Top, green, young leaves reddish purple; underside, light green, reddish perimeter. Leaf nearly round; sinus wide open. Leaf size: 9.5 in. (24 cm). Leaf spread: 5–7.5 ft. (1.5–2.3 m). Stem color: Bronze to red. Fine hairs on peduncle and petiole.

COMMENTS. *Nymphaea* 'Amabilis', with its very large flowers, is a fine waterlily for medium or large pools.

Nymphaea 'American Star'
Slocum 1985

Chance seedling of *N.* 'Rose Arey'

PLATE 137

CHARACTERISTICS. Odorata rhizome, fairly free flowering.

FLOWERS. Petal color: Rich salmon-pink, tips

lighter pink (*RHS* 62B; tips, 62C). Sepal color: Rich salmon-pink, border greenish (*RHS* 62C; border, 143C). Anther color: Yellow (*RHS* 20B). Stamen color: Inner rows yellow; outer rows pinkish orange. Flower shape: Stellate. Flower size: 6–7 in. (15–18 cm). Fragrance: Pleasant. Number of petals: 30 or 31. Number of sepals: 4.

LEAVES. Color: Top, green, new leaves purple-green; underside, red, prominent green V along midvein on new leaves. Leaves round; lobes cover three-fourths of sinus. Leaf size: 10–11 in. (25–28 cm). Leaf spread: 4–5 ft. (1.2–1.5 m). Stem color: Purple. Peduncle and petiole stems very fuzzy.

COMMENTS. This waterlily, which has very long, narrow petals, was named by Ray Davies of Stapeley Water Gardens, England, while visiting the seedling beds at Perry's Water Gardens (zone 6b). It was introduced by Stapeley Water Gardens. For best results plant *Nymphaea* 'American Star' in a large planter and allow a colony of several rhizomes to develop. It will then bloom fairly well. I recommend this plant for medium or large pools and natural ponds.

Nymphaea 'Andreana'

Marliac 1895

Nymphaea alba var. *rubra* × *N. mexicana*

CHARACTERISTICS. Upright rhizome, very free flowering.

FLOWERS. Petal color: Inner petals reddish orange then rusty orange; outer petals medium pale yellow then peach-yellow. My stock came from Bennett's Water Gardens in England. However, Latour-Marliac Water Gardens (now owned by Stapeley Water Gardens) claims that the color of bloom is all red. (*RHS* inner, first day, orange-red 34B; third day, red 42B; outer, first day, 19B; third day, 41D). Sepal color: Yellowish (*RHS* 19B). Anther color: Golden yellow (*RHS* 19A). Stamen color: Deep yellow. Flower shape: Cuplike then peony-style. Flower size: 5–7 in. (13–18 cm). Fragrance: Very slight, if any. Number of petals: 20–22. Number of sepals: 4.

LEAVES. Color: Top, green, dark reddish brown blotches; underside, green, numerous dark reddish brown spots and blotches. Leaf nearly round; sinus wide open. Leaf size: 7–8 in. (18–20 cm). Leaf spread: 3–4 ft. (0.9–1.2 m). Stem color: Green, brown when young. No pubescence on peduncle or petiole.

COMMENTS. *Nymphaea* 'Andreana' is frequently confused with *N.* 'Aurora', which it resembles very closely. The main difference is *N.* 'Andreana' has larger blooms, larger leaves, and larger leaf spread. 'Andreana' is one of the choicest of the changeable hardies and I recommend it for any size pool.

Nymphaea 'Anna Epple'

Epple 1970

Parentage unknown

PLATE 138

CHARACTERISTICS. Free flowering, Marliac rhizome, perennial.

FLOWERS. Petal color: Medium pink (*RHS* 13B). Sepal color: Inner: medium pink (*RHS* 65A); outer, dark green (*RHS* 138B) Anther color: Inner, yellow (*RHS* 13B). Stamen color: yellow (*RHS* 13A). Flower shape: Cuplike. Flower size: 5–6 in. (12–15 cm). Fragrance: Very slight. Number of petals: 24–28. Number of sepals: 4.

LEAVES. Color: Top, olive green (*RHS* 146A); underside, reddish brown (*RHS* 185A) and green center (*RHS* 193A). Round leaf; sinus open. Leaf size: 6–10 in. (15–25 cm). Leaf spread: 40–48 in. (100–120 cm).

COMMENTS BY ERNST EPPLE. The preferred depth of water is 24–28 in. (60–80 cm). I recommend *Nymphaea* 'Anna Epple' for small or medium ponds.

Nymphaea 'Apple Blossom Pink'

Slocum 1988

Chance seedling of *N.* 'Perry's Pink'

PLATE 139

CHARACTERISTICS. Odorata rhizome, fairly free flowering.

FLOWERS. Petal color: Shell pink (*RHS* 56D or paler). Sepal color: Shell pink (*RHS* 56D or paler). Anther color: Deep yellow (*RHS* 13B). Stamen color: Deep yellow. Flower shape: Peony-style. Flower size: 7–9 in. (18–23 cm). Fragrance: Delightful. Number of petals: 38–40. Number of sepals: 4.

LEAVES. Color: Top, green; underside, pinkish brown. Leaf round; sinus an open V. Leaf size: 10–11 in. (25–28 cm). Leaf spread: 6–7 ft. (1.8–2.1 m). Stem color: Brown. No pubescence on peduncle or petiole.

COMMENTS. Blooms are quite double. *Nymphaea* 'Apple Blossom Pink' is a volunteer seedling from one of the clay-bottom propagating ponds at Perry's Water Gardens. Due to its remarkable beauty and huge size, I recommend it for medium or large pools or even the natural pond. Note, however, that in the natural pond it may travel 2 ft. (0.6 m) or more per year. I recommend planting in a container at least 24 × 24 × 12 in. (60 × 60 × 30 cm) for optimum performance.

Nymphaea 'Arc-en-Ciel'

Marliac 1901

Parentage unknown

PLATE 140

CHARACTERISTICS. Odorata rhizome, fairly free flowering, beautiful leaves.

FLOWERS. Petal color: Usually shell pink on first day, white or nearly white by second day (*RHS* first day, 36D; second day, 155B). Sepal color: Medium pink then off-white (*RHS* First day, 36C; second day 56D). Anther color: Deep yellow (*RHS* 12A). Stamen color: Deep yellow. Flower shape: Stellate, long narrow petals and sepals. Flower size: 5–6 in. (13–15 cm). Fragrance: Pronounced sweet scent on larger blooms. Number of petals: 18–24. Number of sepals: 4.

LEAVES. Color: Top, olive green, frequently splashed yellow, cream, pink, and even red radiating from center or large pink or reddish areas; underside, reddish brown. Leaf round; sinus wide open. Leaf size: 9.5 in. (24 cm). Leaf spread: 4–5 ft. (1.2–1.5 m). Stem color: Green; some peduncles display prominent, light yellow stripes. No pubescence on peduncle or petiole.

COMMENTS. *Nymphaea* 'Arc-en-Ciel' has magnificent leaves and is a wonderful plant for the collector. Some leaf colorations are truly beautiful and no two leaves are exactly alike. I recommend this cultivar for medium and large pools.

Nymphaea 'Arethusa'

Syn. 'Bateau'

Marliac, date unknown

Nymphaea alba var. *rubra* × *N. mexicana*

CHARACTERISTICS. Marliac rhizome, free flowering.

FLOWERS. Petal color: Dark red center then deep purplish red; outer petals lighter then deepening (*RHS* center, 59B; third day, 59A; outer, 64D; third day, 59D). Sepal color: Nearly white then rosy pink (*RHS* 155A then 65C). Anther color: Burnt orange (*RHS* 32C). Stamen color: Orange-red. Flower shape: Globular. Flower size: 5–5.5 in. (13–14 cm). Fragrance: Slight. Number of petals: 27. Number of sepals: 4.

LEAVES. Color: Top, green, blotched purple, newest leaves purplish; underside, red. Leaves round; sinus a wide-open V. Leaf size: 8 in. (20 cm). Leaf spread: 3–4 ft. (0.9–1.2 m). Stem color: Red to reddish brown. Some fuzz on peduncle and petiole.

COMMENTS. Flowers are more globular than cuplike, in a shape similar to that of the cultivar *Nymphaea* 'Marliacea Rubra Punctata'. Magnificent leaves and beautiful flowers make this waterlily an excellent choice for any size pool.

Nymphaea 'Atropurpurea'

Marliac 1901

Parentage unknown

PLATE 141

CHARACTERISTICS. Marliac rhizome, free flowering except in very hot climates.

FLOWERS. Petal color: Deep red, deepening each day, occasional flecking in tips (*RHS* 61A and darker). Sepal color: Deep pink then pinkish red; veins darker (*RHS* 63 then 64A; veins, 61A). Anther color: Very deep yellow (*RHS* 13A). Stamen color: Burnt orange. Flower shape: Round, flat, then stellate. Flower size: 7–8 in. (18–20 cm). Fragrance: Very slight. Number of petals: 30–33. Number of sepals: 4.

LEAVES. Color: Top, green, new leaves purple; underside, purple, green V along midvein. Leaf round; sinus a very large V. Leaf size: 9–10 in. (23–25 cm). Leaf spread: 4 ft. (1.2 m). Stem color: Peduncle, purple; petiole green. No pubescence on peduncle or petiole.

COMMENTS. With its deep, rich red petals and sepals, *Nymphaea* 'Atropurpurea' is extremely striking. Center petals on second-day flowers sometimes burn, however, when this plant is grown in hot summer climates (comparable to zones 7–10). Also, when grown in zone 7 this cultivar blooms all summer; in zone 9 blooming slows in the summer. I recommend this waterlily for medium and large pools.

Nymphaea 'Attorney Elrod'

Strawn 1986

Parentage unknown

CHARACTERISTICS. Free flowering, Marliac rhizome, perennial.

FLOWERS. Petal color: Bright red with intermixing white (interior petals) and the opposite coloration on outer petals. Sepal color: Inner, light yellowish green that becomes dark olive at tips; outer, dark green. Anther color: Inner, dark reddish orange; outer, dark red with yellow tips. Stamen color: Bright yellow with reddish orange. Flower shape: Globular. Flower size: 3–4 in. (7.5–10 cm). Fragrance: Yes. Number of petals: 25–28. Number of sepals: 6 or 7.

LEAVES. Color: Top, immature leaves are a deep green with a burgundy tint and outlay on the margins; mature leaves are green with slightly lighter yellowish green markings in random areas; underside, light bronze brown that transitions into light green at the midvein. Round leaf with open sinus. Leaf size: 5–6 in. (12.5–15 cm). Leaf spread: 6–12 ft. (1.8–3.6 m). Stem color: Light brown, almost tan. No pubescence on peduncle or petiole.

COMMENTS BY LILYPONS WATER GARDENS. Joe Tomocik of Denver Botanic Gardens said that he has had Nymphaea 'Attorney Elrod' for about 16–18 years, so the longevity of this plant is fabulous. Bruce McLane of Florida Aquatic Nurseries suggests that it can be used in a small container garden because of its tight Marliac root system.

Nymphaea 'Attraction'

Marliac 1910

Parentage unknown

PLATE 142

CHARACTERISTICS. Marliac rhizome, free flowering.

FLOWERS. Petal color: Inner petals deep garnet red; outer petals lighter (RHS inner, 64A; outer, 64B). Sepal color: White, striped pink; pink base developing on older flowers (RHS 155C; stripes, 64D; base, 65A). Anther color: Golden yellow (RHS 19A). Stamen color: Glowing orange. Flower shape: Cup-

like then stellate. Flower size: 6–8 in. (15–20 cm). Fragrance: Very slight. Number of petals: 26–28. Number of sepals: 4 or 5, usually 5.

LEAVES. Color: Top, green, new leaves light bronze; underside, green, light bronze perimeter. Leaf oval; lobes overlap at sinus, one lobe usually raised. Leaf size: 10–12 in. (25–30 cm). Leaf spread: 4–5 ft. (1.2–1.5 m). Stem color: Purplish. No pubescence on peduncle or petiole.

COMMENTS. This cultivar is among the largest of the red hardy waterlilies and one of the best red hardy cultivars to use for cut flowers. Inner petals are subject to burn and blackening on hot days, however. This waterlily is also subject to crown rot.

Nymphaea 'Aurora'

Marliac 1895

Probably N. alba var. rubra × N. mexicana

PLATE 143

CHARACTERISTICS. Upright rhizome, very free flowering.

FLOWERS. Petal color: First day, yellow-apricot, darker center; second day, orange-red, slightly flecked; third day, deep burgundy-red, slightly flecked (RHS first day, 24D and 29A; second day, 35B; third day, 47A). Sepal color: Creamy white, flushing pink and white (RHS 155A; second and third days, 55C). Anther color: Yellow then orange (RHS 13A then 23A). Stamen color: Glowing, golden orange, especially on second and third days. Flower shape: Cuplike, later flattening. Flower size: 4–4.5 in. (10–11 cm). Fragrance: Very slight. Number of petals: 24 or 25. Number of sepals: 4 or 5.

LEAVES. Color: Top, green, new leaves blotched purple; underside, light purple, many small red-purple mottles. Leaf slightly longer than wide; sinus a wide-open V. Leaf size: 6–6.5 in. (15–16 cm). Leaf spread: 3 ft. (0.9 m). Stem color: Bright green. No pubescence on peduncle or petiole.

COMMENTS. I think Nymphaea 'Aurora' is one of the most beautiful waterlilies ever created. It has the widest color range of any changeable until late summer, and flowers stay open very late in the day. In late summer, new blooms open orange in North Carolina. In spring and most of the summer, new blooms are yellow. This waterlily is ideal for the tub garden or small to medium pool.

Nymphaea 'Barbara Dobbins'

Strawn 1996

Nymphaea odorata × *N. mexicana*

CHARACTERISTICS. Nonviviparous, odorata rhizome, free flowering, perennial.

FLOWERS. Petal color: Soft yellow blushed with soft pink; inner petals shade to apricot. Sepal color: Inner, creamy white, medium green tips; outer, green with dark green tips, soft pink on edges. Anther color: Inner, bright yellow; outer, bright yellow. Stamen color: Bright yellow. Flower shape: Stellate. Flower size: 4–6 in. (10–15 cm). Fragrance: Pleasant. Number of petals: 30–32. Number of sepals: 4.

LEAVES. Color: Top, new leaves have faint mottling on green; underside, light red-purple with noticeable flecking; young leaves more green than red. Leaf nearly round with convolutions; sinus slightly open. Leaf size: 8–10 in. (20–25 cm). Leaf spread: 5–7 ft. (1.5–2.1 m). Stem color: Brown. No pubescence on peduncle or petiole.

COMMENTS BY DEAN MCGEE. This hybrid has a strikingly unique blend of color, with a mixture of pink, yellow, and apricot colors, and stands out as an exceptional bloomer. Flowers stand 4–6 in. (10–15 cm) above the water.

COMMENTS BY PERRY SLOCUM. *Nymphaea* 'Barbara Dobbins' is truly a beautiful waterlily, but, after a year of doing well here in North Carolina, it died from crown rot. I recommend it for the southern states.

Nymphaea 'Berit Strawn'

Strawn 1993

Nymphaea 'Rembrandt' × *N. mexicana*

PLATE 144

CHARACTERISTICS. Nonviviparous, upright rhizome, free flowering, perennial.

FLOWERS. Petal color: Deep peach. Sepal color: Inner, greenish white with faint pink at base; outer, dark green. Anther color: Inner, bright yellow; outer, bright yellow. Stamen color: Bright yellow. Flower shape: Cuplike. Flower size: 3–4 in. (7.5–10 cm). Fragrance: Pleasant. Number of petals: 22–24. Number of sepals: 4.

LEAVES. Color: Top, dark green with heavy flecking and faint mottling; underside, reddish purple with heavy flecking, newer leaves have almost bronze color. Leaf slightly ovate; sinus open. Leaf size: 4–5 in. (10–13 cm). Leaf spread: 2–4 ft. (0.6–1.2 m). Stem color: Bronze. Pubescence on peduncle and petiole.

COMMENTS BY DEAN MCGEE. This cultivar provides a great combination of unique pink-peach blossoms with leaves uncharacteristic of hardy waterlilies. Excellent for small tub gardens or medium ponds.

COMMENTS BY PERRY SLOCUM. *Nymphaea* 'Berit Strawn' is a great waterlily for southern states in United States, but in North Carolina it died from crown rot.

Nymphaea 'Bernice Ikins'

Strawn, date unknown

Parentage unknown

CHARACTERISTICS. Nonviviparous, odorata rhizome, free flowering, perennial.

FLOWERS. Petal color: Deep fuchsia. Sepal color: Inner, deep fuchsia, dark green on outer edges; outer, green with deep pink on edges. Anther color: Inner, golden yellow; outer, fuchsia with golden yellow anthers. Stamen color: Golden yellow. Flower shape: Cuplike, then stellate. Flower size: 4–5 in. (10–12.5 cm). Fragrance: Strong. Number of petals: 40–42. Number of sepals: 4

LEAVES. Color: Top, leaves vary in color between green, plum, and deep plum; underside, reddish plum color with green veins stemming from peduncle. Nearly round; sinus open. Leaf size: 8–10 in. (20–25 cm). Leaf spread: 5–7 ft. (1.5–2.1 m). Stem color: Brown. No pubescence on peduncle or petiole.

COMMENTS BY DEAN MCGEE. *Nymphaea* 'Bernice Ikins' gives an exceptional display of intense, deep fuchsia color with double flowers. This very large plant makes for an eye-catching centerpiece, and it is one of Kirk Strawn's best hybrids.

Nymphaea 'Berthold'

Berthold 1985

Nymphaea 'Froebeli' × *N.* 'Bee Pod'

PLATE 145

CHARACTERISTICS. Very free flowering, Marliac rhizome, perennial.

FLOWERS. Petal color: Light pink, fading with

age. Anther color: Inner, golden orange; outer, dark green. Stamen color: Golden yellow. Flower shape: Cup, with wide petals. Flower size: 4 in. (10 cm). Fragrance: Faint. Number of petals: 19. Number of sepals: 4.

LEAVES. Color: Top, green; underside, reddish brown, green center with green rib. Leaf slightly oval; sinus wide open. Leaf size: 7 in. (18 cm). Leaf spread: 24 in. (61 cm). Stem color: Light green. No pubescence on peduncle or petiole.

COMMENTS BY REG HENLEY. In habit and general flowering ability, *Nymphaea* 'Berthold could be a pink version of *N*. 'Froebeli', flowering constantly throughout the summer months.

Nymphaea 'Betsy Sakata'
Strawn 1997
Nymphaea 'Princess Elizabeth' × *N. mexicana*

CHARACTERISTICS. Nonviviparous, odorata rhizome, very free flowering, perennial.

FLOWERS. Petal color: Light yellow throughout with very faint pink on outer petals; deeper yellow toward inner petals. Sepal color: Inner, greenish yellow; outer, medium green, blushed pink on some edges Anther color: Inner, bright yellow; outer, bright yellow. Stamen color: Bright yellow. Flower shape: Stellate, then wide open. Flower size: 5–6 in. (12.5–15 cm). Fragrance: Strong. Number of petals: 28–30. Number of sepals: 4.

LEAVES. Color: Top, medium green; underside, light plum colored with moderate flecking; darker plum color toward outer edges. Leaf nearly round; sinus slightly open. Leaf size: 8–10 in. (20–25.5 cm). Leaf spread: 6–8 ft. (1.8–2.4 m). Stem color: Light green. No pubescence on peduncle or petiole.

COMMENTS BY DEAN MCGEE. Named after International Waterlily and Water Gardening Society Hall of Fame member Betsy Sakata, this unique waterlily has large soft yellow blossoms that open wide for a beautiful display. Flowers stand 3–4 in. (7.5–10 cm) above the water; excellent for a large pond setting.

Nymphaea 'Black Princess'
Slocum 1995
Nymphaea 'Perry's Fire Opal' × *N*. 'Pamela'
PLATE 146

CHARACTERISTICS. Free flowering, Marliac rhizome, perennial.

FLOWERS. Petal color: Dark red petals first day; second day inner petals turn much darker; by third day all inner petals are almost black. Sepal color: Reddish purple. Anther color: Inner, dark green; outer, dark green. Stamen color: Purple. Flower shape: Cuplike changing to peony-shaped. Flower size: 5–6 in. (12.7–15.2 cm). Fragrance: Slight, pleasant. Number of petals: 36–38. Number of sepals: 4.

LEAVES. Color: Top, new leaves are purple changing after a few weeks to olive green; underside, reddish with prominent green veins. Leaf round; sinus variable. Usually open but sometimes closed or partly closed. Leaf size: 8–9 in. (20.3–23 cm). Leaf spread: 3.5–6.5 ft. (1–2 m). Stem color: Brown. Short thick fuzz on peduncle and petiole.

COMMENTS. This cultivar clearly represents a breakthrough in waterlily color (U.S. plant patent 9662). The first- and second-day blooms are held 6–8 in. (15.2–20.3 cm) above the water and provide lovely reflections. Demand for this waterlily is high and, even though it is a good propagator, it is difficult to keep sufficient stock on hand. I must mention, however, that in the Deep South the center petals will burn.

Nymphaea 'Bleeding Heart'
Perry's Water Gardens 1993
Natural hybrid, parentage unknown
PLATE 147

CHARACTERISTICS. Mediocre flowering (free flowering after colony has formed), odorata rhizome, perennial.

FLOWERS. Petal color: Blood red. Sepal color: Red on inside, dark green on outside. Anther color: Inner, deep yellow; outer, deep yellow. Stamen color: Inner, deep yellow; outer, red. Flower shape: Cuplike. Flower size: 3.5 in. (9 cm). Fragrance: Very slight. Number of petals: 38–50. Number of sepals: 6.

LEAVES. Color: Top, bronzy purple at first turning olive green; underside, red with prominent green veins. Nearly round; sinus wide open. Leaf size: 6.5 in. (16.5 cm). Leaf spread: 3–4 ft. (0.9–1.2 m). Stem color: peduncle green or brown; petiole brown. No pubescence on peduncle or petiole.

COMMENTS. Although this is an odorata-type

waterlily, the flower is such a shocking red that it should have a place in the collector's pond or large pool.

Nymphaea 'Blushing Bride'
Perry's Water Gardens 1997
Natural hybrid, N. 'Texas Dawn' and N. 'Perry's Red Beauty' probable parents
PLATE 148
CHARACTERISTICS. Free flowering, Marliac rhizome, perennial.

FLOWERS. Petal color: Light yellow flushed with pink. Sepal color: Inner, cream with a touch of pink; outer, dark green. Anther color: Inner, dark yellow; outer, dark yellow. Stamen color: Dark yellow. Flower shape: Cuplike on first day, then opening wide. Flower size: 6–7 in. (15–17.8 cm). Fragrance: Slight, pleasant. Number of petals: 54–59. Number of sepals: 4.

LEAVES. Color: Top, green flecked with purple; underside, red changing to green, both stages heavily flecked with purple. Nearly round; sinus partly closed or fully open. Leaf size: About 9 in. (23 cm). Leaf spread: 5–6 ft. (1.5–1.8 m). Stem color: peduncle reddish purple; petiole greenish brown. A little fuzz on peduncle and petiole.

COMMENTS. Nymphaea 'Blushing Bride' is a very vigorous grower and, with its many blooms, it receives many comments and praise from visitors to our gardens. From a distance, the blooms appear as a double white, but close up the blush of pink shows on cream. I highly recommend N. 'Blushing Bride' for medium and large pools.

Nymphaea 'Bory de Saint-Vincent'
Latour-Marliac Nursery 1937
Parentage unknown
CHARACTERISTICS. Marliac rhizome, very free flowering.

FLOWERS. Petal color: Inner petals red; outer petals pink, lighter tips (RHS inner, 48A; outer petals, 48D, tips, 49C). Sepal color: White, greenish veins and border (RHS 155B; veins and border, 193C). Anther color: Burnt orange (RHS 29B). Stamen color: Orange. Flower shape: Full star. Flower size: 5.5–6 in. (14–15 cm). Fragrance: Very slight. Number of petals: 24. Number of sepals: 4.

LEAVES. Color: Top, green, new leaves mottled purple; underside, brownish green. Leaf nearly round; sinus open. Leaf size: 9–10 in. (23–25 cm). Leaf spread: 4–5 ft. (1.2–1.5 m). Stem color: Greenish bronze. No pubescence on peduncle or petiole.

COMMENTS. Nymphaea 'Bory de Saint-Vincent', with its four-colored blooms (red-and-pink petals, orange centers, and white sepals), is certainly among the most striking of the hardy waterlilies. I highly recommend it for any size pool.

Nymphaea 'Brackleyi Rosea'
Parentage unknown
CHARACTERISTICS. Odorata rhizome, fairly free flowering.

FLOWERS. Petal color: Shell pink (RHS 36D). Sepal color: Slightly darker than petals, one prominent central pink vein (RHS 36C; vein, 36B). Anther color: Deep yellow (RHS 11A). Stamen color: Deep yellow. Flower shape: Stellate. Flower size: 5 in. (13 cm). Fragrance: Very sweet. Number of petals: 21. Number of sepals: 4.

LEAVES. Color: Top, green, new leaves purple; underside, bronzy green, new leaves purple. Leaf nearly round; sinus open. Leaf size: 9–10 in. (23–25 cm). Leaf spread: 4–5 ft. (1.2–1.5 m). Stem color: Bronzy green. No pubescence on peduncle or petiole.

COMMENTS. Nymphaea 'Brackleyi Rosea', available since 1909, is one of the older pink waterlilies. Today many other pink hardy lilies that are freer blooming with more striking shades of pink are available. For best results N. 'Brackleyi Rosea' should be planted in a large container and allowed to form a colony of several plants. Suitable for medium or large pools or natural ponds, where it can be expected to spread about 1 ft. (0.3 m) or more per year.

Nymphaea 'Burgundy Princess'
Strawn 1983
Nymphaea 'Pink Beauty' × N. 'Perry's Pink'
CHARACTERISTICS. Nonviviparous, Marliac rhizome, fairly free flowering, perennial.

FLOWERS. Petal color: Outer petals blushed red, deepening to an intense red at inner petals. Sepal color: Inner, red, olive green at tips and outer edges;

outer, green with dark green tips. Anther color: Inner, deep red with golden yellow tips; outer, golden yellow. Stamen color: Golden yellow. Flower shape: Cuplike. Flower size: 2–4 in. (5–10 cm). Fragrance: Slight. Number of petals: 28–30. Number of sepals: 4.

LEAVES. Color: Top, medium green, newer leaves slightly olive green; underside, faint reddish brown with green tips; newer leaves more reddish brown underneath. Leaf round; lobes overlap at sinus. Leaf size: 4–5 in. (10–12.5 cm). Leaf spread: 2–4 ft. (0.6–1.2 m). Stem color: Brown. No pubescence on peduncle or petiole.

COMMENTS BY DEAN MCGEE. The striking red blossoms rest on the surface of the water. This cultivar makes an excellent centerpiece or in contrast with softer color lilies in a small or medium pond.

Nymphaea 'Carolina Sunset'

Slocum 1991

Seedling of N. 'Texas Dawn'

PLATE 149

CHARACTERISTICS. Marliac rhizome, free flowering.

FLOWERS. Petal color: Inner petals deep yellow; middle petals light yellow, blushed peach (RHS inner, 18C,D; middle, 7A; blush, lighter than 62D). Sepal color: Pale green, tips darker green (RHS 1D; tips, 139D and lighter). Anther color: Deep yellow (RHS 11A). Stamen color: Deep yellow. Flower shape: Cuplike; sepals turn down, touch petiole. Flower size: 7–8 in. (18–20 cm). Fragrance: Very pleasant. Number of petals: 29–33. Number of sepals: 4.

LEAVES. Color: Top, green, new leaves chartreuse, heavily mottled purple and/or green; underside, pinkish, heavily blotched purple. Leaf nearly round; sinus a wide-open V. Leaf size: 11 × 11.5 in. (28 × 29 cm). Leaf spread: 4–5 ft. (1.2–1.5 m). Stem color: Peduncle purplish brown, petiole purple. Heavy fuzz on both peduncle and petiole.

COMMENTS. Flowers of Nymphaea 'Carolina Sunset' display a beautiful pastel color. The yellow petals are suffused with a blush of peach—a rare color combination for hardy waterlilies. Flower color and the unique chartreuse of new leaves set this cultivar apart. I recommend it for medium or large pools.

Nymphaea 'Caroliniana Perfecta'

Marliac 1893

Parentage unknown

CHARACTERISTICS. Odorata rhizome, fairly free flowering.

FLOWERS. Petal color: Salmon-pink (RHS 36A). Sepal color: Light salmon-pink (RHS 36D). Anther color: Yellow (RHS 11A). Stamen color: Yellow. Flower shape: Cuplike. Flower size: 5–6 in. (13–15 cm). Fragrance: Very sweet. Number of petals: 30. Number of sepals: 4.

LEAVES. Color: Top, dark green, new leaves bronzy; underside, reddish brown. Leaf nearly round; sinus open. Leaf size: 9–10 in. (23–25 cm). Leaf spread: 4–5 ft. (1.2–1.5 m). Stem color: Peduncle, brownish green; petiole green. No pubescence on peduncle or petiole.

COMMENTS. This was one of the first pink cultivars. There are many better pink hardies among the newer creations. I recommend planting Nymphaea 'Caroliniana Perfecta' in a planter at least 24 × 24 × 12 in. (60 × 60 × 30 cm), where it can form a colony of several plants. It is suitable for medium and large pools.

Nymphaea 'Celebration'

Strawn 1994

Nymphaea 'Peter Slocum' × N. 'Pink Beauty'

CHARACTERISTICS. Nonviviparous, odorata rhizome, free flowering, perennial.

FLOWERS. Petal color: Fuchsia pink. Sepal color: Inner, fuchsia, white at base; outer, olive green with dark green tips. Anther color: Inner, deep yellow; outer, deep yellow. Stamen color: Fuchsia. Flower shape: Stellate. Flower size: 3–4 in. (7.5–10 cm). Fragrance: Pleasant. Number of petals: 34–36. Number of sepals: 4.

LEAVES. Color: Top, medium green, some leaves are olive green with orange-brown tint; some newer leaves are plum color; underside, deep plum. Leaf nearly round; lobes slightly overlap at sinus. Leaf size: 3–5 in. (7.5–12.5 cm). Leaf spread: 2–4 ft. (0.6–1.2 m). Stem color: Light green. No pubescence on peduncle or petiole.

COMMENTS BY DEAN MCGEE. Resembling a smaller version of Nymphaea 'Mayla', this waterlily boasts fuchsia blossoms that open wide and rest on the surface of the water. It is an excellent selection for small or medium ponds.

Nymphaea 'Charlene Strawn'
Strawn 1969
Parentage unknown
PLATE 150
CHARACTERISTICS. Marliac rhizome, quite free flowering.

FLOWERS. Petal color: Inner petals, rich yellow; outer petals lighter yellow (*RHS* inner, 2B,C; outer, 2D). Sepal color: Greenish yellow, tips green, edges often blushed pink (*RHS* 1D; tips, 145C; edges, 73D). Anther color: Deep yellow (*RHS* 12A). Stamen color: Yellow. Flower shape: Stellate. Flower size: 6–8 in. (15–20 cm). Fragrance: Very sweet. Number of petals: 27–29. Number of sepals: 4.

LEAVES. Color: Top, green, new leaves display small purple specks and mottles; underside, light purple and green, mottled purple, newest leaves red, mottled purple. Leaf nearly round; lobes sometimes overlap at sinus, more often sinus an open V. Leaf size: 8–9 in. (20–23 cm). Leaf spread: 3–5 ft. (0.9–1.5 m). Stem color: Brown. Thick fuzz on peduncle and petiole.

COMMENTS. This is the most fragrant hardy waterlily I know, and it makes an excellent cut flower. The plant develops an abundance of leaves, however, which sometimes hide the flowers. Kirk Strawn named this waterlily after his wife. I recommend it for medium and large pools.

Nymphaea 'Charles de Meurville'
Latour-Marliac Nursery 1931
Parentage unknown
CHARACTERISTICS. Marliac rhizome, very free flowering.

FLOWERS. Petal color: Inner petals, dark pinkish red; outer petals, pink (*RHS* inner, 64B; outer, 65A). Sepal color: Very pale pink (*RHS* 65D). Anther color: Golden orange (*RHS* 19A). Stamen color: Brilliant orange. Flower shape: Stellate. Flower size: 6–7 in. (15–18 cm). Fragrance: Slight. Number of petals: 22. Number of sepals: 4.

LEAVES. Color: Top, dark green; underside, dark green, light green veins. Leaf very long; sinus a long V. Leaf size: 10 × 8 in. (25 × 20 cm). Leaf spread: 4–5

ft. (1.2–1.5 m). Stem color: Purple. Very short fuzz on peduncle and petiole.

COMMENTS. Many petals are raised rather than flat. This waterlily is a very good choice for a medium or large pool.

Nymphaea 'Charlie's Choice'
Syn. 'Charles' Choice'
Strawn 1995
Nymphaea 'Rembrandt' × *N. mexicana*
PLATE 151
CHARACTERISTICS. Nonviviparous, pineapple rhizome, free flowering, perennial.

FLOWERS. Petal color: Blushed bright red, darker red at base. Sepal color: Inner, greenish white, dark green pin stripes; outer, bronze striped with lighter green edges, red base. Anther color: Inner, golden yellow; outer, golden yellow. Stamen color: Red. Flower shape: Cuplike. Flower size: 2–3 in. (5–7.5 cm). Fragrance: Slight. Number of petals: 20–22. Number of sepals: 4.

LEAVES. Color: Top, dark green with distinctive mottling, newer leaves have reddish tint; underside, reddish plum with moderate flecking, newer leaves olive green. Leaf slightly ovate with slight convolutions, lobes overlapping; open sinus. Leaf size: 3–5 in. (7.5–12.5 cm). Leaf spread: 2–3 ft. (0.6–0.9 m). Stem color: Olive green. No pubescence on peduncle or petiole.

COMMENTS BY DEAN MCGEE. Unique characteristics make this a charming waterlily for smaller ponds and tub gardens. Dedicated to International Waterlily and Water Gardening Society Hall of Fame member and hybridizer Charles Thomas.

Nymphaea 'Cherokee'
Syn. 'Orange Hybrid'
Perry's Water Gardens 1989
Nymphaea 'Colonel A. J. Welch' × *N.* 'Aurora'
CHARACTERISTICS. Upright rhizome, occasionally viviparous from blossom (new plants and rhizomes develop from about 5 percent of flowers or less), free flowering.

FLOWERS. Petal color: Rich red; outer petals cream, flushed pink, becoming deep red by third day (*RHS* 53D; outer petals, 11D; flush, 36D; third day, 44A). Sepal color: Creamy white (*RHS* 11D).

Anther color: Bright orange (*RHS* 24A). Stamen color: Orange-red. Flower shape: Cuplike. Flower size: 3–4 in. (8–10 cm). Fragrance: Slight, lemony. Number of petals: 21. Number of sepals: 4.

LEAVES. Color: Top, green, newest leaves richly mottled maroon; underside, purple. Leaves round; sinus a wide-open V. Leaf size: 4–6 in. (10–15 cm). Leaf spread: 3–4 ft. (0.9–1.2 m). Stem color: Maroon. No pubescence on peduncle or petiole.

COMMENTS. The second- and third-day flower color of *Nymphaea* 'Cherokee' is quite similar to the flower color of *N.* 'Aurora'. 'Cherokee' is also similar to *N.* 'Perry's Red Star' and *N.* 'Colonel A. J. Welch' in that some of the flowers are viviparous, developing new plants from blooms. The new plants produced in this manner have yellow flowers that soon turn the normal color. This plant does better in the Deep South than in northern states, where it is subject to crown rot.

Nymphaea 'Chrysantha'

Formerly 'Graziella'
Marliac 1905
Parentage unknown
PLATE 152

CHARACTERISTICS. Changeable, upright rhizome, very free flowering.

FLOWERS. Petal color: Outer, cream-yellow, large green patch on outside; inner, deeper cream-yellow; all petals flushed orange, deepening (*RHS* outer, first day, 10D; third day, 29C,D; green patch, 152B; inner, first day, 24C,D; third day, 31B,C; flush, 29D). Sepal color: Creamy, deepening, usually a few short red stripes on one or more sepals; slight red blush and flecks by third day (*RHS* first day, 11D; third day, 12D; stripes, 64C; blush and flecks, 54D). Anther color: Golden yellow (*RHS* 23B). Stamen color: Inner rows, golden yellow; outer rows, orange-pink. Flower shape: Cuplike. Flower size: 3–4 in. (8–10 cm). Fragrance: None. Number of petals: 16–19. Number of sepals: 4 or 5.

LEAVES. Color: Top, green, new leaves blotched purple; underside, reddish, freckled purple, new leaves bronzy. Leaf almost round; sinus a wide-open V. Leaf size: 6.5 × 5.5 in. (16 × 14 cm). Leaf spread: 2–3 ft. (0.6–1 m). Stem color: Green to purple. Short fuzz and tiny hairs on peduncle and petiole.

COMMENTS. *Nymphaea* 'Chrysantha' is frequently mislabeled and sold in some nurseries in the United States as *N.* 'Paul Hariot' or *N.* 'Graziella'. Flower color is quite similar among the three, though the 'Paul Hariot' flower is larger. The rhizome of 'Paul Hariot' is subject to crown rot, however, while that of 'Chrysantha' is fairly free from such problems. 'Chrysantha' is an ideal plant for a tub garden or a small pool except in very hot regions, where it does not bloom well.

Nymphaea 'Chubby'

Strawn 1993
Nymphaea 'Dallas' × *N.* 'Hollandia'

CHARACTERISTICS. Nonviviparous, Marliac rhizome, very free flowering, perennial.

FLOWERS. Petal color: White with a hint of pink throughout. Sepal color: Inner, light pink; medium green on edges; outer, medium green. Anther color: Inner, bright yellow; outer, bright yellow. Stamen color: Bright yellow. Flower shape: Cuplike. Flower size: 3–4 in. (7.5–10 cm). Fragrance: Slight. Number of petals: 30–32. Number of sepals: 4.

LEAVES. Color: Top, medium green; underside, plum. Leaf nearly round, sinus open. Leaf size: 5–6 in. (12.5–15 cm). Leaf spread: 3–5 ft. (0.9–1.5 m). Stem color: Olive green. Pubescence on petiole.

COMMENTS BY DEAN MCGEE. This cultivar has a simply beautiful double flower with a tinge of pink. It is a prolific bloomer whose blossoms are just above the surface of the water. Well suited for medium ponds as a compliment with a wide range of other colors.

Nymphaea 'Clyde Ikins'

Strawn, year unknown
Nymphaea 'Nigel' × *N. mexicana*
PLATE 153

CHARACTERISTICS. Nonviviparous, Marliac rhizome, very free flowering, perennial.

FLOWERS. Petal color: Outer petals creamy yellow with a hint of pink, shading to light yellow apricot at inner petals. Sepal color: Inner, creamy white, faint pink on edges; dark green pin stripes; outer, medium green with olive green tips. Anther color: Inner, bright yellow; outer, bright yellow. Stamen color: Bright yellow. Flower shape: Stellate. Flower size: 4–6 in. (10–15 cm). Fragrance: Strong. Number of petals: 32–34. Number of sepals: 4.

LEAVES. Color: Top, medium green, newer leaves more olive with hint of mottling; underside, reddish brown with green veining on peduncle. Leaf slightly ovate, sinus slightly open. Leaf size: 6–8 in. (15–20 cm). Leaf spread: 6–8 ft. (1.8–2.4 m). Stem color: Medium green. No pubescence on peduncle or petiole.

COMMENTS BY DEAN MCGEE. Very large flowers with an awesome yellow apricot appeal. One of the best Kirk Strawn hardy waterlilies. Stands 4–6 in. (10–15 cm) above the water. Dedicated to Dr. Clyde Ikins of Lakeside Gardens, Bandera, Texas.

Nymphaea 'Colonel A. J. Welch'

Marliac, date unknown

Parentage unknown

Plates 154, 155

CHARACTERISTICS. Viviparous from the blossom, Marliac rhizome, not free flowering.

FLOWERS. Petal color: Lemon yellow, inner row slightly deeper yellow (*RHS* 12C; inner row, 12B). Sepal color: Lemon yellow, tips and borders touched green (*RHS* 12D; tips and borders, 151D). Anther color: Bright yellow (*RHS* 13C). Stamen color: Bright yellow. Flower shape: Stellate. Flower size: 5.5–6 in. (14–15 cm). Fragrance: Pleasant in new blooms. Number of petals: 22 or 23. Number of sepals: 4.

LEAVES. Color: Top, olive green, perimeter of newest leaves flecked purple; underside, green, newest leaves display small purple blotches and specks. Leaves round; lobes may overlap one-third to half of sinus or sinus may be an open V. Leaf size: 9 in. (23 cm). Leaf spread: 6 ft. (1.8 m). Stem color: Peduncles usually purple; petioles yellow-green, striped purple, or solid purple. No pubescence on peduncle or petiole.

COMMENTS. This cultivar is a viviparous hardy that frequently develops new plants with rhizomes directly from the old blossom head. It is sometimes mistakenly sold as *N.* 'Sunrise' (syn. *Nymphaea odorata* 'Sulphurea Grandiflora'), which it closely resembles. *Nymphaea* 'Colonel A. J. Welch' is a poor substitute, however, since it produces very few blooms and its abundant foliage crowds together above the water. It is best used in a pond that is very deep, 4–7 ft. (1.2–2.1 m) or so, or as a novelty plant for its viviparous trait.

Nymphaea 'Colorado'

Strawn 1994

Nymphaea 'Louise Villemarette' × *N. mexicana*

PLATE 156

CHARACTERISTICS. Nonviviparous, Marliac rhizome, very free flowering, perennial.

FLOWERS. Petal color: Outer petals soft pink shading to light peach on innermost petals. Sepal color: Inner, light blushed pink; dark green tips; outer, medium green with plum color along some edges. Anther color: Inner, medium yellow; outer, soft pink with yellow anthers. Stamen color: Medium yellow. Flower shape: Stellate. Flower size: 3–4 in. (7.5–10 cm). Fragrance: Very pleasant. Number of petals: 26–28. Number of sepals: 4.

LEAVES. Color: Top, medium green, newer leaves more olive with faint mottling; underside, reddish plum, newer leaves have more green than red. Leaf nearly round; sinus open. Leaf size: 5–7 in. (12.5–18 cm). Leaf spread: 3–5 ft. (0.9–1.5 m). Stem color: Medium green. No pubescence on peduncle or petiole.

COMMENTS BY DEAN MCGEE. One of Kirk Strawn's more classic hybrids, this medium flower has a unique salmon pink color. Very prolific bloomer that will bloom late into the season. Stands 3–4 in. (7.5–10 cm) above the water. Needs room to grow.

Nymphaea 'Colossea'

Marliac 1901

Parentage unknown

CHARACTERISTICS. Marliac rhizome, very free flowering.

FLOWERS. Petal color: Light pink, paling (*RHS* 65D, paling to 155D). Sepal color: Medium pink, paling (*RHS* 65D then 49D). Anther color: Yellow (*RHS* 11A). Stamen color: Yellow. Flower shape: Cuplike then stellate. Flower size: 6–8 in. (15–20 cm). Fragrance: Slight. Number of petals: 23–25. Number of sepals: 4.

LEAVES. Color: Top, green, new leaves bronzy; underside, green. Leaf a little longer than wide;

sinus wide open. Leaf size: 10–12 in. (25–30 cm). Leaf spread: 5–6 ft. (1.5–1.8 m). Stem color: Greenish. A few tiny hairs on peduncle and petiole.

COMMENTS. Flower color of N. 'Colossea' is quite similar to that of N. 'Marliacea Rosea', but 'Colossea' flowers are larger and petals are more rounded on tips. According to Paul Stetson, owner of Paradise Water Gardens, Whitman, Massachusetts, this waterlily produces more flowers over a longer period than any other Marliac variety. I recommend it for medium or large pools.

Nymphaea 'Comanche'

Formerly 'J. C. N. Forestier'
Marliac 1908
Parentage unknown
PLATE 157

CHARACTERISTICS. Pineapple rhizome, very free flowering.

FLOWERS. Petal color: First day, yellow-apricot, deeper toward center; second day, gold-orange flushed pink; third day, deep orange, center petals flushed red, pale yellow tips (RHS first day, 11B, 1B by second day; 43D, 54C by second day; third day, 54B; tips 12D). Sepal color: Creamy, more orange with age, pink base (RHS 1D; third day, 13B; base, 54C). Anther color: Deep golden yellow, more orange with age (RHS first day, 13B; third day, 21D). Stamen color: Golden yellow, orange outer row. Flower shape: Cuplike then stellate. Flower size: 5–6 in. (13–15 cm). Fragrance: Very pleasant. Number of petals: 22–26. Number of sepals: 4.

LEAVES. Color: Top, green, newest leaves bronzy green, few purple flecks; underside, red, flecked purple, flecks prominent on new leaves. Leaves nearly round; sinus usually a wide-open V, some lobes may overlap partially even on same plant. Leaf size: Up to 12 × 11 in. (30 × 28 cm). Leaf spread: 4–5 ft. (1.2–1.5 m). Stem color: Brown. Fine fuzz and small hairs on peduncle and petiole.

COMMENTS. Nymphaea 'Comanche' is the largest and showiest of the orange changeables, but it is also more subject to crown rot than most of the others. This waterlily does well in both southern and northern areas and is an excellent choice for medium and large pools.

Nymphaea 'Conqueror'

Marliac 1910
Parentage unknown

CHARACTERISTICS. Marliac rhizome, very free flowering.

FLOWERS. Petal color: Inner, deep red then deeper; outer, white then light pink (RHS inner, 64C; third day, 61B; outer, 155C; then 68D). Sepal color: White, pink veins (RHS 155C; veins, 68D). Anther color: Bright yellow (RHS 13B). Stamen color: Brilliant orange. Flower shape: Stellate. Flower size: 7–8 in. (18–20 cm). Fragrance: Slight. Number of petals: 28. Number of sepals: 4 or 5.

LEAVES. Color: Top, deep green, new leaves slightly bronzed; underside, green, perimeter bronze, new leaves purple, green V in center. Leaf almost round; sinus usually a wide-open V. Leaf size: Up to 10–11 in. (25–28 cm). Leaf spread: 5 ft. (1.5 m). Stem color: Purple. No pubescence on peduncle or petiole.

COMMENTS. Nymphaea 'Conqueror' is really a tricolored waterlily (red and pink petals with white sepals) and a very satisfactory plant on the whole. In hot weather, however, the inner deep red petals nearly always burn and blacken. I recommend it for medium and large pools.

Nymphaea 'Cynthia Ann'

Strawn, year unknown
Parentage unknown

CHARACTERISTICS. Nonviviparous, odorata rhizome, very free flowering, perennial.

FLOWERS. Petal color: Apricot with faint pink blush at base. Sepal color: Inner, light green, green pin stripes; outer, olive green. Anther color: Inner, bright yellow; outer, bright yellow. Stamen color: Bright yellow. Flower shape: Stellate. Flower size: 3–4 in. (7.5–10 cm). Fragrance: Very pleasant. Number of petals: 26–28. Number of sepals: 4.

LEAVES. Color: Top, medium green, newer leaves are lighter green and have faint mottling; underside, reddish purple, newer leaves have more green than red. Leaf round, tips on lobes; sinus slightly open. Leaf size: 4–5 in. (10–12.5 cm). Leaf spread: 2–4 ft. (0.6–1.2 m). Stem color: Olive green. Pubescence on petiole.

COMMENTS BY DEAN MCGEE. Nymphaea 'Cynthia Ann' has a small apricot blossom that stands 2–3 in. (5–7.5 cm) above the water. This cultivar is great for small to medium ponds. Reminiscent of a smaller version of *N*. 'Clyde Ikins'.

Nymphaea 'Dallas'

Strawn 1991

Parentage unknown

CHARACTERISTICS. Nonviviparous, odorata rhizome, free flowering, perennial.

FLOWERS. Petal color: Intense fuchsia throughout. Sepal color: Inner, deep fuchsia; outer, dark green, olive green at tips. Anther color: Inner, deep yellow; outer, fuchsia with deep yellow anthers. Stamen color: Deep yellow. Flower shape: Stellate. Flower size: 3–5 in. (7.5–12.5 cm). Fragrance: Strong. Number of petals: 24–26. Number of sepals: 4

LEAVES. Color: Top, medium green, some leaves have olive green with plum shading to outer edges; underside, deep plum. Nearly round with overlapping lobes; sinus slightly open. Leaf size: 3–4 in. (7.5–10 cm). Leaf spread: 2–3 ft. (0.6–0.9 m). Stem color: Medium green. Pubescence on petiole.

COMMENTS BY DEAN MCGEE. The attractive deep pink blossoms of *Nymphaea* 'Dallas' make it an excellent waterlily for tub gardens or small to medium ponds.

Nymphaea 'Darwin'

Formerly 'Hollandia'

Marliac 1909

Probably a mutation of *N*. 'Madame Wilfron Gonnère'

PLATE 158

CHARACTERISTICS. Marliac rhizome, free flowering.

FLOWERS. Petal color: Inner, light pink then deeper; outer petals white, pinkish by third day (*RHS* inner, 65A then 73B; outer, 155B; third day, 73D). Sepal color: Pinkish white, pink flush by third day, green border (*RHS* 155B; flush, 73D; border, 144A). Anther color: Golden yellow (*RHS* 13B). Stamen color: Pinkish yellow. Flower shape: Double, peony-style. Flower size: 6–7.5 in. (15–19 cm). Fragrance: Slight. Number of petals: 36 or 37. Number of sepals: 4.

LEAVES. Color: Top, green; underside, green,

new leaves brownish. Leaf round. Sinus varies considerably, even on same plant; some lobes overlap, some separated by an open V. Leaf size: 10–11 in. (25–28 cm). Leaf spread: 4–5 ft. (1.2–1.5 m). Stem color: Purple underwater, green above water. Short fuzz on underwater stems.

COMMENTS. *Nymphaea* 'Darwin' is a great favorite and makes a terrific cut flower. I highly recommend this waterlily for medium and large pools.

Nymphaea 'Denver'

Strawn 1997

Nymphaea 'Rembrandt' × *N. mexicana*

CHARACTERISTICS. Nonviviparous, Marliac rhizome, free flowering, perennial.

FLOWERS. Petal color: Soft white with a hint of yellow. Sepal color: Inner, white with faint green pin stripes; outer, bronze. Anther color: Inner, bright yellow; outer, bright yellow. Stamen color: Bright yellow. Flower shape: Cuplike, double flower. Flower size: 3–4 in. (7.5–10 cm). Fragrance: Slight. Number of petals: 46–48. Number of sepals: 4.

LEAVES. Color: Top, medium green with faint mottling toward perimeter; underside, reddish brown with green veins, veins more noticeable on newer leaves. Leaf slightly ovate, overlapping lobes; closed sinus. Leaf size: 4–5 in. (10–12.5 cm). Leaf spread: 3–4 ft. (0.9–1.2 m). Stem color: Light green. No pubescence on peduncle or petiole.

COMMENTS BY DEAN MCGEE. Double cream blossoms give an outstanding floral display. This waterlily is excellent in the small tub garden or medium pond.

Nymphaea 'Doll House'

Strawn, year unknown

Parentage unknown

PLATE 159

CHARACTERISTICS. Nonviviparous, odorata rhizome, very free flowering, perennial.

FLOWERS. Petal color: Very light pink throughout, petals lighten toward tips. Sepal color: Inner, light pink; outer, olive green. Anther color: Inner, bright yellow; outer, bright yellow. Stamen color: Soft pink. Flower shape: Stellate. Flower size: 2–3 in. (5–7.5 cm). Fragrance: Strong. Number of petals: 36–38. Number of sepals: 4.

LEAVES. Color: Top, medium green, newer leaves olive green; underside, deep reddish plum color. Leaf nearly round, lobes rounded; sinus wide open. Leaf size: 5–6 in. (12.5–15 cm). Leaf spread: 2–4 ft. (0.6–1.2 m). Stem color: Light green. No pubescence on peduncle or petiole.

COMMENTS BY DEAN MCGEE. *Nymphaea* 'Doll House' provides an elegant display of small light pink blossoms that rest just at the water surface. Great for small tub gardens or small to medium ponds.

Nymphaea 'Ellisiana'

Marliac 1896

Parentage unknown

CHARACTERISTICS. Marliac rhizome, very free flowering.

FLOWERS. Petal color: Very brilliant red (*RHS* 61B). Sepal color: Greenish white, pink veins, pink toward base (*RHS* 193D; veins, 62B; base, 62C). Anther color: Rich golden yellow (*RHS* 22A). Stamen color: Orange-red. Flower shape: Full, stellate. Flower size: 4–5 in. (10–13 cm). Fragrance: Strong. Number of petals: 21 or 22. Number of sepals: 4.

LEAVES. Color: Top, green, new leaves dark green, blotched purple; underside, green, new leaves purple-bronze. Leaf a little longer than wide; lobes overlap slightly on new leaves; sinus wide open on older leaves. Leaf size: 7–8 in. (18–20 cm). Leaf spread: 3 ft. (0.9 m). Stem color: Bronze. A few short hairs on peduncle and petiole.

COMMENTS. This is a first-rate plant for a tub garden or small pool. Note, however, that it performs best in northern regions, and it blooms freely all summer in North Carolina (zone 6b). As it tends to stop blooming in very hot weather, I do not recommend it for zones 8–10.

Nymphaea 'Ernst Epple sen'

Epple 1970

Nymphaea 'Maxima' × *N.* 'Gloire du Temple-sur-Lot'

PLATE 160

CHARACTERISTICS. Fairly free flowering, tuberosa rhizome, perennial.

FLOWERS. Petal color: Pure white (*RHS* 155D). Sepal color: Inner, pure white (*RHS* 155D); outer, green (*RHS* 141B). Anther color: Inner, yellow (*RHS* 12B), outer, yellow (*RHS* 12B). Stamen color: Yellow (*RHS* 12A). Flower shape: Cuplike. Flower size: 5–7 in. (12.5–18 cm). Fragrance: Pleasant. Number of petals: 46. Number of sepals: 8, plus 4 more white and green striped second sepals.

LEAVES. Color: Top, dark green (*RHS* 141B); underside, light green (*RHS* 140A). Round leaf with wavy edges; lobes overlap at sinus. Leaf size: 12–16 in. (30–40 cm). Leaf spread: 5.6–6 ft. (1.5–1.8 m).

COMMENTS BY ERNST EPPLE. I recommend *Nymphaea* 'Ernst Epple sen' for medium to large ponds. On the second and third days, flowers close late in the evening.

Nymphaea 'Escarboucle'

Syn. 'Aflame'

Marliac 1909

Parentage unknown

PLATE 161

CHARACTERISTICS. Marliac rhizome, very free flowering.

FLOWERS. Petal color: Very bright vermilion-red, outer petal row tipped white (*RHS* 64B; tips, 155A). Sepal color: Pink, deepening; white tips (*RHS* 62D; last day, 66D; tips, 155A). Anther color: Golden yellow (*RHS* 26B). Stamen color: Burnt orange. Flower shape: Cuplike then stellate. Flower size: 6–7 in. (15–18 cm). Fragrance: Some, even in older flowers. Number of petals: 25. Number of sepals: 4.

LEAVES. Color: Top, green, newer leaves brownish; underside, green, perimeter brownish near sinus, newer leaves brownish. Leaf almost round; lobes overlap about 1 in. (2.5 cm) at sinus. Leaf size: 10–11 in. (25–28 cm). Leaf spread: 4–5 ft. (1.2–1.5 m). Stem color: Bronzy green, sometimes fine red lengthwise stripes. No pubescence on peduncle or petiole.

COMMENTS. This is undoubtedly one of the very best red hardies for medium and large pools. Blooms stay open very late in the afternoon—long after most other red hardies have closed.

Nymphaea 'Eugene de Land'

Latour-Marliac Nursery, year unknown

Parentage unknown

CHARACTERISTICS. Odorata rhizome, fairly free flowering.

FLOWERS. Petal color: Light to medium pink (*RHS* 36A). Sepal color: Light to medium pink (*RHS* 36A). Anther color: Deep yellow (*RHS* 15B). Stamen color: Deep yellow. Flower shape: Full, cuplike, star effect from very long outer petals. Flower size: 7–8 in. (18–20 cm). Fragrance: Very pleasant. Number of petals: 21 or 22. Number of sepals: 4.

LEAVES. Color: Top, green; underside, salmon-pink. Leaf nearly round; sinus usually open. Leaf size: Up to 10–11 in. (25–28 cm). Leaf spread: 4–5.5 ft. (1.2–1.7 m). Stem color: Bronzy green. No pubescence on peduncle or petiole.

COMMENTS. *Nymphaea* 'Eugene de Land' is a very attractive waterlily. For optimal blooming, it should be planted in a large planter, where it can form a colony of several plants. I recommend it for medium and large pools.

Nymphaea 'Fabiola'

Formerly 'Mrs. Richmond'
Marliac Latour Nursery 1913
Parentage unknown

CHARACTERISTICS. Marliac rhizome, very free flowering.

FLOWERS. Petal color: Inner petals pinkish red, highly flecked; outer petals lighter, highly flecked, white tips (*RHS* inner, 64B; outer, 62C,D; tips, 155C). Sepal color: Whitish, pink developing at base (*RHS* 155B; third day, base, 62C). Anther color: Yellow (*RHS* 22B). Stamen color: Orange, pink outer row. Flower shape: Peony-style. Flower size: 6–7 in. (15–18 cm). Fragrance: Pleasant and noticeable in new flowers. Number of petals: 24 or 25. Number of sepals: 4.

LEAVES. Color: Top, green, new leaves bronzy purple; underside, brownish purple. Leaf longer than wide; lobes overlap almost entirely. Leaf size: 12 × 11 in. (30 × 28 cm). Leaf spread: 5 ft. (1.5 m). Stem color: Purple. Thick fuzz on peduncle and petiole.

COMMENTS. Due to its profusion of beautiful large bicolored flowers, *Nymphaea* 'Fabiola' is a wonderful plant for medium and large pools.

Nymphaea 'Fantastic Pink'

Slocum 1987
Seedling or mutation of *N.* 'Pink Sensation'

CHARACTERISTICS. Marliac rhizome, quite free flowering yet somewhat slow in starting.

FLOWERS. Petal color: Shell pink (*RHS* 65D). Sepal color: Shell pink; 11–12 bluish pink lengthwise veins (*RHS* 65D; veins, 65A). Anther color: Deep golden yellow (*RHS* 5B). Stamen color: Deep golden yellow, same as anthers. Flower shape: Full, stellate. Flower size: 6–8 in. (15–20 cm). Fragrance: Slight. Number of petals: 24–30. Number of sepals: 4.

LEAVES. Color: Top, olive green, new leaves deep purple; underside, red or reddish purple. Leaf quite large, nearly round; lobes usually raised at sinus, overlap partially; sinus open or open 1 in. (2.5 cm). Leaf size: 10–12 in. (25–30 cm). Leaf spread: 5–6 ft. (1.5–1.8 m). Stem color: Peduncle, yellow-green, slight purple flecking; petiole green. Pubescence on peduncle and petiole, heavier on peduncle.

COMMENTS. This selection developed in the *Nymphaea* 'Pink Sensation' bed at Perry's Water Gardens in North Carolina (zone 6b). It is rare for a seedling or mutation to suddenly appear with a thick Marliac rhizome. This particular waterlily is especially striking with its very broad petals and sepals. I recommend *N.* 'Fantastic Pink' for medium or large pools.

Nymphaea 'Fiesta'

Henley 1992
Nymphaea 'Firecrest' × *N.* 'Firecrest'
PLATE 162

CHARACTERISTICS. Free flowering, odorata rhizome, perennial.

FLOWERS. Petal color: Intense pink. Sepal color: Inner, pink; outer, pale olive green. Anther color: Inner, light orange; outer, cerise pink. Stamen color: Golden yellow. Flower shape: Stellate. Flower size: 4 in. (10 cm). Fragrance: Medium. Number of petals: 26. Number of sepals: 4.

LEAVES. Color: Top, red brown turning to plain green; underside, reddish brown. Lobes along sinus overlapping on new leaves, opening slightly on maturity with extended tips of lobes along sinus. Leaf size: 6 in. (15 cm). Leaf spread: About 3 ft. (0.9 m). Stem color: Pale olive green. Pubescence on peduncle (new stems have fuzz that disappears with age) and petiole.

COMMENTS BY REG HENLEY. *Nymphaea* 'Fiesta'

is a good-flowering odorata. Close to *N.* 'Firecrest' but with a strong orange-red center with heavy leaf cover; flowers often float on water surface.

Nymphaea 'Fireball'

Perry's Water Gardens 1994

Natural hybrid, parents probably *N.* 'Splendida' × *N.* 'Atropurpurea'

PLATE 163

CHARACTERISTICS. Fairly free flowering, Marliac rhizome, perennial.

FLOWERS. Petal color: Very vivid pinkish red. Sepal color: Inner, greenish with pink veins; outer, deep green. Anther color: Inner, deep yellow; outer, dark yellow. Stamen color: Inner, orange; outer, pinkish red. Flower shape: Cuplike at first, the spreading like a huge peony. Flower size: 5.5–7 in. (14–17.8 cm). Fragrance: Pleasant. Number of petals: 48–51. Number of sepals: 4–6.

LEAVES. Color: Top, bronzy green at first changing to deep green; underside, reddish with prominent green veins. Sinus closed with leaf lobes raised 1 in. (2.5 cm) at junction. Leaf size: 10.5 in. (26.6 cm). Leaf spread: 4–6 ft. (1.2–1.8 m). Stem color: Brownish green. Short fuzz on peduncle and petiole, thicker on peduncle.

COMMENTS. *Nymphaea* 'Fireball' makes a beautiful, richly colored double flower that pleases everyone. Due to its large leaves and fairly large leaf spread, I recommend it only for medium to large pools.

Nymphaea 'Firecrest'

Parentage unknown

PLATE 164

CHARACTERISTICS. Odorata rhizome, moderately free flowering.

FLOWERS. Petal color: Lavender-pink (*RHS* 65B, C). Sepal color: Lavender-pink, greenish margin (*RHS* 65B; margin, 194D). Anther color: Burnt orange (*RHS* 31B). Stamen color: Inner rows, orange; outer rows, pink. Flower shape: Stellate. Flower size: 5.5–6 in. (14–15 cm). Fragrance: Slight. Number of petals: 29. Number of sepals: 4.

LEAVES. Color: Top, green, new leaves very deep purple; underside, deep purple. Leaf round; sinus usually an open V. Leaf size: 9 in. (23 cm). Leaf spread: 4 ft. (1.2 m). Stem color: Green. Considerable fuzz on peduncle and petiole.

COMMENTS. Flowers are held above the water with sepals and outer petals hanging down. For most frequent blooming, plant in a large container at least 2 ft. (0.6 m) in diameter and 1 ft. (0.3 m) deep so that a colony of several roots can form. This waterlily will spread 12 in. (30 cm) or more per year. If space is plentiful, it is a fine waterlily for medium or large pools or natural ponds.

Nymphaea 'Florida Sunset'

Slocum 1995

Nymphaea 'Perry's Fire Opal' × *N. mexicana* f. *canaveralensis*

PLATE 165

CHARACTERISTICS. Free flowering, Marliac rhizome, perennial.

FLOWERS. Petal color: Yellow with pink blush heavier at base. Sepal color: Creamy white on inside with flush of pink. Dark olive green, frequently with deep pink margin on outside. Anther color: Inner, dark yellow; outer, dark yellow. Stamen color: Dark yellow. Flower shape: Cuplike, then peony-shaped. Flower size: 6–8.5 in. (15.2–21.5 cm). Fragrance: Slight. Number of petals: 35 or 36. Number of sepals: 4.

LEAVES. Color: Top, new leaves are dark olive green and heavily blotched with purple; underside, reddish, heavily blotched with purple. Leaves round; sinus closed as leaf lobes overlap; each lobe has 0.5-in. (1.2-cm) sharp point at tip. Leaf size: 9 in. (22.8 cm). Leaf spread: 4–6.5 ft. (1.2–1.9 m). Stem color: Brown. Thick, short fuzz on peduncle and petiole.

COMMENTS. *Nymphaea* 'Florida Sunset' is a free-blooming waterlily that has received many raving comments from visitors to Perry's Water Gardens. I highly recommend it for medium and large pools.

Nymphaea 'Formosa'

Marliac 1909

Parentage unknown

CHARACTERISTICS. Marliac rhizome, very free flowering.

FLOWERS. Petal color: Outer petals medium pink, deepening toward flower center, highly flecked throughout (*RHS* outer, 62D; inner, 62B). Sepal color: Nearly white, blushed pink (*RHS* 155A; blush, 65D or lighter). Anther color: Deep yellow (*RHS* 13A). Stamen color: Yellow. Flower shape: Full, cuplike. Flower size: 5–6 in. (13–15 cm). Fragrance: Very slight. Number of petals: 26. Number of sepals: 4.

LEAVES. Color: Top, olive green, some new leaves purple, others bronzy; underside, red. Leaf nearly round; sinus usually open except for 0.5 in. (1.3 cm) near leaf center. Leaf size: 8 in. (20 cm). Leaf spread: 4–5 ft. (1.2–1.5 m). Stem color: Peduncle, bright green; petiole bronzy yellow. No pubescence on peduncle or petiole.

COMMENTS. An excellent plant for any size pool. One possibly disappointing feature is the large amount of unevenly distributed flecking on the petals.

Nymphaea 'Franz Berthold'

Berthold 2001

Nymphaea 'Fritz Junge' × unknown

PLATE 166

CHARACTERISTICS. Fairly free flowering, Marliac rhizome, perennial.

FLOWERS. Petal color: Raspberry red, strongest at center of flower; color becomes darker with age. Sepal color: Creamy white with raspberry red in fine lines. Anther color: Inner, raspberry red with yellow pollen cells; outer, raspberry red with yellow pollen cells. Stamen color: Orange-red. Flower shape: Stellate with medium wide petals. Flower size: 8.5 in. (21.5 cm). Fragrance: Strongly perfumed. Number of petals: 28. Number of sepals: 4.

LEAVES. Color: Top, green; underside, wine red. Center rib is light green. Round leaf, upturned around most of edge; wide-open sinus terminating in sculptured tip. Leaf size: 11 in. (28 cm). Leaf spread: About 5 ft. (1.5 m). Stem color: Light green. No pubescence on peduncle or petiole.

COMMENTS BY FRANZ BERTHOLD. This waterlily has a very good size ratio of flower to leaf. A strong blooming variety with good fragrance, *Nymphaea* 'Franz Berthold' is great for medium or large pools.

Nymphaea 'Fritz Junge'

Junge 1975, named in 1987

Parentage unknown

PLATE 167

CHARACTERISTICS. Marliac rhizome, free flowering, perennial.

FLOWERS. Petal color: Reddish around the center becoming much lighter toward tips. Sepal color: Cream to white with faint magenta lines. Inner, dark green; outer, dark green. Sepals are sometimes reflexed. Anther color: Inner, orange; outer, orange-yellow. Stamen color: Yellow. Flower shape: Stellate. Flower size: 7.5 in. (19 cm). Fragrance: Faint anise scent. Number of petals: 28. Number of sepals: 4.

LEAVES. Color: Top, dark green; underside, greenish brown. Leaf size: 9 in. (23 cm). Leaf spread: 4–5 ft. (1.2–1.5 m). Stem color: Reddish brown. No pubescence on peduncle or petiole.

COMMENTS BY FRITZ JUNGE. The flowers stay open late on days without sunshine and very long into the evening. It makes a very good cut flower. The leaves can grow up out of the water, when the plant is grown in less than 20 in. (50 cm) of water. Deeper growing depths will improve this problem.

Nymphaea 'Froebeli'

Froebel 1898

Seedling of *N. alba* var. *rubra*

CHARACTERISTICS. Marliac rhizome, free flowering.

FLOWERS. Petal color: Deep burgundy-red (*RHS* 64B). Sepal color: Light pink, deepening; deeper pink lengthwise veins; white tips (*RHS* 62D then 63C; veins, 64D; tips, 155B). Anther color: Yellow (*RHS* 10B). Stamen color: Orange-red. Flower shape: Cuplike then stellate. Flower size: 4.5–5 in. (11–13 cm). Fragrance: Slight. Number of petals: 18. Number of sepals: 4.

LEAVES. Color: Top, green, new leaves bronzy; underside, purplish. Leaf almost round; sinus a wide-open V. Leaf size: 6 in. (15 cm). Leaf spread: 3 ft. (0.9 m). Stem color: Purple. A few fine hairs on peduncle and petiole.

COMMENTS. Otto Froebel of Zurich, Switzerland, developed this waterlily by selective breeding over a 40-year period. *Nymphaea* 'Froebeli' performs best in cooler regions. It is a fine choice for tub gardens or small pools.

Nymphaea 'Fulva'

Marliac 1894

Parentage unknown

CHARACTERISTICS. Upright rhizome, free flowering.

FLOWERS. Petal color: First day, orange, turning to red by third day (*RHS* first day, 24B,C; third day, base, 54A; tip, 50C). Sepal color: White turning to light pink at base (*RHS* first day, 155A; third day, tip, 155A; base, 56B,C). Anther color: Yellow-orange turning to orange-red (*RHS* first day, 14B,C; third day, 30D or 32C). Stamen color: Orange. Flower shape: Cuplike. Flower size: 3–4 in. (8–10 cm). Fragrance: None or slight. Number of petals: 22 or 23. Number of sepals: 4.

LEAVES. Color: Top, green mottled purple; underside, pink with reddish purple flecks. Leaf nearly round but a little longer than wide; sinus wide open. Leaf size: 3.5–4 in. (9–10 cm). Leaf spread: 1.5–4 ft. (0.5–1.2 m). Stem color: Yellowish green. Peduncle and petiole are glabrous.

COMMENTS. This richly colored changeable waterlily is suitable for any size pool, but *Nymphaea* 'Fulva' is especially suited for the tub garden or small pool.

Nymphaea 'George L. Thomas'

Strawn 1996

Parentage unknown

PLATE 168

CHARACTERISTICS. Free flowering when given ample space for rhizome to develop, odorata rhizome, perennial.

FLOWERS. Petal color: Bright, yet subtle fuchsia that fades slightly at the base. Sepal color: Inner, lime green with magenta pink edging and tips; outer, dark green. Anther color: Inner, bright yellow with purple edges around pollen sacs; outer, bright yellow with pinkish tips. Stamen color: Light pinkish yellow. Flower shape: Peony-style. Flower size: 4–5 in. (10–12.5 cm). Fragrance: Spicy, sweet.. Number of petals: 36–38. Number of sepals: 4.

LEAVES. Color: Top, new leaves emerge a solid burgundy brown and mature into a lime green; underside, light burgundy to a lighter green at midvein. Round leaf with slightly overlapping sinus on immature leaf and becoming more open as it matures. Leaf size: 9–11 in. (23–28 cm). Leaf spread: 6–12 ft. (1.8–3.6 m). Stem color: Dark brownish tan. No pubescence on peduncle or petiole.

COMMENTS BY LILYPONS WATER GARDENS. Recommended for medium or large ponds since the plant has an odorata rhizome. The plant has a large gorgeous flower that spreads quickly in a soil-bottom pond. This waterlily is dedicated to four men named George Leicester Thomas, all of whom enriched Lilypons Water Gardens with their contributions.

Nymphaea 'Georgia Peach'

Strawn 1998

Nymphaea 'Louise Villemarette' × *N. mexicana*

PLATE 169

CHARACTERISTICS. Nonviviparous, odorata rhizome, free flowering, perennial.

FLOWERS. Petal color: Outer, light yellow with blushed pink toward base, inner, slightly deeper yellow. Sepal color: Inner, light peach, dark green pin stripes; outer, medium green with dark green tips. Anther color: Inner, golden yellow; outer, golden yellow. Stamen color: Golden yellow. Flower shape: Stellate. Flower size: 4–6 in. (10–15 cm). Fragrance: Strong. Number of petals: 28–30. Number of sepals: 4.

LEAVES. Color: Top, medium green, newer leaves have significant, but faint mottling; underside, red with green toward outer edges. Leaf round; sinus wide open. Leaf size: 5–7 in. (12.5–18 cm). Leaf spread: 3–5 ft. (0.9–1.5 m). Stem color: Medium green. No pubescence on peduncle or petiole.

COMMENTS BY DEAN McGEE. This waterlily has remarkable peach blossoms that lighten to a creamy yellow by its last day of bloom and stand 3–4 in. (7.5–10 cm) above the water. *Nymphaea* 'Georgia Peach' blooms well into the season and is recommended for medium to large ponds.

Nymphaea 'Gladstoniana'

Syn. 'Gladstone'

Richardson 1897

Nymphaea tuberosa × unknown

PLATE 170

CHARACTERISTICS. Marliac rhizome, fairly free flowering.

FLOWERS. Petal color: White (*RHS* 155C). Sepal color: White; purple veins, green tips (*RHS* 155C; veins, 70B; tips, 144C). Anther color: Yellow (*RHS* 9B). Stamen color: Yellow. Flower shape: Stellate, full. Flower size: 5.5–7 in. (14–18 cm). Fragrance: Very slight. Number of petals: 22–25. Number of sepals: 4.

LEAVES. Color: Top, green, new leaves bronzy; underside, bronzy brown. Leaf nearly round, perimeter usually quite wavy; sinus occasionally a wide-open V; both lobes generally raised, overlapping, frequently crimped along sinus. Leaf size: 11–12 in. (28–30 cm). Leaf spread: 5–8 ft. (1.5–2.4 m). Stem color: Usually green, striped purple. Fine fuzz and numerous hairs on peduncle and petiole.

COMMENTS. George Richardson developed this waterlily while working in Lordstown, Ohio. *Nymphaea* 'Gladstoniana' is an ideal plant for a large water garden or natural pond.

Nymphaea 'Gloire du Temple-sur-Lot'

Latour-Marliac Nursery 1913
Parentage unknown
PLATE 171

CHARACTERISTICS. Odorata rhizome, not free flowering.

FLOWERS. Petal color: Shell pink then white (*RHS* 62D paling to 155B). Sepal color: Greenish, blushed shell pink, white by second day (*RHS* 147D; blush, 62D; second day, 155B). Anther color: Yellow (*RHS* 4A). Stamen color: Yellow. Flower shape: Like a double chrysanthemum. Flower size: 5–6 in. (13–15 cm). Fragrance: Very slight. Number of petals: 128 or 129. Number of sepals: 4–6.

LEAVES. Color: Top, green, new leaves brown, orange spot in center; underside, red. Leaf round; lobes overlap completely at sinus. Leaf size: 10 in. (25 cm). Leaf spread: 4–5 ft. (1.2–1.5 m). Stem color: Green. A little fuzz on peduncle and petiole.

COMMENTS. Many people consider *Nymphaea* 'Gloire du Temple-sur-Lot' the most beautiful hardy waterlily. For the greatest number of blooms, plant in a large container at least 2 ft. (0.6 m) in diameter and place under 1 ft. (0.3 m) of water to allow a colony of several rhizomes to develop. This plant is suitable for natural ponds or very large pools.

Nymphaea 'Gloriosa'

Marliac 1896
Parentage unknown
PLATE 172

CHARACTERISTICS. Marliac rhizome, very free flowering.

FLOWERS. Petal color: Bright red, some flecking (*RHS* 66C). Sepal color: White, flushed pink, deeper pink veins (*RHS* 155B; flush, 65D; veins, 66C). Anther color: Bright yellow (*RHS* 16A). Stamen color: Orange-red. Flower shape: Cuplike, somewhat stellate. Flower size: 5 in. (13 cm). Fragrance: Slight. Number of petals: 27–30. Number of sepals: 4 or 5, usually 5.

LEAVES. Color: Top, green, new leaves light purple, dark purple blotches; underside, purple-brown, prominent green veins. Leaf oval; lobes on new leaves usually overlap at sinus, overlap may be absent on older leaves. Leaf size: 8–9 in. (20–23 cm). Leaf spread: 5 ft. (1.5 m). Stem color: Purplish brown. No pubescence on peduncle or petiole.

COMMENTS. *Nymphaea* 'Gloriosa' used to be considered the very best red hardy. Unfortunately, crown rot has decimated this cultivar in many parts of the world. Nurseries are learning how to combat crown rot by segregation of susceptible varieties. Chances are good that this waterlily will become plentiful again, although today it is still scarce. When grown under the right conditions, *N.* 'Gloriosa' is hard to beat in any size pool.

Nymphaea 'Gold Medal'

Slocum 1991
Seedling of *N.* 'Texas Dawn'
PLATE 173

CHARACTERISTICS. Marliac rhizome, free flowering.

FLOWERS. Petal color: Inner petals, rich yellow; outer petals, light yellow (*RHS* inner, 1C; outer, 4D). Sepal color: Greenish yellow (*RHS* 1D). Anther color: Deep yellow (*RHS* 6A). Stamen color: Deep yellow. Flower shape: Round then like chrysanthemum. Flower size: 6–8 in. (15–20 cm). Fragrance: Strong, delightful. Number of petals: 27–31. Number of sepals: 4.

LEAVES. Color: Top, olive green, mottled purple, yellow blotches prominent on new leaves, yellow pattern sometimes retained; underside, pinkish, many reddish purple blotches. Leaf nearly round; sinus usually wide open, lobes may overlap sinus halfway. Leaf size: 10 in. (25 cm). Leaf spread: 4–5 ft. (1.2–1.5 m). Stem color: Brownish purple. Thick fuzz on peduncle and petiole.

COMMENTS. *Nymphaea* 'Gold Medal' has a more double flower (up to 31 petals) than many of the yellow hardy waterlilies currently available. Although the flower color is paler than *N*. 'Texas Dawn', its many petals and freedom of bloom make it highly desirable. I recommend it for medium or large pools.

Nymphaea 'Gonnère'

Syn. 'Snowball', 'Crystal White'

Latour-Marliac Nursery 1914

Nymphaea tuberosa 'Richardsonii' seedling × unknown

PLATE 174

CHARACTERISTICS. Marliac rhizome, fairly free flowering.

FLOWERS. Petal color: White (*RHS* 155C). Sepal color: White, flushed pink, usually bordered and striped green (*RHS* 155C; flush, 62D; border and stripes, 146D). Anther color: Yellow (*RHS* 7A). Stamen color: Yellow. Flower shape: Sphere. Flower size: 4–6 in. (10–15 cm). Fragrance: Pleasant, noticeable in new blooms. Number of petals: 57–62. Number of sepals: 4.

LEAVES. Color: Top, green, newest leaves slightly bronzed; underside, green, newest leaves deep bronze. Leaf round; sinus usually a wide-open V. Leaf size: Usually 6–8 in. (15–20 cm), up to 10 in. (25 cm). Leaf spread: 3–4 ft. (0.9–1.2 m). Stem color: Mostly green. Fairly thick fuzz and hairs on peduncle and petiole.

COMMENTS. Except in very hot regions, particularly zones 8–10, this is a fine choice for a beautiful white waterlily. *Nymphaea* 'Gonnère' is ideal for any size pool. One excellent feature is that blooms stay open late in the day. Though many hardy waterlily flowers close in early afternoon, *N*. 'Gonnère' matches the benefits of all the orange changeables plus other hardies that stay open late in that its flowers stay open until 5:30 p.m. or so.

Nymphaea 'Gregg's Orange Beauty'

Perry's Water Gardens 1996

Natural hybrid, parents probably *N*. 'Texas Dawn' and *N*. 'Perry's Red Beauty'

PLATE 175

CHARACTERISTICS. Free flowering, Marliac rhizome, perennial.

FLOWERS. Petal color: Three inner rows, medium to dark yellow; outer rows, dark pink. Sepal color: Inner, dark pink; outer, bronzy green usually with pink edging. Anther color: Inner, medium yellow; outer, medium yellow. Stamen color: Light yellow. Flower shape: Cuplike. Flower size: 4–5 in. (10–12.7 cm). Fragrance: Slight. Number of petals: 36 or 37. Number of sepals: 4.

LEAVES. Color: Top, new leaf purple, becoming dark green with many purple speckles and blotches; finally, the leaf becomes dark green. Oval shape; sinus may be wide open or partly closed. Leaf size: 8 × 7.5 in. (20.3 × 19 cm). Leaf spread: 4–5 ft. (1.2–1.5 m). Stem color: peduncle greenish brown; petiole reddish brown. No pubescence on peduncle or petiole.

COMMENTS. The color change in the flower is remarkable: The three rows of center petals are yellow; outer petals are deep pink. This rare combination of colors commands everyone's attention. My grandson, Gregg Gibson, discovered this waterlily growing in one of the ponds at Perry's Water Gardens. I recommend *Nymphaea* 'Gregg's Orange Beauty' for any size pond.

Nymphaea 'Gypsy'

Strawn 1998

Nymphaea 'Red Conqueror' × *N. mexicana*

CHARACTERISTICS. Nonviviparous, Marliac rhizome, free flowering, perennial.

FLOWERS. Petal color: Deep blush red that lightens toward outer petals. Sepal color: Inner, light green, faint dark green stripes; outer, medium green with dark green tips. Anther color: Inner, bright yellow; outer, bright yellow. Stamen color: Deep blush red. Flower shape: Stellate. Flower size: 4–5 in. (10–12.5 cm). Fragrance: Pleasant. Number of petals: 28–30. Number of sepals: 4.

LEAVES. Color: Top, medium green; underside, reddish brown with green veining, newer leaves more green than red. Leaf slightly ovate, distinctive tips on lobes; open sinus. Leaf size: 4–6 in. (10–15 cm). Leaf spread: 3–5 ft. (0.9–1.5 m). Stem color: Medium green. Short pubescence on peduncle and petiole.

COMMENTS BY DEAN McGEE. *Nymphaea* 'Gypsy' produces a remarkable display of scarlet hues. It gives off a reddish orange appearance, and blossoms stand 2–3 in. (5–7.5 cm) above the surface of the water. It is a great choice for small or medium ponds.

Nymphaea 'Helen Fowler'

Shaw, year unknown

Parentage unknown

CHARACTERISTICS. Odorata rhizome, fairly free flowering.

FLOWERS. Petal color: Medium pink (*RHS* 65B). Sepal color: Deeper pink than petals (*RHS* 49A). Anther color: Deep golden yellow (*RHS* 20A). Stamen color: Deep yellow. Flower shape: Stellate. Flower size: 6–8 in. (15–20 cm). Fragrance: Very sweet. Number of petals: 19 or 20. Number of sepals: 4.

LEAVES. Color: Top, green, new leaves bronzy; underside, brownish, new leaves purple. Leaves round; sinus narrow, usually open. Leaf size: 9 in. (23 cm). Leaf spread: 4–5 ft. (1.2–1.5 m). Stem color: Brownish. Fine fuzz on peduncle and petiole.

COMMENTS. *Nymphaea* 'Helen Fowler' was named for W. B. Shaw's daughter. Mr. Shaw operated the Shaw Water Gardens (later known as the Kenilworth Aquatic Gardens) in Washington, D.C. This waterlily has a particularly beautiful color. For best performance, plant it in a large planter so that it can form a colony of plants. I recommend it for medium or large pools.

Nymphaea 'Helvola'

Syn. 'Yellow Pygmy'

Marliac 1879

Probably *N. tetragona* × *N. mexicana*

PLATE 176

CHARACTERISTICS. Finger-type rhizome, very free flowering.

FLOWERS. Petal color: Medium yellow (*RHS* 3C). Sepal color: Pale yellow (*RHS* 1D). Anther color:

Yellow (*RHS* 8A). Stamen color: Yellow. Flower shape: Cuplike then stellate. Flower size: 2–3 in. (5–8 cm). Fragrance: Very slight. Number of petals: 16 or 17. Number of sepals: 4.

LEAVES. Color: Top, green, heavily mottled and blotched deep purple; underside, red, small deep purple mottles. Leaf egg-shaped; sinus an open V. Both lobes have an extra projection at the tips. Leaf size: 5 × 3.5 in. (13 × 9 cm). Leaf spread: 2–3 ft. (0.6–0.9 m). Stem color: Green and/or brown; both colors sometimes appear on same plant. No pubescence on peduncle or petiole.

COMMENTS. Flowers do not open until early afternoon in North Carolina, but they do stay open until quite late in the afternoon. *Nymphaea* 'Helvola' is ideal for a tub garden or a small pool.

Nymphaea 'Hermine'

Marliac 1910

Parentage unknown

PLATE 177

CHARACTERISTICS. Marliac rhizome, very free flowering.

FLOWERS. Petal color: White (*RHS* 155D). Sepal color: White (*RHS* 155D). Anther color: Bright yellow (*RHS* 9B). Stamen color: Yellow. Flower shape: Stellate. Flower size: 5–5.5 in. (13–14 cm). Fragrance: Very slight. Number of petals: 17–20. Number of sepals: 4.

LEAVES. Color: Top, olive green, new leaves slightly bronzed; underside, bronzy or purplish, new leaves red. Leaf heart-shaped; sinus wide open. Leaf size: 7 × 6 in. (18 × 15 cm). Leaf spread: 30 in. (75 cm). Stem color: Peduncle green, some tinged bronze; petiole bronzy purple. No pubescence on peduncle or petiole.

COMMENTS. Flowers are quite single and very lovely. I recommend this plant very highly for the small pool or tub garden.

Nymphaea 'Highlight'

Strawn 1998

Nymphaea 'Nigel' × *N. mexicana*

CHARACTERISTICS. Nonviviparous, odorata rhizome, very free flowering, perennial.

FLOWERS. Petal color: inner, creamy yellow; outer, lightens to soft white. Sepal color: Inner, creamy yellowish green; outer, medium green. Anther color: Inner, deep yellow; outer, deep yellow. Stamen color: Deep yellow. Flower shape: Cuplike. Flower size: 3–5 in. (7.5–12.5 cm). Fragrance: Strong. Number of petals: 26–28. Number of sepals: 4.

LEAVES. Color: Top, medium green, newer leaves have faint mottling towards perimeter; underside, reddish brown with green veining at peduncle. Leaf nearly round, slightly pointed tips on lobes; sinus open. Leaf size: 6–8 in. (15–20 cm). Leaf spread: 5–7 ft. (1.5–2.1 m). Stem color: Medium green. No pubescence on peduncle or petiole.

COMMENTS BY DEAN MCGEE. Elegantly large blossoms work well in large ponds with need for lighter colors. This prolific bloomer stands 3–4 in. (7.5–10 cm) above the water and blooms late into the season.

Nymphaea 'Indiana'

Latour-Marliac Nursery 1912

Parentage unknown

PLATE 178

CHARACTERISTICS. Upright rhizome, very free flowering.

FLOWERS. Petal color: Apricot then apricot-orange then deep orange-red (RHS 39A; second day, 41B; third day, 51A). Sepal color: Pale yellow, pinkish veins (RHS 159D; veins, 37C,D). Anther color: Golden orange (RHS 23B). Stamen color: Glowing orange. Flower shape: Cuplike then wide open. Flower size: 3.5–4 in. (9–10 cm). Fragrance: Very slight. Number of petals: 15–19. Number of sepals: 4.

LEAVES. Color: Top, green, purple blotches, new leaves bronzy green, quite heavily mottled deeper purple; underside, bronzy pink, many red speckles and small blotches. Leaf small, nearly round; sinus wide open. Leaf size: 5 × 4.5 in. (13 × 11 cm). Leaf spread: 30 in. (75 cm). Stem color: Peduncle, yellow-green; petiole, darker green. Many fine hairs on peduncle and petiole.

COMMENTS. Nymphaea 'Indiana', with its freedom of bloom, wide color variation, and small leaf spread, is one of the best of the changeable waterlilies. It is very similar to N. 'Aurora' in flower color and shape and in leaf color, shape, and spread, yet

N. 'Indiana' flowers have about six fewer petals. 'Indiana' is an excellent plant for the tub garden and small pool.

Nymphaea 'Inner Light'

Strawn 1997

Nymphaea 'Nigel × N. mexicana

PLATE 179

CHARACTERISTICS. Free flowering, odorata rhizome, perennial.

FLOWERS. Petal color: Inner petals appear darker yellow than outer petals; soft pink base. Sepal color: Inner, light green with darker green tips; outer, dark green. Anther color: Inner, bright yellow; outer, bright yellow. Stamen color: Bright deep yellow. Flower shape: Stellate. Flower size: 5–6 in. (12.5–15 cm). Fragrance: Pleasant. Number of petals: 34–36. Number of sepals: 4.

LEAVES. Color: Top, immature leaves have slight brownish purple mottling and are darker green toward midvein and lighter toward margins; mature leaves brighter green; underside, light reddish brown with light green veining at peduncle. Nearly round leaf, sinus slightly open with overlapping lobes. Leaf size: 6–8 in. (15–20 cm). Leaf spread: 5–7 ft. (1.5–2.1 m). Stem color: Dark green. No pubescence on peduncle or petiole.

COMMENTS BY DEAN MCGEE. Nymphaea 'Inner Light' was named for its luminescent center and is definitely a spectacular addition to any pond, as it holds its large blossoms above the water surface.

Nymphaea 'Irene Heritage'

Slocum 1988

Chance seedling, N. 'Atropurpurea' probable parent

CHARACTERISTICS. Marliac-odorata rhizome, fairly free flowering.

FLOWERS. Petal color: Brilliant glowing red, deepening; outer petals somewhat flecked (RHS 63A then 64A). Sepal color: Pale pink, about 8 lengthwise deep pink stripes, much flecking (RHS 70C; stripes, 64A). Anther color: Golden yellow (RHS 10B). Stamen color: Inner rows, mostly orange; outer rows, red. Flower shape: Stellate. Flower size: 5–6 in. (13–15 cm). Fragrance: Slight. Number of petals: 29–34. Number of sepals: 4.

LEAVES. Color: Top, green, new leaves bronzy

purple; underside, green, new leaves purplish bronze. Leaves oval; lobes usually overlap at sinus, a few sinuses wide open. Leaf size: 9 × 8 in. (23 × 20 cm). Leaf spread: 4–5 ft. (1.2–1.5 m). Stem color: Dark brown. Thick fuzz on all stems.

COMMENTS. *Nymphaea* 'Irene Heritage' is a waterlily of exceptionally good color. It honors Bill and Irene Heritage, who have spent a lifetime with waterlilies. Bill managed two waterlily companies in England and wrote two excellent books on water gardens (see Further Reading). He also received one of the two 1989 Hall of Fame awards presented by the International Waterlily and Water Gardening Society. *Nymphaea* 'Irene Heritage' has moderate-sized leaves and restricted leaf coverage. This makes it especially well suited to small and medium pools, though it is an excellent choice for pools of any size. For maximum success, plant it in a large container and allow it to form a colony of plants. Unfortunately, after doing well in North Carolina for several years, my plants developed crown rot.

Nymphaea 'James Brydon'

Dreer Nurseries 1900
Probably includes *N. alba* var. *rubra*, *N. candida*, and at least one from the *N.* 'Laydekeri' hybrid group
PLATE 180

CHARACTERISTICS. Marliac rhizome, very free flowering.

FLOWERS. Petal color: Brilliant rose-red (*RHS* 66C). Sepal color: Brilliant rose-red (*RHS* 66C). Anther color: Bright orange-yellow (*RHS* 24B). Stamen color: Orange-red. Flower shape: Cuplike. Flower size: 4–5 in. (10–13 cm). Fragrance: Reminiscent of ripe apples. Number of petals: 27. Number of sepals: 4.

LEAVES. Color: Top, green, new leaves purplish brown, dark purple blotches; underside, purple-red, prominent green V from apex to sinus. Leaf round; lobes overlap at sinus. Leaf size: 7 in. (18 cm). Leaf spread: 3–4 ft. (0.9–1.2 m). Stem color: Purple. Some fuzz on lower portion of petiole.

COMMENTS. Unlike *Nymphaea* 'Gloriosa', for many years the finest red waterlily available, *N.* 'James Brydon' is not at all subject to crown rot. It is a first choice for tub garden or small pool and is also excellent for medium and large pools.

Nymphaea 'Japanese Pygmy Red'

Parentage unknown

CHARACTERISTICS. Marliac rhizome, free flowering.

FLOWERS. Petal color: Pale pink then deep red, flecked (*RHS* 62D; third day, 53B). Sepal color: White then pink; veins prominent, greenish then red (*RHS* 195D then 55D; veins, 138C then 53B). Anther color: Deep yellow-orange (*RHS* 20A). Stamen color: Deep yellow. Flower shape: Cuplike then stellate. Flower size: 3–4 in. (8–10 cm). Fragrance: None. Number of petals: 14. Number of sepals: 4.

LEAVES. Color: Top, dark green, new leaves purplish; underside, bronzy brown. Leaf nearly round; sinus open. Leaf size: 7–8 in. (18–20 cm). Leaf spread: 3–3.5 ft. (0.9–1.2 m). Stem color: Brownish. No pubescence on peduncle or petiole.

COMMENTS. This waterlily grows successfully in England but does not do well in warm regions of the middle and southern United States. *Nymphaea* 'Japanese Pygmy Red' does well in zones 3–5, is doubtful in zone 6, and does poorly and usually dies in zones 7–10. I recommend it for northern regions, and then only for the collector. My experience in growing it in Florida (zone 9) and North Carolina (zone 6b) is that it starts to grow and bloom but then dies out.

Nymphaea 'Jasmine'

Henley 1995
Nymphaea 'Caroliniana' × *N.* 'Bee Pod'
PLATE 181

CHARACTERISTICS. Fairly free flowering, odorata rhizome, perennial.

FLOWERS. Petal color: White. Sepal color: Inner, white with slight green at tips; outer, green. Anther color: Inner, golden yellow with faint reddish staining; outer, golden yellow. Stamen color: Golden yellow. Flower shape: Stellate, with medium wide petals. Flower size: 4 in. (10 cm). Fragrance: Quite exceptional, very strong, like jasmine. Number of petals: 24. Number of sepals: 4.

LEAVES. Color: Top, green; underside, bright reddish brown. Round leaf; sinus usually open. Leaf size: 9 in. (23 cm). Leaf spread: 30 in. (75 cm). Stem color: Reddish brown. No pubescence on peduncle or petiole.

COMMENTS BY REG HENLEY. *Nymphaea* 'Jasmine' is not an outstanding improvement on other white odoratas except for the exceptional perfume, which is reminiscent of jasmine. It is without doubt the most highly perfumed waterlily we have ever encountered, of a strength compatible to *Aponogeton distachyos* (cape pondweed). While not a particular outstanding flower, we feel that there is potential here for developing more scent in future waterlilies hybrids.

Nymphaea 'Jim Saunders'

Henley 1996
Nymphaea 'Firecrest' × *N. tetragona*
PLATE 182

CHARACTERISTICS. Fairly free flowering, Marliac rhizome, perennial.

FLOWERS. Petal color: Rich pink. Sepal color: Inner, pink; outer, green. Anther color: Inner, golden yellow, tinged pink; outer, pink. Stamen color: Golden yellow. Flower shape: Cuplike. Flower size: 1.5 in. (3.5 cm). Fragrance: Faint. Number of petals: 34. Number of sepals: 4.

LEAVES. Color: Top, leaf emerging as dark brown slowly fading to plain green; underside, dark brown. Round leaf; sinus open. Leaf size: 4 in. (10 cm). Leaf spread: 12 in. (30 cm). Stem color: Dark brown then light brownish green. No pubescence on peduncle or petiole.

COMMENTS BY REG HENLEY. *Nymphaea* 'Jim Saunders' is a miniature waterlily with good petal numbers and one of the strongest pink colors of all the miniatures.

COMMENTS BY PERRY SLOCUM. This looks like a winner.

Nymphaea 'Joanne Pring'

Pring 1942
Mutation of *N. tetragona*

CHARACTERISTICS. Marliac rhizome, free flowering.

FLOWERS. Petal color: Inner petals light to medium pink, outer petals pale pink; all deepening (*RHS* inner, 73C; third day, 72C; outer, 62D; third day, 73C). Sepal color: White, pink flush, green border (*RHS* 155B; flush, 73D; border, 138D). Anther

color: Golden yellow (*RHS* 15A). Stamen color: Orange. Flower shape: Cuplike. Flower size: 3–4 in. (8–10 cm). Fragrance: Slight. Number of petals: 15 or 16. Number of sepals: 4.

LEAVES. Color: Top, green, new leaves bronzy light purple, deep purple blotches; underside, reddish brown, new leaves reddish purple. Leaf a little longer than wide; sinus a wide-open V. Leaf size: 5.5 in. (14 cm). Leaf spread: 3 ft. (0.9 m). Stem color: Purplish brown. No pubescence on peduncle or petiole.

COMMENTS. This cultivar is somewhat subject to crown rot; otherwise, it is an excellent performer and an ideal choice for a tub garden or small pool.

Nymphaea 'Joey Tomocik'

Strawn 1993
Nymphaea odorata × *N. mexicana*
PLATE 183

CHARACTERISTICS. Nonviviparous, odorata rhizome, very free flowering, perennial.

FLOWERS. Petal color: Bright yellow with slightly rounded petals. Sepal color: Inner, yellowish green, medium green pin stripes; outer, light green with light pink on some edges. Anther color: Inner, deep yellow; outer, deep yellow. Stamen color: Deep yellow. Flower shape: Full, stellate. Flower size: 4–5 in. (10–12.5 cm). Fragrance: Pleasant. Number of petals: 26–28. Number of sepals: 4.

LEAVES. Color: Top, medium green; underside, reddish brown with noticeable flecking, new leaves lighter shades of red. Leaf nearly round; sinus slightly open. Leaf size: 8–10 in. (20–25.5 cm). Leaf spread: 4–5 ft. (1.2–1.5 m). Stem color: Medium green. No pubescence on peduncle or petiole.

COMMENTS BY DEAN MCGEE. A Strawn favorite, this beautiful hybrid boasts one of the brightest yellow hardy blooms. Large flowers stand 3–4 in. (7.5–10 cm) above the water. Dedicated to Mr. Joe Tomocik, curator of the Denver Botanical Gardens, and named after his daughter.

COMMENTS BY PERRY SLOCUM. This is a beautiful waterlily, but in North Carolina it lived for two years and then died from crown rot. It is great for southern states, however.

Nymphaea 'Karl Epple'

Epple 1972

Parentage unknown

PLATE 184

CHARACTERISTICS. Moderately free flowering, tuberosa rhizome, perennial.

FLOWERS. Petal color: Deep pink (*RHS* 63B). Sepal color: Inner, rich pink (*RHS* 62A); outer, olive green (*RHS* 146A). Anther color: Inner, yellow (*RHS* 12B); outer, yellow (*RHS* 12B). Stamen color: Yellow (*RHS* 14B). Flower shape: Cuplike. Flower size: 3–4 in. (7.5–10 cm). Fragrance: Delightful. Number of petals: 24. Number of sepals: 4.

LEAVES. Color: Top, new leaves, purple (*RHS* 185B) changing to olive green (*RHS* 146A). Leaf round; sinus open. Leaf size: 5–7 in. (12.5–18 cm). Leaf spread: 40–48 in. (100–120 cm).

COMMENTS BY ERNST EPPLE. I recommend *N.* 'Karl Epple' for small to medium ponds with a preferred depth of 20–32 in. (50–80 cm). Flowers stand 3–5 in. (7.5–12.5 cm) above the water.

Nymphaea 'Laura Strawn'

Strawn 1997

Nymphaea 'Rosy Morn' × unknown

CHARACTERISTICS. Nonviviparous, Marliac rhizome, very free flowering, perennial.

FLOWERS. Petal color: Creamy yellow throughout petals, faint blush pink stripes on outer petals. Sepal color: Inner, creamy white; greenish gray toward tips and outer edges; outer, light green with dark green tips, faint blush pink on some edges. Anther color: Inner, medium yellow; outer, medium yellow. Stamen color: Medium yellow. Flower shape: Full, stellate. Flower size: 4–5 in. (10–12.5 cm). Fragrance: Pleasant. Number of petals: 34–36. Number of sepals: 4.

LEAVES. Color: Top, medium green; underside, light green with reddish brown and moderate flecking toward perimeter. Leaf ovate, sinus open, definitive tips on lobes. Leaf size: 5–7 in. (12.5–18 cm). Leaf spread: 4–5 ft. (1.2–1.5 m). Stem color: Brown. Pubescence on petiole.

COMMENTS BY DEAN MCGEE. The blossoms of *Nymphaea* 'Laura Strawn' exhibit a very graceful display of yellow. The blooms rest at the water surface. Best suited for large ponds.

Nymphaea 'Laydekeri Alba'

Syn. 'White Laydeker'

Latour-Marliac Nursery, year unknown

Parentage unknown

CHARACTERISTICS. Upright rhizome, very free flowering.

FLOWERS. Petal color: Waxy white (*RHS* 155A). Sepal color: Greenish cream, green lengthwise stripes (*RHS* 160D; stripes, 193C). Anther color: Yellow (*RHS* 12A). Stamen color: Yellow. Flower shape: Cuplike. Flower size: 3–4 in. (8–10 cm). Fragrance: Noticeable in first-day flowers. Number of petals: 17–19. Number of sepals: 4.

LEAVES. Color: Top, deep green, prominent yellow veins, new leaves quite purplish, a few deep purple blotches; underside, red, usually green V along midvein. Leaf round; lobes usually overlap two-thirds down sinus. Leaf size: 8 in. (20 cm). Leaf spread: 3–4 ft. (0.9–1.2 m). Stem color: Green. No pubescence on peduncle or petiole.

COMMENTS. I have seen first-year plants with 8–10 blooms at a time. This beautiful waterlily, which is in very short supply, is in most respects ideal for a tub garden or a small pool. It occasionally dies back, especially in very hot weather.

Nymphaea 'Laydekeri Fulgens'

Syn. 'Red Laydeker'

Marliac 1895

Parentage unknown

PLATE 185

CHARACTERISTICS. Marliac rhizome, extremely free flowering.

FLOWERS. Petal color: Vivid burgundy-red, deepening, flecked (*RHS* 64B; last day, 64A). Sepal color: Pale pink, deepening; white tips (*RHS* 64D; last day, 60C; tips, 155A). Anther color: Golden yellow (*RHS* 20A). Stamen color: Deep orange-red. Flower shape: Cuplike. Flower size: 5–6 in. (13–15 cm). Fragrance: Slight. Number of petals: 20. Number of sepals: 4.

LEAVES. Color: Top, green, new leaves purplish green, dark purple blotches; underside, purple, prominent V on new leaves. Leaf almost round; lobes overlap, covering two-thirds of sinus. Leaf size: 8.5 × 7.5 in. (22 × 19 cm). Leaf spread: 4–5 ft. (1.2–1.5 m). Stem color: Purple-brown. No pubescence on peduncle or petiole.

COMMENTS. This is one of the most magnificent waterlilies of all time. It is one of the very best bloomers and also has the largest flowers and largest leaf spread of any of the Laydekeri waterlilies. A bed of these commands instant attention. *Nymphaea* 'Laydekeri Fulgens' is one of the first to bloom in spring and keeps on flowering through summer and far into autumn. I highly recommend it for any size pool.

Nymphaea 'Laydekeri Lilacea'

Syn. 'Pink Laydeker'

Latour-Marliac Nursery, year unknown

Parentage unknown

CHARACTERISTICS. Marliac rhizome, very free flowering.

FLOWERS. Petal color: Lilac-pink, paling toward outer petals (*RHS* inner, 73C; outer, 73D). Sepal color: Pale pink, deepening; prominent greenish veins (*RHS* 69B or lighter; third day, 73D; veins, 192C). Anther color: Deep yellow (*RHS* 19A). Stamen color: Deep yellow. Flower shape: Cuplike. Flower size: 2.5–3.5 in. (6–9 cm). Fragrance: Slight. Number of petals: 16. Number of sepals: 4.

LEAVES. Color: Top, olive green, a few purple mottles; underside, green, newer leaves purplish. Leaf nearly round; sinus open. Leaf size: 7–8 in. (18–20 cm). Leaf spread: 3–4 ft. (0.9–1.2 m). Stem color: Brownish. No pubescence on peduncle or petiole.

COMMENTS. *Nymphaea* 'Laydekeri Lilacea' is a fine waterlily for the tub garden or small pool. The blooms are an unusual lilac-pink, very close to the color of the common lilac (*Syringa vulgaris*). It is in short supply and may be hard to find. Caution: An inferior substitute is being sold.

Nymphaea 'Laydekeri Purpurata'

Syn. 'Laydekeri Carmine'

Marliac 1895

Parentage unknown

CHARACTERISTICS. Upright rhizome, extremely free flowering.

FLOWERS. Petal color: Tips white; inner rows pinkish red, deepening; outer rows slightly paler, deepening, flecked (*RHS* tips, 155A; inner, 62B then 63A,B; outer, 62C then 63D). Sepal color: White, prominent green veins; last day, pink, flecked, prominent gray-green veins (*RHS* 155A; veins, 138B; last day, 62C; veins, 138B). Anther color: Brilliant yellow (*RHS* 21B). Stamen color: Orange-red. Flower shape: Stellate. Flower size: 5 in. (13 cm). Fragrance: None. Number of petals: 22 or 23. Number of sepals: 4.

LEAVES. Color: Top, green, newest leaves purplish green, dark purple blotches; underside, purple, prominent green lengthwise V on new leaves. Leaves nearly round; sinus a wide-open V. Leaf size: 8–9 in. (20–23 cm). Leaf spread: 4–5 ft. (1.2–1.5 m). Stem color: Purple. No pubescence on peduncle or petiole.

COMMENTS. This cultivar is a very reliable waterlily that I highly recommend for any size pool. Despite the high degree of flecking in the petals, which some consider to detract from the flower, its very free-blooming habit makes *Nymphaea* 'Laydekeri Purpurata' a great waterlily.

Nymphaea 'Laydekeri Rosea'

Marliac 1893

Probably *N. tetragona* × *N. alba* var. *rubra*

PLATE 186

CHARACTERISTICS. Upright rhizome, free flowering.

FLOWERS. Petal color: Pink, inner petals deeper (*RHS* outer, 65C; inner, 64D). Sepal color: Light pink, slightly deeper pink veins and borders (*RHS* 73D; veins and borders, 65B). Anther color: Deep yellow (*RHS* 24B). Stamen color: Orange. Flower shape: Cuplike. Flower size: 4–5 in. (10–13 cm). Fragrance: None. Number of petals: 25–26. Number of sepals: 4.

LEAVES. Color: Top, green, newest leaves purple, mottled deeper purple; underside, purple-brown. Leaf a little longer than wide; lobes overlap about 1.5 in. (4 cm). Leaf size: 9 × 7.5 in. (23 × 19 cm). Leaf spread: 4–5 ft. (1.2–1.5 m). Stem color: Brown. A few hairs on peduncle and petiole.

COMMENTS. Of all the *Nymphaea* Laydekeri pinks and those close to pink, this is perhaps the finest with its rich pink color, abundance of blooms, and adaptability to small pools and tub gardens. I recommend it for medium pools as well.

Nymphaea 'Lemonade'

Lilypons Water Gardens 1996
Parentage unknown
PLATE 187

CHARACTERISTICS. Free flowering, Marliac rhizome, perennial.

FLOWERS. Petal color: Very soft yellow. Sepal color: Inner, light green with light pink outlay; outer, green. Anther color: Inner, bright yellowish orange; outer, bright yellow. Stamen color: Bright sunshine yellow. Flower shape: Stellate. Flower size: 5–6 in. (12.5–15 cm). Fragrance: Subtle, sweet. Number of petals: 22–24. Number of sepals: 4.

LEAVES. Color: Top, new leaves are yellowish green and mature to a bright green with deep purple specks that tend to become sparse toward the midvein; underside, bright reddish pink with a deep red mottling that fades to a lighter red at midvein; underside also turns more greenish yellow at the midvein and petiole. Round leaf; sinus open. Leaf size: 8–8.5 in. (20–21.25 cm). Leaf spread: 6–12 ft. (1.8–3.6 m). Stem color: Dark reddish brown. Pubescence on peduncle and petiole.

COMMENTS BY LILYPONS WATER GARDENS. Nymphaea 'Lemonade' has a very substantial elongated Marliac rhizome, which makes it easy to start for beginning water gardeners. It is also the palest yellow waterlily. We recommend it for medium ponds.

Nymphaea 'Lemon Chiffon'

Strawn 1993
Nymphaea 'Rembrandt' × N. mexicana
PLATE 188

CHARACTERISTICS. Nonviviparous, Marliac rhizome, free flowering, perennial.

FLOWERS. Petal color: Soft yellow throughout, with green stripes on outer petals. Sepal color: Inner, greenish yellow, dark green toward tips; outer, dark green with lighter green edges. Anther color: Inner, medium yellow; outer, medium yellow. Stamen color: Medium yellow. Flower shape: Cuplike. Flower size: 2–4 in. (5–10 cm). Fragrance: Slight. Number of petals: 34. Number of sepals: 4.

LEAVES. Color: Top, dark green with mottling and some flecking; underside, light brown with moderate flecking, newer leaves have light greenish tint.

Leaf is slightly ovate with distinctive points on lobes; overlapping lobes at sinus. Leaf size: 4–6 in. (10–15 cm). Leaf spread: 2–4 ft. (0.6–1.2 m). Stem color: Brown. No pubescence on peduncle or petiole.

COMMENTS BY DEAN McGEE. This waterlily has elegant double yellow flowers that make for a nice contrast with its darker, mottled leaves. Nymphaea 'Lemon Chiffon' is great for a small tub garden or medium pond.

Nymphaea 'Lemon Mist'

Strawn 1997
Nymphaea 'Louise Villemarette' × N. mexicana

CHARACTERISTICS. Nonviviparous, odorata rhizome, very free flowering, perennial.

FLOWERS. Petal color: Medium yellow throughout petals. Sepal color: Inner, light green; outer, medium green. Anther color: Inner, bright yellow; outer, bright yellow. Stamen color: Bright yellow. Flower shape: Stellate, then wide open. Flower size: 4–5 in. (10–12.5 cm). Fragrance: Pleasant. Number of petals: 38–40. Number of sepals: 4.

LEAVES. Color: Top, medium green; underside, slightly red with green veining, newer leaves mostly green. Leaf round; sinus wide open. Leaf size: 7–9 in. (18–23 cm). Leaf spread: 4–5 ft. (1.2–1.5 m). Stem color: Medium green. No pubescence on peduncle or petiole.

COMMENTS BY DEAN McGEE. Nymphaea 'Lemon Mist' produces a large double flower with a beautiful contrast of yellow between the petals and stamens. Blossoms stand 3–4 in. (7.5–10 cm) above the water and bloom late into the season.

Nymphaea 'Lily Pons'

Perry's Water Gardens 1992
Natural hybrid, probably N. 'Perry's Fire Opal' × N.
    'Gloire du Temple-sur-Lot'
PLATE 189

CHARACTERISTICS. Odorata rhizome, moderate bloomer until colony has formed, perennial.

FLOWERS. Petal color: Beautiful medium to light pink. Sepal color: Nearly white on the inside, dark green on outside. Anther color: Inner, deep yellow; outer, deep yellow. Stamen color: Inner, deep yellow; outer, pink-orange. Flower shape: Like multi-petaled peony. Flower size: 5.5–7 in. (14–17.8 cm).

Fragrance: Very slight. Number of petals: 76–103. Number of sepals: 7 or 8.

LEAVES. Color: Top, dark green; underside, red with prominent green veins. Leaf round; sinus open. Leaf size: 8 in. (20.2 cm). Leaf spread: 4–6 ft. (1.2–1.8 cm). Stem color: Bright green. Peduncle has very short fuzz, none on petiole.

COMMENTS. Nymphaea 'Lily Pons' was originally named N. 'Perry's Double Pink' due to its many petals. When Charles Thomas, president of Lilypons Water Gardens, saw it, he fell in love with it and asked if he could rename it after the famous opera singer, Lily Pons. I agreed, of course. It has been a big seller for Lilypons Water Gardens. The bloom of N. 'Lily Pons' is magnificent. However, to really appreciate its beauty, one needs to give it plenty of room and let it form a colony of rhizomes. For this reason, I recommend it for the medium or large pond.

Nymphaea 'Liou'

Strawn 1993

Nymphaea 'Radiant Red' × N. 'Perry's Pink'

CHARACTERISTICS. Nonviviparous, Marliac rhizome, free flowering, perennial.

FLOWERS. Petal color: Deep burgundy red. Sepal color: Inner, greenish white, burgundy at base; outer, medium green. Anther color: Inner, deep yellow; outer, deep yellow. Stamen color: Burgundy red with deep yellow anthers. Flower shape: Cuplike. Flower size: 2–3 in. (5–7.5 cm). Fragrance: Slight. Number of petals: 24–26. Number of sepals: 4.

LEAVES. Color: Top, medium green; underside, reddish brown with green veining present. Leaf slightly ovate, overlapping lobes at sinus. Leaf size: 4–5 in. (10–12.5 cm). Leaf spread: 2–4 ft. (0.6–1.2 m). Stem color: Brown. No pubescence on peduncle or petiole.

COMMENTS BY DEAN MCGEE. The deep, intense red flowers open early, and blossoms rest at the surface of the water. Nymphaea 'Liou' is similar to N. 'Burgundy Princess' but with richer color. Excellent for tub gardens or small or medium ponds.

Nymphaea 'Louise'

Thomas 1962

Nymphaea 'Escarboucle' × N. 'Mrs. C. W. Thomas'

CHARACTERISTICS. Odorata rhizome, fairly free flowering.

FLOWERS. Petal color: Red (RHS 42A). Sepal color: Light pink, white tips (RHS 50C; tips, 155B). Anther color: Deep yellow (RHS 20A). Stamen color: Deep yellow. Flower shape: Cuplike, full. Flower size: 6 in. (15 cm). Fragrance: Very sweet. Number of petals: 20. Number of sepals: 4.

LEAVES. Color: Top, green, new leaves slightly bronzy; underside, brown, new leaves purplish. Leaf nearly round; sinus wide open. Leaf size: 9–10 in. (23–25 cm). Leaf spread: 4–5 ft. (1.2–1.5 m). Stem color: Brownish. No pubescence on peduncle or petiole.

COMMENTS. Plant Nymphaea 'Louise' in a large container so that it can form a colony, and it will then produce more blooms. I recommend 'Louise' for any size pool and especially medium and large pools.

Nymphaea 'Louise Villemarette'

Strawn 1993

Nymphaea 'Peter Slocum' × N. 'Sunrise'

CHARACTERISTICS. Nonviviparous, odorata rhizome, free flowering, perennial.

FLOWERS. Petal color: Fuchsia pink. Sepal color: Inner, fuchsia; outer, olive green with dark green tips, fuchsia on some edges. Anther color: Inner, deep yellow; outer, deep yellow. Stamen color: Fuchsia pink. Flower shape: Cuplike. Flower size: 2–4 in. (5–10 cm). Fragrance: Strong. Number of petals: 32–34. Number of sepals: 4.

LEAVES. Color: Top, medium green, some leaves reddish bronze; underside, reddish plum. Leaf nearly round; sinus closed, lobes overlapping. Leaf size: 4–5 in. (10–12.5 cm). Leaf spread: 2–4 ft. (0.6–1.2 m). Stem color: Brown. No pubescence on peduncle or petiole.

COMMENTS BY DEAN MCGEE. Nymphaea 'Louise Villemarette' produces small, intense fuchsia, double blossoms that rest on the surface of the water. It is an excellent choice for small or medium ponds.

Nymphaea 'Lucida'

Marliac 1894

Parentage unknown

CHARACTERISTICS. Marliac rhizome, free flowering.

FLOWERS. Petal color: Inner petals, red; outer petals whitish pink, pink veins (*RHS* inner, 51A; outer, 36D; veins, 51D). Sepal color: White, pink base (*RHS* 155A; base, red 36D). Anther color: Yellow-orange (*RHS* 14A). Stamen color: Deep yellow. Flower shape: Stellate. Flower size: 5–6 in. (13–15 cm). Fragrance: Slight, if any. Number of petals: 18–20. Number of sepals: 4.

LEAVES. Color: Top, green, scattering of large purple mottles and blotches; underside, purple-brown. Leaf a little longer than wide; sinus open. Leaf size: Up to 10×9 in. (25×23 cm). Leaf spread: 4–5 ft. (1.2–1.5 m). Stem color: Greenish bronze, striped purple. No pubescence on peduncle or petiole.

COMMENTS. *Nymphaea* 'Lucida' has attractive leaves, beautiful flower color, and a very free-flowering habit. It is a fine choice for any size pool.

Nymphaea 'Lustrous'
Parentage unknown

CHARACTERISTICS. Marliac rhizome, very free flowering.

FLOWERS. Petal color: Light salmon-pink (*RHS* 36C). Sepal color: Medium salmon-pink (*RHS* 37C). Anther color: Yellow (*RHS* 9C). Stamen color: Yellow. Flower shape: Cuplike. Flower size: 5–6 in. (13–15 cm). Fragrance: Slight. Number of petals: 28–30. Number of sepals: 4.

LEAVES. Color: Top, green, new leaves bronzy; underside, brownish purple, new leaves red. Leaf oval, wavy edges; sinus usually open. Leaf size: 9 × 8 in. (23 × 20 cm). Leaf spread: 3–5 ft. (0.9–1.5 m). Stem color: Brownish green. Some fuzz on peduncle and petiole.

COMMENTS. This North American hybrid makes an excellent waterlily for any size pool. Unlike most hardy waterlily cultivars, *Nymphaea* 'Lustrous' develops viable seeds. It is believed to be a parent of *N*. 'Pink Sensation'.

Nymphaea 'Madame Wilfron Gonnère'
Syn. 'Pink Gonnère'
Latour-Marliac Nursery after 1912
Parentage unknown

CHARACTERISTICS. Marliac rhizome, very free flowering.

FLOWERS. Petal color: Inner petals rich pink; outer petals lighter (*RHS* inner, 62C; outer, 62D). Sepal color: Greenish white, veins slightly darker; older flowers blushed pink (*RHS* 193D; veins, 193A; blush, 62D or paler). Anther color: Golden yellow (*RHS* 12A). Stamen color: Gold, pink outer row. Flower shape: Peony-style. Flower size: 5 in. (13 cm). Fragrance: None. Number of petals: 33. Number of sepals: 4.

LEAVES. Color: Top, green, new leaves slightly bronzed; underside, same as top. Early spring leaves display an attractive broad yellow lengthwise stripe on top that disappears completely when warm weather arrives. Leaf round; lobes overlap considerably at sinus. Leaf size: 9.5–10 in. (24–25 cm). Leaf spread: 4 ft. (1.2 m). Stem color: Greenish brown, faint purple stripes; oldest stems brown. Short fuzz and hairs on peduncle and petiole.

COMMENTS. *Nymphaea* 'Madame Wilfron Gonnère', with its very double blooms, is a beautiful waterlily for any size pool.

Nymphaea 'Marguerite Laplace'
Latour-Marliac Nursery 1913
Parentage unknown

CHARACTERISTICS. Marliac rhizome, free flowering.

FLOWERS. Petal color: Medium pink (*RHS* 68C). Sepal color: White, flushed pink, pink veins near base (*RHS* 155C; flush, 62D; veins, 62C). Anther color: Yellow (*RHS* 13A). Stamen color: Yellow-orange. Flower shape: Cuplike, full. Flower size: 6.5–7 in. (16–18 cm). Fragrance: Slight. Number of petals: 30. Number of sepals: 4.

LEAVES. Color: Top, deep green; underside, bronzy green. Leaves round; sinus usually about one-third open. Leaf size: 9 in. (23 cm). Leaf spread: 5 ft. (1.5 m). Stem color: Green. A few hairs on peduncle and petiole.

COMMENTS. *Nymphaea* 'Marguerite Laplace' is a very beautiful pink waterlily developed in France. I recommend it for medium and large water gardens.

Nymphaea 'Marie Clara'
Henley 2000
Nymphaea 'Perry's Darkest Red' × *N*. 'Perry's Almost Black'
PLATE 190

CHARACTERISTICS. Free flowering, Marliac rhizome, perennial.

FLOWERS. Petal color: Dark red with black sheen. Sepal color: Inner, delicate pink; outer, dark green edged with rose. Anther color: Inner, yellow overlaid with dark red; outer, red. Stamen color: Orange. Flower shape: Cuplike. Flower size: 6.5 in. (16 cm). Fragrance: Faint. Number of petals: 48. Number of sepals: 5.

LEAVES. Color: Top, emerge reddish brown aging to plain green. Leaves are round, with slight indent on new leaves on side away from sinus; sinus either open or closed; leaf lobes overlap; lobe tips either rounded or pointed. Leaf size: 10 in. (25.5 cm). Leaf spread: About 4.5 ft. (1.4 m). Stem color: Peduncle green with brown shading, petiole plain green. Pubescence slight on both stems.

COMMENTS BY REG HENLEY. Nymphaea 'Marie Clara' is the development of two of Perry's dark red varieties acclimated to the United Kingdom's cool climate (zones 7–9). It is a strong grower with good flowering potential at our latitude, carrying on the work to an ultimate black flower.

Nymphaea 'Marliacea Albida'

Syn. 'Marliac White'
Marliac 1880
Parentage unknown

CHARACTERISTICS. Marliac rhizome, very free flowering.

FLOWERS. Petal color: White (RHS 155C). Sepal color: Pale green, pink tint and veins evident in older blooms (RHS 1D; tint and veins, 55B). Anther color: Yellow (RHS 9A). Stamen color: Yellow. Flower shape: Cuplike. Flower size: 5–6 in. (13–15 cm). Fragrance: Very slight. Number of petals: 23–26. Number of sepals: 4.

LEAVES. Color: Top, green; underside, green, new leaves slightly bronzed. Leaf round; sinus on older leaves generally an open V, lobes on younger leaves overlap to cover one-third to three-fourths of sinus. Lobes sometimes raised. Leaf size: 9 in. (23 cm). Leaf spread: 3–4 ft. (0.9–1.2 m). Stem color: Greenish brown. Fine fuzz and numerous hairs on peduncle and petiole.

COMMENTS. Due to its moderate leaf spread and abundance of blooms, Nymphaea 'Marliacea Albida' is a great waterlily for any size pool.

Nymphaea 'Marliacea Carnea'

Syn. 'Marliac Flesh', 'Morning Glory'
Marliac 1887
Parentage unknown

CHARACTERISTICS. Marliac rhizome, very free flowering.

FLOWERS. Petal color: Light pink (RHS 62D or lighter). Sepal color: Slightly deeper pink than petals, still deeper pink veins (RHS 62D; veins, 62C). Anther color: Deep yellow (RHS 12A). Stamen color: Deep yellow. Flower shape: Cuplike. Flower size: 4.5–5 in. (11–13 cm). Fragrance: Slight. Number of petals: 23. Number of sepals: 4.

LEAVES. Color: Top, green, new leaves purplish; underside, red. Leaf a little longer than wide; lobes may overlap sinus completely, halfway, or not at all. Leaf size: 7.5–8 in. (19–20 cm). Leaf spread: 4–5 ft. (1.2–1.5 m). Stem color: Yellowish green. No pubescence on peduncle or petiole.

COMMENTS. Nymphaea 'Marliacea Carnea' is one of Marliac's finest creations. Some people confuse this waterlily with his N. 'Marliacea Rosea', which is very similar but whose flowers are one or two shades deeper. Also, differences are found in stem color, sinuses, and pubescence on stems (lacking in N. 'Marliacea Carnea'). I recommend N. 'Marliacea Carnea' for any size pool, especially medium and large ones.

Nymphaea 'Marliacea Chromatella'

Syn. 'Golden Cup', 'Marliac Yellow'
Marliac 1887
Nymphaea alba × N. mexicana

CHARACTERISTICS. Pineapple rhizome, very free flowering.

FLOWERS. Petal color: Light yellow (RHS 2D). Sepal color: Pale greenish yellow, faint pink blush, pinkish veins at base (RHS 1D; blush, 62D or lighter; veins, 62D). Anther color: Deep yellow (RHS 10A). Stamen color: Yellow. Flower shape: Cuplike. Flower size: 4–5.5 in. (10–14 cm). Fragrance: Strong in new blooms. Number of petals: 22–25. Number of sepals: 4 or 5.

LEAVES. Color: Top, green, young leaves blotched and mottled purple; underside, reddish purple, new leaves green, small purple blotches. Leaf round; sinus an open V. Leaf size: 8–9 in. (20–23 cm). Leaf spread: 3 ft. (0.9 m). Stem color: Green. Short fuzz and hairs on peduncle and petiole.

COMMENTS. For beauty and performance, *Nymphaea* 'Marliacea Chromatella' rates among the very best of the hardy waterlilies. It is very satisfactory for any size pool, including the tub garden. The rhizome of a mature plant does actually resemble a pineapple.

Nymphaea 'Marliacea Rosea'

Syn. 'Marliac Rose'
Marliac(?) 1879(?)
Parentage unknown
PLATE 191

CHARACTERISTICS. Marliac rhizome, very free flowering.

FLOWERS. Petal color: Pale pink near base, lighter toward tip (*RHS* 65D or lighter). Sepal color: Shell pink, darker pink veins (*RHS* 69A; veins, 63A). Anther color: Golden yellow (*RHS* 12A). Stamen color: Same as anthers or very close. Flower shape: Cuplike then stellate. Flower size: 5–6 in. (13–15 cm). Fragrance: Very slight. Number of petals: 17–23. Number of sepals: 4 or 5.

LEAVES. Color: Top, green, new leaves bronzy purple; underside, red. Leaf nearly round; sinus wide open. Leaf size: 8–9 in. (20–23 cm). Leaf spread: 4–6 ft. (1.2–1.8 m). Stem color: Peduncle, bronzy; petiole, bronzy green. Many fine hairs on peduncle and petiole.

COMMENTS. *Nymphaea* 'Marliacea Rosea' is one of the choicest waterlilies for any size pool. It is quite similar to 'Marliacea Carnea' but deeper in color.

Nymphaea 'Marliacea Rubra Punctata'

Marliac 1889
Parentage unknown

CHARACTERISTICS. Marliac rhizome, moderately free flowering.

FLOWERS. Petal color: Deep purple-red, some flecking (*RHS* 64B). Sepal color: Pinkish (*RHS* 62C). Anther color: Golden yellow (*RHS* 20B). Sta-

men color: Bright orange. Flower shape: Globular or cuplike. Flower size: 4 in. (10 cm). Fragrance: Pleasant, noticeable even in older flowers. Number of petals: 20–22. Number of sepals: 4.

LEAVES. Color: Top, green; underside, bronzy purple. Leaf round; lobes overlap 1 in. (2.5 cm) at sinus. Leaf size: 9 in. (23 cm). Leaf spread: 3 ft. (0.9 m). Stem color: Purplish brown. Thick fuzz on peduncle and petiole.

COMMENTS. Petals and sepals alike are short and rounded. The very unusual flower shape makes this a collector's waterlily for a small or medium pool.

Nymphaea 'Martha'

Strawn 1993
Nymphaea 'Pink Sensation' × *N*. 'Flammea'
PLATE 192

CHARACTERISTICS. Nonviviparous, Marliac rhizome, very free flowering, perennial.

FLOWERS. Petal color: Soft pink throughout with light fading at tips; outer petals have olive green stripes. Sepal color: Inner, pinkish green with dark green pin stripes, dark green at tips; outer, olive green. Anther color: Inner, deep yellow; outer, soft pink with deep yellow anthers. Stamen color: Deep yellow. Flower shape: Cuplike, then stellate. Flower size: 3–4 in. (7.5–10 cm). Fragrance: Slight. Number of petals: 30–32. Number of sepals: 4.

LEAVES. Color: Top, medium green; underside, reddish plum. Leaf slightly ovate with slight convolutions; sinus open. Leaf size: 4–5 in. (10–12.5 cm). Leaf spread: 3–5 ft. (0.9–1.5 m). Stem color: Medium green. Pubescence on peduncle and petiole.

COMMENTS BY DEAN McGEE. The gorgeous light pink flowers with long petals make for a very elegant display in a medium or large pond. Blossoms of *Nymphaea* 'Martha' sit directly on the surface of the water, and it blooms late into the season.

Nymphaea 'Mary'

Strawn 1993
Nymphaea 'Rembrandt' × unknown

CHARACTERISTICS. Nonviviparous, Marliac rhizome, fairly free flowering, perennial.

FLOWERS. Petal color: Faint red blush turning deeper on inner petals; outer petals striped medium green. Sepal color: Inner, blush red, dark green tips; outer, very dark green with soft pink on some edges. Anther color: Inner, medium yellow; outer, medium yellow. Stamen color: Blush red. Flower shape: Cuplike. Flower size: 3–5 in. (7.5–12.5 cm). Fragrance: Strong. Number of petals: 36. Number of sepals: 4.

LEAVES. Color: Top, dark green with plum toward edges, newer leaves deep plum; underside, reddish purple. Leaf is nearly round, lobes overlapping at sinus. Leaf size: 4–5 in. (10–12.5 cm). Leaf spread: 3–5 ft. (0.9–1.5 m). Stem color: Red-purple. No pubescence on peduncle or petiole.

COMMENTS BY DEAN MCGEE. The bold red color with darker leaf color makes Nymphaea 'Mary' a nice stand-alone waterlily. It is well suited for medium ponds.

Nymphaea 'Masaniello'

Marliac 1908
Parentage unknown
PLATE 193

CHARACTERISTICS. Marliac rhizome, very free flowering.

FLOWERS. Petal color: Inner petals, strawberry pink; outer petals, lighter (RHS inner, 65A; outer, 65C). Sepal color: White; pink flush at base, deepening (RHS 155A; flush, 65D then 65C). Anther color: Golden yellow (RHS 19A). Stamen color: Golden orange. Flower shape: Cuplike. Flower size: 5–6 in. (13–15 cm). Fragrance: Slight. Number of petals: 25. Number of sepals: 4.

LEAVES. Color: Top, green; underside, green, new leaves slightly bronzed. Leaf nearly round; sinus usually open; lobes may overlap 1 in. (2.5 cm) at petiole. Leaf size: Up to 10 × 9 in. (25 × 23 cm). Leaf spread: 4 ft. (1.2 m). Stem color: Brown, occasional faint purple stripes; petiole green near leaf base. No pubescence on peduncle or petiole.

COMMENTS. Nymphaea 'Masaniello', with its bicolor flowers, is an excellent plant for any size pool.

Nymphaea 'Maurice Laydeker'

Latour-Marliac Nursery, year unknown
Parentage unknown

CHARACTERISTICS. Marliac rhizome, free flowering.

FLOWERS. Petal color: Inner petals strawberry red; outer petals paler (RHS inner, 62B; outer, 62D). Sepal color: White, base develops pink blush (RHS 155D; blush, 62D). Anther color: Yellow-orange (RHS 26C). Stamen color: Burnt orange. Flower shape: Cuplike. Flower size: 4 in. (10 cm). Fragrance: Slight. Number of petals: 20 or 21. Number of sepals: 4.

LEAVES. Color: Top, green; underside, purple-brown. Leaf almost round; sinus usually a wide-open V yet lobes sometimes overlap at sinus. Leaf size: 6–7 in. (15–18 cm). Leaf spread: 2–3 ft. (0.6–0.9 m). Stem color: Green. No pubescence on peduncle or petiole.

COMMENTS. With its red-and-white bicolor combination, small leaves, and small leaf spread, Nymphaea 'Maurice Laydeker' makes a fine choice for the tub garden, small, or medium pool. In North Carolina, however, it is frequently afflicted with crown rot.

Nymphaea 'Mayla'

Strawn 1993
Nymphaea 'Peter Slocum' × N. 'Fabiola'
PLATE 194

CHARACTERISTICS. Nonviviparous, odorata rhizome, very free flowering, perennial.

FLOWERS. Petal color: Fuchsia pink throughout petals. Sepal color: Inner, fuchsia; outer, medium green with dark green tips, some edges are fuchsia. Anther color: Inner, bright yellow; outer, bright yellow. Stamen color: Pink. Flower shape: Stellate, then wide open. Flower size: 5–6 in. (12.5–15 cm). Fragrance: Strong. Number of petals: 40. Number of sepals: 4.

LEAVES. Color: Top, medium green, some leaves are plum colored, newer leaves deep plum; underside, reddish purple, center vein leading from peduncle usually light green. Leaf nearly round, tips of lobes slightly pointed with lobes overlapping at sinus. Leaf size: 8–10 in. (20–25 cm). Leaf spread: 6–8 ft. (1.8–2.4 m). Stem color: Bronze. Pubescence on petiole.

COMMENTS BY DEAN MCGEE. Known for its fascinating flower and leaf colors, Nymphaea 'Mayla' boasts a large bloom that opens wide and sits just on top of the water surface. This waterlily is the showpiece for any large pond, and is one of Kirk Strawn's most popular hybrids.

Nymphaea 'Meteor'

Marliac 1909

Parentage unknown

PLATE 195

CHARACTERISTICS. Marliac rhizome, free flowering.

FLOWERS. Petal color: Inner petals red; outer petals pink, white tips (RHS inner, 63A; outer, 63C; tips, 155D). Sepal color: Light pink, light green border (RHS 62D or lighter; border, 142D). Anther color: Yellow (RHS 13B). Stamen color: Orange. Flower shape: Stellate. Flower size: 6–7 in. (15–18 cm). Fragrance: Slight. Number of petals: 26 or 27. Number of sepals: 4.

LEAVES. Color: Top, medium green; underside, medium green, young leaves bronzy. Leaf round; sinus closed. Leaf size: 9 in. (23 cm). Leaf spread: 4–6 ft. (1.2–1.8 m). Stem color: Rhubarb red, some purple stripes. Fuzz on peduncle and petiole, especially on peduncle.

COMMENTS. This cultivar's flowers are a brilliant, glowing color. Nymphaea 'Meteor' is a fine waterlily for medium and large pools.

Nymphaea 'M. Evelyn Stetson'

Paul Stetson Sr. 1986

Parentage unknown

CHARACTERISTICS. Odorata rhizome, free flowering.

FLOWERS. Petal color: Inner, yellow; outer, white (RHS inner, 6A; outer, 155B). Sepal color: Greenish yellow (RHS 142C). Anther color: Deep yellow (RHS 6A). Stamen color: Yellow. Flower shape: Stellate. Flower size: 6–8 in. (15–20 cm). Fragrance: Very sweet. Number of petals: 40–42. Number of sepals: 5.

LEAVES. Color: Top, deep green; underside, yellow to pink. Leaves nearly round; lobes have pointed tips, overlap at sinus. Leaf size: 8–9 in. (20–23 cm). Leaf spread: 6 ft. (1.8 m). Stem color: Brown and red. Some fuzz on peduncle and petiole.

COMMENTS. Nymphaea 'M. Evelyn Stetson', with its very double flowers and distinctive long petals, grows quite large if given room. I recommend this plant for medium or large pools.

Nymphaea 'Michael Berthold'

Berthold 1997

Nymphaea 'Frita' × N. 'Bee Pod'

PLATE 196

CHARACTERISTICS. Free flowering, Marliac rhizome, nonviviparous, perennial.

FLOWERS. Petal color: Pink increasing in intensity to center, fading with age to pale pink. Sepal color: Inner, white with pink lines; outer, green. Anther color: Inner, golden yellow; outer, deep pink to red. Stamen color: Golden yellow. Flower shape: Narrow petals, stellate. Flower size: 4.25 in. (11 cm). Fragrance: Strong, like vanilla. Number of petals: 23. Number of sepals: 8.

LEAVES. Color: Top, new leaf is reddish brown aging to plain green; underside, light wine red, center has green rib. Leaf emerges with upturned edge, reducing with age but never totally flat. Leaf size: 4.75 in. (12 cm). Leaf spread: 4 ft. (1.2 m). Stem color: Reddish brown. No pubescence on peduncle or petiole.

COMMENTS BY FRANZ BERTHOLD. Nymphaea 'Michael Berthold' is a smaller plant than the seed parent (N. 'Frita') but with the same style of flowers and more red in the center of the flowers. The pink increases in intensity with age.

Nymphaea 'Moon Dance'

Florida Aquatic Nursery 1996

Nymphaea mexicana × N. odorata

PLATE 197

CHARACTERISTICS. Free flowering, Marliac-odorata rhizome, perennial.

FLOWERS. Petal color: Creamy white petals and petaloids. Sepal color: Inner, creamy white with pink blush; outer, green to bronze. Anther color: Inner, golden yellow; outer, golden yellow. Stamen color: Golden yellow. Flower shape: Stellate. Flower size: 6 in. (15 cm). Fragrance: Slight sweet scent. Number of petals: 30. Number of sepals: 4.

LEAVES. Color: Top, olive green with chocolate and burgundy blotches; underside, grayish red with burgundy blotches. Oval leaf; sinus open. Leaf size: 10 × 8 in. (25.5 × 20 cm). Leaf spread: 4–6 ft. (1.2–1.8 m). Stem color: Reddish brown. Pubescence on peduncle and petiole.

COMMENTS BY BRAD AND BRUCE MCLANE. Nymphaea 'Moon Dance' won first prize in its category at the International Waterlily and Water Gardening Society 2001 Banksian Trials. The honors really belong to mother nature because it is a natural cross of *N. mexicana* × *N. odorata* collected from Lake Okeechobee, Florida. *Nymphaea* 'Moon Dance' would make a fine addition to any medium or large pool.

Nymphaea 'Moorei'

Adelaide Botanic Gardens 1900

Nymphaea alba × *N. mexicana*

PLATE 198

CHARACTERISTICS. Upright rhizome, fairly free flowering.

FLOWERS. Petal color: Medium yellow (*RHS* 1C). Sepal color: Greenish white, tips greenish yellow; veins and edges pinkish, especially in older flowers (*RHS* 157B; tips, 145C; veins and edges, 38C). Anther color: Deep yellow (*RHS* 10A). Stamen color: Yellow. Flower shape: Cuplike then stellate. Flower size: 4–5 in. (10–13 cm). Fragrance: Very slight, if any. Number of petals: 25 or 26. Number of sepals: 4 or 5.

LEAVES. Color: Top, green, numerous purple specks and small mottles around perimeter of new leaves; underside, red, newest leaves brown, all leaves covered with numerous purple specks and small purple mottles. Leaf a little longer than wide; sinus an open V. Leaf size: 9 in. (23 cm). Leaf spread: 3–4 ft. (0.9–1.2 m). Stem color: Green. No pubescence on peduncle or petiole.

COMMENTS. Flowers are a lovely shade of yellow, a shade deeper than those of *Nymphaea* 'Marliacea Chromatella'; however, this plant does not match *N.* 'Marliacea Chromatella' in the number of blooms produced. *Nymphaea* 'Moorei' could be used in any size pool. I have found it subject to crown rot in North Carolina.

Nymphaea 'Mrs. C. W. Thomas'

Thomas 1931

Parentage unknown

PLATE 199

CHARACTERISTICS. Odorata rhizome, fairly free flowering.

FLOWERS. Petal color: Inner petals pale pink; outer petals shell pink (*RHS* inner, 36D; outer, 62D). Sepal color: Shell pink (*RHS* 62D). Anther

color: Deep yellow (*RHS* 13A). Stamen color: Deep yellow. Flower shape: Peony-style. Flower size: 6–7 in. (15–18 cm). Fragrance: Delightful. Number of petals: 36. Number of sepals: 4.

LEAVES. Color: Top, green, new leaves bronzy; underside, brown, new leaves purplish. Leaf nearly round, edges smooth; sinus open. Leaf size: 9–10 in. (23–25 cm). Leaf spread: 4–6 ft. (1.2–1.8 m). Stem color: Brownish. Fine fuzz and hair on peduncle and petiole.

COMMENTS. *Nymphaea* 'Mrs. C. W. Thomas', originally a chance seedling from Lilypons Water Gardens, is a beautiful cultivar. If planted in a large container so that it can form a colony of rhizomes, it will bloom quite freely. I recommend it for medium and large pools.

Nymphaea 'Mt. Shasta'

Slocum 1993

Nymphaea 'Pink Starlet' × *N.* 'Queen of Whites'

PLATE 200

CHARACTERISTICS. Fairly free flowering, Marliac rhizome, perennial.

FLOWERS. Petal color: Pure white. Sepal color: Pale green, almost white on inside; dark green on outside. Anther color: Inner, dark yellow; outer, dark yellow. Stamen color: medium to light yellow. Flower shape: Cuplike at first, like a fountain as it fully opens. Flower size: 7–9 in. (17.5–22.5 cm). Fragrance: None. Number of petals: 24–26. Number of sepals: 4.

LEAVES. Color: Top, olive green; underside, pinkish with prominent green veins. Leaf round with wavy edges; sinus wide open. Leaf size: 7–9 in. (17.5–22.5 cm). Leaf spread: 5–6 ft. (1.5–1.8 m). Stem color: Peduncle greenish brown, petiole either greenish or brownish. No pubescence on peduncle or petiole.

COMMENTS. With its long petals and large blooms, this has been a favorite at Perry's Water Gardens. Due to its fairly large leaf spread, I recommend *Nymphaea* 'Mt. Shasta' for medium and large pools.

Nymphaea 'Newton'

Marliac 1910

Parentage unknown

PLATE 201

CHARACTERISTICS. Marliac rhizome, very free flowering.

FLOWERS. Petal color: Red (*RHS* 51A). Sepal color: Pink, white tips (*RHS* 55D; tips, 155A). Anther color: Orange (*RHS* 21A). Stamen color: Deep yellow. Flower shape: Stellate, long narrow petals. Flower size: 6–8 in. (15–20 cm). Fragrance: Slight. Number of petals: 19. Number of sepals: 4.

LEAVES. Color: Top, green, purple blotches; underside, brownish red. Leaf nearly round; sinus open. Leaf size: 9 in. (23 cm). Leaf spread: 3.5–5 ft. (1.1–1.5 m). Stem color: Reddish brown. Some short fuzz on peduncle and petiole.

COMMENTS. Long narrow petals and sepals are found in only a few hardy waterlilies: *Nymphaea* 'Newton', *N.* 'Perry's Red Beauty', and *N.* 'Yellow Queen'. New flowers closely resemble many tropical waterlilies and are held about 3 in. (7.5 cm) above the water; last-day flowers float. *Nymphaea* 'Newton' is an exquisite waterlily, and I recommend it for any size pool.

Nymphaea 'Norma Gedye'

Gedye 1973
Parentage unknown
PLATE 202

CHARACTERISTICS. Marliac rhizome, fairly free flowering.

FLOWERS. Petal color: Medium pink, deepening toward base (*RHS* 65A; base, 68B or lighter). Sepal color: Pink (*RHS* 68B or lighter). Anther color: Yellow (*RHS* 12A). Stamen color: Inner rows golden yellow; outer rows pink. Flower shape: Stellate, open. Flower size: 6.5–7.5 in. (16–19 cm). Fragrance: Slight. Number of petals: 19 or 20. Number of sepals: 4.

LEAVES. Color: Top, green, new leaves purplered; underside, red. Leaf a little longer than wide; sinus usually a wide-open V. Leaf size: Up to 11 in. (28 cm). Leaf spread: 4–5 ft. (1.2–1.5 m). Stem color: Green, striped purple. Fine hairs on peduncle and petiole, more on petiole.

COMMENTS. This beautiful waterlily, developed at Gedye's Water Gardens in Doncaster East, Australia, is named for the wife of the nursery owner, Laurence Gedye. Truly, a large specimen of *Nymphaea* 'Norma Gedye' is one of the most beautiful of all waterlilies. I highly recommend it for medium and large pools.

Nymphaea 'Odalisque'

Marliac 1908
Parentage may include *N. tuberosa*

CHARACTERISTICS. Tuberosa rhizome, fairly free flowering.

FLOWERS. Petal color: Pinkish (*RHS* 36A). Sepal color: Pinkish (*RHS* 36A). Anther color: Yellowish orange (*RHS* 22C). Stamen color: Yellowish orange. Flower shape: Stellate; sepals and outer petals point downward when flower is open. Flower size: 5–6 in. (13–15 cm). Fragrance: Some. Number of petals: 23. Number of sepals: 4 or 5, usually 5.

LEAVES. Color: Top, apple green; underside, dark brownish red. Leaves nearly round, unusually a little broader than long; sinus a small V. Leaf size: 6.5 × 7 in. (16 × 18 cm). Leaf spread: 4–5 ft. (1.2–1.5 m). Stem color: Green. No pubescence on peduncle or petiole.

COMMENTS. *Nymphaea* 'Odalisque' has unusual features for a hardy: The flowers are held 5–6 in. (13–15 cm) above water and the sepals and outer petals hang down. To become a frequent bloomer, *N.* 'Odalisque' needs to be planted in a large container and allowed to form a colony. I recommend it for medium and large pools.

Nymphaea odorata 'Sulphurea'

Marliac 1879
Seedling of *N. odorata*

CHARACTERISTICS. Odorata rhizome, fairly free flowering.

FLOWERS. Petal color: Rich yellow (*RHS* 4A). Sepal color: Pale yellowish green (*RHS* 1D). Anther color: Yellow (*RHS* 7A,B). Stamen color: Yellow. Flower shape: Cuplike then stellate. Flower size: 6–7 in. (15–18 cm). Fragrance: Quite sweet. Number of petals: 21–24. Number of sepals: 4.

LEAVES. Color: Top, green, new leaves speckled and blotched purple; underside, red or purple, deep purple mottles. Leaves nearly round; lobes pointed at tips. Sinus usually an open V; lobes may overlap somewhat, especially on new leaves. Leaf size: Up to 10 × 9 in. (25 × 23 cm). Leaf spread: 3–4 ft. (0.9–1.2 m). Stem color: Peduncle, yellowish green, occasional purple stripe; petiole, purple or brown. Fine hairs on peduncle and petiole.

COMMENTS. *Nymphaea odorata* 'Sulphurea' flowers have a very good color and scent. The blooms are open only a short time, however, opening late in the morning and closing in midafternoon. This waterlily is suited for medium or large pools.

Nymphaea odorata 'Turicensis'

Seedling of *N. odorata*

CHARACTERISTICS. Odorata rhizome, fairly free flowering.

FLOWERS. Petal color: Soft pink (*RHS* 62D). Sepal color: Greenish yellow (*RHS* 145D). Anther color: Deep yellow (*RHS* 13A). Stamen color: Deep yellow. Flower shape: Stellate. Flower size: 5–6 in. (13–15 cm). Fragrance: Lovely and pleasant. Number of petals: 25 or 26. Number of sepals 4.

LEAVES. Color: Top, green; underside, bronzy red. Leaf nearly round with rounded lobes; sinus usually open. Leaf size: 5–6 in. (13–15 cm). Leaf spread: 2.5 ft. (0.8 m). Stem color: Greenish. No pubescence on peduncle or petiole.

COMMENTS. For best performance, as with other odorata types, this waterlily should be planted in a large container so that it can form a colony of plants. It will then bloom fairly well. *Nymphaea odorata* 'Turicensis' is currently more widely known in England than in the United States. I recommend it for medium or large pools.

Nymphaea 'Osceola'

Connelly 1989

Natural hybrid of *N. mexicana* No. 1 × *N. odorata*

CHARACTERISTICS. Free flowering, Marliac-odorata rhizome, perennial.

FLOWERS. Petal color: Center petals deep yellow, outer petals lighter. Sepal color: Inner, light yellowish green; outer, dark green. Anther color: Inner, very deep yellow; outer, deep yellow. Stamen color: Deep yellow. Flower shape: Cuplike then stellate. Flower size: 6–7 in. (15–18 cm). Fragrance: Fairly sweet first two days. Number of petals: 21 or 22. Number of sepals: 4.

LEAVES. Color: Top, new leaves flecked purple; underside, reddish blotched with dark brown and purple. Nearly round leaf with lobe tips projecting;

open sinus. Leaf size: 9 × 8.5 in. (23 × 21.5 cm). Leaf spread: 4–5 ft. (1.2–1.5 m). Stem color: Reddish purple. Peduncle and petiole covered with fine hairs.

COMMENTS. Leeann Connelly discovered a large group of *Nymphaea* 'Osceola', which she named after the famous Seminole war chief, in Lake Okeechobee, Florida. The flower color is rich and flowers are freely produced. A good choice for any size pool in southern states, but here in North Carolina *N.* 'Osceola' dies from crown rot. So, I do not recommend it for northern regions.

Nymphaea 'Patio Joe'

Strawn, year unknown

Parentage unknown

CHARACTERISTICS. Nonviviparous, odorata rhizome, very free flowering, perennial.

FLOWERS. Petal color: Blushed pink throughout petals, then lighten to creamy white at tips. Sepal color: Inner, soft pink, dark green tips; outer, medium green with pink on some edges. Anther color: Inner, deep yellow; outer, deep yellow. Stamen color: Blush pink. Flower shape: Cuplike. Flower size: 3–4 in. (7.5–10 cm). Fragrance: Very pleasant. Number of petals: 30–32. Number of sepals: 4.

LEAVES. Color: Top, medium green, newer leaves olive green with faint mottling; underside, reddish brown with faint green edges, newer leaves have more green than red. Leaf nearly round; sinus slightly open, slight distinguished tips on lobes. Leaf size: 5–7 in. (13–18 cm). Leaf spread: 3–5 ft. (0.9–1.5 m). Stem color: Medium green. No pubescence on peduncle or petiole.

COMMENTS BY DEAN MCGEE. *Nymphaea* 'Patio Joe' has characteristics similar to *N.* 'Colorado', but with more pink in hues. It is a very prolific bloomer that stands 3–4 in. (7.5–10 cm) above the water and blooms late into the season.

Nymphaea 'Paul Hariot'

Marliac 1905

Parentage unknown

CHARACTERISTICS. Upright rhizome, very free flowering, perennial.

FLOWERS. Petal color: Inner petals orange, deepening; outer petals apricot, by third day deep pinkish orange (*RHS* inner, first day, 38B; third day, 38A; outer, first day, 29D; third day, 49C or 41D). Sepal color: Creamy apricot then light pink (*RHS* 29D; third day, 36D). Anther color: Golden yellow (*RHS* 21C). Stamen color: Burnt orange. Flower shape: Cuplike. Flower size: 4–5 in. (10–13 cm). Fragrance: Slight. Number of petals: 22. Number of sepals: 4 or 5.

LEAVES. Color: Top, green, yet variable. New leaves on young plants olive green, speckled and freckled; larger leaves from main plant very deep green with covering of large and small purple blotches. Underside, smallest leaves light purple, purple specks and freckles; larger leaves green or purple, purple specks and mottles. Leaves oval; sinus an open V or lobes overlap about halfway. Lobes rounded at tips. Leaf size: 6–7 in. (15–18 cm). Leaf spread: 3–4 ft. (0.9–1.2 m). Stem color: Brown. A few fine hairs on peduncle and petiole.

COMMENTS. *Nymphaea* 'Paul Hariot' blooms very freely once it is established. I consider this waterlily an ideal plant for a tub garden or a small or medium pool. Some commercial water gardens in the United States and England sell both *N.* 'Sioux' and *N.* 'Chrysantha' (see description) for this fine plant, which is not currently available from most nurseries. Propagation can be difficult due to the rhizome of *N.* 'Paul Hariot' being subject to crown rot in Europe, the United States, and Japan. Currently Australian nurseries have a good supply of the true *N.* 'Paul Hariot'.

Nymphaea 'Peace Lily'

Strawn 1999

Parentage unknown

CHARACTERISTICS. Nonviviparous, odorata rhizome, very free flowering, perennial.

FLOWERS. Petal color: Blushed pink on outer petals, moving toward light yellow at inner petals. Sepal color: Inner, creamy yellow, faint pink on edges; outer, olive green, blushed pink on some edges. Anther color: Inner, bright yellow; outer, bright yellow. Stamen color: Bright yellow. Flower shape: Full, stellate. Flower size: 4–5 in. (10–12.5 cm). Fragrance: Pleasant. Number of petals: 24–26. Number of sepals: 4.

LEAVES. Color: Top, medium green; underside, reddish brown with noticeable flecking, newer leaves have more green than red shade. Leaf nearly round; sinus open. Leaf size: 6–8 in. (15–20 cm). Leaf spread: 3–5 ft. (0.9–1.5 m). Stem color: Bronze. Light pubescence on petiole.

COMMENTS BY DEAN MCGEE. The very unique combination of peach and apricot hues in *Nymphaea* 'Peace Lily' makes for a beautiful large blossom display. A prolific bloomer, this waterlily stands 2–3 in. (5–7.5 cm) above the water surface and blooms late into the season. It is a great choice for medium to large ponds.

Nymphaea 'Peaches and Cream'

Slocum 1992

Nymphaea 'Texas Dawn' × *N.* 'Perry's Viviparous Pink'

PLATE 203

CHARACTERISTICS. Free flowering, Marliac rhizome, perennial.

FLOWERS. Petal color: Pink outer petals, yellow inner petals with pink base. Sepal color: Inner, light pink; outer, olive green. Anther color: Inner, deep yellow; outer, deep yellow. Stamen color: Deep yellow. Flower shape: Like a peony. Flower size: 6–8 in. (15.2–20.3 cm). Fragrance: Delightful. Number of petals: 32–37. Number of sepals: 4.

LEAVES. Color: Top, at first, olive green heavily mottled with purple blotches, which disappear after a few weeks; leaf turns to a brighter green; underside, bright red with purple blotches. Leaves are nearly round; sinus open. Leaf size: 7.5 × 8.5 in. (19 × 21.5 cm). Leaf spread: 3.5–5 ft. (1–1.5 m). Stem color: Deep purple. Pubescence quite thick on stems.

COMMENTS. *Nymphaea* 'Peaches and Cream' is an outstanding cultivar that receives much praise from viewers. The first- and second-day flowers are held 6–8 in. (15–20 cm) above the water, which adds to their beauty. I highly recommend this waterlily for any size pool. It holds U.S. plant patent 9676 (issued October 29 1996).

Nymphaea 'Peach Glow'

Strawn 1997

Nymphaea 'Rembrandt' × *N. mexicana*

CHARACTERISTICS. Nonviviparous, odorata rhizome, very free flowering, perennial.

FLOWERS. Petal color: Light yellow-orange color

throughout petals. Sepal color: Inner, creamy yellowish green; outer, medium green with dark green tips. Anther color: Inner, bright yellow; outer, bright yellow. Stamen color: Bright yellow. Flower shape: Full, stellate. Flower size: 4–5 in. (10–12.5 cm). Fragrance: Pleasant. Number of petals: 34–36. Number of sepals: 4.

LEAVES. Color: Top, medium green; underside, light reddish brown with green veining at center. Leaf nearly round; sinus slightly open. Leaf size: 7–8 in. (18–20 cm). Leaf spread: 5–7 ft. (1.5–2.1 m). Stem color: Medium green. No pubescence on peduncle or petiole.

COMMENTS BY DEAN McGEE. *Nymphaea* 'Peach Glow' has an awesome display of large light peach flowers that lightens to almost white by its last day of bloom. A vigorous bloomer, this waterlily is ideal for medium to large ponds.

Nymphaea 'Pearl of the Pool'

Slocum 1946

Nymphaea 'Pink Opal × N. 'Marliacea Rosea'

CHARACTERISTICS. Odorata rhizome, moderately free flowering.

FLOWERS. Petal color: Medium pink (*RHS* 62C). Sepal color: Medium pink (*RHS* 62C). Anther color: Yellow (*RHS* 12B). Stamen color: Pinkish orange. Flower shape: Stellate, open. Flower size: 5–6 in. (13–15 cm). Fragrance: Very nice. Number of petals: 40–48. Number of sepals: 4.

LEAVES. Color: Top, green, first leaves bronzy; underside, red, green V along midvein. Leaf round; lobes may or may not overlap at sinus, one or both lobes may be raised. Leaf size: Up to 10 in. (25 cm). Leaf spread: 4–5 ft. (1.2–1.5 m). Stem color: Light brown, purple stripes. Occasionally fine fuzz on some stems.

COMMENTS. This was the first hardy waterlily ever patented in the United States, U.S. plant patent 666, issued to Perry D. Slocum in January 1946. *Nymphaea* 'Pearl of the Pool' blooms most freely when planted in a large container, where it can form a colony of several plants. A planter 24 × 24 × 12 in. (60 × 60 × 30 cm) is ideal. I recommend it for medium or large pools or the natural pond.

Nymphaea 'Perry's Autumn Sunset'

Perry's Water Gardens 2003

Natural hybrid, parents probably N. 'Perry's Orange Sunset' × N. 'Blushing Bride'

PLATE 204

CHARACTERISTICS. Free flowering, Marliac rhizome, nonviviparous, perennial.

FLOWERS. Petal color: Salmon pink middle and outer petals, center petals orange. Sepal color: Inner, orange-pink; outer, olive green, often edged with red or pink. Anther color: Inner, dark yellow; outer, yellow. Stamen color: Inner, yellow; outer, orange. Flower shape: Cuplike on first day, opening wide on second and third days like a dahlia. Flower size: 5–7 in. (12.5–18 cm). Fragrance: Slight and pleasant. Number of petals: 35–37. Number of sepals: 4.

LEAVES. Color: Top, round leaf is dark green at first and very heavily mottled with purple; purple blotches disappear in a few weeks; underside, medium purple heavily covered with deep purple blotches. Sinus is variable but usually half open. A projection is distinctive on tip of each lobe. Leaf size: 8–10 in. (20–25.5 cm). Leaf spread: 4–5 ft. (1.2–1.5 m). Stem color: Purple. A little fuzz on peduncle and petiole.

COMMENTS. *Nymphaea* 'Perry's Autumn Sunset' has a rare color that commands instant attention and praise. It is quite double for a sunset variety, and on the first two days flowers are held high above the water. I highly recommend it for medium to large ponds.

Nymphaea 'Perry's Baby Pink'

Perry's Water Gardens 2001

Natural hybrid, parentage unknown

PLATE 205

CHARACTERISTICS. Fairly free flowering, Marliac rhizome, perennial.

FLOWERS. Petal color: Inner, deep pink; outer, variable from light pink to nearly white in outer row. Sepal color: Inner, white; outer, deep green. Anther color: Inner, deep yellow; outer, also deep yellow. Stamen color: Inner, deep yellow; outer, pinkish. Flower shape: Cuplike. Flower size: About 3.5 in. (9 cm). Fragrance: None. Number of petals: 18–20. Number of sepals: 4.

LEAVES. Color: Top, dark green becoming a little

lighter with age; underside, reddish brown with prominent green veins. Leaves oblong; sinus open. Leaf size: 5–7 × 4.5–6.5 in. (12.5–17.5 × 11.3–16.3 cm). The leaf spread is about 3 ft. (0.9 m). Stem color: Variable: Reddish purple on petioles to brown on peduncles. No pubescence on peduncle or petiole.

COMMENTS. The waterlily industry has needed a free-flowering, very small, pink hardy waterlily for tub gardens and small pools. Ben Gibson discovered this volunteer growing in one of the ponds at Perry's Water Gardens. After testing for two years, I feel that this is it. Here in North Carolina, *Nymphaea* 'Perry's Baby Pink' has been outstanding in early season but slows down as real hot weather arrives in late summer.

Nymphaea 'Perry's Baby Red'
Slocum 1989
Probably *N.* 'Alba Plenissima' × *N.* 'Atropurpurea'
PLATE 206
CHARACTERISTICS. Marliac rhizome, very free flowering.

FLOWERS. Petal color: Deep red (*RHS* 61A,B). Sepal color: Pink, prominent red veins (*RHS* 69B; veins, 61B). Anther color: Yellow-orange (*RHS* 19A). Stamen color: Orange. Flower shape: Cuplike. Flower size: 3–3.5 in. (8–9 cm). Fragrance: Slight. Number of petals: 24–31. Number of sepals: 4.

LEAVES. Color: Top, green, newest leaves purple; underside, brown, newest leaves red. Leaves heart-shaped; sinus a wide-open V. Lobe tips usually pointed. Leaf size: 4.5–6 in. (11–15 cm). Leaf spread: 30 in. (75 cm). Stem color: Peduncle brown, petiole red. Thick short fuzz on peduncle and petiole.

COMMENTS. *Nymphaea* 'Perry's Baby Red' is a waterlily with excellent qualities for the tub garden or small pool. Unfortunately, the high demand for this waterlily may exceed supply. It has become very popular throughout the waterlily world.

Nymphaea 'Perry's Black Opal'
Slocum 1990
Probably *N.* 'Vesuve' × *N.* 'Splendida'
PLATE 207
CHARACTERISTICS. Marliac rhizome, free flowering.

FLOWERS. Petal color: Very dark red (*RHS* 71A).

Sepal color: Lighter than petals (*RHS* 64A). Anther color: Orange (*RHS* 23C). Stamen color: Deep orange-red. Flower shape: Stellate. Flower size: 6–7 in. (15–18 cm). Fragrance: None. Number of petals: 24. Number of sepals: 4.

LEAVES. Color: Top, green, new leaves bronzy red; underside, reddish, wide green stripe in middle. Leaf nearly round; sinus wide open. Leaf size: 10 × 9.5 in. (25 × 24 cm). Leaf spread: 3.5–5 ft. (1.1–1.5 m). Stem color: Purple. Thick fuzz on peduncle and petiole.

COMMENTS. I recommend this cultivar for any size pool, especially medium and large pools. This is one of the darkest red hardy waterlilies. Furthermore, flowers do not burn or melt (at least in North Carolina, zone 6b) during the very hot summer days, as do many red-flowered cultivars, and *Nymphaea* 'Perry's Black Opal' blooms freely in hot weather. A comparison of flower color with *N.* 'Atropurpurea' (another dark red waterlily that blooms throughout the summer) reveals 'Perry's Black Opal' to be several shades deeper. In the mid-1990s, two new even darker waterlilies were hybridized: *N.* 'Black Princess' (U.S. plant patent 9662) and *N.* 'Almost Black'.

Nymphaea 'Perry's Cactus Pink'
Slocum 1990
Probably *N.* 'Perry's Pink' × *N.* 'American Star'
PLATE 208
CHARACTERISTICS. Odorata rhizome, fairly free blooming, petals uniquely rolled, narrow.

FLOWERS. Petal color: Shell pink, base deeper pink (*RHS* 65D; base, 65A). Sepal color: Deep pink (*RHS* 67C,D). Anther color: Deep yellow (*RHS* 13A). Stamen color: Orange. Flower shape: Stellate. Flower size: 5–6 in. (13–15 cm). Fragrance: Delightful. Number of petals: 28. Number of sepals: 4.

LEAVES. Color: Top, green, new leaves purplish; underside, red. Leaf nearly round; sinus usually two-thirds open, sometimes completely open or closed. Leaf size: 7–8 in. (18–20 cm). Leaf spread: About 4 ft. (1.2 m). Stem color: Reddish purple. Thick fuzz on peduncle and petiole.

COMMENTS. The unique long, rolled petals of *N.* 'Perry's Cactus Pink' distinguish this waterlily from all others and instantly command attention. I have never seen any other waterlily with these flower features. Plant this cultivar in a large container and let it form a colony for best results. I recommend it for medium or large pools.

Nymphaea 'Perry's Crinkled Pink'

Slocum 1989

Nymphaea 'Gloire du Temple-sur-Lot' × *N.* 'Vesuve'

CHARACTERISTICS. Marliac rhizome, fairly free flowering.

FLOWERS. Petal color: Deep shell pink (*RHS* 62C). Sepal color: Light pink (*RHS* 62D). Anther color: Deep yellow (*RHS* 12A). Stamen color: Deep yellow. Flower shape: Stellate, full. Flower size: 4.5–5.5 in. (11–14 cm). Fragrance: Slight. Number of petals: 27–33. Number of sepals: 4.

LEAVES. Color: Top, green, newest leaves purplish brown; underside, iridescent red, prominent green veins. Leaves round; sinus a wide-open V. Leaf size: 8–9 in. (20–23 cm). Leaf spread: 4 ft. (1.2 m). Stem color: Brown, petioles darker brown than peduncles. No pubescence on peduncle or petiole.

COMMENTS. *Nymphaea* 'Perry's Crinkled Pink', with its crinkled petals, is unique among pink hardy waterlilies. I recommend it for any size pool.

Nymphaea 'Perry's Double White'

Slocum 1990

Seedling of *N. tuberosa* 'Richardsonii' No. 2 and probably *N.* 'Perry's Super Red'

PLATE 209

CHARACTERISTICS. Marliac-tuberosa rhizome, free flowering.

FLOWERS. Petal color: Pure white (*RHS* 155D). Sepal color: White, tipped green, prominent dark gray veins (*RHS* 155A; tips, 144A; veins, 201B). Anther color: Yellow (*RHS* 8A). Stamen color: Deep yellow. Flower shape: Stellate, open. Flower size: 6–7 in. (15–18 cm). Fragrance: None. Number of petals: 39–46, usually 44. Number of sepals: 4.

LEAVES. Color: Top, deep green, new leaves slightly bronzed; underside, green. Leaves nearly round, edges slightly ruffled; sinus an open V. Leaf size: 9–10 in. (23–25 cm). Leaf spread: 4–5 ft. (1.2–1.5 m). Stem color: Brown, dense red mottling. No pubescence on peduncle or petiole.

COMMENTS. *Nymphaea* 'Perry's Double White'

has a beautiful flower form and is quite free flowering. Its bloom season is unusually long, frequently lasting April through October in North Carolina (zone 6b). Plant in a large container, about 24 × 24 × 12 in. (60 × 60 × 30 cm), so that it can form a colony and produce its maximum number of blooms. I consider it one of the best, if not *the* best, of all the large white hardies. Suitable for any size pool.

Nymphaea 'Perry's Double Yellow'

Slocum 1996

Natural hybrid from *N.* 'Texas Dawn'

PLATE 210

CHARACTERISTICS. Free flowering, Marliac rhizome, perennial.

FLOWERS. Petal color: Medium yellow growing paler with age. Sepal color: Inner, greenish white, darker green toward tip; outer, dark green. Anther color: Inner, dark yellow; outer, dark yellow. Stamen color: Dark to medium yellow. Flower shape: Like peony. Flower size: 5.5–7 in. (14–17.8 cm). Fragrance: Pleasant. Number of petals: 47 or 48. Number of sepals: 4.

LEAVES. Color: Top, dark green flecked and speckled purple at first but soon turning all green. Leaf nearly round; sinus either wide open or partly closed. Leaf size: 8 in. (20.3 cm). Leaf spread: 4–5 ft (1.2–1.5 m). Stem color: Reddish purple. Pubescence on peduncle and petiole, except top 4 in. (10 cm) of peduncle above water.

COMMENTS. *Nymphaea* 'Perry's Double Yellow' is an outstanding, impressive waterlily. On hot sunny days, the last-day blooms become nearly white, which seems to be its only bad feature. I recommend it for medium and large pools.

Nymphaea 'Perry's Fire Opal'

Slocum 1987

Nymphaea 'Peter Slocum' × *N.* 'Director George T. Moore'

PLATE 211

CHARACTERISTICS. Odorata rhizome, free flowering, unusual vein pattern radiates from leaf center.

FLOWERS. Petal color: Very rich pink, darker pink lengthwise stripe (*RHS* 66D; stripe, 66C). Sepal color: Pink (*RHS* 63D). Anther color: Golden yellow (*RHS* 13A). Stamen color: Orange. Flower shape: Peony-style. Flower size: 5–6 in. (13–15 cm). Fragrance: Delightful. Number of petals: 40–50. Number of sepals: 4.

LEAVES. Color: Top, green, new leaves purplish red, veins light green on green leaves, purplish on new leaves; underside, red. Leaf round; lobes usually overlap at sinus. Leaf size: 7–10 in. (18–25 cm). Leaf spread: 3–4 ft. (0.9–1.2 m). Stem color: Green. Thick fuzz on peduncle and petiole.

COMMENTS. *Nymphaea* 'Perry's Fire Opal' is one of the very best odorata waterlilies for the tub garden or small pool; it can also be used in medium and large pools. It blooms quite well in a restricted area, and its flower color is wonderful. To achieve the best possible performance, plant it in a large planter and allow it to form a colony. Flowers are very double and often nearly as large as the leaves. As *N.* 'Perry's Fire Opal' is becoming more widely known, it is displacing *N.* 'Pink Opal' as *the* pink odorata for the tub garden. Recipient of the International Waterlily and Water Gardening Society's America Award for 1990, it was the first odorata waterlily ever given such an award.

Nymphaea 'Perry's Magnificent'

Slocum 1990
Nymphaea 'Perry's Pink' × *N.* 'Director George T. Moore'
PLATE 212

CHARACTERISTICS. Odorata rhizome, fairly free flowering.

FLOWERS. Petal color: Very deep dusty rose; center petals edged yellow (*RHS* 63B; edge, 1D). Sepal color: Deep pink (*RHS* 185C). Anther color: Orange (*RHS* 32C). Stamen color: Orange. Flower shape: Stellate. Flower size: 6–7 in. (15–18 cm). Fragrance: Delightful. Number of petals: 33–38. Number of sepals: 4.

LEAVES. Color: Top, green, new leaves bronzy purple; underside, red. Leaf round; sinus frequently two-thirds open, sometimes fully open or nearly closed. Leaf size: 10 in. (25 cm). Leaf spread: 4–5 ft. (1.2–1.5 m). Stem color: Brown, striped purple. No pubescence on peduncle or petiole.

COMMENTS. *Nymphaea* 'Perry's Magnificent', with a prominent red center dot in the stigmal area

and deep, evenly textured petals, is one of the most striking of the new pink hardy waterlilies. Plant it in a large planter, about 24 × 24 × 12 in. (60 × 60 × 30 cm), and allow it to form a colony to maximize bloom. I recommend this cultivar for medium or large pools as well as the natural pond.

Nymphaea 'Perry's Orange Sunset'

Perry's Water Gardens 1996
Natural hybrid of *N.* 'Texas Dawn' × *N.* 'Perry's Red Beauty'
PLATE 213

CHARACTERISTICS. Free flowering, Marliac rhizome, perennial.

FLOWERS. Petal color: Glowing salmon and pinkish orange. Sepal color: Inner, salmon orange; outer, dark green usually with some pink on one or two edges of sepal. Anther color: Inner, dark yellow; outer, dark yellow. Stamen color: Dark yellow, except outermost are orange. Flower shape: Cuplike. Flower size: 5–5.5 in. (12.7–14 cm). Fragrance: Slight and pleasant. Number of petals: 30–33. Number of sepals: 4.

LEAVES. Color: Top, brownish green, flecked with purple turning all green in a few weeks; underside, pinkish red with purple blotches. Leaf nearly round; sinus partly closed or fully open. Leaf size: About 9 in. (22.8 cm). Leaf spread: 3.5–5 ft. (1–1.5 m). Stem color: Peduncle reddish brown, petiole brown. No pubescence on peduncle or petiole.

COMMENTS. *Nymphaea* 'Perry's Orange Sunset' is truly a showstopper. It won First Prize in its class at the International Waterlily and Water Garden Symposium in 2002 held at Portland, Oregon. It is a favorite with thousands of visitors at Perry's Water Gardens, and I highly recommend it for any size pool.

Nymphaea 'Perry's Pink'

Slocum 1984
Chance seedling of *N.* 'Rose Arey'
PLATE 214

CHARACTERISTICS. Odorata rhizome, moderately free flowering.

FLOWERS. Petal color: Rich pink (*RHS* 64D). Sepal color: Rich pink (*RHS* 64D). Anther color: Golden yellow (*RHS* 31C,D). Stamen color: Inner stamens, yellow; outer stamens orange. Flower shape: Stellate, many petals. Flower size: 6–7 in. (15–18 cm). Fragrance: Delightful. Number of petals: 35–39. Number of sepals: 4.

LEAVES. Color: Top, green, new leaves purple; underside, purple, new leaves red, persistent bright green lengthwise V along midvein. Leaves round; sinus on older leaves a wide-open V, lobes overlap on new leaves. Leaf size: Up to 11 in. (28 cm). Leaf spread: 4–5 ft. (1.2–1.5 m). Stem color: Greenish brown, purple stripes. No pubescence on peduncle or petiole.

COMMENTS. Nymphaea 'Perry's Pink' has an unusual red dot in the center of every flower (precisely in the middle of the stigmal area). For best flowering, it should be planted in a large container and allowed to form a colony of several plants. This is an excellent choice for medium or large pools as well as natural ponds.

Nymphaea 'Perry's Pink Bicolor'

Slocum 1989

Nymphaea alba (from New Zealand) × N. 'Fabiola'

CHARACTERISTICS. Marliac rhizome, free flowering.

FLOWERS. Petal color: Center petals deep pink, outer petals whitish pink, pink veins (RHS center, 64B,C; outer, 69B,C; veins, 70D). Sepal color: White, pink veins (RHS 155A; veins, 70D). Anther color: Golden yellow (RHS 13C). Stamen color: Orange. Flower shape: Stellate. Flower size: 5.5–6 in. (14–15 cm). Fragrance: Slight. Number of petals: 20–21. Number of sepals: 4.

LEAVES. Color: Top, green, newest leaves bronzy; underside, purplish, green lengthwise stripe, 2 in. (5 cm) wide. Leaves egg-shaped; sinus a wide-open V. Leaf size: Up to 11 × 10 in. (28 × 25 cm). Leaf spread: 5–6 ft. (1.5–1.8 m). Stem color: Purplish. Short fuzz on peduncle and petiole.

COMMENTS. Nymphaea 'Perry's Pink Bicolor' is a very pleasing pink-and-white combination. I recommend it for medium and large pools.

Nymphaea 'Perry's Pink Delight'

Slocum 1990

Probably N. 'Colonel A. J. Welch' × N. 'Splendida'

CHARACTERISTICS. Marliac rhizome, mildly vi-

viparous from the flower, moderately free blooming.

FLOWERS. Petal color: Evenly pink, paling (RHS 63B then 62D). Sepal color: Light pink, striped darker pink (RHS 62D; stripes, 62A). Anther color: Orange (RHS 15C). Stamen color: Yellow. Flower shape: Stellate. Flower size: 5.5–7 in. (14–18 cm). Fragrance: None. Number of petals: 28. Number of sepals: 4.

LEAVES. Color: Top, green, new leaves purplish red; underside, reddish. Leaf nearly round; sinus open. Leaf size: Up to 10 in. (25 cm). Leaf spread: 4–5 ft. (1.2–1.5 m). Stem color: Peduncle reddish, striped purple; petiole chartreuse, striped purple. No pubescence on peduncle or petiole.

COMMENTS. Flowers of Nymphaea 'Perry's Pink Delight' are in the same color group as N. 'Pink Sensation' yet average 8–10 more petals. Being a Marliac type and free flowering, it should make a name for itself for use in medium and large pools. A decided plus is its occasional ability to produce plantlets from the base of the flowers. In North Carolina, blooms become fewer in late summer.

Nymphaea 'Perry's Pink Heaven'

Slocum 1990

Probably N. 'Perry's Fire Opal' × N. 'Pearl of the Pool'

PLATE 215

CHARACTERISTICS. Odorata rhizome, fairly free flowering.

FLOWERS. Petal color: Pink, darker pink base and center vein (RHS 62C; base and vein, 62B). Sepal color: Deep pink, fairly even texture (RHS 65A). Anther color: Very deep yellow (RHS 19A). Stamen color: Orange. Flower shape: Stellate. Flower size: 6–8 in. (15–20 cm). Fragrance: Slight yet pleasant. Number of petals: 44 or 45. Number of sepals: 4.

LEAVES. Color: Top, green, new leaves bronzy; underside, red. Leaf nearly round; lobes overlap sinus. Leaf size: 7.5 × 8 in. (19 × 20 cm). Leaf spread: 4–5 ft. (1.2–1.5 m). Stem color: Bright green. Sparse short hairs on peduncle and petiole.

COMMENTS. This cultivar develops flowers remarkably close to its leaves in size, the closest of any waterlily I know. The many-petaled, large, fragrant flowers are delightful. I recommend planting Nym-

phaea 'Perry's Pink Heaven' in a large container so that it can form a colony of plants. It is suitable for medium or large pools.

Nymphaea 'Perry's Red Beauty'

Slocum 1989

Nymphaea 'Vesuve' one parent

PLATE 216

CHARACTERISTICS. Marliac rhizome, free flowering.

FLOWERS. Petal color: Very deep red, deepening (*RHS* 61B; last day, 61A). Sepal color: White, splashed pale pink, green tips (*RHS* 155A; splashes, 62C; tips, 144A,B). Anther color: Yellow (*RHS* 11B). Stamen color: Orange-red. Flower shape: Stellate. Flower size: 6.5–7 in. (16–18 cm). Fragrance: Slight. Number of petals: 24–30. Number of sepals: 4.

LEAVES. Color: Top, green, newest leaves purplish brown; underside, reddish. Leaves oblong; lobes overlap at sinus. Leaf size: Up to 10 × 8.5 in. (25 × 22 cm). Leaf spread: 4 ft. (1.2 m). Stem color: Reddish brown. Thick fuzz on peduncle and petiole.

COMMENTS. *Nymphaea* 'Perry's Red Beauty' fills the need for a very deep red, stellate, hardy waterlily. It resembles *N.* 'Newton' in flower shape, yet has a much deeper color. Many of its petals curl inward in a unique way. A fine waterlily for any size pool.

Nymphaea 'Perry's Red Bicolor'

Slocum 1989

Nymphaea 'Vesuve' is probable parent

PLATE 217

CHARACTERISTICS. Marliac rhizome, free flowering.

FLOWERS. Petal color: Inner petals deep rich red; outer petals pinkish red (*RHS* inner, 64B; outer, 66D). Sepal color: White, green tips and margins, pink base, usually pink veins (*RHS* 155B; tips and margins, 145B; veins and base, 70D). Anther color: Yellow-Orange (*RHS* 18A). Stamen color: Orange. Flower shape: Stellate. Flower size: 5.5–6 in. (14–15 cm). Fragrance: Slight. Number of petals: 16–19. Number of sepals: 4–6.

LEAVES. Color: Top, green, ragged purple circle about 1 in. (2.5 cm) in diameter midleaf at petiole, newest leaves purplish; underside, red. Leaves nearly round; sinus a wide-open V. Leaf size: 7.5 × 7 in. (19 × 18 cm). Leaf spread: 4 ft. (1.2 m). Stem color: Peduncle, brown; petiole purplish. Thick fuzz on peduncle and petiole.

COMMENTS. *Nymphaea* 'Perry's Red Bicolor', with its contrasting red-and-white flowers, is a striking waterlily for any size pool.

Nymphaea 'Perry's Red Glow'

Slocum 1989

Probably *N.* 'Alba Plenissima' × *N.* 'Atropurpurea'

CHARACTERISTICS. Marliac-tuberosa rhizome, fairly free flowering.

FLOWERS. Petal color: Very deep red (*RHS* 61A, B). Sepal color: Rich green, slightly deeper at tips and margins, red veins and splashes (*RHS* 146D; veins and splashes, 64C). Anther color: Inner anthers, medium orange; outer anthers burnt orange (*RHS* inner, 29B; outer, 42D). Stamen color: Purple-red. Flower shape: Stellate. Flower size: 3.5–4 in. (9–10 cm). Fragrance: Slight. Number of petals: 23–30. Number of sepals: 4.

LEAVES. Color: Top, green, newest leaves purple; underside, red. Leaves heart-shaped; sinus a wide-open V. Leaf size: 6–7 in. (15–18 cm). Leaf spread: 3 ft. (1 m). Stem color: Brownish purple. Thick fuzz on peduncle and petiole.

COMMENTS. *Nymphaea* 'Perry's Red Glow', one of the deepest red lilies I have ever seen, has excellent flower color. Its 16 carpels are especially pronounced—more so than on any other hardy I know. I recommend it for small or medium pools.

Nymphaea 'Perry's Red Wonder'

Syn. 'Perry's Red Volunteer'

Slocum 1989

Nymphaea 'Splendida' probable parent

PLATE 218

CHARACTERISTICS. Marliac rhizome, free flowering.

FLOWERS. Petal color: Bright red (*RHS* 67B). Sepal color: Pale pink, reddish pink center veins; green flush at edges (*RHS* 73D; veins, 63B; flush, 145D). Anther color: Orange (*RHS* 24B). Stamen color: Orange. Flower shape: Stellate. Flower size: 5.5–6.5 in. (14–16 cm). Fragrance: Slight. Number of petals: 21 or 22. Number of sepals: 4.

LEAVES. Color: Top, green, newest leaves purplish; underside, brown, newest leaves red. Leaves round; sinus a wide-open V. Leaf size: 5.5–7 in. (14–18 cm). Leaf spread: 30–36 in. (75–90 cm). Stem color: Peduncle, reddish brown; petiole, red. Thick fuzz on peduncle and petiole.

COMMENTS. Nymphaea 'Perry's Red Wonder' is a brilliantly colored newcomer with two outstanding features: It is one of the freest-blooming hardy waterlilies I have ever seen, and the blooms are nearly as large as the leaves. I highly recommend it for the tub garden or small or medium pool.

Nymphaea 'Perry's Rich Rose'

Slocum 1990
Nymphaea 'Perry's Pink' × N. 'Mrs. Martin E. Randig'
PLATE 219

CHARACTERISTICS. Odorata rhizome, fairly free flowering.

FLOWERS. Petal color: Rich old rose (RHS 64C,D). Sepal color: Red (RHS 64B). Anther color: Orange (RHS 29B). Stamen color: Orange. Flower shape: Stellate. Flower size: 6–8 in. (15–20 cm). Fragrance: Slight, pleasant. Number of petals: 29–30. Number of sepals: 4.

LEAVES. Color: Top, green, new leaves purple then bronze; underside, red, broad green midstripe lengthwise and inside lobes. Leaves round; sinus usually two-thirds open. Leaf size: 9 in. (23 cm). Leaf spread: 4–4.5 ft. (1.2–1.4 m). Stem color: Peduncle, bright chartreuse; petiole, medium green; both striped purple. No pubescence on peduncle or petiole.

COMMENTS. The flowers of this cultivar are often nearly as large as the leaves, and they stay open quite late in the afternoon, long after most other odoratas have closed. Although one parent is a tropical waterlily (N. 'Mrs. Martin E. Randig'), this cultivar has survived temperatures of –5°F (–21°C); from this tropical parent, N. 'Perry's Rich Rose' undoubtedly received its very rich and even flower color and long bloom period. A rare identifying feature is the pink dot in the middle of the stigmal area. Plant in a large container so that it can form a colony of rhizomes, and then it will flower freely. I recommend it for any size pool.

Nymphaea 'Perry's Strawberry Pink'

Slocum 1989
Probably N. alba (from New Zealand) × N. 'Vesuve'
PLATE 220

CHARACTERISTICS. Marliac rhizome, free flowering.

FLOWERS. Petal color: Inner petals deep strawberry pink; outer petals deeper (RHS inner, 66D; outer, 65C). Sepal color: Pink, greenish white tips (RHS 65D; tips, 145D). Anther color: Orange (RHS 19A). Stamen color: Orange. Flower shape: Cuplike, petals stellate. Flower size: 5–5.5 in. (13–14 cm). Fragrance: Slight. Number of petals: 29 or 30. Number of sepals: 4.

LEAVES. Color: Top, green, newest leaves purplish; underside, bronze, newest leaves iridescent purple. Leaves round; lobes overlap at sinus. Leaf size: 7 in. (18 cm). Leaf spread: 4–5 ft. (1.2–1.5 m). Stem color: Brownish purple. Fine fuzz on peduncle and petiole.

COMMENTS. Due to its small leaves, I recommend Nymphaea 'Perry's Strawberry Pink' for any size pool. The freedom of bloom and beautiful flowers make it an excellent choice.

Nymphaea 'Perry's Super Red'

Slocum 1989
Nymphaea 'Charles de Meurville' × N. 'Gloire du Temple-sur-Lot'
PLATE 221

CHARACTERISTICS. Marliac rhizome, free flowering.

FLOWERS. Petal color: Inner petals brilliant vermilion-red; outer petals pink (RHS inner, 67A; outer, 61D). Sepal color: Greenish white, pink center veins (RHS 147D; veins, 61D). Anther color: Inner anthers yellow-orange; outer anthers scarlet-orange (RHS inner, 11A; outer, 37A). Stamen color: Orange-red. Flower shape: Full, peony-style. Flower size: 5.5–7.5 in. (14–19 cm). Fragrance: Slight. Number of petals: 38–43. Number of sepals: 4.

LEAVES. Color: Top, green, newest leaves brown; underside, red, green veins. Leaves round; lobes usually overlap, cover sinus, occasionally sinus partly open. Leaf size: Up to 10 in. (25 cm). Leaf spread: 5 ft. (1.5 m). Stem color: Reddish purple. Thick fuzz on peduncle and petiole.

COMMENTS. *Nymphaea* 'Perry's Super Red' flowers are more double than any other red waterlily I know, the color is particularly glowing and brilliant, and their size places this cultivar (along with *N.* 'Atropurpurea' and *N.* 'Attraction') among the largest of the red hardy waterlilies. Blooms stay open later in the day than most red waterlilies. I recommend 'Perry's Super Red' for medium and large pools. It is especially suited to deep-water pools, up to 7 ft. (2.1 m) in depth. A Texan with a large pool told me that it does not burn for him and it is his favorite.

Nymphaea 'Perry's Super Rose'

Slocum 1990
Probably *N.* 'Perry's Pink' × *N.* 'Sirius'
PLATE 222

CHARACTERISTICS. Odorata rhizome, fairly free flowering.

FLOWERS. Petal color: Rich deep rose-pink (*RHS* 72C). Sepal color: Rich deep rose-pink (*RHS* 72C). Anther color: Golden orange (*RHS* 26C). Stamen color: Orange. Flower shape: Stellate. Flower size: 6.5–7.5 in. (16–19 cm). Fragrance: Very pleasant. Number of petals: 37 or 38. Number of sepals: 4.

LEAVES. Color: Top, green, new leaves reddish brown; underside, reddish. Leaf wider than long, distinct indentation at apex; sinus usually open in young leaves, lobes overlap in mature leaves. Leaf size: Up to 10.5 × 11 in. (27 × 28 cm). Leaf spread: 4–5 ft. (1.2–1.5 m). Stem color: Olive green, striped purple. Heavy fuzz on peduncle and petiole.

COMMENTS. This cultivar is somewhat similar to *Nymphaea* 'Rose Arey', but flower color is deeper and less subject to fading and spring leaves are not distorted. Inner petals are beautifully rolled. Plant *N.* 'Perry's Super Rose' in a large container, allowing it to form a colony of rhizomes, and it will produce several blooms at a time. I highly recommend it for medium and large pools.

Nymphaea 'Perry's Super Yellow'

Perry's Water Gardens 1996
Natural hybrid, probably *N.* 'Texas Dawn' × *N.* 'Perry's Red Beauty'
PLATE 223

CHARACTERISTICS. Free flowering, Marliac rhizome, perennial.

FLOWERS. Petal color: Medium yellow, growing paler with age; outermost petals have pink blush. Sepal color: Inner, pale yellowish green; outer, olive green often with broad band of pink along border. Anther color: Inner, dark yellow; outer, dark yellow. Stamen color: Dark yellow. Flower shape: Very full star. Flower size: 6–9 in. (15–23 cm). Fragrance: Very pleasant. Number of petals: 36 or 37. Number of sepals: 4.

LEAVES. Color: Top, new leaf is bright green with purple blotches, which soon turn green; underside, reddish with prominent green veins and purple blotches. Round leaf, sinus usually open. Leaf size: 8–8.5 in. (20–21.5 cm). Leaf spread: 5–6 ft. (1.5–1.8 m). Stem color: Reddish. Pubescence on peduncle and petiole.

COMMENTS. *Nymphaea* 'Perry's Super Yellow' is a magnificent new hybrid that people rave about after seeing it close up. The fragrance is noticeable but not pronounced. I highly recommend it for medium and large pools.

Nymphaea 'Perry's Vivid Rose'

Slocum 1990
Nymphaea 'Perry's Pink' × *N.* 'Pamela'
PLATE 224

CHARACTERISTICS. Odorata rhizome, fairly free flowering.

FLOWERS. Petal color: Pinkish red; inner petals edged yellow (*RHS* 74C; edging, 19B). Sepal color: Deep pinkish red (*RHS* 61B). Anther color: Orange (*RHS* 29B). Stamen color: Orange. Flower shape: Cuplike, full. Flower size: 5.5–6 in. (14–15 cm). Fragrance: Very pleasant. Number of petals: 38 or 39. Number of sepals: 4.

LEAVES. Color: Top, green, new leaves reddish; underside, light brown, new leaves pinkish. Leaf round; sinus an open V. Leaf size: 8–8.5 in. (20–22 cm). Leaf spread: 4–5 ft. (1.2–1.5 m). Stem color: Peduncle, brown; petiole, greenish brown. No pubescence on peduncle or petiole.

COMMENTS. Flowers of *Nymphaea* 'Perry's Vivid Pink' are certainly one of the most striking deep pinks of any waterlily. As it is an odorata, plant in a large container and allow it to form a colony to maximize bloom. I recommend it for medium and large pools and natural ponds.

Nymphaea 'Perry's Viviparous Pink'

Slocum 1990

Nymphaea 'Perry's Pink' × *N*. 'Colonel A. J. Welch'

PLATE 225

CHARACTERISTICS. Mildly viviparous from blossom, odorata rhizome, free flowering.

FLOWERS. Petal color: Deep pink (*RHS* 68B). Sepal color: Deep pink; base lighter (*RHS* 68B; base, 68C). Anther color: Orange (*RHS* 15B). Stamen color: Orange. Flower shape: Stellate. Flower size: 6–7.5 in. (15–19 cm). Fragrance: Slight to none. Number of petals: 44–47. Number of sepals: 4.

LEAVES. Color: Top, green, new leaves red, brilliant orange-red spot at petiole; underside, red. Leaf round; sinus usually open, may be partly closed. Leaf size: Up to 10.5 in. (27 cm). Leaf spread: About 5 ft. (1.5 m). Stem color: Brownish purple. A few fine, short hairs on peduncle and petiole.

COMMENTS. *Nymphaea* 'Perry's Viviparous Pink' is much admired for its beautiful new red leaves and vivid, very double, rich pink blooms with a glowing red spot in the flower center. Bloom season is unusually long for a pink hardy, continuing well into late October in North Carolina (zone 6b). Expect first-day flowers to close by midday on hot sunny days. Although it is less than 5 percent viviparous, even this percent production of plantlets from its spent flowers is a definite plus. Watching the new plantlet form and develop while still attached to the mother plant can be a very gratifying experience. Another pink hardy that develops plantlets is *N*. 'Perry's Pink Delight'. I recommend *N*. 'Perry's Viviparous Pink' for medium and large pools.

Nymphaea 'Perry's White Star'

Slocum 1990

Nymphaea 'Pink Starlet' × *N*. 'Pamela'

PLATE 226

CHARACTERISTICS. Marliac-tuberosa rhizome, free blooming.

FLOWERS. Petal color: White (*RHS* 155B). Sepal color: Grayish green, grayish green prominent veins, green tips and borders (*RHS* 195C; veins, 194C; tips and borders, 145B). Anther color: Yellow (*RHS* 6B). Stamen color: Yellow. Flower shape: Stellate, long narrow petals. Flower size: 5.5–7 in. (14–18 cm). Fragrance: Very pleasant. Number of petals: 32–34. Number of sepals: 4.

LEAVES. Color: Top, green, new leaves bronzy; underside, reddish. Leaf slightly longer than wide; sinus usually an open V. Leaf size: 8–9.5 × 7.5–9 in. (20–24 × 19–23 cm). Leaf spread: 4–5 ft. (1.2–1.5 m). Stem color: Peduncle, reddish brown; petiole, red. Thick fuzz on peduncle and petiole.

COMMENTS. *Nymphaea* 'Perry's White Star' is a white variation of *N*. 'Pink Starlet'. Blooms are held 2–4 in. (5–10 cm) above the water. Plant it in a large container, about 24 × 24 × 12 in. (60 × 60 × 30 cm), so that it can form a colony of free-flowering plants. I recommend this cultivar for medium and large pools.

Nymphaea 'Perry's White Wonder'

Slocum 1990

Probably *N. tetragona* and *N. alba* (from New Zealand)

CHARACTERISTICS. Marliac rhizome, very free flowering.

FLOWERS. Petal color: White (*RHS* 155A). Sepal color: White; pale pink blush (*RHS* 155A; blush, lighter than 73D). Anther color: Yellow (*RHS* 3A). Stamen color: Deep yellow. Flower shape: Cuplike then stellate. Flower size: 3.5–6 in. (9–15 cm). Fragrance: Very slight. Number of petals: 27–31. Number of sepals: 4.

LEAVES. Color: Top, green, new leaves bronzy; underside, reddish. Leaves nearly round, lobe tips project 0.25 in. (0.5 cm); sinus generally open, may be up to three-fourths closed. Leaf size: Up to 9 × 8 in. (23 × 20 cm). Leaf spread 3.5–4.5 ft. (1.1–1.4 m). Stem color: Bronzy green. A few tiny hairs on peduncle and petiole.

COMMENTS. A lovely white-flowered cultivar with very sturdy stems, *Nymphaea* 'Perry's White Wonder' is not subject to crown rot. Its restrained growth makes it ideal for tub gardens or small to large pools.

Nymphaea 'Perry's Wildfire'

Slocum 1990

Nymphaea 'Perry's Pink' × *N*. 'Mrs. Martin E. Randig'

CHARACTERISTICS. Odorata rhizome, fairly free flowering.

FLOWERS. Petal color: Glowing purplish red (*RHS* 64B). Sepal color: Glowing purplish red (*RHS* 64B). Anther color: Orange (*RHS* 29B). Stamen color: Orange-red. Flower shape: Stellate. Flower size: 6–7 in. (15–18 cm). Fragrance: Delightful. Number of petals: 28 or 29. Number of sepals: 4.

LEAVES. Color: Top, deep green, new leaves purplish brown; underside, pinkish red. Heart-shaped leaves; sinus two-thirds open. Leaf size: Up to 10 × 9 in. (25 × 23 cm). Leaf spread: 4–5 ft. (1.2–1.5 m). Stem color: Greenish, striped purple. A few fine hairs on peduncle and petiole.

COMMENTS. The color of *N.* 'Perry's Wildfire', similar to a brush fire, is new to hardy waterlilies. Because people go wild over it, the name 'Perry's Wildfire' took shape. Flowers also stay open quite late in the afternoon. Although this cultivar has a tropical parent, undoubtedly supplying its deep purple-red color, it has survived winter lows of –5°F (–21°C) in an outdoor pond. Plant 'Perry's Wildfire' in a large container so that it can form a colony of rhizomes. I recommend this cultivar for medium and large pools.

Nymphaea 'Peter Slocum'

Slocum 1984
Chance seedling of *N.* 'Pearl of the Pool'
PLATE 227

CHARACTERISTICS. Odorata rhizome, moderately free flowering, perennial.

FLOWERS. Petal color: Medium pink, fading slightly (*RHS* 62B,C). Sepal color: Medium pink, fading slightly (*RHS* 62B,C). Anther color: Yellow (*RHS* 19A). Stamen color: Yellow; orange and pinkish exterior rows. Flower shape: Peony-style. Flower size: 6–7.5 in. (15–19 cm). Fragrance: Very sweet. Number of petals: 40 or 41. Number of sepals: 4.

LEAVES. Color: Top, green, newest leaves purple; underside, red, prominent green lengthwise V along midvein, underside green when above water. Leaf round; lobes overlap, cover sinus. Leaf size: Up to 11 in. (28 cm). Leaf spread: 5–6 ft. (1.5–1.8m). Stem color: Green. Short fuzz on peduncle and petiole.

COMMENTS. This cultivar is named after my son Peter, owner of Slocum Water Gardens, Winter Haven, Florida. Concave petals give this exquisitely beautiful waterlily a bicolor effect and a silvery

sheen. *Nymphaea* 'Peter Slocum' blooms are also superb as cut flowers. It will bloom plentifully if planted in a large container and allowed to form a colony. Flowers stay open later than most odorata waterlilies. I highly recommend this plant for medium or large pools and natural ponds.

Nymphaea 'Picciola'

Latour-Marliac Nursery 1913
Parentage unknown

CHARACTERISTICS. Marliac rhizome, free flowering, perennial.

FLOWERS. Petal color: Inner petals, rich clear purple-red; outer petals purple-red, flecked, pink toward tips (*RHS* inner, 182A; outer, 47B; tips, 43D). Sepal color: Pink, deep purplish lengthwise stripes, green edges, white tips (*RHS* 68D; stripes, 60D; edges, 134D; tips, 155A). Anther color: Orange (*RHS* 20A). Stamen color: Orange-red. Flower shape: Stellate. Flower size: 5.5–6 in. (14–15 cm). Fragrance: Slight. Number of petals: 29. Number of sepals: 4.

LEAVES. Color: Top, green, heavily blotched purple; underside, red, prominent green veins. Leaf almost round, lobes sharply pointed at tips; lobes overlap 1 in. (2.5 cm) at sinus. Leaf size: 8.5–9 in. (22–23 cm). Leaf spread: 4–5 ft. (1.2–1.5 m). Stem color: Red. No pubescence on peduncle or petiole.

COMMENTS. Leaf and flower colors are quite similar to those of *Nymphaea* 'Sirius', yet *N.* 'Picciola' has a smaller leaf spread and is therefore more suitable for small and medium pools. However, *N.* 'Picciola' is more subject to crown rot than *N.* 'Sirius'.

Nymphaea 'Pink Beauty'

Syn. 'Luciana'
Dreer 1899
Parentage unknown
PLATE 228

CHARACTERISTICS. Marliac rhizome, extremely free flowering.

FLOWERS. Petal color: Medium pink (*RHS* 62B or 65A). Sepal color: Medium pink (*RHS* 62B or 65A). Anther color: Golden yellow (*RHS* 11A). Stamen color: Inner rows, yellow; outer rows pink. Flower shape: Cuplike. Flower size: 4–6 in. (10–15 cm). Fragrance: Very slight. Number of petals: 24 or 25. Number of sepals: 4 or 5.

LEAVES. Color: Top, green, new leaves slightly bronzed; underside, green, new leaves purple. Leaf round; sinus an open V. Leaf size: 8–9 in. (20–23 cm). Leaf spread: 3–4 ft. (0.9–1.2 m). Stem color: Green, striped purple. No pubescence on peduncle or petiole.

COMMENTS. *Nymphaea* 'Pink Beauty' is an excellent waterlily for any size pool. It has become one of the most popular pink hardies in the United States. I highly recommend it for the tub garden or small pool.

Nymphaea 'Pink Grapefruit'
Strawn, year unknown
Parentage unknown
PLATE 229

CHARACTERISTICS. Nonviviparous, Marliac rhizome, very free flowering, perennial.

FLOWERS. Petal color: Light reddish pink outer petals that progress to soft yellow toward inner petals. Sepal color: Inner, greenish white at center; faint pink toward outer edges; outer, light green with dark green tips, reddish pink on some edges. Anther color: Inner, deep yellow; outer, deep yellow. Stamen color: Deep yellow. Flower shape: Stellate. Flower size: 4–5 in. (10–12.5 cm). Fragrance: Strong. Number of petals: 24–26. Number of sepals: 4.

LEAVES. Color: Top, medium green with heavy blotched flecking, newer leaves light green; underside, reddish plum with similar blotched flecking, newer leaves have more green than red. Leaf is nearly round; sinus open, distinct tips on lobes. Leaf size: 5–7 in. (12.5–18 cm). Leaf spread: 4–6 ft. (1.2–1.8 m). Stem color: Bronze. No pubescence on peduncle or petiole.

COMMENTS BY DEAN MCGEE. The unique color patterns of *Nymphaea* 'Pink Grapefruit' resemble its name very well. A prolific bloomer, these blossoms stand 2–3 in. (5–7.5 cm) above the water surface. Excellent choice as a stand-alone or centerpiece waterlily in a medium or large pond.

Nymphaea 'Pink Opal'
Fowler 1915
Parentage unknown

CHARACTERISTICS. Odorata rhizome, moderately free flowering; flowers held 3–5 in. (8–13 cm) above water.

FLOWERS. Petal color: Coral pink (*RHS* 38A). Sepal color: Deep pink (*RHS* 39B). Anther color: Deep yellow (*RHS* 12B). Stamen color: Deep yellow. Flower shape: Cuplike. Flower size: 3–4 in. (8–10 cm). Fragrance: Lovely, sweet. Number of petals: 26. Number of sepals: 4.

LEAVES. Color: Top, green, new leaves bronzy; underside, reddish. Leaf nearly round; lobes usually overlap at sinus. Leaf size: 8–9 in. (20–23 cm). Leaf spread: Up to 3 ft. (0.9 m). Stem color: Brownish. Some fuzz on peduncle and petiole.

COMMENTS. *Nymphaea* 'Pink Opal' holds its blooms above the water on especially strong peduncles. Blooms make fine cut flowers. For many years this waterlily was highly recommended for tub gardens, but it is now superseded by hardy waterlilies such as *N.* 'Perry's Fire Opal', *N.* 'Laydekeri Rosea', *N.* 'Masaniello', and *N.* 'Perry's Baby Red', which have improved all-around performance. I recommend 'Pink Opal' only for collectors.

Nymphaea 'Pink Pumpkin'
Strawn 1994
Nymphaea 'Pink Beauty' × *N.* 'Peter Slocum'

CHARACTERISTICS. Nonviviparous, Marliac rhizome, free flowering, perennial.

FLOWERS. Petal color: Intense fuchsia petals throughout, tips slightly lighter toward inner petals. Sepal color: Inner, fuchsia; dark green tips; outer, medium green, dark green tips. Anther color: Inner, bright yellow; outer, bright yellow. Stamen color: Fuchsia pink. Flower shape: Stellate, then wide open. Flower size: 3–4 in. (7.5–10 cm). Fragrance: Pleasant. Number of petals: 32–34. Number of sepals: 4.

LEAVES. Color: Top, medium green, some leaves are olive green with orange-brown tint; underside, reddish plum. Leaf nearly round; sinus open. Leaf size: 3–5 in. (7.5–12.5 cm). Leaf spread: 2–4 ft. (0.6–1.2 m). Stem color: Bronze. Pubescence on petiole.

COMMENTS BY DEAN MCGEE. *Nymphaea* 'Pink Pumpkin' produces sparkling pink blossoms that open wide and rest on the surface of the water, complimented by unique combination of green and pumpkin colored leaves. Nice selection for small to medium ponds.

Nymphaea 'Pink Sensation'

Slocum 1947

Chance seedling or mutation of N. 'Lustrous'

PLATE 230

CHARACTERISTICS. Marliac rhizome, very free flowering.

FLOWERS. Petal color: Smooth rich pink (*RHS* 62B). Sepal color: Slightly darker than petals (*RHS* 62A,B). Anther color: Golden yellow (*RHS* 11A). Stamen color: Yellow, orange and pink outer rows. Flower shape: Cuplike then stellate. Flower size: 5–6 in. (13–15 cm). Fragrance: Slight. Number of petals: 20. Number of sepals: 4.

LEAVES. Color: Top, green, first leaves purplish green; underside, purplish brown, first leaves red. Leaf round; sinus a narrow, open V. Leaf size: Up to 10 in. (25 cm). Leaf spread: 4 ft. (1.2 m). Stem color: Greenish. Thick fuzz on peduncle and petiole.

COMMENTS. Flowers stay open very late in the afternoon, later than those of any other pink hardy. For all-around performance, this is probably the very best pink hardy for any size pool.

Nymphaea 'Pink Starlet'

Landon 1970

Natural hybrid involving N. tuberosa

CHARACTERISTICS. Tuberosa rhizome, very free flowering early in the season, less so with onset of fruiting.

FLOWERS. Petal color: Light pink (*RHS* 36D). Sepal color: Pinkish, slightly deeper than petals (*RHS* 36C). Anther color: Deep yellow (*RHS* 13B). Stamen color: Yellow. Flower shape: Stellate. Flower size: 5–7 in. (13–18 cm). Fragrance: Lemony. Number of petals: 29 or 30. Number of sepals: 4.

LEAVES. Color: Top, olive green, new leaves bronzy; underside, green suffused with pink and maroon, new leaves bronzy. Leaves round, smooth edges; sinus open. Leaf size: 6–10 in. (15–25 cm). Leaf spread: 3–6 ft. (0.9–1.8 m). Stem color: Reddish brown. No pubescence on peduncle or petiole.

COMMENTS. *Nymphaea* 'Pink Starlet' is an especially delicate-looking waterlily, and the flowers are held 9 in. (23 cm) above the water. I recommend it for any size pool, especially medium and large ones.

Nymphaea 'Pink Sunrise'

Strawn 1993

Nymphaea 'Peter Slocum' × N. 'Sunrise'

CHARACTERISTICS. Nonviviparous, Marliac rhizome, free flowering, perennial.

FLOWERS. Petal color: Medium pink throughout petals. Sepal color: Inner, light green, dark green pin stripes; outer, medium green. Anther color: Inner, bright yellow; outer, bright yellow. Stamen color: Bright yellow. Flower shape: Full, cuplike. Flower size: 3–4 in. (7.5–10 cm). Fragrance: Slight. Number of petals: 38–40. Number of sepals: 4.

LEAVES. Color: Top, medium green; underside, deep plum color. Leaf nearly round; sinus slightly open. Leaf size: 4–5 in. (10–12.5 cm). Leaf spread: 3–5 ft. (0.9–1.5 m). Stem color: Light green. No pubescence on peduncle or petiole.

COMMENTS BY DEAN McGEE. The very elegant solid pink flowers of *Nymphaea* 'Pink Sunrise' sit directly on the surface of the water. Vigorous bloomer that is well suited for medium ponds.

Nymphaea 'Pöstlingberg'

Wendelin Buggele, year unknown

Parentage unknown

CHARACTERISTICS. Tuberosa rhizome, fairly free flowering, very fast, vigorous grower.

FLOWERS. Petal color: White (*RHS* 155C). Sepal color: White; pale pink center (*RHS* 155C; center, 65D). Anther color: Golden yellow (*RHS* 13C). Stamen color: Golden yellow. Flower shape: Cuplike, petals stellate. Flower size: 6–7 in. (15–18 cm). Fragrance: Mild and pleasant. Number of petals: 19 or 20. Number of sepals: 4.

LEAVES. Color: Top, green, new leaves bronzy green; underside, green, new leaves bronzy, prominent green veins. Leaf nearly round; lobes sharply pointed, usually overlap sinus to cover all but 1 in. (2.5 cm). Leaf size: 13 × 12 in. (33 × 30 cm). Leaf spread: 6 ft. (1.8 m). Stem color: Yellowish green, purple lengthwise stripes. No pubescence on peduncle or petiole.

COMMENTS. *Nymphaea* 'Pöstlingberg', developed in Linz, Austria, has large leaves and a very large leaf spread if given ample growing room. It is a very pretty waterlily for the collector with a large pool.

Nymphaea 'Pride of Palm Beach'

Connelly 1985

Parentage unknown

CHARACTERISTICS. Fairly free flowering, odorata rhizome, nonviviparous, perennial.

FLOWERS. Petal color: Outer rows are pale pink and the rest are white. Sepal color: Inner, pink; outer, olive green. Anther color: Inner, yellow; outer, yellow. Stamen color: Yellow. Flower shape: Cuplike. Flower size: 5–6 in. (12.5–15 cm). Fragrance: Sweet, spicy. Number of petals: 45. Number of sepals: 4.

LEAVES. Color: Top, new leaves are bronzy, then olive green; underside, pinkish. Nearly round leaf with partly open sinus. Leaf size: 5–7 in. (12.5–18 cm). Leaf spread: 4–5 ft. (1.2–1.5 m). Stem color: Brown. A little pubescence on peduncle and petiole.

COMMENTS BY LEEANN CONNELLY. This is a really nice compact waterlily that grows well in tubs and small ponds. I discovered it in the small town of Loridan, Florida. The area it was in goes bone dry in the autumn and winter, and I think that such conditions made it evolve into a dwarf waterlily. In south Florida it blooms up to December and keeps nice leaves all year.

Nymphaea 'Queen of Whites'

Gedye 1970

Parentage unknown

CHARACTERISTICS. Marliac rhizome, very free flowering.

FLOWERS. Petal color: White (RHS 155C). Sepal color: White; sometimes blushed pale pink (RHS 155C; blush, 36C,D). Anther color: Yellow (RHS 12B). Stamen color: Yellow. Flower shape: Cuplike, petals stellate. Flower size: 6–7 in. (15–18 cm). Fragrance: Lovely, mild. Number of petals: 27–29. Number of sepals: 4.

LEAVES. Color: Top, green; underside, red or bronzy red, green if above water. Leaf nearly round; sinus usually an open V; lobes overlap partially on new leaves, one lobe frequently raised. Leaf size: Up to 11.5 × 10.5 in. (29 × 27 cm). Leaf spread: 4–6 ft. (1.2–1.8 m). Stem color: Green or greenish brown. Very fine fuzz and hairs on peduncle and petiole.

COMMENTS. This waterlily, from Gedye's Water Gardens, Doncaster East, Australia, has one more row of petals than Nymphaea 'Marliacea Albida' and usually produces larger and wider flowers. A first-year plant may develop five or six blooms at a time beginning in midsummer. Nymphaea 'Queen of Whites' is ideal for medium and large pools.

Nymphaea 'Radiant Red'

Parentage unknown

CHARACTERISTICS. Marliac rhizome, free flowering.

FLOWERS. Petal color: Red, somewhat flecked (RHS 66C). Sepal color: White, developing green tint and pink stripes (RHS 155C; tint, 149D; stripes, 66D). Anther color: Yellow-orange (RHS 21C). Stamen color: Orange. Flower shape: Full, stellate, long sepals. Flower size: 5–6 in. (13–15 cm). Fragrance: Slight. Number of petals: 22. Number of sepals: 4.

LEAVES. Color: Top, green; underside, green, newer leaves bronze. Leaf nearly round; sinus two-thirds to completely open. Leaf size: Up to 10 in. (25 cm). Leaf spread: 3–4 ft. (0.9–1.2 m). Stem color: Peduncle, brownish purple; petiole purple. Fuzz on peduncle and petiole, especially on peduncle.

COMMENTS. Nymphaea 'Radiant Red' is a fine red hardy waterlily for any size pool.

Nymphaea 'Ray Davies'

Slocum 1985

Seedling of N. 'Rosanna'

CHARACTERISTICS. Odorata rhizome, moderately free flowering.

FLOWERS. Petal color: Inner petals yellow; outer petals light pink, deeper toward base (RHS 5D; outer, 62D; base, 62C). Sepal color: Light pink (RHS 62D). Anther color: Yellow (RHS 6A). Stamen color: Yellow. Flower shape: Peony-style. Flower size: 6–7 in. (15–18 cm). Fragrance: Slight. Number of petals: 53–55. Number of sepals: 4.

LEAVES. Color: Top, deep green, new leaves slightly bronzed; underside, brownish purple, prominent V along midvein, new leaves red. Leaf round; lobes overlap slightly along two-thirds of sinus. Leaf size: Up to 10–11 in. (25–28 cm). Leaf spread: 5 ft. (1.5 m). Stem color: Green, purple stripes. Some fine fuzz and hairs on peduncle and petiole.

COMMENTS. I developed this cultivar in North Carolina (zone 6b) and named it in honor of the owner of Stapeley Water Gardens. *Nymphaea* 'Ray Davies', with its very double blooms, is undoubtedly one of the most beautiful lilies in the world today. It was voted best new hardy waterlily for 1987 by the members of the International Waterlily and Water Gardening Society. For best results, plant it in a large container and allow it to form a colony of rhizomes. It will then produce quite an abundance of flowers. This waterlily is ideal for a large pool or natural pond, yet it will also adapt to a medium-sized pool.

Nymphaea 'Red Joanne Pring'

Perry's Water Gardens 1987
Probable mutation of *N.* 'Joanne Pring'

CHARACTERISTICS. Small Marliac rhizome, very free flowering.

FLOWERS. Petal color: Rich pink then rich red (*RHS* 62B,C; third day, 63A,B). Sepal color: White then pink, flecked lighter pink (*RHS* 155A; third day, 65B). Anther color: Yellow then burnt orange (*RHS* 13B; third day, 24A). Stamen color: Yellow to orange. Flower shape: Cuplike. Flower size: 3–4 in. (8–10 cm). Fragrance: Slight. Number of petals: 15–16. Number of sepals: 4.

LEAVES. Color: Top, green, young leaves mottled purple; underside, red-brown, young leaves red-purple. Leaf a little longer than wide; sinus a wide V. Leaf size: 5.5 in. (14 cm). Leaf spread: 3 ft. (0.9 m). Stem color: Purplish brown. No pubescence on peduncle or petiole.

COMMENTS. *Nymphaea* 'Red Joanne Pring' showed up in a bed of *N.* 'Joanne Pring' at Perry's Water Gardens in North Carolina (zone 6b). Apparently it is a mutation or sport of 'Joanne Pring' and identical to it in every way (including a susceptibility to crown rot) except flower color. The deep red flowers of this chance waterlily are magnificent. I consider it a fine choice for a tub garden or small pool in all climates.

Nymphaea 'Red Paradise'

Perry's Water Gardens 1993
Natural hybrid, one parent probably *N.*
   'Atropurpurea'
PLATE 231

CHARACTERISTICS. Fairly free flowering, Marliac rhizome, perennial.

FLOWERS. Petal color: Very deep red. Sepal color: Inner sepals, outer third of sepal green, inner two-thirds pink; outer, olive green. Anther color: Inner, deep yellow; outer, deep yellow. Stamen color: Red at base. Flower shape: Cuplike. Flower size: 4.5–5 in. (11.5–12.7 cm). Fragrance: Slight. Number of petals: 27 or 28. Number of sepals: 4.

LEAVES. Color: Top, new leaves purple, in a few weeks turning olive green; underside, reddish. Sinus usually open. Leaf size: About 7.5 in. (19 cm). Leaf spread: 3.5–5 ft. (1–1.5 m). Stem color: Brown to reddish brown or purple. No pubescence on peduncle or petiole.

COMMENTS. *Nymphaea* 'Red Paradise' has excellent color and is a moderately free bloomer. First- and second-day flowers are held about 6–8 in. (15–20 cm) above the water. However, in late August in North Carolina, the blooms are produced less freely.

Nymphaea 'Red Queen'

Slocum 1995
Nymphaea 'Perry's Fire Opal' × *N.* 'Blue Beauty'
PLATE 232

CHARACTERISTICS. Free flowering, Marliac rhizome, perennial.

FLOWERS. Petal color: Dark purplish red. Sepal color: inside pinkish, outside olive green often with pink edge. Anther color: inner, dark yellow; outer, dark yellow. Stamen color: Purplish red. Flower shape: Peony shape. Flower size: 4.5–5.5 in. (11.5–14 cm). Fragrance: Slight, pleasant. Number of petals: 41–44. Number of sepals: 4.

LEAVES. Color: Top, new leaves purple, soon changing to olive green; underside, red with prominent green veins. Oval; sinus closed, with lobes overlapping and protruding up. Leaf size: 8 × 7.5 in. (20.3 × 19 cm). Leaf spread: 4–6 ft. (1.2–1.8 m). Stem color: Brownish. Thick, short fuzz on peduncle and petiole.

COMMENTS. This is truly one of the outstanding new hybrids. It is one of the favorites with visitors to Perry's Water Gardens. I highly recommend *N.* 'Red Queen' for medium and large pools.

Nymphaea 'Red Sensation'

Slocum 1991

Probably *N.* 'Alba Plenissima' × *N.* 'Atropurpurea'

PLATE 233

CHARACTERISTICS. Marliac rhizome, free flowering.

FLOWERS. Petal color: Deep red, some flecking (*RHS* 64A). Sepal color: Tip half greenish; base reddish pink (*RHS* tip, 145B; base, 63C). Anther color: Deep yellow (*RHS* 5B). Stamen color: Deep yellow. Flower shape: Peony-style. Flower size: 6–7.5 in. (15–19 cm). Fragrance: Slight. Number of petals: 37 or 38. Number of sepals: 4.

LEAVES. Color: Top, green, new leaves bronzy green; underside, mostly green, new leaves pinkish, prominent green veins. Leaf nearly round, undulating margin; sinus an open V. Leaf size: Up to 10 in. (25 cm). Leaf spread: 4–5 ft. (1.2–1.5 m). Stem color: Brownish. No pubescence on peduncle or petiole.

COMMENTS. *Nymphaea* 'Red Sensation' is one of the most striking new red hardies ever developed at Perry's Water Gardens. The slight flecking on the petals seems to add to the flower's beauty rather than detract. I highly recommend this cultivar for medium or large pools.

Nymphaea 'Red Spider'

Strawn 1993

Nymphaea 'White Sultan' × *N. mexicana*

PLATE 234

CHARACTERISTICS. Nonviviparous, Marliac rhizome, free flowering, perennial.

FLOWERS. Petal color: Blushed red becoming more intense red toward inner petals. Sepal color: Inner, yellowish green; outer, dark green, medium green at base. Anther color: Inner, bright yellow; outer, bright yellow. Stamen color: Deep blushed red. Flower shape: Stellate, with crinkled petals. Flower size: 3–4 in. (7.5–10 cm). Fragrance: Slight. Number of petals: 34–36. Number of sepals: 4.

LEAVES. Color: Top, dark green with flecking toward outer edges; underside, reddish brown with heavier flecking, newer leaves more green than brown. Leaf is slightly ovate with convolutions; sinus slightly open. Leaf size: 3–5 in. (7.5–12.5 cm). Leaf spread: 2–3 ft. (0.6–0.9 m). Stem color: Olive green. No pubescence on peduncle or petiole.

COMMENTS BY DEAN MCGEE. *Nymphaea* 'Red Spider' gives a truly outstanding display of radiant scarlet hues and has full stellate crinkled petals complemented with unique heavily flecked leaves. This waterlily is an excellent choice for a medium pond.

Nymphaea 'Regann'

Henley 1991

PLATE 235

CHARACTERISTICS. Free flowering, Marliac rhizome, perennial.

FLOWERS. Petal color: Uniform strong red. Sepal color: White with red showing at base reducing to tip. Anther color: Inner, red with yellow pollen; outer, red. Stamen color: Red. Flower shape: Cuplike. Flower size: 5 in. (12.5 cm). Fragrance: Faint. Number of petals: 28. Number of sepals: 4.

LEAVES. Color: Top, green; underside, green with slight bronze. Leaf round with notch at top; lobes overlap at sinus, opening at base. Leaf size: 9 in. (23 cm). Leaf spread: 3 ft. (0.9 m). Stem color: Peduncle brown, petiole dark red aging to olive green. No pubescence on peduncle or petiole.

COMMENTS BY REG HENLEY. *Nymphaea* 'Regann' is a strong grower with good flowering ability, and it wants to mass proliferate at this latitude (51°N). I recommend it for any size pool.

Nymphaea 'René Gérard'

Syn. 'La Beaugère'

Latour-Marliac Nursery 1914

Parentage unknown

CHARACTERISTICS. Marliac rhizome, free flowering.

FLOWERS. Petal color: Inner petals deep rosy red, paling toward outer petals; much flecking, especially in outer petals (*RHS* inner, 63B; outer, 65C). Sepal color: White (*RHS* 155A). Anther color: Yellow-orange (*RHS* 14B). Stamen color: Yellow-orange. Flower shape: Stellate. Flower size: 6–9 in. (15–23 cm). Fragrance: Slight. Number of petals: 20–24. Number of sepals: 4.

LEAVES. Color: Top and underside, green, newest leaves bronzy green. Leaves nearly round; sinus usually an open V. Leaf size: Up to 10–11 in. (25–28 cm). Leaf spread: 5 ft. (1.5 m). Stem color: Usually bronzy green. A few hairs may appear on peduncle and petiole.

COMMENTS. With its pleasing flowers, shading from darker center to pale outer petals, *Nymphaea* 'René Gérard' is quite attractive, although some people object to the heavy flecking. I highly recommend it for medium and large pools. The Latour-Marliac Nursery in France now calls this waterlily *N.* 'La Beaugère'.

Nymphaea 'Robinsoniana'

Syn. 'Robinsoni', 'Robinsonii'
Marliac 1895
Probably *N. alba var. rubra* × *N. mexicana*

CHARACTERISTICS. Upright rhizome the size and shape of a pineapple, free flowering.

FLOWERS. Petal color: Orange-red, lighter tips (*RHS* 41D; tips, 39D). Sepal color: Lighter orange-red than petals, greenish cream tips (*RHS* 39C; tips, 149D). Anther color: Yellow-orange (*RHS* 23B). Stamen color: Orange. Flower shape: Inner portion cuplike, outer stellate. Flower size: 4.5–5 in. (11–13 cm). Fragrance: Slight. Number of petals: 24–27. Number of sepals: 4.

LEAVES. Color: Top, beautiful light purple, deep purple blotches, greener with age; underside, deep red, purple specks and mottles. Leaf a little longer than wide; lobes overlap about halfway down sinus. Each lobe, except in some young leaves, has a distinctive notch about halfway down the sinus. Leaf size: 8 in. (20 cm). Leaf spread: 4–5 ft. (1.2–1.5 m). Stem color: Greenish brown, faint purple stripes. No pubescence on peduncle or petiole.

COMMENTS. Leaves are especially beautiful and have a unique notch along the sinus (not always present in late summer). *Nymphaea* 'Robinsoniana' is best suited for medium and large pools, but its restrained growth makes it suitable for small pools as well. I have found this cultivar to be somewhat subject to crown rot.

Nymphaea 'Rosanna'

Ambassador Water Gardens (where it was sold as *N.* 'Rosanna Supreme')
Parentage unknown

CHARACTERISTICS. Odorata rhizome, fairly free flowering.

FLOWERS. Petal color: Base, medium pink; upper portion shell pink (*RHS* base, 62C; upper portion, 62D). Sepal color: Medium pink, some green patches (*RHS* 62D; patches, 135D). Anther color: Deep golden yellow (*RHS* 9A). Stamen color: Deep golden yellow. Flower shape: Stellate. Flower size: 6–7 in. (15–18 cm). Fragrance: Some. Number of petals: 20. Number of sepals: 4.

LEAVES. Color: Top, green, new leaves purplish; underside, red, green V lengthwise along midvein. Leaf round; sinus a wide-open V. Leaf size: 9–9.5 in. (23–24 cm). Leaf spread: 4 ft. (1.2 m). Stem color: Green, purple stripes. Thick fuzz on peduncle and petiole.

COMMENTS. Unusual bicolor pink blooms make this one of the prettiest hardy waterlilies. For best results, plant it in a large container so that a colony of rhizomes can develop. This lovely waterlily was confused with *N.* 'Rosanna Supreme' (see description) for many years. I recommend *N.* 'Rosanna' for medium and large pools.

Nymphaea 'Rosanna Supreme'

Randig, year unknown
Parentage unknown

CHARACTERISTICS. Marliac rhizome, very free flowering.

FLOWERS. Petal color: Inner petals pale pink, some flecking, developing deeper pink base; outer petals lighter pink, turning to a deeper pink (*RHS* inner, first day, 65D or lighter; third day, base, 63C; outer, first day, 63D; third day, 65D or lighter). Sepal color: Nearly white, prominent gray-green veins (*RHS* 155B; veins, 191C). Anther color: Yellow (*RHS* 12B). Stamen color: Inner stamens yellow, outer orange. Flower shape: Stellate. Flower size: 4–5 in. (10–13 cm). Fragrance: None. Number of petals: 24–26. Number of sepals: 4.

LEAVES. Color: Top, green, new leaves deep green, mottled purple; underside, pale red-brown or green, green V along midvein, new leaves red-brown. Leaf nearly round; sinus a wide-open V. Leaf size: 8–9 in. (20–23 cm). Leaf spread: 4 ft. (1.2 m). Stem color: Peduncles, brown; petioles purple. Some hairs on peduncle and petiole.

COMMENTS. *Nymphaea* 'Rosanna Supreme' is very free flowering and can be used in any size pool.

Flowers are highly flecked, lacking the clear smooth pink of the immensely popular N. 'Pink Beauty', N. 'Perry's Pink', N. 'Peter Slocum', N. 'Pink Sensation', N. 'Rose Arey', and other evenly colored pinks. The N. 'Rosanna Supreme' sold by Ambassador Water Gardens is actually N. 'Rosanna'.

Nymphaea 'Rose Arey'

Fowler 1913

Parentage unknown

PLATE 236

CHARACTERISTICS. Odorata rhizome, fairly free flowering.

FLOWERS. Petal color: Very rich medium or deep pink (RHS 63C or 68C). Sepal color: Deep pink (RHS 58D). Anther color: Yellow (RHS 11A). Stamen color: Inner stamens golden yellow; outer orange-pink. Flower shape: Stellate. Flower size: 7–8 in. (18–20 cm). Fragrance: Very sweet. Number of petals: 33–39. Number of sepals: 4.

LEAVES. Color: Top, green, new leaves purple; underside, brown, new leaves purple. Leaves round; sinus narrow and open. Leaf size: 9 in. (23 cm). Leaf spread: 4–5 ft. (1.2–1.5 m). Stem color: Brown, purple stripes. Fine fuzz and hair on peduncle and petiole.

COMMENTS. This is one of the most beautiful lilies known. Plant Nymphaea 'Rose Arey' in a large container, about 24 × 24 × 12 in. (60 × 60 × 30 cm) and allow it to form a colony, and it will produce numerous blooms. Blooms also make fine cut flowers. Nymphaea 'Rose Arey' is an excellent choice for medium or large pools or the natural pond. In ponds, plants may develop at a rate of 1–2 ft. (0.3–0.6 m) per year and may also drop viable seeds. A negative feature is that new leaves in spring are often twisted and ill-shaped.

Nymphaea 'Rose Magnolia'

Parentage unknown

CHARACTERISTICS. Tuberosa rhizome, fairly free flowering if given room to mature.

FLOWERS. Petal color: Shell pink, deeper at base (RHS 56D; base, 56B,C). Sepal color: Light pink (RHS 56C). Anther color: Deep yellow (RHS 18A). Stamen color: Deep yellow. Flower shape: Cuplike. Flower size: 4–5 in. (10–13 cm). Fragrance: Slight. Number of petals: 20. Number of sepals: 4.

LEAVES. Color: Top, green, new leaves bronzy; underside, pinkish brown. Leaf nearly round, edges frequently wavy; sinus either open or closed. Leaf size: Up to 10 in. (25 cm). Leaf spread: 5–6 ft. (1.5–1.8 m). Stem color: Brownish. No pubescence on peduncle or petiole.

COMMENTS. This is an older, North American hybrid. As there are much more free-blooming and more richly colored pink hardies available today, I recommend Nymphaea 'Rose Magnolia' only for the collector with a large pool.

Nymphaea 'Rosennymphe'

Junge 1911

Parentage unknown

CHARACTERISTICS. Moderately free flowering, odorata rhizome, perennial.

FLOWERS. Petal color: First day, salmon pink; second day, turns light pink; third day, almost white. Sepal color: Inner, white and pink; outer, green with touch of pink. Anther color: Inner, golden yellow and pale pink; outer, golden yellow. Stamen color: Pale pink. Flower shape: Irregular star shape with medium width petals. Flower size: 4.7 in. (12 cm). Fragrance: Sweet. Number of petals: 22. Number of sepals: 4.

LEAVES. Color: Top, brown aging to plain green; underside, light brown. Round leaf; sinus open. Leaf size: 9–12 in. (23–30 cm). Leaf spread: 5 ft. (1.5 m). Stem color: yellow-green. No pubescence on peduncle or petiole.

COMMENTS BY HENRICH JUNGE. The flowers stand above water level when grown in less than 27 in. (70 cm) of water.

COMMENTS BY PERRY SLOCUM. I was advised by several German nurserymen visiting Perry's Water Gardens that the true N. 'Rosennymphe' opens pink and changes to white. Nursery proprietors in the United States and Australia, however, continue to promote a variation as N. 'Rosennymphe'. There are many superior pinks on the market, however. (Those with a Marliac rhizome require less container space and do not require two to three months to become free blooming, as do the odorata.) I recommend N. 'Rosennymphe' for the collector or the water gardener with a large pool.

Nymphaea 'Rosy Morn'

Johnson 1932

Nymphaea 'Rose Arey' × *N.* 'Escarboucle'

PLATE 237

CHARACTERISTICS. Marliac rhizome, very free flowering.

FLOWERS. Petal color: Inner petals rich strawberry pink; outer petals very pale pink, fading (*RHS* inner, 62B; outer, 62D or lighter, fading to 36D or lighter). Sepal color: Pale pink, veins pink, both whitening (*RHS* 65D or lighter; veins, 65B or 65C). Anther color: Deep golden yellow (*RHS* 13B). Stamen color: Yellow. Flower shape: Stellate. Flower size: 6–7 in. (15–18 cm). Fragrance: Very slight. Number of petals: 24. Number of sepals: 4.

LEAVES. Color: Top, green, new leaves purplish, prominent reddish purple blotch at junction with petiole; underside, red, green V along midvein. Leaf round; sinus usually open. Leaf size: 8–9 in. (20–23 cm). Leaf spread: 3–4 ft. (0.9–1.2 m). Stem color: Peduncle, brownish; petiole purple. Thick fuzz on peduncle and petiole.

COMMENTS. *Nymphaea* 'Rosy Morn', with its very striking, abundant, and large flowers, would be an outstanding addition to any pool.

Nymphaea 'Rubra'

Parentage unknown

PLATE 238

CHARACTERISTICS. Free flowering, Marliac rhizome, perennial.

FLOWERS. Petal color: Lovely pinkish red. Sepal color: Inner, white, flushed with green near tip and pink near base; outer, olive green. Anther color: Inner, orange-yellow; outer, orange-yellow. Stamen color: Orange. Flower shape: Cuplike. Flower size: 2.5–3 in. (6.3–7.5 cm). Fragrance: Delightful. Number of petals: 16–18. Number of sepals: 4, sometimes 5.

LEAVES. Color: Top, purple at first changing to dark green with purple blotches; underside, red. Leaf oval; open sinus. Leaf size: About 4 × 3.5 in. (10 × 9 cm). Leaf spread: About 2.5 ft. (0.8 m). Stem color: Peduncle greenish brown, petiole reddish brown. No pubescence on peduncle or petiole.

COMMENTS. Now there are two waterlilies with the same name. The other is a tropical night-blooming species, however, and should be written as *Nymphaea rubra* (see Plate 20). Cathy Green, of Green and Hagstrom Nursery, advises that *N.* 'Rubra' came from a botanical garden in Kunming, in central Yunnan Province, China. *Nymphaea* 'Rubra' has very small, mottled leaves. It is a wonderful little waterlily ideal for a small pool or tub garden, and I highly recommend it.

Nymphaea 'Ruby Red'

Slocum 1992

Nymphaea 'Tetragona' × *N.* 'Perry's Darkest Red'

PLATE 239

CHARACTERISTICS. Free flowering, Marliac rhizome, perennial.

FLOWERS. Petal color: Very brilliant red. Sepal color: Inner, pale pink or white; outer, olive green. Anther color: Inner, dark yellow; outer, dark yellow. Stamen color: Inner, orange; outer, orange-red. Flower shape: Cuplike. Flower size: 3.5–4 in. (9–10 cm). Fragrance: None. Number of petals: 20–24. Number of sepals: 4.

LEAVES. Color: Top, new leaves olive green with purple blotches, which soon disappear, leaving a brilliant green leaf; underside, purple. Leaf round or oblong; sinus open or partly closed. Leaf size: 4.5–6 × 3.5–4.75 in. (11.5–15 × 9–12 cm). Leaf spread: About 3 ft. (0.9 m). Stem color: Peduncle greenish brown, petiole reddish brown. No pubescence on peduncle or petiole.

COMMENTS. *Nymphaea* 'Ruby Red' has just about everything that a person would want for a small pool or tub garden. The only minus is that it opens late in the morning. It is the slowest propagator that we grow at Perry's Water Gardens, but this means it takes a long time for the plant to become crowded. Due to its slow propagating feature, it has not been put on the market as yet. *Nymphaea* 'Ruby Red' won best in the small size class at the 2001 International Waterlily and Water Gardening Society Symposium. I especially recommend it for small pools or tub gardens.

Nymphaea 'Sanguinea'

Marliac 1894, Parentage unknown

CHARACTERISTICS. Marliac rhizome, free flowering.

FLOWERS. Petal color: Crimson red, deepening (*RHS* 63B; third day, 63A). Sepal color: White, light pink near base (*RHS* 155B; base, 73D). Anther color: Yellow (*RHS* 9C). Stamen color: Yellow-orange. Flower shape: Somewhat stellate. Flower size: 5–6 in. (13–15 cm). Fragrance: Slight. Number of petals: 23 or 24. Number of sepals: 4.

LEAVES. Color: Top, green, newest leaves lightly mottled deep purple; underside, red, prominent green lengthwise vein. Leaf nearly round; sinus one- to two-thirds open. Leaf size: 9–10 in. (23–25 cm). Leaf spread: Up to 5 ft. (1.5 m). Stem color: Red. No pubescence on peduncle or petiole.

COMMENTS. The glowing blood-red blooms make this one of the most striking of all the red hardies. I recommend it for medium or large pools.

Nymphaea 'Seignoureti'

Marliac 1893

Possibly *N. alba* var. *rubra* × *N. mexicana*

CHARACTERISTICS. Upright rhizome, changeable, very free flowering.

FLOWERS. Petal color: First day, inner petals apricot-orange, outer petals yellowish white; third day, all petals predominantly orange-red (*RHS* first day, 33C,D; outer, 11C,D; third day, 37A). Sepal color: Light yellow then peach, pink base (*RHS* first day, 2D; third day, 29C; base, 54D). Anther color: Deep yellow (*RHS* 13B). Stamen color: Pale orange. Flower shape: Cuplike. Flower size: 3–4 in. (8–10 cm). Fragrance: None. Number of petals: 18. Number of sepals: 4.

LEAVES. Color: Top, green, new leaves bronzy, all lightly mottled maroon; underside, purplish, many deeper maroon spots. Leaf nearly round; sinus one- to two-thirds open. Leaf size: 6–7 in. (15–18 cm). Leaf spread: 4 ft. (1.2 m). Stem color: Reddish. No pubescence on peduncle or petiole.

COMMENTS. This lovely waterlily is variable. The original *Nymphaea* 'Seignoureti' description was translated by Fr. J. M. Berghs for the *Water Garden Journal* (March 1989, p. 11): "Medium-sized flowers, standing 15 cm (about 6 in) above the water, shaded with pink and carmine on a pale-yellow background; leaves marked with brown; stamens orange-yellow." Based on this description, the *N.* 'Seignoureti' I have described appears to be the original. I recommend 'Seignoureti' for any size pool. However, because this is a very old variety, finding it could be difficult.

Nymphaea 'Sioux'

Marliac 1908

Parentage unknown

PLATE 240

CHARACTERISTICS. Changeable, upright rhizome, extremely free flowering.

FLOWERS. Petal color: Petal coloration deepens each day; progression also from lightest center petal row to deepening outer rows. Inner petals yellowish apricot then orange-red; outer petals yellow then apricot-orange (*RHS* inner, first day, 16C to 25B; third day, 29B to 30D; outer, first day, 11B to 24D; third day, 25C). Sepal color: White then pinkish orange at base (*RHS* 155A; base, 35B or 35C). Anther color: Yellow (*RHS* 20A). Stamen color: Inside stamens, golden yellow; outside, orange. Flower shape: Stellate, lanceolate petals. Flower size: 5–6 in. (13–15 cm). Fragrance: Quite nice, especially in new flowers. Number of petals: 19 or 20. Number of sepals: 4.

LEAVES. Color: Top, green, perimeter dappled purple on new leaves; underside, green, freckled purple, new leaves red, prominent green V along midvein. Leaf almost round; sinus a wide-open V. Leaf size: 8–9 in. (20–23 cm). Leaf spread: 4 ft. (1.2 m). Stem color: Green. Fine fuzz and hairs on peduncle and petiole.

COMMENTS. *Nymphaea* 'Sioux' performs magnificently and flowers stay open very late in the day. It is my first choice among the larger Marliac's orange changeables as an excellent waterlily for medium or large pools.

Nymphaea 'Sirius'

Latour-Marliac Nursery 1913

Parentage unknown

CHARACTERISTICS. Marliac rhizome, very free flowering.

FLOWERS. Petal color: Inner petals, deep purple-red, some flecking; outer petals, purplish red, some flecking, white tips (*RHS* inner, 61A; outer, 70B; tips, 155B). Sepal color: Pink, shading to white at tips, flecked (*RHS* 63C,D; tips, 155B). Anther color: Burnt orange (*RHS* 34B). Stamen color: Deep glowing red. Flower shape: Stellate. Flower size: 6–7 in. (15–18 cm). Fragrance: Very slight. Number of petals: 27. Number of sepals: 4 or 5.

LEAVES. Color: Top, deep green, new leaves lightly blotched purple; underside, green, prominent light green veins. Leaf round; sinus a very wide V. Leaf size: Up to 11 in. (28 cm). Leaf spread: 5–6 ft. (1.5–1.8 m). Stem color: Brownish purple. Some fuzz on all stems.

COMMENTS. *Nymphaea* 'Sirius', named for the brightest star in the heavens, is a strikingly star-shaped waterlily. I highly recommend it for medium and large pools.

Nymphaea 'Solfatare'
Marliac 1906
Parentage unknown

CHARACTERISTICS. Changeable, upright rhizome, free flowering.

FLOWERS. Petal color: Inner petals, yellowish apricot, deepening; outer petals, creamy peach then peach (*RHS* inner, 27A; third day, 31D; outer, 20D; third day, 27C). Sepal color: Pale yellowish apricot (*RHS* 27D). Anther color: Yellowish apricot then orange (*RHS* 23D; third day, 24C). Stamen color: Orange. Flower shape: Cuplike. Flower size: 3–4 in. (8–10 cm). Fragrance: None. Number of petals: 29. Number of sepals: 4.

LEAVES. Color: Top, green, new leaves spotted purple; underside, bronzy green, maroon spots and blotches. Leaf oval; sinus wide open. Leaf size: 6 × 5 in. (15 × 13 cm). Leaf spread: 30–40 in. (75–100 cm). Stem color: Light green. No pubescence on peduncle or petiole.

COMMENTS. *Nymphaea* 'Solfatare', a continuous bloomer, is currently more widely available in Australia than in the United States. It is an ideal waterlily for small or medium pools. Unfortunately, my experience in importing *N.* 'Solfatare' plants from Australia is that they did well for a few months and then succumbed to crown rot.

Nymphaea 'Somptuosa'
Marliac 1909
Parentage unknown

CHARACTERISTICS. Marliac rhizome, free flowering.

FLOWERS. Petal color: Inner petals deep pink then glowing red, flecked except on innermost petals; outer petals white then blushed pink (*RHS* inner first day, 70C; third day, 63A; outer, 155B; third day, blush, 65D or lighter). Sepal color: White then blushed pink (*RHS* 155B; blush, 65D or lighter). Anther color: Golden yellow (*RHS* 16B). Stamen color: Golden yellow. Flower shape: Peony-style. Flower size: 5–6 in. (13–15 cm). Fragrance: Slight. Number of petals: 35. Number of sepals: 4.

LEAVES. Color: Top, bright green, faint purple mottling, new leaves light purple, dark purple mottles; underside, red. Leaf quite round; lobe tips rounded. Lobes usually overlap 0.75 in. (2 cm) at beginning of sinus, rest of sinus wide open. Leaf size: 8 in. (20 cm). Leaf spread: 4–5 ft. (1.2–1.5 m). Stem color: Bronzy green. No pubescence on peduncle or petiole.

COMMENTS. This is a very fine pink-and-white bicolor suited for medium and large pools. Flower color is somewhat flecked, yet the blooms are still quite pretty. For many years nurseries in the United States confused *N.* 'Somptuosa' with *N.* 'Masaniello', but this confusion finally has been sorted out.

Nymphaea 'Splendida'
Marliac 1909
Parentage unknown
PLATE 241

CHARACTERISTICS. Marliac rhizome, very free flowering.

FLOWERS. Petal color: Inner petals, reddish pink, deepening; outer petals, light pink, deepening (*RHS* inner, 63C then 63B; outer, 65D then 63C,D). Sepal color: White, prominent red veins (*RHS* 155A; veins, 63B,C). Anther color: Bright yellow (*RHS* 12B). Stamen color: Orange-red. Flower shape: Quite large, globular after first day. Flower size: 5–6 in. (13–15 cm). Fragrance: Delightful, especially second-day blooms. Number of petals: 30. Number of sepals: 4.

LEAVES. Color: Top, green, new leaves purplish brown; underside, mostly brown, touched purple, prominent greenish yellow veins. Leaf nearly round; sinus usually a small V; lobes in older leaves frequently overlap. Leaf size: 9 in. (23 cm). Leaf spread: 4–5 ft. (1.2–1.5 m). Stem color: Brown. Fuzz completely covers all stems.

COMMENTS. *Nymphaea* 'Splendida' is a magnificent waterlily. Established plants in rich soil develop more deeply colored blooms than young plants in ordinary soil. This cultivar is one of the best for medium or large pools.

Nymphaea 'Starbright'

Strawn 1997

Nymphaea 'Rembrandt' × *N. mexicana*

CHARACTERISTICS. Nonviviparous, Marliac rhizome, free flowering, perennial.

FLOWERS. Petal color: Soft white with faint pink blush at base of outer petals. Sepal color: Inner, greenish white, darker green toward tips; outer, olive green with darker tips. Anther color: Inner, bright yellow; outer, bright yellow. Stamen color: Bright yellow. Flower shape: Full, stellate. Flower size: 4–5 in. (10–12.5 cm). Fragrance: Slight. Number of petals: 32–34. Number of sepals: 4.

LEAVES. Color: Top, dark green with faint mottling, newer leaves more olive green; underside, reddish purple. Leaf slightly ovate; lobes overlap slightly at sinus. Leaf size: 4–6 in. (10–15 cm). Leaf spread: 3–5 ft. (0.9–1.5 m). Stem color: Olive green. Slight pubescence on petiole.

COMMENTS BY DEAN MCGEE. *Nymphaea* 'Starbright' has an elegantly shaped flower with pleasing contrasts of white and yellow with a hint of pink, along with nice mottled leaves. This cultivar is excellent for medium ponds.

Nymphaea 'Starburst'

Strawn 1997

Parentage unknown

CHARACTERISTICS. Nonviviparous, Marliac rhizome, free flowering, perennial.

FLOWERS. Petal color: Outer petals almost white, light red blush at base. Sepal color: Inner, light pink; outer, olive green. Anther color: Inner, medium yellow; outer, medium yellow. Stamen color: Medium yellow. Flower shape: Full, stellate. Flower size: 4–5 in. (10–12.5 cm). Fragrance: Slight. Number of petals: 28–30. Number of sepals: 4.

LEAVES. Color: Top, dark green, newer leaves olive green or bronze; underside, reddish purple. Leaf nearly round; lobes overlap slightly at sinus, distinctive tips on lobes. Leaf size: 4–5 in. (10–12.5

cm). Leaf spread: 3–5 ft. (0.9–1.5 m). Stem color: Brown. No pubescence on peduncle or petiole.

COMMENTS BY DEAN MCGEE. The beautiful stellate flowers have an interesting blend between red and white, giving way to pink hues. *Nymphaea* 'Starburst' is excellent for medium ponds.

Nymphaea 'Steven Strawn'

Strawn, year unknown

Parentage unknown

CHARACTERISTICS. Nonviviparous, Marliac rhizome, free flowering, perennial.

FLOWERS. Petal color: Deep red blushed with creamy yellow undertones toward outer petals. Sepal color: Inner, greenish white, faint red at base; outer, olive green with dark green tips. Anther color: Inner, golden yellow; outer, reddish purple with golden yellow anthers. Stamen color: Golden yellow. Flower shape: Stellate. Flower size: 4–5 in. (10–12.5 cm). Fragrance: None. Number of petals: 24–26. Number of sepals: 4.

LEAVES. Color: Top, dark green; underside, reddish brown with heavy flecking, newer leaves light green. Leaf oval; lobes overlap at sinus, distinctive tips on lobes. Leaf size: 5–7 in. (12.5–18 cm). Leaf spread: 3–5 ft. (0.9–1.5 m). Stem color: Bronze. Slight pubescence on peduncle and petiole.

COMMENTS BY DEAN MCGEE. Very unique red flowers with contrasting dark leaves make *Nymphaea* 'Steven Strawn' a good choice for medium to large ponds.

Nymphaea 'Sultan'

Syn. 'Grésille'

Latour-Marliac Nursery, year unknown

Parentage unknown

PLATE 242

CHARACTERISTICS. Marliac rhizome, very free flowering.

FLOWERS. Petal color: Inner petals, deep pink, deep red by second day; outer petals, pale pink, rich red by second day; flecking develops from inner to outer petals (*RHS* inner, first day, 68C or 66D; second day, 63A; outer, 65D; second day, 63B,C). Sepal color: White, base flushed rose-pink, veins rose-pink (*RHS* 155B; base and veins, 65A,B). Anther color: Yellow (*RHS* 13B). Stamen color: Burnt orange. Flower shape: Cuplike, then wide stellate. Flower size: 6–7 in. (15–18 cm). Fragrance: Slight. Number of petals: 24 or 25. Number of sepals: 4.

LEAVES. Color: Top, green; underside, green, new leaves bronzy. Leaf round; lobes overlap sinus; frequently both lobes turn upward. Leaf size: 10–11 in. (25–28 cm). Leaf spread: 4–5 ft. (1.2–1.5 m). Stem color: Brown; older stems striped purple. Fuzz only on underwater stems.

COMMENTS. *Nymphaea* 'Sultan' is one of the very top red waterlilies for zones 4–10, doing well in the Deep South, Florida, and Texas. (*Nymphaea* 'Charles de Meurville', *N.* 'Escarboucle', *N.* 'Froebeli', *N.* 'James Brydon', *N.* 'Perry's Black Opal', *N.* 'Perry's Baby Red', *N.* 'Perry's Red Wonder', and *N.* 'Splendida' also perform well in southern regions.) The Latour-Marliac Nursery renamed this cultivar *N.* 'Grésille'. It is ideal for medium and large pools.

Nymphaea 'Sunny Pink'

Kirk Strawn 1997

Nymphaea 'Texas Dawn' seedling

CHARACTERISTICS. Nonviviparous, odorata rhizome, very free flowering, perennial.

FLOWERS. Petal color: Outer, blushed medium pink; inner, medium yellow. Sepal color: Inner, light pink blushed with creamy white at center and base; outer, medium green with olive green tips, medium pink on some edges. Anther color: Inner, bright yellow; outer, bright yellow. Stamen color: Bright yellow. Flower shape: Full, stellate. Flower size: 5–7 in. (12.5–18 cm). Fragrance: Sweet. Number of petals: 28–30. Number of sepals: 4.

LEAVES. Color: Top, green, newer leaves more olive green with flecking toward outer edge; underside, red with heavy purple flecking. Leaf nearly round; sinus slightly open. Leaf size: 8–10 in. (20–25 cm). Leaf spread: 6–8 ft. (1.8–2.4 m). Stem color: Bronze. No pubescence on peduncle or petiole.

COMMENTS BY DEAN MCGEE. *Nymphaea* 'Sunny Pink' is a very prolific large blooming waterlily with a good blend of pink and yellow petals. It blooms late into the season and makes for a great large pond display.

Nymphaea 'Sunrise'

Syn. *N. odorata* 'Sulphurea Grandiflora'

Marliac 1888

Seedling of *N. odorata*

PLATE 243

CHARACTERISTICS. Marliac-odorata rhizome, free flowering in zones 6–10, less so in zones 3–5.

FLOWERS. Petal color: Yellow, outer petals lighter (*RHS* inner, 4B; outer, 1D). Sepal color: Light green, veins greenish gray; tips greenish (*RHS* 157A; veins, 194B,C; tips, 145C). Anther color: Deep yellow (*RHS* 6B). Stamen color: Yellow. Flower shape: Stellate. Flower size: 7–9.5 in. (18–24 cm). Fragrance: Very slight. Number of petals: 23–28. Number of sepals: 4 or 5.

LEAVES. Color: Top, green, tiny purple mottles on new leaves; underside, red, small dark purple blotches on new leaves lighten with age. Leaf a little longer than wide; sinus usually a wide-open V. Leaf size: 11 × 10 in. (28 × 25 cm). Leaf spread: 4–5 ft. (1.2–1.5 m). Stem color: Yellow-green, usually striped purple. Fine fuzz on peduncle and petiole.

COMMENTS. Around 1930, this waterlily was renamed *Nymphaea* 'Sunrise' by Johnson Water Gardens, Hynes, California. With its huge blooms and long narrow pointed petals, it can be a real show waterlily for warm or temperate regions. In cool regions expect fewer blooms. It is currently one of the four largest-flowered hardy waterlilies (the others are *N.* 'Perry's Super Red', *N.* 'Yellow Queen', and *N.* 'Apple Blossom Pink'). New spring leaves are frequently twisted and poorly formed, but with warmer weather, leaves develop perfectly. This waterlily is a good choice for medium and large pools, but has had crown rot at some nurseries.

Nymphaea 'Texas Dawn'

Landon 1985

Nymphaea 'Pink Starlet' × *N. mexicana* No. 1

PLATE 244

CHARACTERISTICS. Tuberosa-Marliac rhizome, very free flowering.

FLOWERS. Petal color: Inner petals, rich yellow; outer petals blushed pink (*RHS* inner, 4C; outer, 8D; blush, 36D). Sepal color: Greenish yellow, pink border (*RHS* 1D; border, 36C). Anther color: Deep yellow (*RHS* 6A). Stamen color: Yellow. Flower shape: Stellate, long narrow petals. Flower size: 6–8 in. (15–20 cm). Fragrance: Delightful, lemony. Number of petals: 26–28. Number of sepals: 4.

LEAVES. Color: Top, green, new leaves speckled purple; underside, purplish. Leaf nearly round; sinus two-thirds to completely open. Leaf size: 8 in. (20 cm). Leaf spread: 3–5 ft. (0.9–1.5 m). Stem color: Red or purple. Some fuzz on peduncle and petiole.

COMMENTS. This lovely waterlily was developed by Kenneth Landon in San Angelo, Texas (zone 7b). *Nymphaea* 'Texas Dawn' is probably one of the best yellow-flowered waterlilies since *N.* 'Marliacea Chromatella' made its appearance in 1887, and it received the International Waterlily and Water Gardening Society's 1990 American Award. When grown in zones 6–10, spring-planted specimens can be expected to produce seven or eight blooms at a time by midsummer. In late summer and fall the flowers may take on an attractive pinkish cast. The flowers are frequently held 10 in. (25 cm) above water. I highly recommend *N.* 'Texas Dawn' for any size pool in zones 6–10; possibly the rhizome will survive zone 5 if given winter protection.

Nymphaea 'Thomas O'Brien'

Strawn, year unknown

Parentage unknown

CHARACTERISTICS. Nonviviparous, Marliac rhizome, fairly free flowering, perennial.

FLOWERS. Petal color: Medium pink at base of petals, then creamy white toward tips. Sepal color: Inner, blushed red; olive green at tips; outer, olive green with blushed pink on some edges. Anther color: Inner, soft yellow; outer, soft yellow. Stamen color: Soft yellow. Flower shape: Cuplike. Flower size: 3–4 in. (7.5–10 cm). Fragrance: Pleasant. Number of petals: 38–40. Number of sepals: 4.

LEAVES. Color: Top, medium green with light flecking on outer edges, newer leaves have more prominent blotchy flecks throughout; underside, medium plum color with similar flecked patterns. Leaf nearly round; sinus open, distinctive tips on lobes. Leaf size: 5–6 in. (12.5–15 cm). Leaf spread: 3–5 ft. (0.9–1.5 m). Stem color: Olive green. Slight pubescence on petiole.

COMMENTS BY DEAN MCGEE. *Nymphaea* 'Thomas O'Brien' is an outstanding waterlily that

boasts a gorgeous carnation pink and creamy white combination. Double blossoms open wide and stand 2–3 in. (5–7.5 cm) above the water surface. Excellent for medium to large ponds.

Nymphaea tuberosa 'Maxima'

Formerly *N. tuberosa* 'Richardsonii' No. 2

Seedling of *N. tuberosa*

CHARACTERISTICS. Tuberosa rhizome, not free blooming though moderate in early summer.

FLOWERS. Petal color: Pure white (*RHS* 155C). Sepal color: Greenish white (*RHS* 1D). Anther color: Bright yellow (*RHS* 12A). Stamen color: Yellow. Flower shape: Peony-style, petals stellate. Flower size: 5 in. (13 cm). Fragrance: Pleasant, strong. Number of petals: 30. Number of sepals: 4 or 5.

LEAVES. Color: Top, green; underside, green, prominent green veins. Leaves round; lobes generally overlap at sinus on large leaves; on small leaves sinus frequently open or partly open. Leaf size: 8–9 in. (20–23 cm). Leaf spread: 6 ft. (1.8 m). Stem color: Green, purple stripes. Very thick fuzz on peduncle and petiole.

COMMENTS. Although moderately free flowering early in the season, by midsummer *Nymphaea tuberosa* 'Maxima' has rampant leaf growth and fewer blooms. Leaves are produced so abundantly that they crowd above the water. I consider it most suited to the natural pond.

Nymphaea tuberosa 'Richardsonii'

Richardson 1894

Parentage unknown

PLATE 245

CHARACTERISTICS. Tuberosa rhizome, moderately free flowering.

FLOWERS. Petal color: White (*RHS* 155D). Sepal color: Greenish cream (*RHS* 1D). Anther color: Yellow (*RHS* 11A). Stamen color: Yellow. Flower shape: Full, peony-style. Flower size: 6–8 in. (15–20 cm). Fragrance: Some. Number of petals: 46–50. Number of sepals: 4 or 5.

LEAVES. Color: Top, green; underside, green. Leaf large, nearly round, wavy edges; sinus open. Leaf size: 10–11 in. (25–28 cm). Leaf spread: 6–7 ft. (1.8–2.1 m). Stem color: Green, purple stripes. No pubescence on peduncle or petiole.

COMMENTS. *Nymphaea tuberosa* 'Richardsonii', which I consider the genuine or original strain, is a truly beautiful white hardy. It will grow in water 3 ft. (0.9 m) deep, but it is not suitable for many water gardens due to its large leaf spread and limited number of blooms. I recommend it only for the collector with a large pool or natural pond, where it would have plenty of room to spread.

Nymphaea 'Venus'

Slocum 1991
Nymphaea 'Pink Starlet' × *N.* 'Pamela'
PLATE 246

CHARACTERISTICS. Marliac-tuberosa rhizome, free flowering.

FLOWERS. Petal color: White, very pale pink blush (*RHS* 155D; blush too pale to show on chart). Sepal color: White, very pale pink blush, tips green, veins deep purplish (*RHS* 155D; blush too pale to show on chart; tips, 146D; veins, 77A). Anther color: Yellow (*RHS* 6C). Stamen color: Yellow. Flower shape: Stellate. Flower size: 6–7 in. (15–18 cm). Fragrance: Slight in new flowers. Number of petals: 29–32. Number of sepals: 4.

LEAVES. Color: Top, green, new leaves bronzy; underside, reddish, wide green midstripe. Leaf nearly round; sinus usually open. Leaf size: 10.5 in. (27 cm). Leaf spread: 4–5 ft. (1.2–1.5 m). Stem color: Peduncle brown, petiole reddish; both faintly striped purple. A few sparse hairs on peduncle and petiole.

COMMENTS. Flowers on this cultivar appear totally white when viewed from a distance, and the delicate pink is discovered up close. Although one of its parents is a tropical waterlily, this plant has survived in North Carolina temperatures of 0°F (–18°C) without loss. As the planet Venus is frequently one of the most brilliant objects in the sky, so too does *N.* 'Venus' attract much attention, with its large double blooms held 3–6 in. (8–15 cm) above the water. I recommend *N.* 'Venus' for medium or large pools.

Nymphaea 'Vesuve'

Marliac 1906
Parentage unknown
PLATE 247

CHARACTERISTICS. Marliac rhizome, very free flowering.

FLOWERS. Petal color: Brilliant, glowing red, deepening (*RHS* 61B; last day, 61A). Sepal color: Pink, white tips (*RHS* 70D; tips, 155B). Anther color: Rich yellow (*RHS* 14C). Stamen color: Burnt orange. Flower shape: Stellate. Flower size: 7 in. (18 cm). Fragrance: Especially noticeable in first-day flowers. Number of petals: 22 or 23. Number of sepals: 4 or 5.

LEAVES. Color: Top, green; underside, bronzy brown. Leaf nearly round; sinus a wide-open V. Leaf size: 9–10 in. (23–25 cm). Leaf spread: 4 ft. (1.2 m). Stem color: Purple. No pubescence on peduncle or petiole.

COMMENTS. *Nymphaea* 'Vesuve', with a flower color somewhat similar to *N.* 'Escarboucle', is one of the great lilies of all time. It has a very long blooming season, and flowers open early in the day and stay open late. Most petals are concave and many have two lengthwise creases, giving the flowers a unique appearance. I recommend this waterlily for any size pool.

Nymphaea 'Virginalis'

Marliac 1910
Parentage unknown
PLATE 248

CHARACTERISTICS. Marliac rhizome, very free flowering.

FLOWERS. Petal color: White (*RHS* 155D). Sepal color: White (*RHS* 155B). Anther color: Yellow (*RHS* 7B). Stamen color: Yellow. Flower shape: Cuplike. Flower size: 4.5–5.5 in. (11–14 cm). Fragrance: Noticeable in new blooms. Number of petals: 21 or 22. Number of sepals: 4.

LEAVES. Color: Top, green, newest leaves purple or bronze; underside, bronzy green, newest leaves purple. Leaves round; lobes overlap at sinus, frequently one lobe is raised; each lobe apex tipped up to 0.25 in. (0.6 cm). Leaf size: 9 in. (23 cm). Leaf spread: 3–4 ft. (0.9–1.2 m). Stem color: Green to light brown. Heavy fuzz on peduncle and petiole.

COMMENTS. Because of its freedom of bloom and always-dependable performance, many nursery people consider *Nymphaea* 'Virginalis' one of the best all-around white hardies. I highly recommend it for any size pool.

Nymphaea 'Virginia'

Thomas 1962

Nymphaea odorata 'Sulphurea Grandiflora' × N. 'Gladstoniana'

PLATE 249

CHARACTERISTICS. Marliac rhizome, free flowering.

FLOWERS. Petal color: Inner petals, pale yellow, deeper toward flower center; outer petals white (RHS inner, 2D to 6A; outer, 155B). Sepal color: White, green flush and edges (RHS 155B; flush and edges, 145D). Anther color: Yellow (RHS 13A). Stamen color: Yellow. Flower shape: Quite full and stellate. Flower size: 7–8 in. (18–20 cm). Fragrance: Noticeable in new blooms. Number of petals: 23–27. Number of sepals: 4.

LEAVES. Color: Top, green, perimeter blotched purple, new leaves green, heavily blotched with small purple blotches; underside, reddish, many small purple blotches. Leaf egg-shaped; sinus usually an open V. Lobes occasionally overlap near petiole. Leaf size: 10 × 8.5 in. (25 × 22 cm). Leaf spread: 5–6 ft. (1.5–1.8 m). Stem color: Dark olive green. Fuzz and fine hairs on peduncle and petiole.

COMMENTS. Nymphaea 'Virginia' held U.S. plant patent 2172. It is similar to N. odorata 'Sulphurea Grandiflora' in every way except flower color. It could be considered a white version of this classic waterlily. I recommend it for medium and large pools.

Nymphaea 'Walter Pagels'

Strawn 1993

Nymphaea 'Hollandia' × N. 'Perry's Pink'

PLATE 250

CHARACTERISTICS. Nonviviparous, Marliac rhizome, free flowering, perennial.

FLOWERS. Petal color: Soft white throughout petals. Sepal color: Inner, greenish white; medium green pin stripes; outer, medium green, dark toward tips. Anther color: Inner, bright yellow; outer, bright yellow. Stamen color: Bright yellow. Flower shape: Cuplike. Flower size: 3–4 in. (7.5–10 cm). Fragrance: Slight. Number of petals: 30–32. Number of sepals: 4.

LEAVES. Color: Top, medium green with faint mottling toward edge; underside, reddish plum with green veins around center at peduncle. Leaf slightly ovate; lobes slightly overlapping at sinus, sinus more open on mature leaves. Leaf size: 4–5 in. (10–12.5 cm). Leaf spread: 2–3 ft. (0.6–0.9 m). Stem color: Light green. No pubescence on peduncle or petiole.

COMMENTS BY DEAN McGEE. This hybrid was named for the first president of the International Waterlily and Water Gardening Society. Nymphaea 'Walter Pagels' has small to medium ivory white blossoms that stand just above the water surface. A great choice to contrast with other colorful waterlilies in small to medium ponds or as a stand-alone for small tub gardens.

Nymphaea 'Weymouth Red'

Bennett 1991

Parentage unknown

PLATE 251

CHARACTERISTICS. Free flowering, Marliac rhizome, perennial.

FLOWERS. Petal color: Inner, dark red purple (RHS 59A); outer, a lighter dark red purple (RHS 61A). Sepal color: Inner, white, striped with purple (RHS 64A). Anther color: Inner, deep yellow (RHS 11A); outer, deep yellow (RHS 3A). Stamen color: Deep yellow (RHS 11A). Flower shape: Stellate with long petals. Flower size: 5 in. (12.5 cm). Fragrance: Pleasing. Number of petals: 16–22. Number of sepals: 4.

LEAVES. Color: Top, uniform dark green (RHS 147A); underside, green (RHS 146A); center triangle: slight red purple (RHS 60C). Round leaf, very slightly pointed; sinus open about 40 degrees. Leaf size: 6.5 in. (16.5 cm). Leaf spread: 3 ft. (0.9 m). Flower stem color: Brown (RHS 177A). Leaf stem: Light brown (RHS 177D). No pubescence on peduncle or petiole.

COMMENTS BY NORMAN BENNETT. After growing Nymphaea 'Weymouth Red' for 12 years, it is still a pleasing variety. It is better than average among waterlilies with small to medium dark red blooms with somewhat long petals and modestly sized leaves.

Nymphaea 'White Cup'

Slocum 1986

Nymphaea 'Peter Slocum' × *N*. 'Panama Pacific'

CHARACTERISTICS. Odorata rhizome, fairly free flowering.

FLOWERS. Petal color: Pure white (*RHS* 155D). Sepal color: White, flushed chartreuse, especially along edges (*RHS* 155D; flush and edges, 145B). Anther color: Golden yellow (*RHS* 5A). Stamen color: Golden yellow. Flower shape: Cuplike. Flower size: 3–4 in. (8–10 cm). Fragrance: Some. Number of petals: 19 or 20. Number of sepals: 4.

LEAVES. Color: Top, green, newest leaves purple; underside, red, green on perimeter above water. Leaf round; sinus an open V. Lobe usually has a sharply pointed tip. Leaf size: 8–10 in. (20–25 cm). Leaf spread: 4–5 ft. (1.2–1.5 m). Stem color: Chartreuse. Fine fuzz on peduncle and petiole.

COMMENTS. For an odorata type, this cup-shaped white waterlily blooms quite freely. Because there are many better white hardies on the market, *Nymphaea* 'White Cup' is for the collector or the water gardener with a medium or large pool.

Nymphaea 'White Sensation'

Slocum 1995

Nymphaea 'Pink Starlet' × *N*. 'Pamela'

PLATE 252

CHARACTERISTICS. Marliac rhizome, free flowering, perennial.

FLOWERS. Petal color: Brilliant white, four outer petals have prominent green middle on the outside. Sepal color: Inside, outer half is green, inner half is white flushed with green; outer, olive green. Anther color: Inner, dark yellow; outer, dark yellow. Stamen color: Dark yellow. Flower shape: Wide and spread out. Flower size: 6–8.5 in. (15–21.5 cm). Fragrance: Slight, pleasant. Number of petals: 46 or 47, usually 47. Number of sepals: 4.

LEAVES. Color: Top, olive green; underside, mostly reddish, greenish center. Leaves round; sinus variable, usually open but some leaves overlap at least halfway up. Leaf size: 8.5–10 in. (21.5–25 cm). Leaf spread: 5–6 ft. (1.5–1.8 m). Stem color: Peduncle mostly brown, petiole reddish brown. No pubescence on peduncle or petiole.

COMMENTS. *Nymphaea* 'White Sensation', with its large and numerous very double flowers, is a real show waterlily. We planted a bed of it right next to *N*. 'Virginalis', and it outperformed *N*. 'Virginalis' by many times. Due to its large leaf spread, it is not suitable for the small pond, but we highly recommend it for medium or large pools.

Nymphaea 'White Sultan'

Strawn 1991

Mutation of *N*. 'Sultan'

CHARACTERISTICS. Nonviviparous, Marliac rhizome, very free flowering, perennial.

FLOWERS. Petal color: Bright white. Sepal color: Inner, white with medium green on edges; outer, medium green. Anther color: Inner, bright yellow; outer, bright yellow. Stamen color: Bright yellow. Flower shape: Cuplike with slightly rounded petals. Flower size: 4–5 in. (10–12.5 cm). Fragrance: Slight. Number of petals: 24–26. Number of sepals: 4.

LEAVES. Color: Top, medium green; underside, brown with green veins at peduncle. Leaf round, overlapping lobes at sinus. Leaf size: 5–6 in. (12.5–15 cm). Leaf spread: 3–5 ft. (0.9–1.5 m). Stem color: Reddish brown. No pubescence on peduncle or petiole.

COMMENTS BY DEAN MCGEE. The pristine white flowers of *Nymphaea* 'White Sultan' stand out well in any pond. Blossoms sit at the water surface. Excellent choice for combining with other waterlilies with contrasting colors, and best for medium to large ponds.

Nymphaea 'White 1000 Petals'

Perry's Water Gardens 1998

Natural hybrid, *N*. 'Lily Pons' probably a parent

PLATE 253

CHARACTERISTICS. Odorata rhizome, moderate flowering, perennial.

FLOWERS. Petal color: Pure white. Sepal color: Inner, white; outer, olive green. Anther color: Inner, medium to light yellow; outer, medium to light yellow. Stamen color: Medium to light yellow. Flower shape: Peony shape, then opening wide. Flower size: 5.5–6.5 in. (14–16.5 cm). Fragrance: Slight. Number of petals: 131–150. Number of sepals: 4 or 5.

LEAVES. Color: Top, bronzy green turning to olive green; underside, reddish with prominent green veins. Leaf nearly round; sinus closed. Leaf size: About 10 in. (25.5 cm). Leaf spread: 4.5–6 ft. (1.4–1.9 m). Stem color: Brownish. Pubescence on peduncle and petiole.

COMMENTS. *Nymphaea* 'White 1000 Petals' has more petals than any other hardy waterlily that I know. Although it is a moderate bloomer, when given plenty of room and allowed to form a colony of rhizomes, it puts on a delightful performance. I recommend it for the large pool or the collector with lots of room.

Nymphaea 'William Falconer'

Dreer 1899

Parentage unknown

CHARACTERISTICS. Marliac rhizome, very free flowering in cool-summer areas, moderately free flowering in milder zones.

FLOWERS. Petal color: Very deep red (*RHS* 64A). Sepal color: Very deep pink (*RHS* 63C). Anther color: Burnt orange (*RHS* 31B). Stamen color: Burgundy-red. Flower shape: Cuplike. Flower size: 4.5–5 in. (11–13 cm). Fragrance: None. Number of petals: 25. Number of sepals: 4.

LEAVES. Color: Top, green, new leaves purple, dark purple blotches; underside, purple, bright green lengthwise V. Leaf slightly longer than wide; sinus an open V. Leaf size: 8 × 7.5 in. (20 × 19 cm). Leaf spread: 3 ft. (0.9 m). Stem color: Purple. Fine hairs on peduncle and petiole.

COMMENTS. This waterlily performs magnificently where summer temperatures remain moderate, but it will stop flowering during prolonged hot periods. *Nymphaea* 'William Falconer' blooms not at all or very little in places such as Florida and the other Gulf states. Inner petals blacken during very hot periods. I recommend this waterlily for any size pool in the temperate zones, but it is the wrong choice for hot-summer areas.

Nymphaea 'Wow'

Slocum 1990

Nymphaea 'Perry's Pink' × *N.* 'Pamela'

PLATE 254

CHARACTERISTICS. Odorata rhizome, moderately free flowering, very striking flower color, red dot in center of stigmal area.

FLOWERS. Petal color: Reddish purple (*RHS* 58A). Sepal color: Reddish purple (*RHS* 59A). Anther color: Yellowish orange (*RHS* 29A). Stamen color: Orange. Flower shape: Cuplike, full. Flower size: 5–6 in. (13–15 cm). Fragrance: Very pleasant. Number of petals: 31–35. Number of sepals: 4.

LEAVES. Color: Top, green, new leaves reddish; underside, brown, new leaves reddish. Leaf nearly round, pointed tips at lobe ends; sinus either fully open or two-thirds closed. Leaf size: Up to 10 in. (25 cm). Leaf spread: 3–5 ft. (0.9–1.5 m). Stem color: Peduncle brownish, petiole yellowish green, both striped purple. No pubescence on peduncle or petiole.

COMMENTS. The flower color of *Nymphaea* 'Wow' is striking and somewhat similar to *N.* 'Perry's Wildfire', yet the flower form is more rigid and flowers make excellent cut flowers. When using as a cut flower, be sure the whole stem is placed in water. I recommend this cultivar for medium and large pools.

Nymphaea 'Yellow Princess'

Slocum 1991

Seedling of *N.* 'Texas Dawn'

PLATE 255

CHARACTERISTICS. Marliac rhizome, free flowering.

FLOWERS. Petal color: Inner petals, rich yellow; outer petals, light yellow (*RHS* inner, 3A; outer, 1D). Sepal color: Greenish yellow, base paler (*RHS* 145C; base, 1D). Anther color: Deep yellow (*RHS* 6B). Stamen color: Deep yellow. Flower shape: Stellate. Flower size: 6–7.5 in. (15–19 cm). Fragrance: Very pleasant. Number of petals: 24–28. Number of sepals: 4.

LEAVES. Color: Top, deep olive green, perimeter flecked purple on new leaves; underside, yellowish green, heavily blotched reddish purple. Leaf nearly round, pointed tips at lobe ends; sinus a wide-open V. Leaf size: Up to 12 in. (30 cm). Leaf spread: 4–5 ft. (1.2–1.5 m). Stem color: Brownish. Thick fuzz on peduncle and petiole.

COMMENTS. *Nymphaea* 'Yellow Princess', with its freedom of bloom and excellent stellate flowers, has earned a place among the outstanding yellow hardies. I recommend it for any size pool.

Nymphaea 'Yellow Queen'

Slocum 1991
Seedling of *N.* 'Texas Dawn'
PLATE 256

CHARACTERISTICS. Marliac rhizome, free flowering.

FLOWERS. Petal color: Inner petals, rich yellow; outer, lighter (*RHS* inner, 8B; outer, 2D). Sepal color: Greenish yellow (*RHS* 145D). Anther color: Deep yellow (*RHS* 13B). Stamen color: Deep yellow. Flower shape: Unique star-shape. Flower size: 7–10 in. (18–25 cm). Fragrance: Delightful. Number of petals: 30–32. Number of sepals: 4.

LEAVES. Color: Top, deep olive green, new leaves heavily mottled purple, mottling fades slightly with age; underside, red or deep pink, heavily mottled reddish purple. Leaf nearly round; sinus a wide-open V. Leaf size: Up to 12 in. (30 cm). Leaf spread: 4–5 ft. (1.2–1.5 m). Stem color: Purplish brown. Thick fuzz on peduncle and petiole.

COMMENTS. One outstanding trait of *Nymphaea* 'Yellow Queen' is the flower's resemblance to a tropical day bloomer with an unusual upward curl to the petal tips. Blooms open much earlier than any other yellow hardy cultivar (about 9:30 a.m.) and the beautiful, heavily mottled leaves are among the prettiest of hardies, ranking with *N.* 'Arc-en-Ciel' in their beauty. I recommend this cultivar for medium or large pools.

Nymphaea 'Yellow Sensation'

Slocum 1991
Nymphaea alba (from New Zealand) × *N. mexicana*
     No. 2
PLATE 257

CHARACTERISTICS. Upright rhizome, free flowering, very double flower for a yellow hardy.

FLOWERS. Petal color: Rich yellow (*RHS* 3C). Sepal color: Pale greenish yellow, green tips and border (*RHS* 145D and lighter; tips and border, 145B). Anther color: Deep yellow (*RHS* 11A). Stamen color: Deep yellow. Flower shape: Cuplike. Flower size: 5–8 in. (13–20 cm). Fragrance: Slight, pleasant. Number of petals: 33–36. Number of sepals: 4.

LEAVES. Color: Top, olive green, new leaves greenish, flecked purple, perimeter blotched purple; underside, yellowish green, perimeter flecked reddish purple. Leaf nearly round; lobes frequently overlap in new leaves, partially overlap in medium-sized leaves; sinus completely open in large leaves. Leaf size: Up to 10 in. (25 cm). Leaf spread: 3–5 ft. (0.9–1.5 m). Stem color: Peduncle brownish, petiole greenish brown, striped purple. Thick fuzz on peduncle and petiole.

COMMENTS. *Nymphaea* 'Yellow Sensation' is so striking that it has become one of the most popular contemporary yellow hardies. It shares one parent with *N.* 'Marliacea Chromatella', yet flowers are larger, more richly colored, and have more petals (33–36 compared to the 22–25 of *N.* 'Chromatella'). Blooms are held up to 6 in. (15 cm) above water. I hybridized this cultivar using the larger form of *N. mexicana* (No. 2), whereas Joseph Marliac probably did not have access to this rare plant over a century ago when he hybridized 'Marliacea Chromatella'. I recommend 'Yellow Sensation' for small, medium, or large pools. It does well in water that is 3–4 ft. (0.9–1.2 m) deep, and it is not recommended for shallow ponds, as its leaves will crowd each other on the water surface. Unfortunately, in some northern areas it may suffer from crown rot.

Nymphaea 'Yogi Gi'

Strawn, year unknown
Parentage unknown
PLATE 258

CHARACTERISTICS. Nonviviparous, odorata rhizome, free flowering, perennial.

FLOWERS. Petal color: Deep fuchsia throughout with slightly rounded petals. Sepal color: Inner, fuchsia; outer, olive green, medium green base. Anther color: Inner, bright yellow; outer, bright yellow. Stamen color: Bright yellow. Flower shape: Cuplike. Flower size: 5–6 in. (12.5–15 cm). Fragrance: Slight. Number of petals: 24–26. Number of sepals: 4.

LEAVES. Color: Top, medium green blushed with plum on edges; some leaves have green and plum on same leaf; underside, reddish plum. Leaf slightly ovate; lobes slightly overlapping, sinus open. Leaf size: 8–10 in. (20–25.5 cm). Leaf spread: 4–6 ft. (1.2–1.9 m). Stem color: Brown. Pubescence on peduncle and petiole.

COMMENTS BY DEAN MCGEE. This uniquely large waterlily that resembles Nymphaea 'Mayla', but with deeper colors similar to N. 'Bernice Ikins'. Nymphaea 'Yogi Gi' has the distinctive characteristic of dual shades of color on certain individual leaves. Excellent as a centerpiece for large ponds.

Nymphaea 'Yuh-Ling'

Strawn 1992
Nymphaea 'Pink Sensation' × N. 'Princess Elizabeth'
PLATE 259

CHARACTERISTICS. Nonviviparous, Marliac rhizome, free flowering, perennial.

FLOWERS. Petal color: Deep fuchsia. Sepal color: Inner, deep fuchsia; outer, bronze, deep fuchsia on some edges. Anther color: Inner, bright yellow; outer, deep fuchsia with bright yellow. Stamen color: Bright yellow. Flower shape: Cuplike. Flower size: 3–4 in. (7.5–10 cm). Fragrance: Strong. Number of petals: 30–32. Number of sepals: 4.

LEAVES. Color: Top, medium green with plum shading on edges; some leaves have olive green with plum shading around perimeter; underside, deep reddish plum. Leaf nearly round; sinus slightly open. Leaf size: 4–5 in. (10–12.5 cm). Leaf spread: 3–5 ft. (0.9–1.5). Stem color: Brown. Pubescence on peduncle and petiole.

COMMENTS BY DEAN MCGEE. Nymphaea 'Yuh-Ling' provides a stunningly bold contrast between deep fuchsia and bright yellow stamens. Blossom color similar to N. 'Bernice Ikins'. Excellent for medium to large ponds.

CHAPTER 7

Other Genera in the Waterlily Family

THIS CHAPTER covers the five remaining genera of the waterlily family: *Nuphar, Victoria, Euryale, Barclaya,* and *Ondinea*. Linnaeus originally classified *Nuphar* as *Nymphaea*, and indeed these two genera have many similarities. *Victoria* and *Euryale* also share many similar characteristics, whereas *Barclaya* and *Ondinea* have only a slight resemblance.

The Genus *Nuphar*

Members of the genus *Nuphar* (spatterdock, yellow pond lily, yellow cow lily) are aquatic herbs distributed primarily in the Northern Hemisphere. Some of the species and varieties have beautiful submerged leaves, a feature highly desirable for aquaria. *Nuphar japonica* develops orange-red flowers and reddish leaves, which makes it a good choice for the tub garden, small pool, or aquarium.

The genus *Nuphar* was once thought to include 26 species, one subspecies, and 17 varieties, as presented by Henkel, Rehnelt, and Dittman in their 1907 study, *Das Buch der Nymphaeaceen oder Seerosengewächse*. According to *Hortus Third* (1976) the genus includes 25 species. However, in 1956 Dr. Ernest O. Beal reduced the genus to two species, *N. japonica* and *N. lutea*, with nine subspecies. In his intensive study, Beal examined 4000 specimens, and I accept it as the primary authority. I do not consider this taxonomic review of *Nuphar* definitive, however, as it principally covers the American and European nuphars and passes over the Japanese species in brief. Much more study is needed on this plant group before the earlier classifications can be discarded. Beal's findings are further discussed under *N. lutea*.

Nuphars are quite different in floral structure from waterlilies and lotuses (Figure 27), so different categories are required to describe them. *Nuphar lutea* subsp. *macrophylla* grows in central Florida, and I have been able to study it very carefully and include in its description all the categories used for hardy waterlilies. For the other *Nuphar lutea* subspecies, I concentrate on the traits that distinguish them from each other. Flower size, number of sepals, length of anthers, number of stigmatic rays, and shape of leaf and sinus are all such distinguishing traits. Sepal color, usually green and yellow for each subspecies, is omitted as a descriptive category. Likewise, petals, anthers, and stamens are generally yellow. Flower shape; fragrance; leaf color, size, and spread; and stem color cannot be considered suitable distinguishing characteristics.

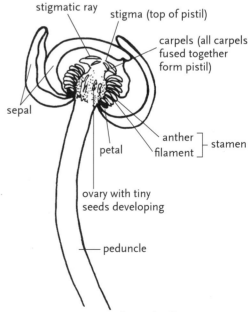

FIGURE 27. Cross section of a *Nuphar* flower.

Nuphars are not generally included in a water garden planting except perhaps by the collector of rare plants. Hardiness zone information is not detailed. Furthermore, as nuphars are hardy perennials, there is no specific planting period other than spring and summer. In areas comparable to zones 8–10, nuphars can be planted year-round.

Nuphars develop from thick rhizomes growing in mud in pond, lake, or stream bottoms in water up to 10 ft. (3 m) deep. *Nuphar japonica* and *N. lutea* subsp. *sagittifolia* are exceptions, producing small rhizomes, and are suitable for aquarium use. Nuphars are day blooming at first, occasionally becoming day and night blooming.

Leaf shape varies from nearly round to lanceolate with overlapping to widely divergent lobes, smooth above and smooth to densely hairy on the underside. Leaves may be floating, emersed, or submerged. They are arranged spirally, with round, somewhat flattened or winged petioles at the base of a long sinus. Petioles and peduncles are smooth to densely pubescent.

Sepals, varying in number from 5 to 14, are greenish or tinged yellow or red. These are casually recognized as "petals" because they are the larger and more colorful parts of the flower. The actual petals are generally yellow, quite small, numerous, thick, and oblong or sometimes thin and spatulate. Petals are often notched, sometimes scalelike, and are located directly under the stamens. Stamens are numerous, tinged yellow or red, attached in spiral rows below the seed capsule, recurving, exposing anthers that are 0.05–0.4 in. (0.1–1 cm) long. Carpels are fused together with few to many stigmatic rays. Flowers are borne just above water to 12 in. (30 cm) above water. Seed pods usually ripen above water.

Linnaeus included *Nuphar lutea* with white waterlilies in the genus *Nymphaea*, but Sibthorp and Smith designated the separate genus *Nuphar* in 1809. After examining both herbarium and living specimens, Beal realized that a close morphological relationship exists among previously recognized North American and Eurasian species. He also noted that plants are extremely variable and therefore advised recognizing only those forms associated with geographical or ecological features.

The subspecies of *Nuphar lutea* are separated and classified according to shape of fruit, variations in stigmatic disk, anthers, petals, number of sepals, and variations in leaves and petioles. The descriptions overlap in many instances, and there are many intermediate specimens showing a combination of features. As a result, any decision to assign an intermediate plant to a nearby subspecies is arbitrary. Plants intermediate between *N. lutea* subsp. *lutea* and *N. lutea* subsp. *pumila*, as well as between the latter and *N. lutea* subsp. *variegata*, are especially abundant in areas of overlap. Therefore, they are not recognized as subspecies but as natural hybrids.

Nuphar japonica de Candolle
Japanese pond lily
Native to Japan
PLATE 260

CHARACTERISTICS. Day blooming, small finger-type rhizome (sometimes larger, especially in rich soil), fairly free flowering, sepals moderately large, petals very small (hidden beneath anthers); develops both submerged and floating leaves, which become aerial in shallow water. Leaf color differs above and below water; both submerged and floating leaves smooth.

FLOWERS. Petal color: Deep yellow (*RHS* 21C). Sepal color: Outer, deep green center surrounded with rich yellow changing to orange by second or third day and then to red; inner, green at base with yellow above (*RHS* outer, 144D,B [darker in center]; outside, 11B to 25A by second or third day, then to 34B; inner, base, 144D; above, 14B). Anther color: Yellowish orange (*RHS* 14C). Anther length: 0.2–0.4 in. (0.5–1 cm). Stamen color: Yellowish orange. Flower shape: Cuplike. Flower size: 1–2 in. (2.5–5 cm). Fragrance: None. Number of petals: 16–18. Number of sepals: 6 or 7. Number of stigmatic rays: Usually 12 or 13.

LEAVES. Color: Top, floating leaves reddish brown at first, turning to olive green; underside, same. Submerged leaves reddish purple on both sides. Floating leaves heart-shaped, leathery; sinus open. Submerged leaves heart-shaped, thin, undulating. Leaf size: Floating leaves 4.5 × 3 in. (11 × 8 cm); submerged leaves 3.5 × 2.5 in. (9 × 6 cm). Leaf spread: 18–24 in. (45–60 cm). Stem color: Peduncle bronzy green; petioles greenish, submerged petioles to submerged leaves reddish. No pubescence on peduncle or petiole.

COMMENTS. This species makes a very desirable aquarium plant with its yellow to orange to red blooms and red submerged leaves and small rhizome. Where all the conditions are right and the soil is rich, however, I have seen much larger rhizomes. Its small leaf spread also makes it an excellent choice for tub gardens or small pools.

Nuphar lutea subsp. *lutea*

Native to Eurasia; throughout Europe except the far north, south to Algeria, Palestine, Iran, eastward in central Asia to southern Siberia and Manchuria

CHARACTERISTICS. Day blooming, exposed leaves floating, petiole more or less flattened, petals thin and broadly spatulate, most longer than stamens. Fruit displays a narrowly constricted neck below the notched stigmatic disk.

FLOWERS. Petal color: Yellow. Anther length: 0.1–0.4 in. (0.3–1 cm). Flower shape: Cuplike. Flower size: 1.25–2.5 in. (3–6 cm). Number of sepals: 5. Number of stigmatic rays: 5–28.

LEAVES. Egg-shaped, lobes close or overlapping; sinus usually closed.

COMMENTS. In its natural habitats, *Nuphar lutea* subsp. *lutea* grows in ponds, lakes, and slow-moving streams. In the average water garden I see no future for this plant. In the plant's native areas, fish farmers may find this plant provides fine coverage.

Nuphar lutea subsp. *macrophylla* (Small) Beal

Syn. *Nuphar advena* (Aiton) Aiton f.

American spatterdock

Native to North and Central America, Cuba; eastern United States, southern Maine west to southern Wisconsin, south to northeastern Mexico and Central America

PLATE 261

CHARACTERISTICS. Day blooming, thick, fleshy, frequently branching, long rhizome, fairly free flowering, sepals large, many leaves carried above water.

FLOWERS. Petal color: Deep yellow, underside tipped orange (*RHS* 13B; tips, 24B). Sepal color: Outer three, deep green; inner three mostly deep yellow, patch of deep green same color of outer sepals (*RHS* outer three, 144A; inner, 12A). Anther color: Deep yellow (*RHS* 12A). Anther length: 0.2–0.4 in. (0.5–1 cm). Stamen color: Yellow. Flower shape: Cuplike. Flower size: 2–2.5 in. (5–6 cm). Fragrance: None. Number of petals: 20. Number of sepals: 6. Number of stigmatic rays: 5–18.

LEAVES. Color: Top, green, new leaves bronzy brown, red spot at petiole; underside, green, new leaves yellowish green. Leaf egg-shaped; sinus usually wide open. Leaf size: 14.5 × 10 in. (37 × 25 cm). Leaf spread: 5–8 ft. (1.5–2.4 m). Stem color: Bright green. No pubescence on peduncle or petiole.

COMMENTS. In its natural habitats, found growing in ponds, lakes, sluggish streams, marshes, swamps, ditches, and canals. *Nuphar lutea* subsp. *macrophylla*, compared to the waterlily *Nymphaea odorata*, has several drawbacks for water garden use. Blooms are small relative to leaf size, flowers are not scented, leaves rise up out of the water, sometimes hiding the blooms, and a deeper water depth of 4–6 ft. (1.2–1.8 m) is required for optimum growth. Due to its large leaf spread and small blooms, I recommend it only for collectors or for use by fish farmers for coverage.

Nuphar lutea subsp. *orbiculata* (Small) Beal

Native to southeastern United States, particularly south-central and southwestern Georgia, north-central Florida

CHARACTERISTICS. Day blooming, exposed leaves floating, densely pubescent underneath, petiole round. Fruit slightly constricted below a round to irregularly scalloped stigmatic disk. Stigmatic disk green, yellow, or sometimes tinged red.

FLOWERS. Petal color: Yellow. Anther length: 0.2–0.4 in. (0.5–1 cm). Flower shape: Cuplike. Flower size: 1.5–2.5 in. (4–6 cm). Number of sepals: 6. Number of stigmatic rays: 12–28.

LEAVES. Color, green. Leaves round to egg-shaped; thick, leathery, rounded lobes may or may not overlap at sinus; submerged leaves similar yet thin, flaccid. Sinus may or may not be open. Pubescence on peduncle and petiole.

COMMENTS. In its natural habitats, found growing in acidic pools and ponds. Probable best used by fish farmers for coverage.

Nuphar lutea subsp. *ozarkana* (Miller & Standley) Beal

Native to Ozark region of Missouri and north-western Arkansas

CHARACTERISTICS. Day blooming, exposed leaves usually floating. Differs from *N. lutea* subsp. *variegata* in having round petioles. Differs from the highly variable *N. lutea* subsp. *macrophylla* in leaf shape and presence of red pigmentation in sepals and fruit.

FLOWERS. Petal color: Yellow. Anther length: 0.2–0.4 in. (0.5–1 cm). Flower shape: Cuplike. Flower size: 2–2.5 in. (5–6 cm). Number of sepals: 6. Number of stigmatic rays: 5–18.

LEAVES. Oblong to egg-shaped to nearly round; lobes close or nearly parallel; sinus slightly open.

COMMENTS. In its natural habitats, found growing in ponds, lakes, and slow-moving streams. This plant is not usually sought by water gardeners due to its small blooms relative to leaf size, but it could provide good coverage for fish in a lake or fish farm.

Nuphar lutea subsp. *polysepala* (Engelmann) Beal

Native to North America; Alaska southward along the Pacific Coast and Sierra Nevada range to San Luis Obispo County, California, southeastward in the Rocky Mountains to northeastern Colorado and Utah

CHARACTERISTICS. Day blooming, leaves usually floating, sometimes emersed. Petioles round. Filament often extending 0.05–0.2 in. (0.1–0.5 cm) beyond the anther. Stigmatic disk round to deeply notched.

FLOWERS. Petal color: Usually yellow, sometime tinged red. Anther color: Tinged yellow to deep red. Anther length: 0.2–0.4 in. (0.5–1 cm). Flower shape: Cuplike. Flower size: 3.5–5 in. (9–13 cm). Number of sepals: 7–9. Number of stigmatic rays: 9–36, usually 20–25.

LEAVES. Round to oblong, smooth; lobes rounded to acute, may or may not overlap. Sinus either closed or open.

COMMENTS. In its natural habitats, found growing in ponds, lakes, streams. This plant could be used in mountain ponds too cold for waterlilies to thrive.

Nuphar lutea subsp. *pumila* (Timm) Beal

Syn. *Nuphar microphylla* Beal

Native to north temperate regions of Europe, Asia, and northeastern North America

CHARACTERISTICS. Day blooming, petals thin to thicker, broadly spatulate, sometimes thicker. Exposed leaves floating, sometimes only 1 in. (2.5 cm) in diameter, underside varying from smooth to densely pubescent. Petioles vary from nearly round to angular near leaf. Fruit with narrowly constricted neck below a deeply dentate disk. Stigmatic disk tinged yellow to red.

FLOWERS. Anther length: 0.05–0.1 in. (0.1–0.3 cm). Flower shape: Cuplike. Flower size: 0.6–1.25 in. (1.5–3 cm). Number of sepals: Usually 5. Number of stigmatic rays: 5–14.

LEAVES. Round or nearly round, lobes lined up close, sinus slightly open. Leaf size: 5.5 in. (14 cm) or smaller.

COMMENTS. In its natural habitats, found growing in ponds, lakes, and streams. Though representatives of *Nuphar* from southeastern China and Japan appear to be closely related to *N. lutea* subsp. *pumila*, Beal noted that a scarcity of material from southeastern China and Japan had prevented a determination of the position of those plants within the genus *Nuphar*.

Nuphar lutea subsp. *sagittifolia* (Walter) Beal

Cape Fear spatterdock

Native to Virginia, North Carolina, South Carolina

CHARACTERISTICS. Day blooming, leaves glabrous, exposed leaves floating, submerged leaves numerous, thin, translucent.

FLOWERS. Petal color: Yellow (*RHS* 13A). Sepal color: Outer three, bright green; inner three, rich yellow (*RHS* outer, 144A; inner, 12A). Anther color: Rich yellow (*RHS* 12A). Anther length: About 0.1 in. (0.3 cm). Stamen color: Yellow. Flower shape: Cuplike. Flower size: 1 in. (2.5 cm). Fragrance: None. Number of petals: 16. Number of sepals: 6. Number of stigmatic rays: 12–18.

LEAVES. Color: Top, bright green; underside, yellowish green. Leaves oblong to lanceolate; sinus not over 1.5 in. (4 cm) deep. Leaf size: 6–16 × 2–4 in. (15–40 × 5–10 cm); submerged leaves usually larger.

Leaf spread: 24–30 in. (60–75 cm). Stem color: Bright green.

COMMENTS. This riverine subspecies has beautiful underwater leaves and is sold widely in the aquarium trade. Its common name, Cape Fear spatterdock, comes from the fact that many of the plants are collected from the Cape Fear River, North Carolina. The blooms are too small to generate much interest as a pool plant, so I do not recommend it for the water garden.

Nuphar lutea subsp. *ulvacea* (Miller & Standley) Beal
Native to United States; Blackwater River, western Florida

CHARACTERISTICS. Day blooming, exposed leaves floating, smooth, submerged leaves numerous, thin, translucent. Stigmatic rays usually elliptical.

FLOWERS. Anther length: About 0.1 in. (0.3 cm). Flower shape: Cuplike. Flower size: 1–1.25 in. (2.5–3 cm). Number of sepals: 6–9. Number of stigmatic rays: 9–12.

LEAVES. Lanceolate; sinus one-fourth length of leaf or less. Leaf size: 8–10 × 3–4 in. (20–25 × 8–10 cm).

COMMENTS. Small flowers rule out this plant for pool use, but it should make an excellent aquarium plant due to its numerous submerged leaves. Because of its scarcity, however, it is rarely used in aquaria.

Nuphar lutea subsp. *variegata* (Engelmann) Beal
Native to North America; Yukon Territory and the Great Bear Lake to Newfoundland, south to western Montana, Nebraska, Iowa, northern Illinois, northern Ohio and Delaware; possibly in northwestern Arkansas and Kentucky

CHARACTERISTICS. Day blooming, exposed leaves usually floating, smooth. Petiole flattened, winged. Fruit slightly constricted. Somewhat notched stigmatic disk, greenish, often tinged red.

FLOWERS. Anther length: 0.2–0.4 in. (0.5–1 cm). Flower shape: Cuplike. Flower size: 1.5–2.5 in. (4–6 cm). Number of sepals: Usually 6. Number of stigmatic rays: 7–26.

LEAVES. Oblong to round; lobes either close or overlapping; sinus either partly open or closed.

COMMENTS. In its natural habitats, found growing in ponds, lakes, and slow-moving streams. I do not see any future for this small-bloomed plant in the water garden. Undoubtedly, it provides good coverage for fish in lakes and ponds.

The Genus *Victoria*

Members of the genus *Victoria* (giant waterlilies, water platters), with their huge pie-plate–shaped leaves reaching 8 ft. (2.4 m) in diameter and with blooms as large as 16 in. (40 cm) across, are without a doubt the queens of the waterlily world. If a thin plywood disk is placed on the leaf to distribute the weight evenly, the gigantic pads can support the weight of a full-grown person. These dramatic plants are worth going many miles to see. There are two species, both originating from South America. *Victoria amazonica* (Poeppig) Sowerby (syn. *V. regia* Lindley) mostly grows along the Amazon River basin and is the more tropical and tender of the two. *Victoria cruziana* d'Orbigny, from Paraguay, Bolivia, and Argentina, is somewhat similar but hardier. Patrick Nutt, as the foreman of aquatics and display greenhouses at Longwood Gardens, Kennett Square, Pennsylvania, hybridized these two species and came up with the beautiful *V.* 'Longwood Hybrid', which is far superior in terms of performance to either species. In 1999, Kitt and Ben Knotts, Nancy and Trey Styler, and Joe Summers produced *Victoria* 'Adventure', a hybrid resulting from the opposite cross of the two species.

Victorias have several distinguishing characteristics. First, nearly every part of the plant has sharp spines, including the underside of the pads, the stems, and the exterior of buds. The only exception to this general rule is that *Victoria cruziana* lacks spines on its sepals. Second, the flowers, which change color from day to day, have a distinctive bloom pattern. First-day flowers are white, opening near nightfall and remaining open until late morning the following day. Second-day flowers are pink or reddish (purplish red in the case of *N.* 'Longwood Hybrid'), and reopen in late afternoon. These second-day blooms fold their sepals and petals down and sink into the water during the night. Another distinguishing trait is that the flowers (first-day blooms in particular) have a delightful, potent fragrance that can be detected from a distance of 15–20 ft. (4.5–6 m).

The leaves (pads) are unusual in that they develop heavy trusses with pronounced veining on the underside, and leaf edges are raised. The trusses, an underside support, develop 4–6 in. (10–15 cm) vertically and about 0.5–1 in. (1.3–2.5 cm) in thickness. The raised leaf edges or rims give the leaves a somewhat grand pie-plate look. Rims are not present on young leaves and start forming after several increasingly large flat leaves have been produced. Such rims may be up to 8 in. (20 cm) high in *Victoria cruziana*.

Two notches form on opposite sides in the tops of these vertical rims; the notch closest to the plant center is the deeper of the two. Because pads do not sink after a heavy rain, one theory is that these notches allow excess rainwater to drain out. Yet, I have never observed the notches facilitating rainwater runoff. Because the bottom of this notch is often 0.4–1.25 in. (1–3 cm) above the surface level of the pad, I believe that rainwater dissipates by transmission through the pad.

These very large plants need at least 15 ft. (4.5 m) of pool space. They grow best when water temperatures are 75°F (24°C) or above. *Victoria amazonica* is much more tender than *V. cruziana* and *V. 'Longwood Hybrid'* and yet can be planted successfully at any time of the year in conservatories and greenhouses if water temperatures can be maintained at 85–90°F (29–32°C). Plant *V. cruziana* and *V. 'Longwood Hybrid'* in outside pools when water temperatures reach 65–70°F (18–21°C) or above. (*Victoria 'Adventure'* has not yet been introduced to the market.) Refer to the hardiness zone maps at the end of the book and follow this general planting timetable:

In North America

Zone 10 late March–April, *V. cruziana* and *V. 'Longwood Hybrid'*; May, *V. amazonica*

Zone 9 May–June, *V. cruziana* and *V. 'Longwood Hybrid'*; late May–June, *V. amazonica*

Zone 8 May–June, *V. cruziana* and *V. 'Longwood Hybrid'*; late May–June, *V. amazonica*

Zone 7 25 May–1 July, *V. cruziana* and *V. 'Longwood Hybrid'*; 10 June–1 July, *V. amazonica*

Zone 6 1 June–1 July, *V. cruziana* and *V. 'Longwood Hybrid'*; conservatory planting, *V. amazonica*

Zone 5 10 June–10 July, *V. cruziana* and *V. 'Longwood Hybrid'*

Zone 4 plant in heated or sheltered pools, where water will remain at correct temperatures

In Europe

Zone 10 May–June, *V. cruziana* and *V. 'Longwood Hybrid'*; June, *V. amazonica*

Zone 9 June, *V. cruziana* and *V. 'Longwood Hybrid'*, in areas where water temperatures average 70°F (21°C) or above; conservatory planting, water temperature 85–90°F (29–32°C), *V. amazonica*

Zones 8–4 conservatory planting, water temperature 70°F (21°C) or above, *V. cruziana* and *V. 'Longwood Hybrid'*; conservatory planting, water temperature 85–90°F (29–32°C) or above, *V. amazonica*

In the following descriptions of *Victoria*, "Flower size" is a diameter measurement, "Leaf size" refers to the diameter of a mature leaf, and "Leaf spread" is the area on the water's surface covered by all the leaves of a mature plant.

Victoria 'Adventure'

Kitt and Ben Knotts, Nancy and Trey Styler, and Joe Summers 1999

Victoria amazonica × *V. cruziana*

PLATES 262, 263

CHARACTERISTICS. Night and day blooming, very free flowering, petals somewhat crinkled; thorns on outside of sepals, stems, and under pads.

FLOWERS. Petal color: Creamy white, then medium to light pink. Sepal color: Inner, medium flesh pink; outer, bronzy green. Anther color: Inner, deep red; outer, deep red. Stamen color: Deep red. Flower shape: Somewhat stellate. Flower size: 10–14 in. (25–35 cm). Fragrance: Strong, like pineapple. Number of petals: 62. Number of sepals: 4.

LEAVES. Color: Top of leaf and inside of leaf rim: Bronze-reddish green; underside, deep red with deep red vertical rim (on outside). Round leaf with thorns on underside and outside of rim. Leaf size: 3–8 ft. (0.9–2.4 m) depending on culture. Leaf spread: 10–40 ft. (3–12 m). Stem color: Red, then tan-green. Thorns on peduncle and petiole.

COMMENTS BY KIT KNOTTS. *Victoria* 'Adventure' is intermediate between its parents, tending slightly more to *V. amazonica*. Compared with the reciprocal cross, *V.* 'Longwood Hybrid', *V.* 'Adventure' is slightly larger, rims are slightly lower, pads are more bronzy red-green, and its flowers are larger, have more petals (62 versus 54; 54 is Knott's *V.* 'Longwood Hybrid' count in south Florida; in North Carolina my plants have 73–75 petals), and are a deeper pink on the second night. It is difficult to germinate the seeds but relatively easy to grow as a juvenile and easy as an adult.

COMMENTS. Kit and Ben Knotts and Joe Summers of the Missouri Botanical Gardens made other *Victoria* crosses that had been considered impossible due to uneven chromosomes. They are: *V.* 'Discovery' (*V.* 'Longwood Hybrid' × *V. amazonica*, 1999); *V.* 'Challenger' (*V.* 'Adventure' × *V. cruziana*, 2000); and *V.* 'Atlantis' (*V.* 'Adventure' × *V. amazonica*, 2000). Additional details and images are available at www.Victoria-Adventure.org.

Victoria amazonica (Poeppig) Sowerby

Syn. *Victoria. regia* Lindley

Giant waterlily, Amazon waterlily

Native to the Amazon River region of Brazil, Guiana, Bolivia

PLATES 264, 265

CHARACTERISTICS. Night blooming, nonviviparous, very free flowering in warm climates; propagates by seed, seeds elliptical; smooth, sharp spines on all stems, on underside of leaves, outside of rims, and outer surface of sepals.

FLOWERS. Petal color: Creamy white then pink (*RHS* 158D; second day, 37D). Sepal color: Creamy white then yellow, flushed pink (*RHS* 158D; second day, 8C; flush, 38D). Anther color: Pink (*RHS* 63B). Stamen color: White then pink. Flower shape: Very full, double. Flower size: 9–12 in. (23–30 cm). Fragrance: Strong, like pineapple. Number of petals: 58. Number of sepals: 4.

LEAVES. Color: Top, yellowish green, rim exterior pink, veined red; underside, reddish purple. Leaves round, initially flat, rim developing, 3–6 in. (8–15 cm) in height, exterior sharply spined; leaf undersides sharply spined. No true sinus. Leaf size: 4–6 ft. (1.2–1.8 m). Leaf spread: 15–20 ft. (4.5–6 m), somewhat smaller when crowded. Stem color: Brownish green. No pubescence on peduncle or petiole but lots of sharp spines.

COMMENTS. *Victoria amazonica* is the plant that Joseph Paxton brought to flower and much acclaim at Chatsworth, England, in the mid-19th century. As *V. amazonica* requires a water temperature of 85–90°F (29–32°C), Paxton had a special conservatory and tank built in order to grow it. High winds may severely damage pads. Leaves also tend to become distorted when grown in crowded conditions. In northern latitudes this plant is suited only for a large, warm, heated pool in a conservatory or greenhouse.

Victoria cruziana d'Orbigny

Santa Cruz waterlily

Native to Paraguay, northern Argentina, Bolivia

PLATE 266

CHARACTERISTICS. Night blooming, nonviviparous, very free blooming; propagates by seed, seeds round or spherical, seed surface rough; short, sharp spines on all stems, underside of leaves, outside of rims, but none on sepals.

FLOWERS. Petal color: Creamy white then pink (*RHS* 155A; second day, 56C). Sepal color: Creamy white then pink (*RHS* 155A; second day, 56C). Anther color: Pink (*RHS* 63B). Stamen color: White then pink. Flower shape: Full, double. Flower size: 9–11 in. (23–28 cm). Fragrance: Strong, like pineapple. Number of petals: 65. Number of sepals: 4.

LEAVES. Color: Top, yellowish green, rim exterior green, veined red; new leaves rim exterior veined pinkish; underside, violet-purple. Leaves round, rims 5–8 in. (13–20 cm) high, frequently flared; no true sinus. Leaf size: 4–5.5 ft. (1.2–1.7 m). Leaf spread: 15–18 ft. (4.5–5.4 m). Stem color: Bronzy green. No pubescence on peduncle or petiole but lots of sharp spines.

COMMENTS. *Victoria cruziana* is slightly less free flowering than *V. amazonica*, usually producing two or three new blooms weekly once blooming begins. *Victoria cruziana* is probably a more practical choice than *V. amazonica* for northern water gardeners, as it will take temperatures that are 10–15°F (9–12°C) colder. It grows well in warm climates either in pools or conservatories. *Victoria cruziana* needs water temperatures of at least 65–70°F (18–21°C), and optimum water temperatures are 75–90°F (24–32°C).

Victoria 'Longwood Hybrid'

Nutt 1961

Victoria amazonica × *V. cruziana*

PLATES 267, 268

CHARACTERISTICS. Night blooming, nonviviparous, free flowering; stout sharp purple, black, or brown spines on all stems, underside of leaves, outside of rims, and outside of sepals; seeds globose, 0.3 in. (0.8 cm) long, seed surface rough.

FLOWERS. Petal color: White then rose-pink (*RHS* 155A; second day, 63A). Sepal color: White then rosy pink (*RHS* 155A; second day, 62C). Anther color: Rose-pink (*RHS* 63A). Stamen color: White then pink. Flower shape: Huge, round, full. Flower size: 10–16 in. (25–40 cm). Fragrance: Very wonderful, like pineapple. Number of petals: 73–75. Number of sepals: 4.

LEAVES. Color: Top, yellowish green, rim exterior red, spiny; underside, purple, spiny. Leaves round, initially flat, 2.5–4 in. (6–10 cm) rim developing; no true sinus. Leaf size: 4–8 ft. (1.2–2.4 m). Leaf spread: 12–40 ft. (3.6–12 m). Stem color: Greenish brown. No pubescence on peduncle or petiole.

COMMENTS. *Victoria* 'Longwood Hybrid' was crossed in September 1960 by Patrick Nutt, Longwood Gardens. He used a first-day bloom from *V. cruziana* as the seed parent and a second-day bloom from *V. amazonica* as the pollen parent. (The reverse scenario did not produce viable seed, although *V.* 'Adventure' represents such a cross.) The first seed was collected five weeks later and stored moist for 12 weeks—six weeks in moist sand at 65°F (18°C) and six weeks in water at 50°F (10°C). *Victoria* 'Longwood Hybrid' first flowered in 1961.

Victoria 'Longwood Hybrid' is a true giant among aquatic plants and in many respects is superior to its parents. Increased vigor is reflected in its larger pads, better ability to withstand higher winds and lower water and air temperatures, its flowering 3–11 days earlier, and producing 11–16 more flowers in a season. Blooms open earlier in the evening, and once the plant begins to bloom there is a new blossom every second or third day.

On large leaves, trusses can be about 3 in. (7.5 cm) in height under the center of the pad. Spines, characteristic of *Victoria*, develop on the outside of sepals and flowers as well as on stems. Hybrid seeds germinate quite readily once water temperature nears 70°F (21°C). Most seed propagation is done at Longwood Gardens although other sources are now available (such as Luster Aquatic Nursery

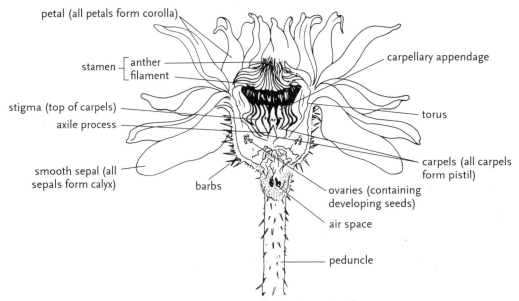

FIGURE 28. Cross section of a *Victoria cruziana* flower.

in Delray Beach, Florida). *Victoria* 'Longwood Hybrid' requires a growing area at least 12 ft. (3.6 m) wide, so is appropriate only for large, warm pools and conservatories.

The Genus *Euryale*

The genus *Euryale* (prickly waterlily, Gorgon plant) has a single species, *Euryale ferox* Salisbury, native to tropical East Africa, Southeast Asia, and China. A perennial in warm climates, it is cultivated in the same manner as the victorias. The leaves, which float on the water surface, are large, spiny, and veined, somewhat similar to those of *Victoria* but lacking rimmed edges. Plants have sharp spines on the exterior surface of the sepals, the stems, and both sides of the leaves. Neither the pads nor the flowers are considered as attractive as those of the victorias.

In its native habitat people highly prize *Euryale ferox* as part of the diet, sometimes baking the pea-sized starchy seeds, known as fox nuts. In Japan the young stems and the roots are eaten as vegetables. The Chinese reputedly have cultivated *E. ferox* for 3000 years.

Large botanic gardens in the United States, such as the Missouri Botanical Garden and Longwood Gardens, tend to have these unusual plants on display. I have also seen one growing in a conservatory at the Royal Botanic Gardens, Kew. I am always impressed by the large purple-veined leaves covered with spines and the deep violet flowers with white center petals. *Euryale* plants are not widely available, and I know of no listing in any commercial aquatic nursery. A few commercial water gardens do have them for sale, however, even though they do not list them. At Perry's Water Gardens in North Carolina, the seeds survive the winter in outdoor ponds and germinate by the hundreds. They become a pest, and we have to pull them out.

Plant *Euryale ferox* outside when water temperature averages 75°F (24°C) or above. Optimum water temperature range is 70–80°F (21–27°C). For maximum bloom number, set planter about 3–10 in. (8–25 cm) below the water surface. I have seen plants bloom in 3 ft. (0.9 m) of water in a natural pond in North Carolina (zone 6b), but they seem to come into flower later when grown in deeper water. Seeds germinate readily if they have not been allowed to dry out during storing or shipping. Refer to the hardiness zone maps at the end of the book and follow this general planting timetable:

In North America		In Europe	
Zone 10	late March–April	Zone 10	May–June
Zone 9	April–May	Zone 9	late May–June, where water temperatures average 75°F (24°C) or above
Zone 8	late May–June		
Zone 7	25 May–1 July		
Zone 6	1 June–1 July		
Zone 5	10 June–10 July		
Zone 4	plant in heated or sheltered pools, where water temperatures average 75°F (24°C) or above	Zones 8–4	conservatory planting, where water can be heated to 75°F (24°C) or above

Euryale ferox Salisbury

Prickly waterlily, Gorgon plant
Native to tropical East Africa, Southeast Asia, China
PLATES 269–271

CHARACTERISTICS. Day blooming, nonviviparous, fairly free flowering; sharp spines on all stems, both sides of leaves, and on outside of sepals; propagates readily from seed.

FLOWERS. Petal color: Inside row, white; outer rows, deep violet (*RHS* 155D; outer, 86B,C). Sepal color: Reddish purple (*RHS* 70A). Anther color: Yellow (*RHS* 3C). Stamen color: White. Flower shape: Cuplike. Flower size: 1.5–3 in. (4–8 cm). Fragrance: Slight. Number of petals: 23 or 24. Number of sepals: 4.

LEAVES. Color: Top, dark green, numerous purple-red veins, purple barbs; underside, purple-violet, numerous purple barbs. Leaf nearly round, sharply barbed, purple-red veins, small bulges over surface. Leaf edge indented (usually rounded) 0.25–1 in. (0.6–2.5 cm) toward plant center. Occasional sinus, 1 in. (2.5 cm). Leaf size: 4–5 ft. (1.2–1.5 m). Leaf spread: 10–15 ft. (3–4.5 m). Stem color: Burgundy-red. No pubescence on peduncle or petiole, but lots of barbs.

COMMENTS. I find this plant to be an attractive addition to medium and large water gardens. For maximum growth *Euryale ferox* needs a growing

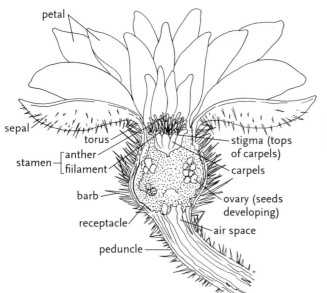

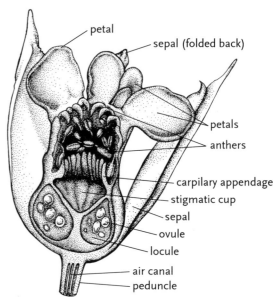

FIGURE 29. Cross section of a *Euryale ferox* flower.

FIGURE 30. Cross section of a *Barclaya* flower.

area 8–15 ft. (2.4–4.5 m) with a minimum of 3–4 in. (8–10 cm) of water over the planter. I have seen this plant adapt to a 5–8 ft. (1.5–2.4 m) wide space and produce blooms. In the larger area, however, flowers are double the size of those grown in the smaller area, with two to three blooms produced at a time. Although I have seen many blooms develop with only 1–2 in. (2.5–5 cm) of water over the planter, a depth of 12–24 in. (30–60 cm) allows maximum bloom formation. This species is easily propagated from seed, but it is very important that seed be stored moist.

The Genus *Barclaya*

The genus *Barclaya* was named in honor of G. W. Barclay, English gardener and plant collector. *Barclaya* plants develop from egg-shaped tubers that produce short runners and a basal leaf rosette. Plants require water temperatures of 78°F (26°C) or above. As such it is not suitable for pools or outdoor culture in either North America or Europe, but it can be planted in aquaria or deep tanks as long as the water temperature requirement can be maintained. Because all leaves are submerged, *Barclaya* makes a desirable show plant for aquarium use.

Leaves are wavy, linear, narrow toward the apex,

blunt, up to 20 in. (50 cm) long and 1.5 in. (4 cm) wide, though smaller when grown in an aquarium. Upperside of leaf is olive green, usually with darker diagonal lines; underside is reddish green. Under optimum growing conditions the stellate flower bud comes to the top of the water to open. Under less-than-ideal conditions the buds will stay underwater and remain closed. Flowers have four or five divided sepals and eight or more petals. Figure 30 illustrates a representative cross section of a *Barclaya* flower.

In the following descriptions, "Flower size" is either a diameter measurement or the length × width, in that order, of the bloom. "Leaf size" is the length × width, in that order, of a submerged mature leaf, and "Leaf spread" is the diameter of the underwater leaf growth of a mature plant.

Barclaya kunstleri (King) Ridley

Syn. *Barclaya motleyi* var. *kunstleri* King
Native to Singapore, western Malaysia
CHARACTERISTICS. Submerged aquatic herb, rhizome branching, petiole 6 in. (15 cm) long, flowers submerged or emergent depending on depth of stream.

FLOWERS. Petal color: Claret. Sepal color: Green. Anther color: White. Stamen color: Claret. Flower shape: Cuplike. Flower size: 1–2 in. (2.5–5 cm). Fragrance: Slight to none. Number of petals: 12–15. Number of sepals: 5.

LEAVES. Color: Top, dark olive green, magenta dots; underside, magenta. Leaves ovate to elliptic, glabrous, thin, apex rounded to obtuse, base usually cordate; sinus shallow. Leaf size: 3.5 × 2.5–2.75 in. (9 × 6–7 cm). Leaf spread: 12 in. (30 cm). Stem color: Light brown to white. Occasional short fuzz on peduncle.

COMMENTS. This is a rare species of the waterlily family and seldom seen outside its native habitat.

Barclaya longifolia Wallich

Syn. *Hydrostemma longifolium* (Wallich) Mabberley
Native to Southeast Asia: Burma, Thailand, Malaysia
PLATE 272

CHARACTERISTICS. Aquatic herb with egg-shaped tuber about 1–1.25 × 0.5–0.75 in. (2.5–3 × 1.3–2 cm), short runners, new plants develop at runner tips. Petiole length varies 2–3 in. (5–8 cm), peduncle 12–16 in. (30–40 cm), sepals 0.4–1 in. (1–2.5 cm), flowers either emerging or remaining as buds under water.

FLOWERS. Petal color: Claret. Sepal color: Greenish pink, green near base. Anther color: Claret-pink. Stamen color: Purplish. Flower shape: Stellate. Flower size: 1–1.5 in. (2.5–4 cm). Fragrance: None or very slight. Number of petals: 8–10. Number of sepals: 5.

LEAVES. Color: Top, brownish green, darker diagonal lines; underside, purple. Leaf long, wavy, straplike, base cordate, apex blunt, lobes rounded; sinus not present. Leaf size: Up to 20 × 1–3 in. (50 × 2.5–8 cm); average length 6–12 in. (15–30 cm). Leaf spread: 2–3 ft. (0.6–0.9 m). Stem color: Brownish. No pubescence on peduncle or petiole.

COMMENTS. *Barclaya longifolia* can make a fine specimen plant for the large aquarium. It requires a fairly deep tank, 18 in. (45 cm) or deeper, a temperature of approximately 78–85°F (26–29°C), and

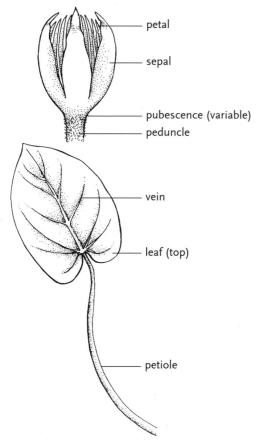

FIGURE 31. *Barclaya kunstleri*, flower and leaf.

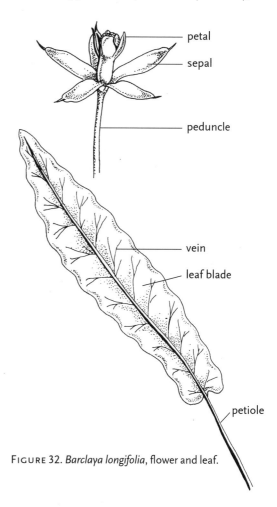

FIGURE 32. *Barclaya longifolia*, flower and leaf.

plenty of nutrients. It is not a desirable pool plant. Propagate it by dividing the young slips that develop on short runners.

Barclaya motleyi Hooker f.

Syn. *Hydrostemma motleyi* (Hooker f.) Mabberley
Native to Sumatra, Borneo, New Guinea

CHARACTERISTICS. Egg-shaped tuber similar to that of *B. longifolia*, petiole usually 2.75–6.5 in. (7–16 cm) long, peduncle 2–5.5 in. (5–14 cm) long; flowers emergent. Sepals 1–1.75 in. (2.5–4.5 cm) long, woolly yellow-brown or gray hairs on exterior surface; anthers oblong, curving in and down. Dense pubescence on lower blade surface.

FLOWERS. Petal color: Pink to red. Sepal color: Green. Anther color: Yellow. Stamen color: Yellow. Flower shape: Stellate. Flower size: 1.5–3 in. (4–8 cm). Fragrance: None or slight. Number of petals: 8–20. Number of sepals: 4 or 5.

LEAVES. Color: Top, olive green, tinted reddish pink; underside, green. Leaf widely obovate, sometimes oblong, apex rounded, base cordate; no sinus present. Leaf size: 2.75–6.5 × 1.25–5.5 in. (7–16 × 3–14 cm). Leaf spread: 24 in. (60 cm). Stem color: Brownish. Pubescence on peduncle and petiole.

COMMENTS. In its natural habitats, it grows from sea level to 5000 ft. (1500 m), in shallow, often muddy pools and often gravelly streams. *Barclaya motleyi* is rarely available to the aquarium plant trade in the United States. I have contacted three of the largest growers and importers of rare aquarium plants and they do not know of anybody importing it. Occasionally Florida Aquatic Nurseries or Suwannee Laboratories (see Sources for Plants and Equipment) has *B. motleyi*. It is not a desirable pool plant, however, due to its high water-temperature requirements of 78–85°F (26–29°C).

Barclaya rotundifolia Hotta

Native to Sarawak (Malaysia)

CHARACTERISTICS. Tuber resembles a small *Nuphar* rhizome, petioles thick, 2.75–6 in. (7–15

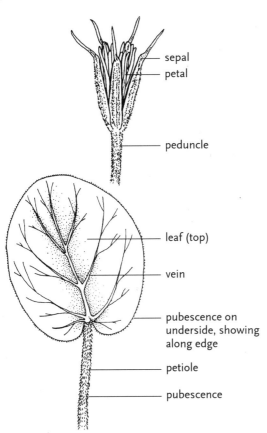

FIGURE 33. *Barclaya motleyi*, flower and leaf.

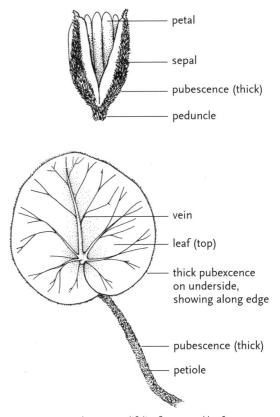

FIGURE 34. *Barclaya rotundifolia*, flower and leaf.

cm) long, peduncles 2–5 in. (5–13 cm) long, sepals 1–1.75 in. (2.5–4.5 cm), round leaves have dense, short pubescence on underside.

FLOWERS. Petal color: Pink to claret. Sepal color: Green. Anther color: Claret to yellow. Stamen color: Claret to yellow. Flower shape: Cuplike. Flower size: 2–3 in. (5–8 cm). Fragrance: Slight. Number of petals: 4 or 5. Number of sepals: 5.

LEAVES. Color: Top, glossy green; underside, light green. Round leaf, base deeply cordate; lobes overlap at sinus. Leaf size: 2.5–3.5 in. (6–9 cm). Leaf spread: 2–3 ft. (0.6–0.9 m). Stem color: Reddish brown to brown. Thick short fuzz on peduncle and petiole.

COMMENTS. *Barclaya rotundifolia* is rare in its native habitat. Partially due to this scarcity, it does not seem to have a commercial future for either aquarium or water garden use.

The Genus *Ondinea*

The genus *Ondinea* is represented by *O. purpurea* and two subspecies. Subspecies *purpurea* produces flowers without petals, whereas subspecies *petaloidea* produces flowers with petals. *Ondinea* is native to the remote Kimberley District of Western Australia, where the aborigines consider its tubers edible. During the winter dry season (June through November) the thumb-sized tubers can be found lodged in the sand of dry streambeds. The streambed soil is composed principally of sand, with 10–30 percent humus. With the onset of the summer wet season (December through May), tubers initiate growth. The tubers, about 1 in. (2.5 cm) long and 0.5 in. (1.3 cm) thick, are somewhat round, brown, with protruding wartlike scars where former leaves, roots, and flowers were attached (Plate 273). Initially the tuber produces roots and submerged, thin, translucent leaves with wavy, undulating margins.

In the following descriptions "Leaf spread" is the area covered by the leaves of the mature plant either on the water's surface or underwater.

Ondinea purpurea Hartog
Native to the Kimberley District, Western Australia
CHARACTERISTICS. Day blooming, flowers with petals.

FLOWERS. Petal color: Blue-violet to purple-pink. Flowers bloom for three consecutive days and are solitary and held above the water. On the first day a small quantity of weak sugar solution develops in the stigmatic cup in the flower center. Major insect pollinators are small *Trigona* bees. Pollen is shaken from the anthers and transported to the pool of nectar on the stigmatic disk, thereby achieving pollination. Numerous small brown seeds are produced from fleshy fruits. Field observations indicate that germination and tuber formation occur before the arrival of the dry season. No field data exist concerning seed germination and dormancy.

LEAVES. Color: Light to dark green above, light green to purple below. Submerged leaves are narrowly egg-shaped to arrow-shaped, ranging 8–24 in. (20–60 cm) in length. In slow-moving or standing water, floating leaves (similar to the floating leaves of small-flowered *Nymphaea*) are also produced. Floating leaves are leathery, narrowly ovate to arrow-shaped, 0.75–4 in. (2–10 cm) in length, green above and green to purple on the underside.

COMMENTS. In its natural habitats, found growing in sun or partial shade in small, clear sandstone streams in a water depth of 1–5 ft. (0.3–1.5 m), with a water temperature usually above 78°F (26°C). A colleague, Don Bryne of Suwannee Laboratories, Lake City, Florida, has tried growing *Ondinea purpurea* commercially for the aquarium trade. He reports that in both northern Florida and Jamaica in autumn, after the blooming season, plants developed tubers and went dormant. He does not predict much of a commercial future for it.

Ondinea purpurea subsp. *petaloidea* Kenneally & Schneider
Native to the Kimberley District, Western Australia
PLATE 274
CHARACTERISTICS. Day blooming, flowers with petals, 27–34 stamens, sepals 0.6–1.5 × 0.25–0.5 in. (1.5–4 × 0.6–1.3 cm), plant-forming tuber.

FLOWERS. Petal color: Lavender-purple (*RHS* 75C). Sepal color: Purplish violet-pink; exterior light green (*RHS* 75D). Anther color: Purple-red (*RHS* 70C). Stamen color: Lavender-purple. Flower shape: Cuplike, pyramidal when calyx and corolla reflex. Flower size: 1.5–1.75 in. (4–4.5 cm); after reflex,

0.75–1 in. (2–2.5 cm). Fragrance: None or slight. Number of petals: 1–5. Number of sepals: 4.

LEAVES. Color: Surface leaves: top, green; underside, green to purplish. Submerged leaves: top, light to dark green; underside, light green to purplish. Surface leaves arrow-shaped, lobe tips rounded, sinus narrow. Submerged leaves longer than wide, thin, base cordate, margins undulate, translucent, nestling on vertical stem, no sinus. Leaf size: Surface leaves 4 × 0.75 in. (10 × 2 cm); submerged leaves 4–7 × 0.75–1.5 in. (10–18 × 2–4 cm). Leaf spread: Surface leaves 8–10 in. (20–25 cm); submerged leaves 8–16 in. (20–40 cm). Stem color: Petioles light green; peduncles light greenish yellow. No pubescence on peduncle or petiole.

COMMENTS. In its natural habitats, found growing in clear sandy streams. Although this plant is a member of the waterlily family, I do not see any commercial future for it, either for pools or aquaria, as it is very susceptible to aquatic bacteria and fungi. Schneider suggests that the pollen may be valuable for intergeneric crosses with *Nymphaea* species.

Ondinea purpurea subsp. *purpurea*

Native to the Kimberley District, Western Australia

CHARACTERISTICS. Day blooming, flower without petals, 14–23 stamens, sepals 0.3–0.6 × 0.06–0.1 in. (0.8–1.5 × 0.15–0.3 cm), plant-forming tuber.

FLOWERS. Petal color: No petals produced. Sepal color: Violet-pink; exterior light green (*RHS* 75D). Anther color: Purple-red (*RHS* 70C). Stamen color: Lavender-purple. Flower shape: Pyramidal when sepals reflexed. Flower size: 0.4–0.6 in. (1–1.5 cm). Fragrance: None or slight. Number of petals: None. Number of sepals: 4.

LEAVES. Color: Surface leaves, top, green; underside, green to purplish. Submerged leaves, top, light to dark green; underside, light green to purplish. Surface leaves narrowly ovate; sinus open. Submerged leaves longer than wide, thin, wavy, translucent, leaf bases closely spaced on vertical stem; no sinus. Leaf size: Surface leaves, 3.5 × 0.75 in. (9 × 2 cm); submerged leaves, 2.75–5 × 0.75–1.25 in. (7–13 × 2–3 cm). Leaf spread: Surface leaves, 8–16 in. (20–40 cm); submerged leaves, 8–12 in. (20–30 cm). Stem color: Petioles light green; peduncles light greenish yellow. No pubescence on peduncle or petiole.

COMMENTS. In its natural habitats, found growing in clear sandy streams. I do not see any commercial future for this member of the waterlily family, either for pools or aquaria.

CHAPTER 8

Lotus Species and Cultivars

Most experts now believe that, due to the great differences between rhizomes, flowers, and leaves of lotuses and waterlilies, lotuses should be in a family by themselves, Nelumbonaceae, rather than within the family Nymphaeaceae.

Nelumbo lutea is native to the eastern and central United States, and *N. nucifera* is native to Asia, the Philippines, north Australia, Egypt (probably introduced from India about 500 B.C.), and the Volga River delta at the Caspian Sea. It should be noted that the "blue lotus of the Nile" and the "blue lotus of India" are not lotuses but *Nymphaea caerulea* and *Nymphaea nouchali* (syn. *N. stellata*), respectively.

Nelumbo nucifera, the sacred lotus, is revered by Buddhists. Over 2500 years ago, Buddha is reputed to have risen up in the heart of a lotus bud out of the murky waters. (Tadpoles, frogs, and fish usually stir up the water around nelumbos.) Lotuses can frequently be seen growing in lagoons close to Buddhist temples.

Decorative lotus seed pods are used extensively in bouquets and wreaths. To my knowledge, all lotus tubers are edible. The tubers and seeds of *Nelumbo lutea* were commonly eaten by Native Americans, and lotus tubers and seeds are still a part of the Asian diet and are available in the United States from specialty markets. The leaves are also eaten or used to wrap various foods for baking. In some areas, particularly Taiwan and China, a very compact, thick-rhizomed variant of *Nelumbo nucifera* is a dietary staple. Commonly called the "edible lotus," its rhizomes are grown, cooked, and used very much like potatoes (Plate 275). In Taiwan particularly, this variant is planted extensively as a food crop, sometimes grown in tanks of pure rotted cow manure, and the short, thick tubers are a staple in

the diet. The flower is pink or white, but little else is known about this lotus. My experience has shown this plant to be difficult to flower; perhaps I have not found the right soil conditions. I do not know of anyone who has been successful in bringing it to flower in the United States.

In North America, lotuses do well over most of the United States and southern Canada as long as there is enough summer heat to bring plants into flower. Lotuses require two to three months of temperatures in the 75–85°F (24–29°C) range. Regions of the United States where lotuses do not perform at their very best are the very hot Southwest, with summer temperatures of 95–115°F (35–46°C), and the cooler mountainous regions of the Pacific Northwest with summer temperatures in the 60–70°F (16–21°C) range.

The summer weather in the British Isles and northern Europe is too cold for lotuses to bloom except in a greenhouse or conservatory. Blooms are produced, however, in the southern half of France, most of Spain, Portugal, Italy, Greece, and western and southern portions of the former Yugoslavia. In southern Australia and New Zealand there is not enough heat for lotuses to bloom except in greenhouses.

While there are many known variants of *Nelumbo nucifera*—in white, pink, red, and bicolor types and single and double blooms—only one variant of *N. lutea*, a natural hybrid, has been identified: *N. lutea* 'Yellow Bird'. It was discovered in 1975 at Lilypons Water Gardens, Buckeystown, Maryland. How all the variants of *N. nucifera* developed is not recorded and many are considered natural hybrids. Although historical details are scant, most of the original cultivars of *N. nucifera* are still being grown and sold today. Over the years aquatic nurseries have assigned trade names to these plants, but the names of decades ago are no longer commonly used in the United States. The names given in this chapter are those most widely used by Western growers. Sometime before 1911, Joseph Marliac hybridized *Nelumbo lutea* and came up with *N.* 'Flavescens', the first recorded *Nelumbo* cultivar in the West. After a void of nearly a century, magnificent new lotus cultivars are again being developed, and some of the most widely available ones are described in this chapter.

These plants, widely acclaimed by water garden experts, perform very well in areas where summer temperatures are in the 75–85°F (24–29°C) range. They should do well in southern Europe, though they are not yet available in many regions. Lotus cultivars grow and bloom quite freely at the Palm House, a conservatory for tropical and semitropical plants at Stapeley Water Gardens, Nantwich, Cheshire, England.

More than 300 types of lotus are grown in the People's Republic of China, but little information is available on these plants. A poster from the Nanjing Botanical Garden displayed at the Fourth Annual Waterlily Symposium, held in Harrogate, England, in 1988, featured a list of an astonishing 125 *Nelumbo nucifera* cultivars grown in their gardens. These likely include botanical varieties and hybrids, whether naturally occurring or the result of planned crosses. The same list, shown opposite, appears in Ni Xueming's *Lotus of China* (1987). Four names include the phrase "thousand petals," and I think one can presume these are cultivars with very double blooms. Only the name 'Red Lotus' coincides with a name used in the West, as red lotus is the common name for *Nelumbo* 'Pekinensis Rubra'. One cannot presume that these are the same plants, however.

All lotuses are day bloomers, with the exception of second- to fifth-day flowers of *Nelumbo* 'Night and Day'. Lotus flowers usually open quite early in the morning and close by midafternoon on the first day. Then they stay open continuously, night and day, for five or six days. The cultivar *N.* 'Momo Botan' is also an exception as older blooms frequently last for nearly a week, often without ever closing. The

blooms of *N.* 'Ben Gibson', a hybrid seedling of *N.* 'Momo Botan', also last several extra days. A "changeable" lotus means that its flower color gradually changes over a three-day period. For example, the flowers of *Nelumbo* 'Mrs. Perry D. Slocum' open dark pink and are a creamy yellow-flushed pink by the third day.

The following dwarf or semidwarf *Nelumbo* cultivars make excellent patio plants: 'Angel Wings', 'Baby Doll', 'Ben Gibson', 'Carolina Queen', 'Charles Thomas', 'Chawan Basu', 'Gregg Gibson', 'Momo Botan', and 'Momo Botan Minima'. Any of these is suitable for planting in a half barrel or comparable container. Round containers are preferable for lotuses because the tubers and runners can jam up in the corners of square planters.

If a wooden half barrel is chosen, line the barrel with black plastic and staple the plastic around the top edge of the barrel. This will prevent leaking as well as the leaching of any toxins from the barrel's former contents. The soil needs to be heavy enough so that it will not float, eliminating for use most of the potting soil mixes found at garden centers. Well-rotted and composted cow manure can be used in the bottom half if mixed one part composted manure to two or three parts topsoil. A heavy loam topsoil from the garden is excellent. Fill the container with soil to within 3–6 in. (8–15 cm) of the top. Fertilizer, such as the convenient tablet forms, can also be added to the soil at this time. Look for an N–P–K ratio of 10–10–5 or 10–14–8. Beware of too much nitrogen, which can burn the plants. I generally use four to six tablets. Finish the container planting by adding 1 in. (2.5 cm) of coarse sand or pea gravel and fill to the top with water.

A bushel (35-L) planter or large plastic pan filled in the same manner can also be used. Place bricks or blocks underneath the tub or barrel to elevate the planter to within 4–6 in. (10–15 cm) of the water's surface. I have used this bushel planter method, placed on top of a concrete block 8 × 8 × 16 in. (20 × 20 × 40 cm), with excellent results. Two or three fertilizer tablets per month during the early summer will provide sufficient fertilization. A sunny location is preferable yet partial shade is usually satisfactory.

For best performance of the large lotuses, plant them in large round containers 20–24 in. (50–60

Lotus (*Nelumbo*) cultivars grown in the People's Republic of China

'Autumn Sky'	'Fresh Flowers'	'Pink Rose'	'Welcoming Guests'
'Bai Wanwan'	'Gui Yang'	'Pink Thousand Petals'	'West Lake Pink'
'Bamboo Joint'	'Hainan'	'Pink Tip White Bowl'	'White Bloom'
'Beijing Pink Flower'	'Han Lotus'	'Qingmaojfe'	'White Bowl'
'Beijing White Flower'	'Hangxhou White Flower'	'Qinglianzi'	'White Cherry'
'Big Green'	'Hong Wanwan'	'Quianling White'	'White Flower Fujian'
'Big Leaf White'	'Hongcha Bowl'	'Red Bowl'	'White Hunan'
'Big Lying Dragon'	'Hunan'	'Red Coat'	'White Peony'
'Big Magpie'	'Hunanpao'	'Red Flower Fujian'	'White Sea'
'Big Red Coat'	'Hundred Petals'	'Red Lotus'	'White Small Gentleman'
'Big Square'	'Jia Yu'	'Red Peony'	'White Stamen Hunan'
'Big Versicolor'	'Jianzuihonghua'	'Red Thousand Petals'	'White Swan'
'Big White'	'Jiaopa'	'Red Tip'	'White Thousand Petals'
'Big White Flower'	'Jifei Lian'	'Sesame Lake'	'Winter Lotus'
'Birthday's Peach'	'June Early'	'Shanxi White'	'Wufei Lian'
'Buddha's Seat'	'Liberation Red'	'Shaoxing Pink'	'Wuxi White'
'Changing Face'	'Little Green'	'Shijiazhuang White'	'Xuanwuhu Red'
'Cherry'	'Long June Early'	'Shuhong Lian'	'Xiamen Bowl'
'Cherry Pink'	'Lushan Pink'	'Single Pink'	'Xiamaojie'
'Children Lotus'	'Lushan White'	'Sino-Japanese Friendship'	'Xiang Cheng'
'Chinese Antique Lotus'	'Lutouzhong'	'Small Magpie'	'Xiangtan Huaye'
'Chongchuantai'	'Maojie'	'Snow Lake'	'Yacheng'
'Chongshihua'	'Nehru Lotus'	'Sparrow'	'Yizhangging'
'Damaojie'	'Ohga Lotus'	'Sunyatsen Lotus'	'Yueyapao'
'Daqingkai'	'Paozi'	'Table Lotus'	'Yushan'
'Early Lotus'	'Phoenix'	'Taibai'	'Yuxiu'
'East Lake Pink'	'Pig Tail'	'Tardy Lotus'	'Zhaohongoha Bowl'
'East Mountain Red Coat'	'Pink Bowl'	'Tenghu Lian'	'Zhouou'
'Falling Flowers'	'Pink Double'	'Thousand Petals'	'Zuifei'
'Fenchuantai'	'Pink Double Palace'	'Two White Flowers'	
'Flower Lotus'	'Pink Jade'	'Wan Er Hong'	
'Fragrant Flower Lotus'	'Pink Lotus'	'Wax Gourd'	

Source: Ni Xueming, *Lotus of China* (1987)

cm) across and 10–12 in. (25–30 cm) deep. This size planter will usually allow for excellent growth and many blooms. See the Source for Plants and Equipment list at the end of the book for places to purchase specialty pools and tubs.

For the bottom half of large containers I recommend mixing one part very well rotted manure to two parts heavy loam or garden soil. Composted cow manure is usually available at garden centers. Other manures, such as sheep manure, are also suitable if well rotted. Use plain garden soil and ten to twelve fertilizer tablets in the top half. Add 1 in. (2.5 cm) of pea gravel to maintain the soil surface.

(If fish complement the pool, the gravel helps prevent them from disturbing the soil.) Add four to six more fertilizer tablets per month during the early summer. Refrain from fertilizing when new plant growth is plentiful because pushing the tablets into the soil may break the new sprouts.

Nearly all lotuses are hardy and can be planted when danger of freezing is over. (*Nelumbo nucifera* 'Waltzing Matilda', known as the "tropical lotus" from northwestern Australia, is an exception.) Plant them at the same time as hardy waterlilies. In Europe, lotuses can be grown in zone 10 and warmer parts of zones 9 and 8 where daytime temperatures reach 75°F (24°C) or above for long periods during the summer. Refer to the hardiness zone maps at the end of the book and follow this general planting timetable:

In North America		In Europe	
Zones 10–9	March through May	Zones 10–9	March–May
Zones 8–5	April–May	Zone 8	April–May
Zone 4	May	Zones 7–4	conservatory planting, where water can be heated to 75°F (24°C) or higher

In the descriptions of the *Nelumbo* species, varieties, and cultivars that follow, common names, if any, are given after the botanical name. Many lotus varieties and cultivars are of unclear or unknown parentage. As a result, some listed names have no botanical standing yet have widespread use among growers and the nursery trade.

Some categories used in describing waterlilies are inappropriate for lotuses. Throughout *Nelumbo*, flower shape (Figure 35) is quite similar, though petal count varies considerably; sepal color is quite similar as well throughout lotuses, though some sepals may have a red spot at the apex. Anthers vary only slightly from flower to flower, whether species

or cultivar. The leaves too are quite standard, either green or bluish green, and the few variations that do exist are mentioned. A sinus is not present, and the stems are hispid, with small spines. Therefore, categories used in describing *Nelumbo* differ from the waterlily descriptions and reflect the distinguishing characteristics of lotus.

Two new categories are added in this chapter: "Seed capsule color" and "Plant height," both of which vary considerably among lotus species and varieties. Seed capsule color can be helpful in identification. Dried capsules, all brown, are widely sought for use in bouquets and wreaths. "Plant height" reflects the measurement above water and can be used as a relative figure to determine whether the plant is dwarf, semidwarf, or full size.

I found it difficult to give a sepal count, as was done for the waterlilies, because it is frequently impossible to distinguish between the sepals and outer petals. "Petal number" therefore includes the tiny outside sepals.

Nelumbo 'Alba Grandiflora'
Asiatic lotus
Parentage unknown
PLATE 276
CHARACTERISTICS. Petal color: White (*RHS* 155A). Seed capsule color: Chartreuse; rim bright

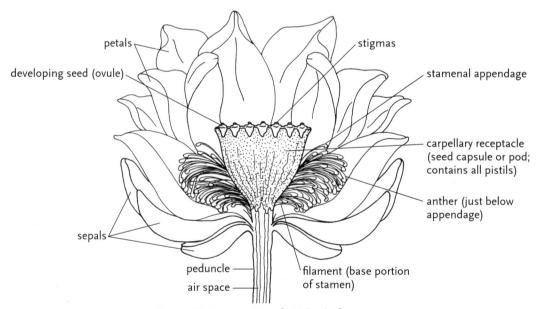

FIGURE 35. Cross section of a *Nelumbo* flower.

green then bluish green; stigmas bright yellow (*RHS* 149D; rim, 136D then 128A; stigmas, 6B). Flower size: 9–10 in. (23–25 cm). Fragrance: Slight in new blooms. Number of petals: 22. Leaf size: 16–23 in. (40–58 cm). Plant height: 4–6 ft. (1.2–1.8 m).

COMMENTS. Asiatic lotus has been the standard white lotus for many decades. The flower is beautiful, the plant is a fairly good bloomer, and the leaves are very impressive with their bluish green color and many convolutions around the edges. The flowers are frequently hidden among the leaves, however. I recommend this plant for medium and large pools.

Nelumbo 'Alba Striata'

Empress lotus
Parentage unknown
PLATES 277, 278

CHARACTERISTICS. Petal color: White; both sides of outer petals flushed pale green; prominent uneven red margins (*RHS* 155C; flush, 149D; margins, 71C). Seed capsule color: Yellow then chartreuse (*RHS* 8C then 145D). Flower size: 10–12 in. (25–30 cm). Fragrance: Pleasant in new flowers. Number of petals: 18 or 19. Leaf size: 19–20 in. (48–50 cm); in rich soil leaves may reach 28 in. (70 cm). Plant height: 4–5 ft. (1.2–1.5 m).

COMMENTS. The empress lotus is very beautiful and, generally, a moderate bloomer. A distinctive flower feature is the jagged red margin on the petals. I recommend it for medium and large pools.

Nelumbo 'Angel Wings'

Slocum 1984
Nelumbo nucifera 'Shirokunshi' × *N.* 'Pekinensis Rubra'
PLATE 279

CHARACTERISTICS. Petal color: White (*RHS* 155C). Seed capsule color: Greenish yellow then green, deeper green rim, prominent yellow stigma (*RHS* 1C then 150C; rim, 142A; stigma, 4A). Flower size: 8–10 in. (20–25 cm). Fragrance: Slight, anise-like. Number of petals: 20–24. Leaf size: 18–23 in. (45–58 cm). Plant height: 2–4 ft. (0.6–1.2 m).

COMMENTS. *Nelumbo* 'Angel Wings' is my favorite of the white lotuses. It is very free flowering and ideal for any size pool, including a tub or barrel garden. The especially beautiful leaves of this plant are highly convoluted, with many waves and a deep cup in the middle of each leaf. The petals roll inward at the edges, making a very pleasing effect. 'Angel Wings' holds U.S. plant patent 5799, issued in 1986 to Perry D. Slocum.

Nelumbo 'Baby Doll'

Slocum 1985
Seedling of *N.* 'Angel Wings'
PLATE 280

CHARACTERISTICS. Petal color: White (*RHS* 155C). Seed capsule color: Chartreuse then green (*RHS* 145C then 130C). Flower size: 4–6 in. (10–15 cm). Fragrance: Very slight. Number of petals: 21. Leaf size: 9–11 in. (23–28 cm). Plant height: 24–30 in. (60–75 cm).

COMMENTS. *Nelumbo* 'Baby Doll' is an ideal plant for a tub or barrel garden. Its tiny seed capsules are only 0.75 in. (2 cm) across, and the cup-shaped flowers are lovely. This lotus is very free flowering. A single plant may produce twelve blooms at a time under ideal conditions. Grown in a more restricted container, *N.* 'Baby Doll' produces less growth and fewer blooms—about twenty blooms total per season when grown in a 30-qt. (33-L) planter.

Nelumbo 'Ben Gibson'

Slocum 1988
Nelumbo nucifera 'Alba Plena' × *N.* 'Momo Botan'
PLATE 281

CHARACTERISTICS. Petal color: Tip pink, paling, veins red; base, pale yellow (*RHS* tip, 63B,C; veins, 63A; base, 4C). Seed capsule color: Yellow then green; about 7 yellow pistils project part way (*RHS* 11A; third day, 142A; pistils, 11A). Flower size: 5.5–6 in. (14–15 cm). Fragrance: Very pleasant. Number of petals: 96–115. Leaf size: 10–13 in. (25–33 cm), small for a lotus. Plant height: 3–4 ft. (0.9–1.2 m).

COMMENTS. *Nelumbo* 'Ben Gibson' is named after one of my twin stepsons, now owner of Perry's Water Gardens. This is an ideal plant for any size pool. A bicolor hybrid, it is very free blooming, quite double, and most pleasing. It has all the outstanding characteristics of *N.* 'Momo Botan', including the long-lasting bloom quality. Each flower lasts up to a week, and older flowers frequently stay open through the night. Blooms are usually held about 3 in. (7.5 cm) above the leaves. The red-veined new flowers are particularly striking.

Nelumbo 'Carolina Queen'

Slocum 1984

Nelumbo lutea × *N.* 'Pekinensis Rubra'

CHARACTERISTICS. Petal color: Pink, creamy yellow base (*RHS* 62B; base, 4A). Seed capsule color: Yellow then green (*RHS* 13A then 145D). Flower size: 9–11 in. (23–28 cm). Fragrance: Slight in new flowers. Number of petals: 21. Leaf size: 18–19 in. (45–48 cm); in rich soil leaves may reach 25 in. (63 cm). Plant height: 3–6 ft. (0.9–1.8 m).

COMMENTS. *Nelumbo* 'Carolina Queen' has two wonderful features—it is very free flowering and it holds its flowers very high, nearly 2 ft. (0.6 m) above the leaves. An excellent choice for pools of any size, it may be placed in a small container and used in small pools, where it will bloom for several years.

Nelumbo 'Charles Thomas'

Slocum 1984

Nelumbo nucifera 'Shirokunshi' × *N.* 'Pekinensis Rubra'

PLATE 282

CHARACTERISTICS. Petal color: Lavender-pink, paling (*RHS* 68B; second and third days, 68C). Seed capsule color: Yellow then chartreuse (*RHS* 13A then 140C). Flower size: 6–8 in. (15–20 cm). Fragrance: Very pleasant anise scent in new flowers. Number of petals: 21. Leaf size: 14–22 in. (35–56 cm). Plant height: 2–3 ft. (0.6–1 m).

COMMENTS. The first lotus ever to receive a U.S. plant patent (5794, to Perry D. Slocum, 1986), *Nelumbo* 'Charles Thomas' is named after the former president of Lilypons Water Gardens, Buckeystown, Maryland. The first-day flower is more pinkish; the lavender-pink flower color that appears on the second day is rare in lotuses. This plant may be placed in a small container—preferably, bushel size (35 L) or larger—and used in pools of any size. It is ideal for a small pool.

Nelumbo 'Chawan Basu'

Parentage unknown

PLATE 283

CHARACTERISTICS. Petal color: Ivory, deep pink margins and veins (*RHS* 11D; margins, 63C; veins, 63B). Seed capsule color: Center light green then deep chartreuse, deep yellow stigma; first day rimmed deep chartreuse (*RHS* center, 142C then 142A; stigma, 11A; rim, 142A). Flower size: 5–9 in. (13–23 cm). Fragrance: Delicate, pleasant in new flowers. Number of petals: 21 or 22. Leaf size: 14–17 in. (35–43 cm). Plant height: 2–3 ft. (0.6–1 m).

COMMENTS. The name *chawan basu* refers to a rice bowl. *Nelumbo* 'Chawan Basu', a dwarf cultivar with small tubers, is a beautiful plant for small or medium pools. Because of its small size, it is well suited to planting in containers. In hot summer climates flowers tend to wilt and in cool climates flowers will not develop. In temperate zones *N.* 'Chawan Basu' is generally a moderate bloomer.

Nelumbo 'First Lady'

Slocum 1995

Nelumbo 'Pekinensis Rubra' × *N.* 'Maggie Belle Slocum'

PLATE 284

CHARACTERISTICS. Petal color: Dark pink at first becoming paler with age. Flower size: 8–10 in. (20.3–25.5 cm). Seed capsule: Yellow with distinctive bright green rim. The yellow of capsule gradually turns all green as flower matures. Number of petals: About 23 counting small outside ones. Leaf size: 18–22 in. (45.7–56 cm). Plant height: Leaves are 3–4 ft. (0.9–1.2 m) above the water. Flowers are usually about 8 in. (20.3 cm) above the leaves.

COMMENTS. *Nelumbo* 'First Lady' is very similar to *N.* 'The President'. Here in North Carolina, *N.* 'First Lady' averages a little smaller flower, a little paler flower on first and second days, a shorter leaf and flower stems, and a distinctive seed capsule. I highly recommend it for any size pool.

Nelumbo 'Flavescens'

Marliac, year unknown

Nelumbo lutea is one parent

CHARACTERISTICS. Petal color: Pale yellow; red spot at base (*RHS* 11D; spot, 39B). Seed capsule color: Yellow then green (*RHS* 8C then 144C). Flower size: 6–8 in. (15–20 cm). Fragrance: Faint, aniselike. Number of petals: 22–25. Leaf size: 13–17 in. (33–43 cm). Plant height: 3–5 ft. (0.9–1.5 m).

COMMENTS. Leaves of *Nelumbo* 'Flavescens' have a conspicuous center red spot that complements the red spots on the petal bases. It produces smaller blooms than its parent, *N. lutea*. Because it is only a moderate bloomer and there are better pale yellow cultivars available, I recommend *N.* 'Flavescens' for the collector only.

Nelumbo 'Glen Gibson'

Slocum 1986

Nelumbo nucifera var. *caspicum* × *N. lutea*

CHARACTERISTICS. Petal color: Pink; base yellowish orange (*RHS* 63D; base, 3A). Seed capsule color: Yellow (*RHS* 10A). Flower size: 8–9 in. (20–23 cm). Fragrance: Slight. Number of petals: 19–20. Leaf size: 15–18 in. (38–45 cm). Plant height: 3 ft. (0.9 m).

COMMENTS. *Nelumbo* 'Glen Gibson' is named after one of my twin stepsons. It is an impressive lotus similar to *N.* 'Carolina Queen' yet of different parentage. Blooms are held very high, about 12 in. (30 cm) above the leaves. I recommend this lotus for pools of any size.

Nelumbo 'Gregg Gibson'

Slocum 1985

Seedling of *N.* 'Charles Thomas'

PLATE 285

CHARACTERISTICS. Petal color: Lavender-pink, paling (*RHS* 70C then 70D). Seed capsule color: Pale chartreuse then darker green (*RHS* 149C,D; third day, 149A). Flower size: 6.5–7 in. (16–18 cm). Fragrance: Pleasant. Number of petals: 22. Leaf size: 13 in. (33 cm). Plant height: 24 in. (60 cm).

COMMENTS. *Nelumbo* 'Gregg Gibson', a dwarf cultivar, is an excellent lotus of unusual color suitable for any size pool. A unique flower feature is the way the inner petals curve, giving a very striking effect. It is named for my grandson.

Nelumbo 'Lavender Lady'

Slocum 1987

Nelumbo 'Charles Thomas' × *N.* 'Shiroman'

PLATE 286

CHARACTERISTICS. Petal color: Petals are cream at base; the rest rich pink taking on a lavender shade with age as petals become paler. Seed capsule: Yellow turning green. Flower size: 11 in. (28 cm). Fragrance: Slight, pleasant. Number of petals: About 25. Leaf size: About 26 in. (71 cm). Plant height: 5–6 ft. (1.5–1.8 m) above water. Leaf height: About 1 ft. (0.3 m) shorter than blooms, which is a wonderful feature as this means that the flowers are held far above leaves and easily visible.

COMMENTS. *Nelumbo* 'Lavender Lady' is a favorite lotus with visitors to Perry's Water Gardens. Due to the large lavender pink blooms with curled petals held high above the pads, the photographers love it. I recommend it for medium and large pools.

Nelumbo 'Linda'

Slocum 1988

Seedling of *N.* 'Mrs. Perry D. Slocum'

PLATE 287

CHARACTERISTICS. Petal color: Deep pink, outer petals flushed yellow, some middle petals flushed yellow (*RHS* 61D; flush, 3C). Seed capsule color: Yellow (*RHS* 8B). Flower size: 7–9 in. (18–23 cm). Fragrance: Very pleasant. Number of petals: 48–52. Leaf size: 18 in. (45 cm). Plant height: 4–5 ft. (1.2–1.5 m).

COMMENTS. *Nelumbo* 'Linda' was named after my stepdaughter. It is unique among lotuses for its pleasing combination of pink and yellow on both inner and outer petals. It is a moderate bloomer, but the blooms are quite double. I recommend this plant for pools of any size.

Nelumbo 'Little Tom Thumb'

An import from China

Parentage unknown

PLATE 288

CHARACTERISTICS. Petal color: First day, deep pink; second day, pink with some creamy white developing in the center of flower; third day, outer petals medium pink with creamy white center petals. On second and third days, greenish petals appear in center. Usually, there are a few green projections on top of the pistils in center. Fragrance: Slight, pleasant. Number of petals: about 40. Seed capsule: Yellow turning green as flower ages. Flower size: 4–5 in. (10–12.5 cm). Leaf size: 5–6.5 in. (12.5–16.5 cm). Plant height: 12–15 in. (30–38 cm).

COMMENTS. *Nelumbo* 'Little Tom Thumb' is

unique among dwarf lotuses with blooms nearly as large as its leaves. Also, there are three colors, pink, creamy white and green, in each flower. I recommend this lovely dwarf lotus for the small pool, tub garden, or even a patio pool that gets some sunshine.

Nelumbo 'Louise Slocum'
Slocum 2001
Nelumbo lutea × N. 'Sweetheart'
PLATES 289–291

CHARACTERISTICS. Petal color: Innermost, pale yellow with a few splashes of green, deep yellow base; middle, pale yellow; outermost, greenish. Seed capsule: Yellow turning to green. Flower size: 8–9 in. (20–23 cm). Slight, pleasant fragrance. Number of petals: 20. Leaf size: 11–13 in. (28–33 cm). Leaf height: 15–18 in. (38–46 cm). Flower height above the water: 24–28 in. (61–71 cm).

COMMENTS. This lotus is named after my wife, Louise. After growing *Nelumbo* 'Louise Slocum' for two years here in North Carolina, I find that it blooms best when planted in a container and placed under about 10–12 in. (20.5–30 cm) of water. This lotus is very impressive with its numerous blooms held high above the leaves. I highly recommend it for any size pool, although it is ideal for the small pool due to its restricted leaf growth and large blooms.

Nelumbo lutea (Willdenow) Persoon
Syn. *Nelumbo pentapetala* (Walter) Fernald
American yellow lotus, water chinquapin
Native to eastern and central United States
PLATE 292

CHARACTERISTICS. Petal color: Rich yellow, slightly lighter tips (*RHS* 3A; tips, 3C). Seed capsule color: Yellow then green (*RHS* 9A then 144D). Flower size: 7–11 in. (18–28 cm). Fragrance: Slight. Number of petals: 22–25. Leaf size: 13–17 in. (33–43 cm); in rich soil leaves may reach 24 in. (60 cm). Plant height: 2.5–5 ft. (0.8–1.5 m).

COMMENTS. *Nymphaea lutea*, the lotus species native to the United States, is a good bloomer that usually holds its flowers 10 in. (25 cm) above its leaves. This plant is suitable for any size pool. American yellow lotus, as this plant is commonly called, has been used extensively in hybridizing and

is the parent of the *Nelumbo* cultivars 'Carolina Queen', 'Glen Gibson', 'Mrs. Perry D. Slocum', 'Patricia Garrett', 'Perry's Giant Sunburst', 'Strawberry Blonde', and 'The Queen', among others.

Nelumbo lutea 'Yellow Bird'
PLATE 293

COMMENTS. This seedling or mutation of the American yellow lotus appeared in a pond at Lilypons Water Gardens, Buckeystown, Maryland, in 1975. 'Yellow Bird' has much broader petals and more rounded tips than *N. lutea*. As it has been only a moderate bloomer for me, I recommend it only for the collector or the owner of a large pool.

Nelumbo 'Maggie Belle Slocum'
Slocum 1984
Nelumbo nucifera 'Shirokunshi' × N. 'Pekinensis Rubra'
PLATE 294

CHARACTERISTICS. Petal color: Very rich, deep lavender-pink, paling; base pale yellow (*RHS* 65A and 68B then 62C; base, 11C). Seed capsule color: Yellow then chartreuse; rim chartreuse then dark green (*RHS* 2A then 149C; rim, 149D then 149C). Flower size: 10–12 in. (25–30 cm). Fragrance: Delightful anise scent, first two days. Number of petals: 22. Leaf size: 20–25 in. (50–63 cm). Plant height: 4–5 ft. (1.2–1.5 m).

COMMENTS. *Nelumbo* 'Maggie Belle Slocum', a hybrid of which I am especially proud, was named after my second wife. It is one of the most striking lotuses ever developed and only the second lotus ever patented in the United States (5798, in 1986). The huge lavender-pink flowers are truly splendid. For the most impressive display, this lotus should be planted in a large container and placed under 3–6 in. (8–15 cm) of water. I highly recommend it for medium or large pools.

Nelumbo 'Momo Botan'
Parentage unknown
PLATE 295

CHARACTERISTICS. Petal color: Very deep rosy pink, yellow toward base (*RHS* 66D; base, 11B). Seed capsule color: Light green then yellow; projecting pistils and stigmas remain yellow (*RHS* 145D then 7A; pistils and stigmas, 12A). Flower size: 5–6 in. (13–15 cm). Fragrance: Strong, pleasant. Number of petals: 106–118. Leaf size: 12–15 in. (30–38 cm). Plant height: 2–4 ft. (0.6–1.2 m).

COMMENTS. *Nelumbo* 'Momo Botan' flowers, which resemble large, deep pink peonies, have some wonderful features. Flowers are open for several days longer than those of most lotuses, and they stay open quite late in the day. While first-day flowers close in midafternoon, second-day flowers stay open until after 6:00 p.m., and older flowers may remain open all night. The plant also has an exceptionally long bloom season. Seed capsules are very small and pretty. Though this lotus is ideal for pools of every size, I especially recommend it for small pools. 'Momo Botan' will bloom in a tub garden and makes an excellent patio plant when placed by itself in a half barrel.

Nelumbo 'Momo Botan Minima'

Miniature *N.* 'Momo Botan'

Parentage unknown

CHARACTERISTICS. Petal color: Deep pink (*RHS* 65A). Seed capsule color: Chartreuse; projecting pistils yellow (*RHS* 149C; pistils, 12A). Flower size: 3–4 in. (8–10 cm). Fragrance: Delightful. Number of petals: 90–110. Leaf size: 5–12 in. (13–30 cm). Plant height: 2–3 ft. (0.6–0.9 m).

COMMENTS. As its name indicates, this cultivar is a smaller version of *Nelumbo* 'Momo Botan'. It has all the fine features of that lotus, including long-lasting blooms that stay open late in the day and a long flowering season. It is ideal for the tub garden or the small pool. In general, it blooms quite well when planted in a 16-qt. (15-L) container and submerged in a pool under 3–4 in. (8–10 cm) of water.

Nelumbo 'Mrs. Perry D. Slocum'

Slocum 1964

Nelumbo lutea × *N.* 'Rosea Plena'

PLATE 296

CHARACTERISTICS. Petal color: First day pink, flushed yellow; second day pink and yellow; third day cream, flushed pink (*RHS* first day, 62A; flush, 3D; second day, 38B, 8B, and 10C; third day, 10B,C; flush, 8D). Seed capsule color: Yellow then green (*RHS* 11A then 139D). Flower size: 9–12 in. (23–30 cm). Fragrance: Strong anise scent, very pleasant. Number of petals: 86. Leaf size: 18–23 in. (45–58 cm). Plant height: 4–5 ft. (1.2–1.5 m).

COMMENTS. *Nelumbo* 'Mrs. Perry D. Slocum', a changeable pink-and-yellow bicolor *Nelumbo*, is reminiscent of the peace rose in flower color. This cultivar is especially free flowering, and one plant may produce three differently colored flowers at the same time. For the most striking display it should be planted in a rounded container (an Aqualite pool is ideal) about 4 × 3 × 1 ft. (1.2 × 0.9 × 0.3 m) and placed under 3–6 in. (8–15 cm) of water. This cultivar will bloom in a tub or barrel garden, but I strongly recommend it for medium or large pools.

Nelumbo 'Night and Day'

Slocum 1996

Nelumbo 'Pekinensis Rubra' × *N.* 'Momo Botan'

PLATE 297

CHARACTERISTICS. Petal color: Dark to medium pink with cream or white base. There are frequently red stripes in the petals running the full length of the pink. Flower size: 7–7.5 in. (17.7–19 cm). Seed capsule: Yellow turning to chartreuse. Fragrance: Very slight. Number of petals: 74–83 plus 17 or 18 staminodes. Some petals are joined together at bottom half. Leaf size: About 18 in. (45 cm). Height above water: 3.5–5 ft. (1–1.5 m).

COMMENTS. *Nelumbo* 'Night and Day' is unique in that after the first day, it stays open night and day without closing, which makes it ideal to cut and bring into the house when one has evening company. In fact, with its extra stout stems, it makes the finest lotus cut flower I know and blooms will last nearly a week fully open in the house. Two negative aspects are that the first few blooms are frequently below the leaves, and the blooms should be bigger in relation to the leaves. However, after the first few blooms, they do appear above the leaves and the flowers are very plentiful. I highly recommend *N.* 'Night and Day' for medium and large pools. I am growing this in a 5-ft. (1.5-m) liner bog garden next to my house in North Carolina. It only has about 6 in. (15.2 cm) of water over it but does very well under these conditions. This double lotus does not droop its blooms after a storm, as several other double lotuses do.

Nelumbo 'Nikki Gibson'

Slocum 1988
Seedling of N. 'Mrs. Perry D. Slocum'
PLATE 298

CHARACTERISTICS. Petal color: Tips pink; midsection whitish yellow; base yellow (*RHS* tips, 66D; midsection, 11D; base, 10B). Seed capsule color: Yellow, rimmed green, then all green (*RHS* 7C; rim, 144B; then all 144B). Flower size: 10–12 in. (25–30 cm). Fragrance: Very pleasant. Number of petals: 20. Leaf size: 18–20 in. (45–50 cm). Plant height: 5 ft. (1.5 m).

COMMENTS. *Nelumbo* 'Nikki Gibson', a true tricolor, is one of the choicest single lotuses. This is a changeable lotus. Blooms are initially cup-shaped and deep pink, then open out flat on the second day as pink and yellow, and on the third day as mostly yellow. All are held high above the leaves. This cultivar is named for my granddaughter. I recommend this plant for medium and large water gardens.

Nelumbo nucifera Gaertner

Syn. *Nelumbo speciosa* Willdenow
Hindu lotus, Egyptian lotus, sacred lotus, speciosa
Native to India, Egypt, China, Japan, the Philippines,
    northern Australia, Thailand, Vietnam, and the
    Volga River delta at the Caspian Sea
PLATE 299

CHARACTERISTICS. Petal color: Deep pink, paling; base one-third creamy yellow, paling (*RHS* 49A then 49C; base, 8B then 8D). Seed capsule color: Yellow then chartreuse (*RHS* 7A then 149D). Flower size: 9–12 in. (23–30 cm). Fragrance: Pleasant, especially noticeable on first and second days. Number of petals: 24. Leaf size: 20–36 in. (50–90 cm). Plant height: 3–5 ft. (0.9–1.5 m).

COMMENTS. This species of lotus, the Hindu lotus, was called the Egyptian lotus for a long time as it also grows along the Nile River and was probably imported to Egypt from India. The Hindu lotus can now be found growing wild throughout Asia. For many years it was the best-selling lotus in the United States, though the cultivar *Nelumbo* 'Mrs. Perry D. Slocum' has now achieved this distinction. This especially beautiful lotus is worthy of a place in pools of every size.

Nelumbo nucifera var. caspicum Fischer

Russian lotus, red Russian lotus
Native to the Volga River delta at the Caspian Sea
PLATE 300

CHARACTERISTICS. The pinkish red flowers are large and quite similar to the cultivar *Nelumbo* 'Pekinensis Rubra' (see description) except that it has a slightly larger bloom and a smaller seed capsule in the flower stage. The flowers average 22 petals and are only slightly fragrant. Leaves average 20–24 in. (50–60 cm) in diameter and are held 3–5 ft. (0.9–1.5 m) above the water.

COMMENTS. This very outstanding lotus is an import from southern Russia by Dr. Creech, former director of the National Arboretum in Washington, D.C. It is worthy of a place in every pool.

Nelumbo nucifera var. rosea

Rose lotus
Native to China and Japan
PLATE 301

CHARACTERISTICS. The flowers, with a rich anise fragrance, are rose-pink with a yellow center and are 8–10 in. (20–25 cm) in diameter. Leaves are 18–20 in. (45–50 cm) in diameter and are held 4–5 ft. (1.2–1.5 m) above the water. The first-day flower somewhat resembles a full rose.

COMMENTS. This variety is similar in many ways to the cultivar *Nelumbo* 'Rosea Plena' (see description) except that *N. nucifera* var. *rosea* develops a single flower, whereas *N.* 'Rosea Plena' forms a double flower. Flowers also closely resemble those of *N. nucifera*, yet those of variety *rosea* are more of a salmon-pink color. I recommend this variety for any size pool.

Nelumbo nucifera 'Alba Plena'

Shiroman lotus
Native to China and Japan
PLATE 302

CHARACTERISTICS. The flowers are creamy white and very double, with 115–120 petals. The blooms are large, 10 in. (25 cm) across, with only a slight fragrance, if any. Leaves average 25 in. (63 cm) in diameter and grow 3–5 ft. (0.9–1.5 m) in height.

COMMENTS. This lotus needs a large planter

and is a fine plant for medium or large pools. For outstanding performance, plant it under 6–8 in. (15–20 cm) of water.

Nelumbo nucifera 'Japanese Double White'

Native to Japan

CHARACTERISTICS. The fragrant white flowers are semidouble. With 52 petals, blooms are more double than most lotuses and have great flower form, displaying an attractive flower center. Leaves are average size, 18–23 in. (45–58 cm), and held 5–6 ft. (1.5–1.8 m) above the water.

COMMENTS. This hybrid was found growing in the Japanese Garden section of the Missouri Botanical Garden. Flowers are occasionally hidden among the leaves. I recommend it for medium or large pools.

Nelumbo nucifera 'Paleface'

Native to northern Australia

CHARACTERISTICS. The fragrant flower is mostly white with pink on the tips of the petals. The flowers are 9–10 in. (23–25 cm) in diameter and are borne quite freely. The leaves average 20 in. (50 cm) and are held 5 ft. (1.5 m) above the water.

COMMENTS. Its unique color pattern sets *Nelumbo* 'Paleface' apart from other lotuses. The cultivar *N.* 'Chawan Basu' (see description), with its pink veins and petal edges, is the closest in color combination. I recommend *N.* 'Paleface' for any size pool.

Nelumbo nucifera 'Shirokunshi'

Tulip lotus
Native to Japan
PLATE 303

CHARACTERISTICS. This slightly fragrant dwarf white lotus develops 7–8 in. (18–20 cm) flowers that are quite single, averaging 16 petals. The 12–18 in. (30–45 cm) leaves are raised only 18–30 in. (45–75 cm) above the water.

COMMENTS. This is a very free-blooming plant ideal for small or medium pools. By planting it in a 30–32 qt. (33–35 L) container and placing it in the pool under 3–6 in. (8–15 cm) of water, one can usually expect several blooms the first season. Consider it, also, for planting in a half barrel on the patio.

Nelumbo nucifera 'Waltzing Matilda'

The tropical lotus
Native to northwestern Australia
PLATE 304

CHARACTERISTICS. Outer three-fourths of the petal is a very deep pink turning to medium pink with age; basal one-fourth is a light yellow. Very fragrant flower is 8–10 in. (20–25 cm) in diameter with 21 petals on the average. Leaves are 24 in. (60 cm) in diameter and held 4–5 ft. (1.2–1.5 m) above the water. Inner petals are uniquely curled, giving the flower a very special beauty. New leaves are unusual in that they are red or reddish purple when they first rise out of water, later turning to green. A unique feature of the leaves is the indentations that appear on opposite sides of each leaf. I have not observed these indentations in any other lotus species or cultivar.

COMMENTS. I grew this cultivar for one full season in zone 6b and a negative feature showed up that may prevent it from becoming popular: the plant does not develop tubers like most lotuses but has only runners, which do not survive the winter outside in North Carolina. However, once it starts to bloom, it gives a great abundance of flowers over a long period where temperatures are 75°F (24°C) or above. Moving the plant into warm quarters such as a greenhouse in autumn in the north would help it to survive. If one can find it, I recommend it for any size pool.

Nelumbo 'Patricia Garrett'

Slocum 1988
Nelumbo 'Maggie Belle Slocum' × *N. lutea*
PLATE 305

CHARACTERISTICS. Petal color: Pink, slightly darker tips, apricot-yellow center (*RHS* 49B; tips, 49A; center, 18B,C). Seed capsule color: Yellow then lime green (*RHS* 10A then 142A). Flower size: 7–10 in. (18–25 cm). Fragrance: Delightful. Number of petals: 22. Leaf size: 17 in. (43 cm). Plant height: 4–5 ft. (1.2–1.5 m).

COMMENTS. *Nelumbo* 'Patricia Garrett', with its lovely pink-and-yellow petal combination, has one of the most beautiful blooms of all the single lotuses. The flowers are held very high, up to 30 in. (75 cm) above the leaves. I highly recommend this lotus, which was named after my stepdaughter, for medium and large pools.

Nelumbo 'Pekinensis Rubra'

Red lotus
Parentage unknown
PLATES 306–309

CHARACTERISTICS. Petal color: Rosy red then deep pink (*RHS* 64C then 64D). Seed capsule color: Yellow; green rim developing in older flowers (*RHS* 6A; rim, 145D). Flower size: 8–12 in. (20–30 cm). Fragrance: Slight. Number of petals: 16 or 17. Leaf size: 20–24 in. (50–60 cm). Plant height: 4–6 ft. (1.2–1.8 m).

COMMENTS. *Nelumbo* 'Pekinensis Rubra' is a splendid plant. It is quite similar to *N. nucifera* var. *caspicum*, though flowers of *N.* 'Pekinensis Rubra' are slightly deeper in color and a bit smaller and plants develop a much larger seed capsule. It is free blooming and may be grown in any size pool.

Nelumbo 'Perry's Double Red Lotus'

Perry's Water Gardens 1995
Volunteer, parents probably *N.* 'Pekinensis Rubra' ×
    N. 'Momo Botan'
PLATE 310

CHARACTERISTICS. Petal color: A glowing red that is very impressive on overcast days, becoming pink as flower ages. Seed capsule: Yellow turning to green and then brown. Flower size: 5–6 in. (12.5–15 cm). Fragrance: Pleasant. Number of petals: More than 60. Leaf size: 12–15 in. (30–38 cm). Leaf height: 3–5 ft. (0.9–1.5 m). Flower height: Usually blooms are held above the leaves but, in early season, sometimes flowers are nestled among the leaves.

COMMENTS. *Nelumbo* 'Perry's Double Red Lotus' is a beautiful semidwarf that fills a void in the smaller lotus group. I highly recommend it for any size pool but especially for small pools. Plant it in a bushel (35-L) or larger container.

Nelumbo 'Perry's Giant Sunburst'

Slocum 1987
Nelumbo nucifera 'Alba Plena' × *N. lutea*
PLATE 311

CHARACTERISTICS. Petal color: Cream; outer petals pale green (*RHS* 1D; outer, 149D). Seed-capsule color: Yellow then lime-yellow; green rim then all-green capsule (*RHS* 11A then 149D; rim, 149D). Flower size: 10–13.5 in. (25–34 cm). Fragrance: Pleasant. Number of petals: 24 or 25. Leaf size: 16–18 in. (40–45 cm). Plant height: 4.5–5.5 ft. (1.4–1.7 m).

COMMENTS. The huge flowers of *Nelumbo* 'Perry's Giant Sunburst' create a magnificent display. A rich, creamy yellow, they are raised high above the leaves. This lotus is very free flowering and is an excellent choice for pools of any size.

Nelumbo 'Perry's Super Star'

Slocum 1988
Seedling of *N.* 'Mrs. Perry D. Slocum'
PLATES 312–314

CHARACTERISTICS. Petal color: First day, rich pink; second day, mostly yellow and pink; third day, mostly cream with some pink tips; 6–8 center petals (petaloids) tipped green, paling slightly (*RHS* 63D then 11C then 11D; green tips, 149C and 142A then 142C; pink tips, 63D then 65C). Seed capsule color: Yellow then chartreuse (*RHS* 11A then 142A). Flower size: 7–8 in. (18–20 cm). Fragrance: Very sweet, aniselike. Number of petals: 75, including petaloids. Leaf size: 17–21 in. (43–53 cm). Plant height: 3–4 ft. (0.9–1.2 m).

COMMENTS. The flower color changes dramatically over three days, and the blooms are beautiful in each phase. The six to eight green-tipped petals at the flower center make this lotus unique. Known as petaloids (or staminodes), these smaller petals arise near the center of double flowers, with an anther at the tip. This free-blooming cultivar is an excellent choice for pools of any size.

Nelumbo 'Pink and Yellow'

An import from China
Parentage unknown
PLATE 315

CHARACTERISTICS. Petal color: Inner third of each petal is medium yellow; middle third, light yellow (cream); outer third, pink. Mostly light yellow by third day with pink edging around petals. Seed capsule: Yellow turning chartreuse. Flower size: 8 in. (20.3 cm). Fragrance: Slight pleasant fragrance.

Number of petals: 20–23. Leaf size: 10.5 in. (26.6 cm). Plant height: 2–3 ft. (0.6–0.9 m).

COMMENTS. Anyone who has ever had this lotus will agree that this is one of the really great lotuses. It is usually the first to bloom each spring, and the blooms are produced in huge quantities. I recommend this lotus for any size pool, especially smaller ones.

Nelumbo 'Rosea Plena'

Double rose lotus
Parentage unknown
PLATE 316

CHARACTERISTICS. Petal color: Very deep rose-pink, yellowing toward base (RHS 58D; base, 11C). Seed capsule color: Yellow then green (RHS 6C then 149D). Flower size: 10–13 in. (25–33 cm). Fragrance: None. Number of petals: 89–102, including petaloids. Leaf size: 18–20 in. (45–50 cm). Plant height: 4–5 ft. (1.2–1.5 m); in rich soil plants may reach 6 ft. (1.8 m).

COMMENTS. The double rose lotus is a very free-flowering plant. With its huge, richly colored double blooms it is among the most striking of lotus cultivars. A distinguishing feature is the small seed capsule, only 1 in. (2.5 cm) across. I highly recommend this impressive lotus for medium and large pools.

Nelumbo 'Sharon'

Slocum 1987
Nelumbo nucifera 'Alba Plena' × N. 'Momo Botan'
PLATE 317

CHARACTERISTICS. Petal color: Pink, deepening; pink veins (RHS 64D then 65A,B; veins, 64C). Seed capsule color: Yellow; rim pale green (RHS 11A; rim, 1C). Flower size: 8 in. (20 cm). Fragrance: Slight. Number of petals: 80, including petaloids. Leaf size: 12–14 in. (30–35 cm). Plant height: 4 ft. (1.2 m).

COMMENTS. Nelumbo 'Sharon', with its double blossoms and the free-blooming habit of N. 'Momo Botan', is a lotus I recommend highly for pools of any size. It resembles 'Momo Botan' somewhat but is taller with larger flowers. It is named after my oldest daughter, who worked with lotuses and waterlilies for many years at the Slocum Water Gardens.

Nelumbo 'Strawberry Blonde'

Perry's Water Gardens 1996
Natural hybrid between N. lutea × N. 'Momo Botan'
PLATE 318–320

CHARACTERISTICS. Petal color: This is a changeable lotus-opening a deep pink and changing to yellow with pink on tips of petals. By second day deep yellow has nearly taken over the base half of each petal except the outer most petals, which are creamy white with flush of pale green and pink. On the third day, yellow predominates with pink petal tips. Seed capsule: Yellow for several days becoming chartreuse. Flower size: 9–10 in. (23–25 cm). Fragrance: Pleasant on new blooms. Number of petals: 83–86 plus 20–27 staminodes. Leaf size: 18–20 in. (46–51 cm). Leaf height above the water: 3–5 ft. (0.9–1.5 m). Flower height above the leaves: 6–8 in. (15–20 cm).

COMMENTS. Nelumbo 'Strawberry Blonde' has a lot of similarity to N. 'Mrs. Perry D. Slocum'. However, it appears that N. 'Strawberry Blonde' has a weaker stem as I find a lot of the flowers are hanging their blooms, especially after a storm. Another minus is that the first blooms are frequently nestled among the leaves. On the positive side, it is a very free bloomer and it is a changeable. One can have different colored flowers in the bed at the same time. I recommend it for medium or large pools and also the collector.

Nelumbo 'Suzanne'

Slocum 1988
Seedling of N. 'Alba Striata'
PLATE 321

CHARACTERISTICS. Petal color: Medium pink, darker pink stripes (RHS 38C; stripes, 62A). Seed capsule color: Yellow, green rim; by third day, rim color develops throughout (RHS 5A; rim, 150C). Flower size: 6–8 in. (15–20 cm). Fragrance: Delightful. Number of petals: 22. Leaf size: 15–20 in. (38–50 cm). Plant height: 4–5 ft. (1.2–1.5 m).

COMMENTS. Flowers of Nelumbo. 'Suzanne' are a rare combination of medium pink petals overlaid with darker stripes, and the effect is very pleasing. I recommend it for pools of any size. It is named for my youngest daughter, who worked with lotuses and waterlilies for many years at the Slocum Water Gardens.

Nelumbo 'Sweetheart'

An import from China

Parentage unknown

PLATE 322

CHARACTERISTICS. Petal color: White with several green or greenish petals near center of bloom. Flower size: 4.5–5 in. (11.5–12.7 cm). Seed capsule: Yellowish green with 8–15 prominent green protuberances on top. Fragrance: Slight. Number of petals: 110–178, plus 5–18 staminodes. Leaf size: About 10 in. (25.5 cm) with wavy edges. Plant height: 2.5 ft. (0.7 m). Flower height: 3 ft. (0.9 m).

COMMENTS. *Nelumbo* 'Sweetheart' is a free flowering semidwarf that is very double. In fact, I do not know of another lotus with as many petals. One bad feature, however, is that nearly all of its first blooms are nestled among the leaves. I recommend it for any size pool, especially the smaller ones.

Nelumbo 'The President'

Slocum 1994

Nelumbo 'Maggie Belle Slocum' × *N.* 'Pekinensis Rubra'

PLATE 323

CHARACTERISTICS. Petal color: Very dark red when it first opens, growing paler with age. Flower size: About 11 in. (28 cm). Seed capsule: Yellow turning green. Fragrance: Slight, aniselike. Number of petals: 24 or 25, counting all smaller outside ones. Leaf size: About 24 in. (61 cm). Plant height: Leaves 3–4 ft. (0.9–1.2 m) above the water. Flowers are raised about 1 ft. (30 cm) above the leaves. Very free flowering.

COMMENTS. With its striking, glowing red first day blooms, the *Nelumbo* 'The President' bed at the entrance to Perry's Water Gardens really stops the traffic. I highly recommend it for medium and large pools.

Nelumbo 'The Queen'

Slocum 1984

Nelumbo 'Alba Striata' × *N. lutea*

CHARACTERISTICS. Petal color: Cream; outer petals green (*RHS* 4D; outer, 139D). Seed capsule color: Yellow then green (*RHS* 11A then 139D). Flower size: 10 in. (25 cm). Fragrance: Very pleasant in first-day flower. Number of petals: 21. Leaf size: 14–23 in. (35–58 cm). Plant height: 4–5 ft. (1.2–1.5 m).

COMMENTS. *Nelumbo* 'The Queen' is a hybrid developed at Perry's Water Gardens in North Carolina. The blooms are held unusually high, 16–18 in. (40–45 cm) above the leaves. Its very free-blooming habit makes this lotus a fine choice for pools of any size.

USDA Hardiness Zone Map

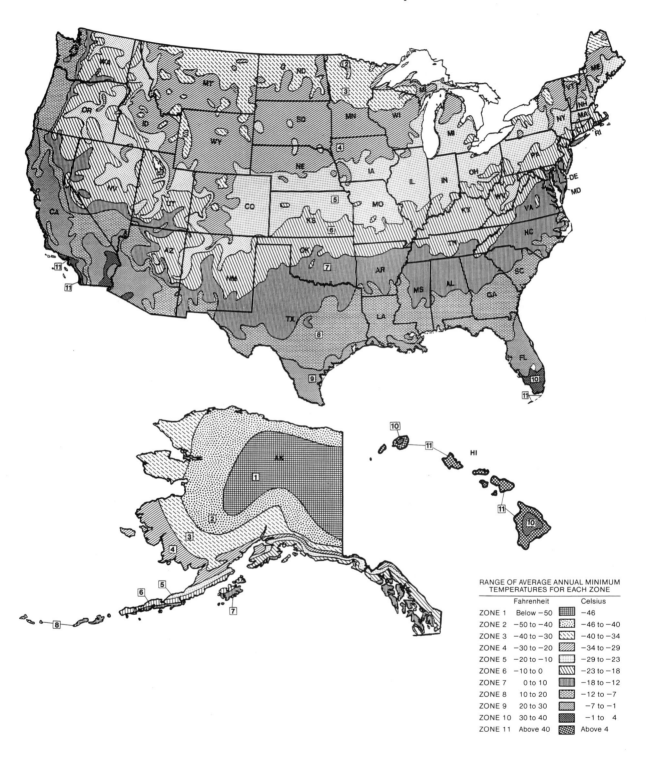

RANGE OF AVERAGE ANNUAL MINIMUM
TEMPERATURES FOR EACH ZONE

	Fahrenheit	Celsius
ZONE 1	Below −50	−46
ZONE 2	−50 to −40	−46 to −40
ZONE 3	−40 to −30	−40 to −34
ZONE 4	−30 to −20	−34 to −29
ZONE 5	−20 to −10	−29 to −23
ZONE 6	−10 to 0	−23 to −18
ZONE 7	0 to 10	−18 to −12
ZONE 8	10 to 20	−12 to −7
ZONE 9	20 to 30	−7 to −1
ZONE 10	30 to 40	−1 to 4
ZONE 11	Above 40	Above 4

European Hardiness Zone Map

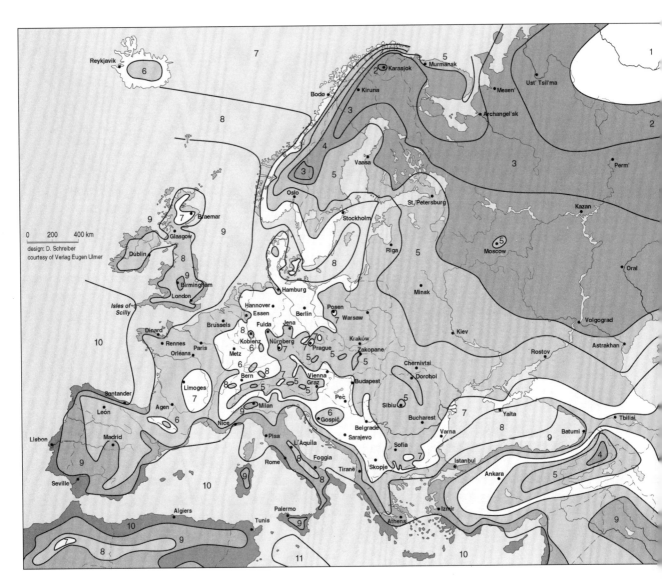

AVERAGE ANNUAL MINIMUM TEMPERATURE

Temperature (°C)	Zone	Temperature (°F)
-45.6 and Below	1	Below -50
-45.5 to -40.0	2	-50 to -40
-40.0 to -34.5	3	-40 to -30
-34.4 to -28.9	4	-30 to -20
-28.8 to -23.4	5	-20 to -10
-23.3 to -17.8	6	-10 to 0
-17.7 to -12.3	7	0 to 10
-12.2 to -6.7	8	10 to 20
-6.6 to -1.2	9	20 to 30
-1.1 to 4.4	10	30 to 40
4.5 and Above	11	40 and Above

Sources for Plants and Equipment

The businesses listed here are likely sources of water gardening supplies. All offer products at retail (unless otherwise noted) in the following categories: plants; fish; pools; biological filters ("filters"); and pumps, fountains, and other equipment ("pumps").

United States

Aloha Lilies
123 N. Regency Place
Tucson, AZ 85711
Tel. (520) 327-2919
plants

American Aquatic Gardens
621 Elysian Fields
New Orleans, LA 70117
Tel. (504) 944-0410
plants

Aqua-Bacta-Aid
Water Quality Science International
P.O. Box 552
Bolivar, MO 65613
Tel. (800) 558-9442
www.wqsii.com
filters • wholesale

Aqualite Pool Co.
430 Bedford Street
Whitman, MA 02382
Tel. (617) 447-4711
pools

Aquatic Gardens and Koi Co.
Box 57, Highway 537
Jobstown, NJ 08041
Tel. (800) 822-5459
www.aquaticgardensandkoico.com
plants, fish, filters • wholesale and retail

Beckett Corporation
5931 Campus Circle Drive W.
Irving, TX 75063
Tel. (888) 232-5388
www.beckettpumps.com
pumps • wholesale

Bee Fork Water Garden
Box 71
Bunker, MO 63629
Tel. (573) 689-2873
plants

Berkshire Mountain Garden Center and Landscaping
1032 South Street
Pittsfield, MA 01201
Tel. (413) 443-7321
plants

Billy Blands Fishery
Route 1
Taylor, AR 71861
Tel. (501) 694-4811
fish • wholesale

Bittersweet Hill Nursery
1274 Governor Bridge Road
Davidsonville, MD 21035
Tel. (401) 798-0231
plants

Blue Ridge Fish Hatchery, Inc.
4536 Kernersville Road
Kernersville, NC 27284
Tel. (800) 334-5257
www.blueridgekoi.com
fish • wholesale

Brents Nursery and Landscape Company
1260 Raymond Road
Jackson, MS 39212
Tel. (601) 372-8464
www.brents-nursery.com
plants

Cal Pump Waterscape Systems
28606 W. Livingston Avenue
Valencia, CA 91355
Tel. (800) 225-1339
www.calpump.com
pumps, filters • wholesale and retail

Corrales Water Lily Gardens
12 Perea Road
Corrales, NM 87048
Tel. (505) 898-6382
plants

Creative Water Gardens
2125 W. Kingsley Road
Garland, TX 75041
Tel. (972) 271-1411
plants

Crystal Palace Perennials
P.O. Box 607
St. John, IN 46373
Tel. (219) 374-9419
www.crystalpalaceperennial.com
plants

Desert Water Gardens
1279 W. 1600 N.
Woods Cross, UT 84087
Tel. (801) 292-8057
plants

Fiber Tech, Inc.
833 Main Street
Southbridge, MA 01550
pools

Florida Aquatic Nursery, Inc.
700 S. Flamingo Road
Davie, FL 33325
Tel. (954) 472-5120
plants • wholesale

Gilberg Perennial Farm
2906 Ossenfort Road
Wildwood, MO 63038
Tel. (636) 458-2033
www.gilbergperennials.com
plants

Hemphill's Garden and Aquatic Center, Inc.
2222 Fallston Road
Fallston, MD 21047
Tel. (410) 803-1688
www.pond-people.com
plants

Hozelock Cyprio
www.hozelock-cyprio.com
pumps • wholesale

Hunting Creek Fisheries, Inc.
6916 Black's Mill Road
Thurmont, MD 21788
Tel. (301) 271-7475
www.huntingcreekfisheries.com
fish • wholesale

Jim's Water Gardening
90760 N. Prairie Road
Eugene, OR 97402
Tel. (541) 461-5537
plants

Landscape Home and Garden Center, Inc.
226 Rt. 17K
Newburgh, NY 12550
Tel. (845) 564-2744
www.thelandscape.com
plants

The Lily Pond
3635 E. Palm Lane
Phoenix, AZ 85003
Tel. (602) 273-1805
plants

Lilypons Water Gardens
6800 Lilypons Road
Buckeystown, MD 21717
Tel. (301) 874-5133
www.lilypons.com
plants, pools

Little Giant Pump Company
P.O. Box 12010
Oklahoma City, OK 73157
Tel. (405) 947-2511
www.littlegiant.com
pumps • wholesale

Maryland Aquatic Nurseries, Inc.
3427 N. Furnace Road
Jarrettsville, MD 21084
Tel. (410) 557-7615
www.marylandaquatic.com
plants

McAllister Water Gardens
7420 St. Helena Highway
St. Helena, CA 94574
Tel. (707) 944-0921
plants

Naranja Water Gardens
31345 SW 194th Avenue
Homestead, FL 33030
Tel. (305) 247-2997
plants • wholesale

Mt. Parnell Fisheries, Inc.
1574 Ft. Loudon Road
Mercersburg, PA 17236
Tel. (800) 438-4652
www.mtparnell.com
fish • wholesale

Nelson Water Gardens and Nursery, Inc.
1502 Ft. Bend Katy Co. Road
Katy, TX 77450
Tel. (281) 391-4769
www.nelsonwatergardens.com
plants

Oasis Water Gardens
404 S. Brandon Street
Seattle, WA 98108
Tel. (206) 767-9776
www.oasiswatergardens.com
plants

Ozark Fisheries, Inc.
HCR 67, Box 20
Stoutland, MO 65567
Tel. (800) 775-3474
scican.net/vmc/fisheries/ozark.html
fish • wholesale

Pacific Water Gardens
354 Pacific Street
San Luis Obispo, CA 93401
Tel. (805) 594-1693
www.pacificwatergardens.com
plants

Paradise Water Gardens
14 May Street
Whitman, MA 02382
Tel. (800) 955-0161
www.paradisewatergardens.com
plants

Patio Garden Ponds
7919 S. Shields Blvd.
Oklahoma City, OK 73149
Tel. (800) 487-5459
www.patio-garden-ponds.com
plants, pools

Perry's Water Gardens
136 Gibson Aquatic Farm Road
Franklin, NC 28734
Tel. (828) 524-3264
plants, fish, pools

Santa Fe Water Gardens
4 Taylor Loop
Santa Fe, NM 87505
Tel. (505) 473-2693
plants

Slocum Water Gardens
1101 Cypress Gardens Blvd.
Winter Haven, FL 33880
Tel. (863) 293-7151
plants, pools

Springdale Water Gardens
Old Quarry Lane
P.O. Box 546
Greenville, VA 24440
Tel. (800) 420-5459
www.springdalewatergardens.com
plants

Strawn Water Gardens
Route 4, Box 142
College Station, TX 77840
Tel. (979) 696-6644
plants • wholesale

Suwannee Laboratories, Inc.
Box 1823
Lake City, FL 32056
Tel. (386) 752-6090
plants • wholesale

Tetra
www.tetra-fish.co.uk
fish, pools, filters, pumps • wholesale

Tropical Pond and Garden
17928 61st Place N.
Loxahatchee, FL 33470
Tel. (561) 791-8994
www.tropicalpond.com
plants, pools

Valley View Farms
11035 York Road
Cockeysville, MD 21030
Tel. (410) 527-0700
www.valleyviewfarms.com
plants

Van Ness Water Gardens
2460 N. Euclid Avenue
Upland, CA 91786-1199
Tel. (800) 205-2425
www.vnwg.com
plants, pools

Walter's Aquatic Plants
6073 Lancaster Drive
San Diego, CA 92120
Tel. (619) 582-5408
plants

Waterford Gardens
74 E. Allendale Road
Saddle River, NJ 07458
Tel. (201) 327-0721
http://waterford-gardens.com
plants, pools

Water Garden Gems, Inc.
3136 Bolton Road
Marion, TX 78124
Tel. (800) 682-6098
www.watergardengems.com
plants

The Water Works
Tilley's Nursery, Inc.
111 E. Fairmount Street
Coopersburg, PA 18036
Tel. (610) 282-4784
www.tnwaterworks.com
plants

Wickleins Aquatic Farm and Nursery
1820 Cromwell Bridge Road
Parkville, MD 21234
Tel. (410) 823-1335
plants

William Tricker, Inc.
7125 Tanglewood Drive
Independence, OH 44131
Tel. (800) 524-3492
www.tricker.com
plants, pools

Canada

Aqua Plantes
221 rue de Liverpool
St Augustine-de-Desmaures,
    Quebec G3A 2M5
Tel. (418) 878-5045
www.aquaplantes.com
plants

Aquatics & Co.
P.O. Box 455
Pickering, Ontario L1V 2R7
Tel. (905) 668-5326
plants

Hydrosphere Water Gardens
RR2 2474 9th Line
Bradford, Ontario L3Z 2A5
Tel. (905) 668-5326
www.pondexperts.ca
plants

Moore Water Gardens
Box 340
Port Stanley, Ontario N0L 2A0
Tel. (519) 782-4052
www.moorewatergardens.com
plants, fish, pools, pumps

Reimer Waterscapes
RR3, Box 34
Tillsonburg, Ontario N4G 4H3
Tel. (519) 842-6049
www.waterscapes.ca
plants, fish, pools, pumps

United Kingdom

Anglo Aquarium Plant Co. Ltd.
Strayfield Road
Enfield
Middlesex EN2 9JE
Tel. (020) 8363 8548
plants • wholesale

Beaver Water Plant and Fish Farm Ltd.
Eastbourne Road (A22)
New Chapel, Lingfield
Surrey RH7 6HL
Tel. (013) 4283 3144
plants, fish

Bennett's Waterlily and Fish Farm
Chickerell
Weymouth
Dorset DT3 4AF
plants, fish, pools, pumps • wholesale and retail

Beresford Pumps Ltd.
Carlton Road
Foleshill
Coventry CV6 7FL
Tel. (024) 7663 8484
pumps

Blagdon Water Gardens
Walrow Industrial Estate
Commerce Way
Highbridge
Somerset TA9 4AG
Tel. (019) 3485 2973
plants, fish, pools, pumps • wholesale

Cougar Pumps Ltd.
Unit 9, Waterloo Industrial Park
Stockport, Cheshire SK1 3BP
Tel. (016) 1476 0006
pumps • wholesale

Dorset Waterlily Company
Yeovil Road
Halstock
Yeovil
Somerset BA22 9RR
Tel. (019) 3589 1668
plants • wholesale

Egmont Water Gardens
132 Tolworth Rise South
Surbiton
Surrey KT5 9NJ
Tel. (020) 8337 9605
plants, fish, pools, pumps

Hertfordshire Fisheries
North Orbital Road
St. Albans
Hertfordshire AL2 2DS
Tel. (017) 2783 3960
plants, fish, pools, pumps

Hozelock Cyprio Ltd.
Waterslade House
Thame Road
Haddenham
Aylesbury
Buckinghamshire HP17 8JD
Tel. (018) 4429 1881
pumps

H. Tisbury and Sons
Spice Pitts Farm
Church Road, Noak Hill
Romford
Essex RM4 1LD
Tel. (017) 0834 1376
plants, fish, pools, pumps

London Aquatics Co. Ltd.
Greenwood Nurseries
Theobalds Park Road
Enfield
Middlesex EN2 9DH
Tel. (020) 8366 4143
plants, fish • wholesale

Lotus Water Garden Products Ltd.
Lodge House
Lodge Square
Burnley
Lancashire BB11 1NW
Tel. (012) 8242 0771
plants, fish, pools, filters, pumps

Newlake Gardens
West Park Road
Copthorne, Crawley
West Sussex RH10 3HQ
Tel. (013) 4271 2332
plants, fish, pools, pumps

Oasis Water Garden Products Ltd.
Knowle Lane, Horton Heath
Eastleigh, Hampshire SO50 7DZ
Tel. (023) 8060 2602
pools, pumps • wholesale

Obart Ltd.
8 Viewpoint Boxley Road
Penenden Heath
Maidstone
Kent ME14 2DZ
Tel. (016) 2235 5000
www.obartpumps.co.uk
pumps • wholesale

Remanoid Ltd.
No. 1 Industrial Estate, Unit 44
Medomsley Road, Consett
Durham DH8 6SZ
Tel. (012) 0759 1089
pools, pumps • wholesale

Shirley Aquatics Ltd.
1355 Stratford Road
Shirley, Solihull
West Midlands B95 5DL
Tel. (012) 1744 1300
plants, fish, pools, pumps

Solesbridge Mill Water Gardens
Tropical Marine Center Ltd.
Solesbridge Lane
Chorleywood, Richmansworth
Hertfordshire WD3 5SX
Tel. (019) 2328 4135
plants, fish, pools

Stapeley Water Gardens
72 London Road
Stapeley, Nantwich
Cheshire CW5 7LH
Tel. (012) 7062 3868
www.stapeleywg.com
plants, fish, pools, filters, pumps •
wholesale and retail

Stuart Turner Ltd.
Henley-on-Thames
Oxfordshire RG9 2AD
Tel. (014) 9157 2655
www.stuart-turner.co.uk
pumps

Water Techniques
Downside Mill
Cobham Park Road
Cobham
Surrey KT11 3PF
Tel. (019) 3286 6588
www.water-techniques.co.uk
pumps • wholesale

Wildwoods Water Gardens Ltd.
Theobalds Park Road
Crews Hill, Enfield
Middlesex EN2 9BP
Tel. (020) 8366 0243
plants, fish, pools, pumps

Wessex Fish Farms
Burton Bradstock
Bridport
Dorset DT6 4NE
Tel. (013) 0889 7685
fish

Wychwood Waterlily and
 Carp Farm
Farnham Road
A28T Odiham
Hook
Hants RG29 1HS
Tel. (012) 5670 2800
plants, fish

Europe

Aquatic D.C.
Chemin des Crahauts
16-B-5980
Boiceau
Belgium
plants

Eberhard Schuster
Garten Baubetrieb
Post Gadebehn
2711 Augustenhof
Germany
Tel. (038) 6322 2705
www.wasserpflanzen-schuster.de
plants

Giardini di Marignolle
Via di Marignolle 69
50124 Florence
Italy
plants

J. Hoogendoorn
Vitvercentrum De Plomp B.V.
Klapwijkseweg 8
2641 RC
The Netherlands
plants

Latour-Marliac
Le Temple-sur-Lot
47110 Sainte Livrade sur Lot
France
Tel. (055) 301 0805
www.latour-marliac.fr
plants

R. Bezancon
15 Avenue du Raincy
94 Saint Maur
France
plants

Australia

Arcadia Lily Ponds
151 Arcadia Road
Arcadia, Sydney Suburbs
New South Wales 2159
Tel. (02) 9655 1670
www.arcadia-lily-ponds.com
plants

Austral Watergardens
1295 Pacific Highway
Cowan
New South Wales 2081
Tel. (02) 9985 7370
E-mail: australwatergardens
    @bigpond.com.au
plants

ClearPond
4 Kingscote Street
Kewdale
Western Australia 6105
Tel. (8) 9353 2266
www.clearpond.com.au
pumps, pools, filters • wholesale

Gedye's Water Gardens
37-41 Elizabeth Street
Doncaster East
Victoria 3109
Tel. (3) 9848 5133
www.gedye.com.au
plants, fish, pools, pumps

Ledora Water Gardens
Pacific Highway
Mt. Kgai
New South Wales 2080
Tel. (02) 9456 1163
plants

Sherringhams Nursery
Lot 1 Wicks Road
North Ryde
New South Wales 2113
Tel. (02) 9888 3133
plants

New Zealand

**Haumoana Fish and Water Plant
    Farm**
5 Haumoana Road
Haumoana, Hawke's Bay
Napier
plants, fish, pools, pumps

New Zealand Water Lily Gardens
RD 2, Pukeauri Road
Waihi
North Island
Tel. (07) 863 8267

Rapaura Watergardens
586 Tapu-Coroglen Road
Tapu
Tel. (07) 868 4821
www.rapaurawatergardens.co.nz
plants

Glossary

adventitious: added from outside; not inherent

anther: pollen-bearing part of stamen

apical: of, at, or constituting the apex

awn: a group of sharp, bristly fibers

carpel: a single pistil or single unit of a compound pistil

changeable waterlily: one with flowers that open lighter colored, deepening on second and third days, or the reverse

cordate: heart-shaped; frequently used to describe leaf shape

crenate: having a notched or scalloped edge; frequently used to describe leaf edges

cultivar: contraction of "cultivated variety"; an induced result of hybridizing or a natural hybrid that has been named, abbreviated cv.

dentate: having a toothed margin; frequently used to describe leaf edges

emersed: having emerged above the surface; standing above the surface water level

filament: basal stalk of the stamen bearing the anthers

finger rhizome: small finger or thumb-sized rhizome; grows erect

glabrous: bald, without hair, down, or fuzz

glaucous: glowing or covered with a whitish "bloom" that can be rubbed off; usually refers to stem or leaf surfaces

hardy waterlily: a perennial aquatic herb

hastate: having a triangular shape like a spearhead; frequently used to describe leaf shape

internode: plant section found between two successive nodes or joints

lanceolate: narrow and tapering toward the end like a lance, several times longer than broad; frequently used to describe leaf shape

mainstem: vertical center of a flower

Marliac rhizome: a thick type of hardy waterlily rhizome developed by Joseph B L Marliac; plants with this type of rhizome are notable for freedom of bloom

mutant: plant with inheritable characteristics that differ from those of the parents

obovate: egg-shaped, the broad end is located at the top; frequently used to describe leaf shape; see also **ovate**

odorata rhizome: a slender type of rhizome common to hardy waterlily species, particularly in eastern North America

ovate: egg-shaped, the broad end is at the base; frequently used to describe leaf shape; see also **obovate**

peduncle: stalk of a single flower or the stalk of a cluster flower

peltate: shaped like a shield; frequently used to describe leaf shape

perfoliate: having a base surrounding the leaf stem; base appears perforated by the stem

perianth: outer part of the flower, including the calyx and corolla

perigynous: refers to flower structure; having the sepals, petals, and stamens attached to the rim surrounding the ovary, unattached to the ovary itself

petaloid: resembling a petal; usually referring to staminodes where several, or all, stamens have changed to petals in the center of flower (usually with anther tips)

petiole: leaf stalk

pineapple rhizome: thick, upright-growing rhizome typical of certain hardy waterlilies

pubescence: surface fuzz, hairs, or down; sometimes present on peduncle or petiole of waterlilies

raceme: unbranched flower cluster consisting of a single central stem; individual flowers grow on small stems off the central stem

radical: in reference to leaves, of or coming from the root

recurved: curved or bent back; often used in reference to flower parts or leaves

reniform: kidney-shaped; frequently used to describe leaf shape

rhizome: modified underground stem from which the plant makes growth

RHS: *Royal Horticultural Society Colour Chart*

sessile: lacking pedicel or peduncle, attachment is direct to main stem

sinus: area between the lobes of the waterlily leaf

spadix: fleshy spike found in tiny flowers, usually enclosed in a **spathe** (see description)

spathe: a large leaflike part or pair of such parts enclosing a flower cluster

stamen: pollen-bearing organ in a flower; includes the slender stalk known as the filament at the base and a pollen sac, the anther, at the tip

staminodes: colored, petal-like organs located just outside the stamens in waterlilies and lotuses; characterized by broad bases and anther-like sacs at the tips

star lily: tropical aquatic herb, mostly resulting from crosses of *Nymphaea flavovirens* (syn. *N. gracilis*) with its own variations or with *N. capensis* var. *zanzibariensis*

stigma: upper tip of the flower pistil that receives pollen; pl. stigmata

stellate: star-shaped; usually used in reference to flowers

stolon: runner, especially a stem running underground

stoma: microscopic opening in the epidermis of plants; it is surrounded by guard cells and serves in gaseous exchange; pl. stomata

style: slender stalk-shaped part of a carpel located between the stigma and ovary

terminal: usually used in reference to the growth at the end of a stem

thumb rhizome: small finger or thumb-sized rhizome; grows erect

tip: staminal appendage in tropical day-blooming waterlilies

translucent: letting light pass through but diffusing it so that objects on other side cannot be clearly distinguished

tuber: short, thickened, fleshy part of an underground stem

tuberosa rhizome: slender hardy waterlily rhizome in which young (new) tubers are attached to the parent tuber only by very fragile, thin pieces; the young tubers usually break off and remain underground when the parent tuber is pulled

tropical waterlily: also known as tender waterlily; species forming an underwater herb, native to warmer countries; may also refer to a cultivar resulting from crossing two tropical waterlily species or crossing a tropical waterlily species and tropical waterlily cultivar

turion: scaly shoot growing from a submerged rootstock

upright rhizome: hardy waterlily rhizome that grows upright

var.: variety or variation

variant: plant displaying variation from the species

viviparous: germination that takes place while new plant is still attached to the parent plant

Further Reading

Books and Journal Articles

Bailey, Liberty Hyde, and Ethel Zoe Bailey. 1976. *Hortus Third*. New York: MacMillan Publishing Co., Inc.

Caillet, Marie, and Joseph K. Mertzweiller. 1988. *The Louisiana Iris*. The Society for Louisiana Irises/ Texas Gardener Press.

Conard, Henry S. 1905. *The Waterlilies: A Monograph of the Genus Nymphaea*. Washington, D.C.: Carnegie Institution of Washington.

Fox, Shirley, ed. 1986. *Aquatic and Wetland Plants of Florida*. 3d ed. Bureau of Aquatic Plant Research and Control, Florida State Department of Natural Resources.

Henkel, Friedrich, F. Rehnelt, and L. Dittman. 1907. *Das Buch der Nymphaeaceen oder Seerosengewächse*. Darmstadt-Neuwiese: Friedrich Henkel.

Heritage, Bill. 1986. *Ponds and Water Gardens*. Rev. 2d ed. New York: Blandford Press Ltd.

International Waterlily and Water Gardening Society. 1993. *Identification of Hardy Nymphaea*. Cheshire, U.K.: Stapeley Water Gardens Ltd.

Jacobs, S. W. L. 1992. New species, lectotypes and synonyms of Australasian *Nymphaea*. *Telopea* 4(4): 635–641.

Nash, Helen. 1994. *The Pond Doctor: Planning and Maintaining a Healthy Water Garden*. New York: Sterling.

Nash, Helen, with Steve Stroupe. 1998. *Aquatic Plants and Their Cultivation: A Complete Guide for Water Gardeners*. Photography by Perry D. Slocum and Bob Romar. New York: Sterling.

Nash, Helen. 2000. *The Living Pond: Water Gardens with Fish and Other Creatures*. New York: Sterling.

Nash, Helen, and Marilyn M. Cook. 1999. *Water Gardening Basics*. New York: Sterling.

Ni Xueming, ed. 1987. *Lotus of China*. Wuhan, China: Wuhan Botanical Institute.

Perry, Frances. 1981. *The Water Garden*. New York: Van Nostrand Reinhold Company.

Reid, George K. 2001. *Pond Life: A Guide to Common Plants and Animals of North American Ponds and Lakes*. Rev. and updated. Ed. Herbert S. Zim, George S. Fichter, Jonathan P. Latimer, Karen Stray Nolting, and John L. Brooks. New York: St. Martin's Press.

Slocum, Perry D., Peter Robinson, with Frances Perry. 1996. *Water Gardening, Water Lilies and Lotuses*. Portland, Oregon: Timber Press.

Swindells, Philip. 1983. *Waterlilies*. Portland, Oregon: Timber Press.

Thomas, Charles B. 1992. *Water Gardens for Plants and Fish*. Neptune City, New Jersey: T.F.H. Publications, Inc. Ltd.

Uber, William C. 1999. *The Basics of Water Gardening*. Upland, California: Dragonfly Press.

Uber, William C. 2001. *Large Ponds, Small Lakes: What Every Water Gardener Needs to Know about Building and Maintaining a Large Pond*. Ed. Tina Littell. Upland, California: Dragonfly Press.

Wiersema, John H. 1987. *A Monograph of Nymphaea Subgenus Hydrocallis (Nymphaeaceae)*. Vol. 16 of *Systematic Botany Monographs*. Ann Arbor, Michigan: The American Society of Plant Taxonomists.

Wieser, K. H., and P. V. Loiselle. 1996. *Your Garden Pond: Practical Tips on Planning, Design, Installation and Maintenance*. Tetra Press.

Journals and Magazines

Pondkeeper Magazine. A full-color magazine for outdoor water gardeners. Published by Vivicon Productions, Inc., 1000 Whitetail Court, Duncansville, PA 16635-6908, Tel. (814) 695-4325.

Pondscapes Magazine. A colorful, well-written publication covering all aspects of outdoor water gardens of all sizes; ten issues per year. Published by the National Pond Society (A. Sperling, ed.), P.O. Box 449, Acworth, GA 30101-0449.

The Water Garden Journal. A quarterly publication for the more experienced hobbyist and water gardening professional, providing informative articles on water gardening techniques, plant husbandry, hybridization, water quality, invasive species issues, and related topics. Published by the International Waterlily and Water Gardening Society, 6828 26th Street W, Bradenton, FL 34027, Tel. (941) 756-0880. Website: http://www.iwgs.org

Water Gardening Magazine: The Magazine for Pond Keepers. Sue Speichert, Ed., P.O. Box 607, St. John, IN 46373, Tel. (219) 374-9419. Website includes a listing of articles in the current and past issues of the magazine, tips and FAQs, a chat room, and subscription information. Website: http://www.watergardening.com

Index